DOCUMENTS

OF THE

31ST AND 32ND

GENERAL CONGREGATIONS

OF THE

SOCIETY OF JESUS

DOCUMENTS
OF THE
31st AND 32nd
GENERAL CONGREGATIONS
OF THE
SOCIETY OF JESUS

An English Translation
of the
Official Latin Texts
of the
General Congregations
and of the
Accompanying Papal Documents

THE INSTITUTE OF JESUIT SOURCES
Saint Louis, 1977

This American Translation was prepared by
the Jesuit Conference, Washington, D.C., and
edited by John W. Padberg, S.J. It is a complete and
authorized version of these official Latin texts:
(1) *Decreta Congregationis Generalis XXXI . . . annis
1965-1966,*
and
(2) *Decreta Congregationis Generalis XXXII . . . annis
1974-1975,* Rome: Generalate of the Society of Jesus,
respectively 1967 and 1975.

IMPRIMI POTEST: Very Reverend Leo F. Weber, S.J.
Provincial of the Missouri Province
January 31, 1977

IMPRIMATUR: Most Reverend George J. Gottwald
Vicar General of St. Louis
February 7, 1977

136

©1977   The Institute of Jesuit Sources
Fusz Memorial, St. Louis University
3700 West Pine Blvd.
St. Louis, Missouri 63108

Printed in the United States of America
Library of Congress Catalog Card Number: 77-70881
ISBN 0-912422-25-4 Smyth sewn flexible Lexotone
ISBN 0-912422-26-2 Smyth sewn paperbound

TABLE OF CONTENTS

VI. Congregations

VII. Government

VIII. Appendix

C. DOCUMENTS PERTAINING TO THE GENERAL CONGREGATION

D. MEMBERS OF THE 31st GENERAL CONGREGATION

THE 32nd GENERAL CONGREGATION
December 2, 1974—March 7, 1975

Abbreviations Used in the Footnotes

AA	*(Apostolicam Actuositatem) Decree on the Apostolate of the Laity.* Vatican II, 1965
AAS	*Acta Apostolicae Sedis*
ActRSJ	*Acta Romana Societatis Iesu*
AG	*(Ad Gentes) Decree on the Church's Missionary Activity.* Vatican II, 1965
CD	*(Christus Dominus) Decree on the Bishops' Pastoral Office in the Church.* Vatican II, 1965
CIC	*Code of Canon Law*
CollDecr	*Collectio Decretorum Congregationum Generalium Societatis Iesu.* 1961
Cons	*Constitutiones Societatis Iesu*
*Cons*MHSJ, I	*Monumenta Constitutionum praevia.* Sources and records previous to the texts of the *Constitutions*
D.	Decree
DH	*(Dignitatis Humanae) Declaration on Religious Freedom.* Vatican II, 1965
DV	*(Dei Verbum) Dogmatic Constitution on Divine Revelation.* Vatican II, 1965
Epit	*Epitome Instituti Societatis Iesu.* 1962
ES	Motu Proprio *Ecclesiae Sanctae.* 1966
ET	Pope Paul VI, Adhortatio Apostolica "Evangelica Testificatio," June 29, 1971. *AAS* (1971), p. 497 sq.
FI	*Formula of the Institute of the Society of Jesus*
GC	General Congregation of the Society of Jesus

1

GE	*(Gravissimum Educationis) Declaration on Christian Education.* Vatican II, 1965
GenExam	*General Examen*
GS	*(Gaudium et Spes) Pastoral Constitution on the Church in the Modern World.* Vatican II, 1965
LG	*(Lumen Gentium) Dogmatic Constitution on the Church.* Vatican II, 1964
MHSJ	Monumenta Historica Societatis Jesu
MI	Monumenta Ignatiana
n.	Number(s)
NA	*(Nostra Aetate) Declaration on the Relationship of the Church to Non-Christian Religions.* Vatican II, 1965
NG	*Normae Generales de Studiis*
OE	*(Orientalium Ecclesiarum) Decree on Eastern Catholic Churches.* Vatican II, 1964
OT	*(Optatam Totius) Decree on Priestly Formation.* Vatican II, 1965
PC	*(Perfectae Caritatis) Decree on the Adaptation and Renewal of the Religious Life.* Vatican II, 1965
PO	*(Presbyterorum Ordinis) Decree on the Ministry and Life of Priests.* Vatican II, 1965
SC	*(Sacrosanctum Concilium) Constitution on the Sacred Liturgy.* Vatican II, 1963
SpEx	*Spiritual Exercises*
UR	*(Unitatis Redintegratio) Decree on Ecumenism.* Vatican II, 1964

THE 31st GENERAL CONGREGATION
OF THE
SOCIETY OF JESUS

May 7–July 15, 1965

and

September 8–November 17, 1966

LETTER OF PROMULGATION
FROM FATHER GENERAL

To the Whole Society

Reverend Fathers and dear Brothers in Christ,
                                    Pax Christi

The decrees of the Thirty-first General Congregation I am sending with this present letter in the name of that Congregation to all the provinces, vice-provinces and missions so that they might be published in the houses of the Society.

In virtue of the powers given to me by the General Congregation[1] I have suspended until January 1, 1968 the date on which Decree 11, on the norms of promotion to last vows, takes effect. This is so that the advancement to final vows of all of those who pronounce such vows after that date might be adapted to these new norms, but not however the advancement of those who take final vows before that date. All the rest of the decrees, in accord with the norm of the Formula of the General Congregation,[2] enter into force from the date of this present letter.

I commend myself earnestly to your Sacrifices and prayers,

> *The servant of all of you in Christ,*
> *Pedro Arrupe*
> *General of the Society of Jesus*

Rome, February 15, 1967

---

1 See D. 56, n. 2, 3°e.
2 Formula C.G., n. 144, § 2, 3°.

A.

HISTORICAL PREFACE

TO THE DECREES

OF THE 31st GENERAL CONGREGATION

Excerpted from the Official Minutes of the Congregation

HISTORICAL PREFACE
TO THE DECREES OF
THE 31st GENERAL CONGREGATION

Excerpted from the Official Minutes of the Congregation

When Very Reverend Father John Baptist Janssens died on October 5, 1964, at the beginning of his nineteenth year as General of the Society of Jesus, Reverend John L. Swain was the same day formally appointed Vicar-General of the Society, in accord with the will left by Fr. Janssens. Father Swain, upon the advice of the Fathers Assistant, announced in his letter of November 13 of the same year that the General Congregation was to take place during the next year, 1965. However, he did not set a specific date for its convocation because of the uncertainty about when the fourth session of the Second Vatican Council would be held and also because of the interval needed to complete the preparations for the work of the Congregation which Father Janssens had begun. In another letter dated January 13, 1965, Father Vicar, again with the consent of his Assistants, set May 6 as the date for the gathering of all the delegates in Rome, so that the first formal session of the Congregation might be held on the following day.

On the day appointed all the members of the Congregation were present in Rome at the curia and at the house of writers next door except for the provincials and the electors of both of the provinces of Poland. (From these provinces the provincials and two of the electors were able to come before the third full meeting of the Congregation. For the other two electors, two substitutes were provided). Also unable to be present were the provincial and the electors of the province of Bohemia and all of the delegates to the Congregation from the province of Hungary and the vice-provinces of Lithuania and Rumania as well as from the missions of Latvia and Estonia. The provincial of Hungary and the vice-provincial of Slovakia were each able to designate a single priest to serve in their stead. In order that these localities of the Society might be present in some way at the Congregation, Father Vicar named as procurators Fathers Wenceslaus Fert from the province of Bohemia and Father Bruno Markaitis from the vice province of Lithuania. In the same way, in order to take advantage of their intimate knowledge of affairs, Father Vicar also named Father Thomas Byrne who had previously held the office as substitute Assistant, and Father Paul Mailleux, the delegate of Father General for the Byzantine Rite.

1. The Beginning of the Congregation

(*From the Minutes,* Acta 1)

On May 7, 1965, the first Friday of May, after the delegates had been received in audience by the Supreme Pontiff, Paul VI, and had received his apostolic benediction, all of the members of the Congregation, that is, all the electors who were present and who had a proven right to be there, entered the assembly hall of the Congregation in the order assigned. After the hymn to the Holy Spirit and the accompanying prayers were recited, the Congregation by unanimous vote declared itself full and legitimate. After this, one of the electors, about whose right to be present some doubt had arisen and who for this reason had been left waiting outside the hall, was admitted to the applause of all those present.

Then Father Vicar gave the prescribed address in which he rendered an account of all that had been done after the death of the General, and he spoke specifically of the preparation for the Congregation and exhorted all those present to that peace, harmony, and faithfulness by which this one desire might flourish in such diversity of opinion, that the Society of Jesus, faithful to the spirit of its founder, might fully respond to the needs of the Church.

After the appropriate voting, Father Pedro M. Abellan, a delegate from the province of Toledo, was elected Secretary. He was also at the same time the Procurator General of the Society. As Assistant Secretary the Congregation elected Father Aloysius Renard from the province of Southern Belgium. The other details normally pertaining to the election of the General of the Society were, with the approval of the Congregation, deferred in order that before that election certain problems might be discussed.

2.   The Election of the Deputies "ad detrimenta"

(*From the Minutes,* Acta 2)

Once the prior meetings of the assistancies had been held, in which, according to the norms of the Formula, names of candidates could be proposed, on May 8 the following were elected as deputies "ad detrimenta" in several ballots and a single counting of the votes:
From the Italian Assistancy, Father Paolo Dezza, delegate from the Venice-Milan province; from the German Assistancy, Father Anthony Pinsker, delegate from the Austrian province; from the French Assistancy, Father Antoine Delchard, delegate from the province of Northern France; from the Spanish Assistancy, Father Lucio Craveiro da Silva, the provincial of Portugal; from the English Assistancy, Father Angus MacDougall, provincial of Upper Canada; from the American Assistancy, Father John J. McMahon, delegate from the New York province; from the Slavic Assistancy, Father John G. Fuček, provincial of Croatia; from the Southern Latin American Assistancy,

Father Anthony Aquino, provincial of Central Brazil; from the Indian Assistancy, Father Edward Mann, provincial of Bombay; from the Northern Latin American Assistancy, Father Henrico Gutierrez Martin del Campo, delegate from the province of Southern Mexico; from the East Asian Assistancy, Father Leo Cullum, delegate from the Philippine province.

Since the Supreme Pontiff had wanted to meet with all the delegates to the Congregation before the Congregation itself began, there was no need to designate certain members to go to him now in order to ask the papal blessing.

3.   The Election of Father General

(*From the Minutes,* Acta 3-8)

1.   Since some postulata had proposed that before the election of the General certain questions should be treated, and especially the question of the length of office of the General, the Congregation thought that in order to proceed to a peaceful election it was necessary to consider this question attentively before the election itself. Therefore, with the inclusion of the delegates who were present for the Congregation only for business and not also for elections, that is the procurators, a discussion took place during five sessions both on the duration of the office of Father General as well as on the prior question of whether the Congregation had the power to pass laws before the election of the General. Finally, on May 17, the Congregation decided not to pass any decree at that time but, once the election had been finished, to examine the matter thoroughly and to make decisions in the plenitude of its power.

2.   It was decided, therefore, that the four days for the gathering of information were to begin on the next day, May 18, and, in accord with the proposal of the Vicar, Father Maurice Giuliani, delegate from the Paris province,

was selected to give the exhortation on the day of election itself. For the job of "Inclusor," that is the one who formally locks the members of the Congregation in the hall, Father George Bottereau, the Superior of the Curia, was chosen. In accord with the provisions of the Formula, the judges who would deal with any question of "ambition" were, besides Father Vicar, the oldest professed from each of the assistancies, that is Fathers Paolo Dezza, Petrus van Gestel, Jean M. Le Blond, Severian Azcona, William J. Murphy, Joannes B. Kozelj, Isidore Griful, Melchior M. Balaguer, Francis Robinson and Leo Cullum.

3.   On May 22, in accord with all the prescriptions of the Formula drawn from the Constitutions and from the decrees of previous General Congregations, Reverend Father Pedro Arrupe was by majority vote on the third ballot elected Superior General of the Society. He had been up to that time provincial of the province of Japan. A formal certification of this election was passed immediately and signed by the Vicar-General. Without any delay Father Paolo Molinari, the Postulator General of the Society, informed the Holy Father and he sent to the new General and to the whole Society his special blessing.

4.   The Election of the Secretaries and the Deputies for the Screening of Postulata

(From the Minutes, Acta 9)

1.   After the election of the General, the delegates who were not formally electors were called back to the hall, that is the Secretary of the Society, Father James W. Naughton, the Treasurer General, Father Romulus Durocher, and the Procurators, Fathers Thomas Byrne, Wenceslaus Fert, Paul Mailleux and Bruno Markaitis.

2.   By majority votes in secret ballots the following were then elected. First, on a separate ballot, as Secretary of the Congregation, Father Pedro M. Abellan who had also pre-

viously been elected secretary for the election of the General. Then on a single ballot his two assistants, Fathers John A. McGrail, provincial of Detroit, and Vincenzo Monachino, delegate from the Roman Province.

3. After the meeting of the various Assistancies, the following were elected deputies for the screening of postulata: From their respective Assistancies: Italian, Father Roberto Tucci, delegate of the Neapolitan province; German, Father Francis von Tattenbach, delegate of the Upper German province; French, Father Maurice Giuliani, delegate of the Paris province; Spanish, Father Victor Blajot, delegate of the Bolivian province; English, Father Piet Fransen, delegate of the Northern Belgian province; American, Father John C. Ford, delegate of the New England province; Slavic, Father Stephan Dzierzek, provincial of the Greater Polish province; Southern Latin American, Father Ferdinand Larrain, delegate of the province of Chile; Indian, Father Aemilius Ugarte, delegate of the province of Madurai; Northern Latin American, Father Aloysius Achaerandio, delegate of the Central American vice-province; East Asian, Father Charles McCarthy, delegate of the Far Eastern province.

5. The Commissions on Substantive Affairs

(*From the Minutes,* Acta 9, 10, 16, 42, 45, 92)

In order better to carry on the work of the Congregation, Father General together with the deputation for screening postulata, to which the Congregation had entrusted this, set up six commissions. Many of them were later divided into subcommissions and even the subcommissions finally into sections. These commissions and subcommissions were as follows:

First Commission: Governance

Subcommissions: 1. Governance in general
2. Universal governance
3. Governance of provinces
4. Congregations

Second Commission: Ministries and Apostolate

Subcommissions: 1. The ordering of ministries in the whole Society
2. Foreign missions
3. Education and the scientific or scholarly apostolate
4. Pastoral ministries and ecumenism
5. Social apostolate and communications media

Third Commission: Studies of Jesuits

Subcommissions: 1. Formation in general
2. The ordinary course of studies
3. Special studies

Fourth Commission: Religious Life

Subcommissions: 1. The nature and purpose of religious and apostolic life in the Society today
2. The vows in general
3. Poverty
4. The spiritual life
5. Spiritual formation
6. Tertianship
7. Common life and discipline

Fifth Commission: Preservation and Renewal of the Institute

Subcommissions: 1. The substantials of the Institute

2. Admission to the Society and to holy orders and dismissal from the Society
3. Grades in the Society
4. Temporal coadjutors
5. Knowledge of the Institute

Sixth Commission: The Mission of the Society Today

In order that the apportionment of the members of the Congregation to the various commissions and subcommissions might be easier and more acceptable, each member was asked to indicate quite freely what commission he would prefer to work on, and the deputation for assigning commission membership took account of these wishes.

Later other commissions or groups or committees were set up. For example, there were a special commission which was to help in writing the texts of decrees, a commission on procedure, a group of canonists who would be of help especially to the first and fifth commissions, a group of experts who were charged with the stylistic editing of the language of the decrees and putting them in order, a group of experts to revise the Formulas of the Congregation, and other groups of delegates established for taking care of whatever necessary work arose.

6. The Two Sessions of the Congregation

(*From the Minutes,* Acta 33-35, 38, 41-43, 46, 49-51, 54, 57, 58)

1. What had never before happened in the history of the Society occurred at this Congregation. It was divided into two sessions. The Congregation took into account the tremendous amount of work generated by the more than 1,900 postulata, the grave and serious nature of the questions to be treated, the immense expectations of the entire Society, the imminence of the fourth session of the Second

Vatican Council and other conditions of both the circumstances and the times. It examined various proposals (for example: establishing a group of deputies who, with the authority of the Congregation would complete the work it had begun, or the calling of another General Congregation within three to five years). Finally after two months of work the Congregation decided to adjourn temporarily on July 15, 1965, and to continue its work in September of the following year, 1966 (cf. d. 49). Later in a letter of Dec. 8, 1965, to all major superiors, the General set September 8, 1966, as the date for convening the second session. At the same time he gave to the members of the Congregation the opportunity for a triduum of spiritual recollection on the 5th, 6th and 7th of the same month at the Curia itself.

2.   During the time between the sessions the work of the Congregation did not cease. Either through letters or by frequent meetings of delegates with other Jesuit experts a variety of reports was prepared and sent to all the members of the Congregation or distributed to them at the beginning of the second session.

3.   After the triduum of recollection in which Father General himself proposed the material for the points for meditation on each of the days, the Congregation began again on September 8, 1966, the feast of the Nativity of Our Lady. The same members were present who had been there at the first session and in addition the new regional assistants and provincials who had in the meantime been named by Father General. Absent, however, were the provincials and delegates from Poland who had not been able to obtain permission from their government to come. Also absent were Fathers Frederic Buuck, delegate from the Lower German province; Edward Mann, former provincial of Bombay; John Rocha, former Assistant for Southern Latin America; John Sehnem, former provincial of Southern Brazil; Anton Pinsker, delegate from the province of Austria; and Jean Richard, former provincial of Montreal, all of whom were hindered by illness or some other obstacle.

The following were also absent at first, but they all later arrived: Fathers John Terpstra, provincial of the Netherlands; Daniel Villanova, provincial of Sicily; John Correia-Afonso, provincial of Bombay; Leo Rosa, provincial of Venice-Milan; Abdallah Dagher, delegate of the vice-province of the Near East; and Ferdinando Larrain, delegate of the province of Chile.

4. In both sessions there were the same secretaries, deputations and commissions. But since Fathers Anton Pinsker and Edward Mann who had been deputies "ad detrimenta" in the first session were now absent, in their place were elected Father John Schasching, provincial of Austria from the German Assistancy, and Father Melchior M. Balaguer, delegate of the province of Bombay from the Assistancy of India.

7. Procedural Matters and Public Information Matters

(*From the Minutes,* Acta 1, 2, 4, 5, 10, 12, 17, 46, 48, 50-52, 54, 56, 61, 62, 87, 88, 92, 96, 98)

1. In order to save time in so large a Congregation and with such an amount of work to be done, certain methods of procedure were adopted right from the beginning which in certain matters differed from the norms of the Formula of the Congregation or added to those norms.. The following are the more important examples. Each delegate had permission to speak only once in the same plenary session on the same business (later the amount of speaking time was cut down to seven minutes); for the balloting on substantive matters red and green electric lights were generally used, the results of which were electronically calculated; the Acta or minutes of the sessions were not read publicly but each of the members of the Congregation received copies of them (see Formula of the General Congregation nn. 16, 24, paragraph 2, 121); the "Relationes praeviae," that is the first formal reports, and the definitive judgments

(see Formula of the General Congregation n. 119) were prepared by subcommissions but they were approved by the chairman of the commission and by the chairmen of all of the subcommissions of that commission; the chairmen of the various commissions helped Father General in arranging all of the work.

2.   In the second session, at the suggestion of the special commission on the manner of proceeding which had been set up toward the end of the first session, the Congregation, first as an experiment and then definitively, approved new rules or norms, the most important of which were the following: (a) Father General named as Vice Chairman of the sessions Fathers Paolo Dezza, the General Assistant; Jean Calvez, delegate of the province of Paris; and George P. Klubertanz, delegate of the province of Wisconsin. They helped him in preparing and chairing the sessions of the Congregation. (b) Those speakers who before a session had asked permission to speak were given seven minutes. Those who during a session sought that permission (see Formula of the General Congregation n. 121), received five minutes. (c) During the discussion any member of the Congregation could propose "a motion of order" which, if the Congregation approved it, could change the order of the agenda which had been proposed by the chairman and the vice chairmen. (d) Speakers were allowed to propose amendments to the text of a decree and these amendments were voted on before the full text itself came to a vote. (e) The commissions and subcommissions could have "open sessions" in which any of the members of the Congregation could be present and speak but could not vote unless they were themselves members of that commission or subcommission. (f) Some Fathers who were not members of the Congregation were brought in to help write the Acta or the minutes of the Congregation. They received permission to attend the plenary sessions.

3.   As far as vernacular languages went, from the beginning of the Congregation approval was given to speakers

to use English, French, Spanish and Italian provided that beforehand they provided a Latin summary of their speech. Very few, however, made use of this permission.

The question of using "simultaneous translations" was more than once taken up. Toward the end of the first session the Congregation decided that such a system was not to be introduced for the present Congregation. But they recommended to Father General that he study the whole thing with a view toward the next general congregation. In the second session, at the proposal of the commission on procedure, the Congregation first gave its approval to use simultaneous translations in the "open sessions of the commissions" and later to use them as an experiment in six of the plenary sessions.

4. Since not a few people asked that in some way Jesuits and also non-Jesuits might be kept informed of the actions of the Congregation, while at the same time the Formula of the General Congregation (n. 25 paragraph 3) as well as the freedom of the Congregation and of the delegates demanded a certain caution, right from the beginning the Congregation set up an "Information Office" after a consideration and discussion of the matter. It was made up of Fathers who were not members of the Congregation but who did have permission to attend its sessions. Newsletters written by them were reviewed according to a set of norms by a commission of delegates which had been established for that purpose by Father General. There were also regulations for the news which the delegates themselves sent out privately.

8. The Introductory Decrees

(*From the Minutes,* Acta 32, 33, 38, 49, 105-108)

The General Congregation wished to preface its decrees with three documents which serve as a sort of general introduction:

1) First, "The Mission of the Society of Jesus Today" (d. 1): The first draft had been prepared in the first session by Commission VI. In the interval between sessions a mixed commission made up of members from the fourth and the sixth commissions was set up which, with the help of many other experts and after several attempts, worked out a new text. Once the comments of the delegates had been received at the beginning of the second session, this new text was again revised and after discussion was approved by the Congregation on November 16, 1966.

2) Secondly, "On the Renewal of Our Law" (d. 2): This decree sets forth the principles and conditions which are to be observed in the renewal of our law. The subcommission on the substantials of the Institute prepared this decree. After the usual deliberation and discusion, it was approved at the same time as the first decree.

3) Thirdly, "The Task of the Society with Regard to Atheism" (d. 3): The sixth commission worked out the text for this decree in the first session in order that the Society might immediately take on the responsibility asked of it by the Supreme Pontiff in his audience on May 7, 1965, "in order that with all your united strength you might oppose atheism most forcefully." The decree was approved on July 5, 1965, and on July 15 by a unanimous vote the Congregation decided on its immediate promulgation so that without delay the Society could put in the public domain its response to the will of the Supreme Pontiff.

9. The Conservation and Renewal of the Institute

(From the Minutes, Acta 52-54, 57)

Not a few postulata which were sent to the Congregation asked either explicitly or implicitly that it be easier to deal with changing the substantials of the Institute, not excepting those which are contained in the Formula of the Institute. On the other hand, other postulata, out of fidelity to the spirit of St. Ignatius, insistently wanted the Congregation to declare that our Institute maintained its full force and obligation even in our times. The Congregation therefore thought that it had to act on the revision of decrees 12-16 of the Collection of Decrees. Having taken on this most serious of questions, the subcommission on the substantials of the Institute prepared two reports. However, because of the length of time needed for their research work, the reports could not be discussed in full session although they had been given to the members in the first period of the Congregation. In the interval between the two sessions, after consulting with other experts, the draft of a decree was written from the material in those two reports and discussions were held on that draft in the usual way in the second session. This discussion, however, brought on a new revision of the draft out of which finally came the definitive text which the Congregation approved on September 19, 1966 (d. 4). In that decree, because of certain extrinsic difficulties, the Congregation did not want to retain the old prohibition against introducing changes in the text of the Constitutions themselves as written by Ignatius, but they expressly committed this matter to the judgment of the General. In addition, the Congregation wanted Title I in the future edition of the collection of decrees to be called "The Institute and its parts," and section III which is to be entitled "The conservation and renewal of the Institute," to be placed before section II which is entitled "Interpretation and dispensation from the Institute."

10. The Distinction in Grades

(From the Minutes, Acta 33-35, 37, 38, 42-43, 55-59, 61, 62, 65, 67-73)

1. This was one of the most serious and one of the most lengthily treated questions in the Congregation. There was a very large number of postulata about it, and they came either from the provincial congregations or from individual

Jesuits. Some of them simply wanted to abolish the distinction of grades in the Society. Others wanted its opportuneness at least to be subject to judgment. Yet others asked that it be preserved absolutely unchanged. Some vehemently complained about the norms presently used for the promotion to solemn profession. . . Given the situation and the time available, the subcommission on grades consulted with experts in law and history, investigated the origin of grades and their establishment, and their development in the old and in the restored Society. It examined the arguments set forth on either side of the question and it proposed to the Congregation various solutions. A very large number of written comments came from the members of the Congregation, and after discussion in many plenary sessions, the Congregation finally came to this conclusion in its first period: (a) A decree would not be passed on removing the distinction of grades between the professed and spiritual coadjutors; (b) There was to be no decision that all the scholastics would first take the vows of the spiritual coadjutor and that some of them could later be promoted to the solemn profession; (c) The current norms for admission to the profession were to be revised; (d) It was recommended to Father General that he set up a commission with the responsibility to investigate the whole problem; this investigation was to include the advantages and disadvantages of granting the solemn profession also to temporal coadjutors (see d. 5 n. 2).

2.   But, among other things, between the two sessions of the Congregation two documents of the Church were published, namely the conciliar decree "Perfectae Caritatis" and the apostolic letter "Ecclesiae Sanctae." At least to some members of the Congregation this seemed to change the whole state of the question; to others, however, it seemed that the distinction of grades in the Society was repugnant neither to the mind nor to the will of the Church. Because of all this, in September, 1966, the controversy started up again. So that everybody might knowledgeably carry on discussion on the disputed questions, first of all, a group

of eleven experts prepared an informational report on the principal points in law which had to be considered with reference to this question. Then four speakers were designated, one by one. Two of them were to give the reasons for removing the distinction of grades and two the reasons for retaining it. Besides this, everyone had plenty of opportunity to speak. A day of consideration, of reflection and prayer was then provided for and all were urged to offer Masses and prayers to God by which they might ask light to find His will in so important and serious a decision. Finally on October 7th, the feast of Our Lady of the Rosary, in secret ballots the Congregation decided the following: (a) The grade of spiritual coadjutor was not to be here and now suppressed, nor were "Definitors" to be set up who could decide together with Father General on the suppression of this grade either in law or in practice; (b) But immediately after the conclusion of this 31st General Congregation a commission was to be established which was to investigate the whole question of the grade of spiritual coadjutor and which would inform the next congregation of procurators about the results of its research in order that the congregation of procurators might decide whether a general congregation should be called in order to deal with this matter (see d. 5 n. 1); (c) A discussion was to begin immediately on revising the norms for promotion to the grade of professed of four solemn vows.

11.   The Permanent Diaconate

(From the Minutes, Acta 43, 45, 48, 81-83, 90)

The question of whether to allow perpetual deacons in the Society was brought up in some postulata in connection with the question of temporal coadjutors. Toward the end of the first session the Congregation decided that the whole question ought to be more accurately investigated in the light of the teachings of the Council and the question of the distinction of grades in the Society. This was done by the appropriate subcommission and by a certain number of experts. Their proposals were discussed in the second session, and the Congregation judged that it ought not to act on the question of introducing the permanent diaconate into the Society at the present time, but rather that it ought to remove whatever obstacles might stand in the way of it being later introduced, committing that to the prudence of the General (d.6). As for the religious vows which would be pronounced by such deacons, whether in the future they would be the vows of the temporal coadjutors or the spiritual coadjutors, the Congregation did not pass a decree because the function of deacons was not yet clearly defined in the documents of the Church, and because the Holy See intended to give further details on this for all religious.

12. Temporal Coadjutors

(From the Minutes, Acta 43, 45, 48, 60-63, 79, 104, 105)

The fact that the number of temporal coadjutors in the Society has been in constant decrease from the beginning of the twentieth century was not the only reason why the General Congregation began to take up this problem. Very many postulata asked for such a treatment, and they desired that the nature of the vocation of the temporal coadjutor would be more clearly defined, that the esteem for this vocation should be shown in actual practice, that the coadjutor brothers would have access to more types of responsibilities and, for these reasons, that their formation—spiritual, cultural and technical—might be further developed. Having all of this before them, the subcommission on temporal coadjutors prepared a draft of the decree and after receiving the comments of the Fathers, corrected it and presented it for debate. The Congregation did not wish to take a vote on this draft in the first session in order that so serious a question could be considered at greater length and allowed to mature. Therefore, with the help of other designated experts a new draft of the decree was written in the interval between the two sessions. Research also took place into what temporal coadjutors themselves from various regions of the Society thought about their vocation and about a decree from the Congregation. These opinions along with the new draft decree were given to the members of the Congregation in the second session. After the usual written comments the question was again discussed in plenary sessions. Finally the Congregation voted on October 12, 1966, on a definitive text and on amendments which had been proposed by the delegates (d. 7). As far as the name of the grade itself, the Congregation decided that in the Latin decree itself the name "coadiutor temporalis" was to be retained but in the vernacular languages it could be translated according to the custom or usage of each region.

13. The Spiritual Formation of Jesuits

(*From the Minutes,* Acta 82-86, 106, 107, 114)

The Congregation received more than 160 postulata in which, for a variety of causes, some complained about the way in which in our times young Jesuits were being formed in the spiritual life. Toward the end of the first session the Fathers of the Congregation received a first report prepared by the appropriate subcommission in which the principles and characteristics of Ignatian spirituality were recalled and in which practical applications to be made here and now for each period of formation were proposed. Because of the lack of time the question could not be pursued any further. In the interval between the sessions there were meetings of masters of novices and of spiritual fathers from many Assistancies. With their opinions taken into account, the subcommission wrote a new report in the second session and distributed it. There was an "open session" of the subcommission with simultaneous translation. From the remarks which were made at that session and from the written comments of the members of the Congregation, the subcommission revised the report and opened it up to discussion, making the comment that the nature of the decree was pedagogical and not doctrinal. The main intention was that it deal in an appropriate manner with the spiritual difficulties of the young Jesuits of our times. In the discussion, quite a few amendments were proposed, and they were voted on too. Finally, a definitive text was approved on November 4 and 5, 1966. A verbal change in that text was allowed as a result of an "intercession" proposed on November 11 (decree 8).

14. The Formation of Scholastics Especially in Studies

(*From the Minutes,* Acta 30-32, 39)

The postulata which dealt with the academic formation of Jesuits numbered around 300. Commission III took very attentive account of them and thought it was better to prepare a single decree which would treat organically of all the material. For many questions this decree would satisfy the desires expressed in the postulata; for other questions which could not immediately be solved, it would provide opportune guidelines. Although a general congregation can indeed revise the decrees of prior congregations, and can even change the Constitutions, it cannot derogate from the universal laws of the Church. Such laws, for example, are the apostolic constitution "Sedes Sapientiae" which, up to the present, still obliges all religious, and the conciliar decree "Optatam Totius" which pertains to all priests. As far as academic degrees go, by decree of the Second Vatican Council, the law on ecclesiastical academic degrees, that is the apostolic constitution "Deus Scientiarum Dominus" is to be revised. Since, for this reason, it is not yet clear what studies will be required in the future for individual degrees, the Congregation was unwilling to set down determinate norms. It did establish this general norm, that Jesuits commonly should acquire those degrees in philosophy and theology which they are able to acquire by our curriculum of studies. Besides, since when it comes to studies, there are many rapid changes in the world and in the Church and, since one region differs from another very greatly, it was difficult to set down laws which were too precise. Wherefore, at the proposal of the commission, the Congregation was satisfied to set down general norms and to put off further determination of those norms either to a new Ratio Studiorum which would apply to the whole Society or to regional orders of studies which were to be prepared soon for the various regions of the society. Therefore, the Congregation gave to Fr. General, with the advice of the commission which was to be set up to revise the Ratio Studiorum, the power even to revise those decrees of preceding general congregations which could not be squared with the new conditions of our times and circumstances. For this reason the decree which had been prepared, discussed and approved in the first session was, by the will of the Congregation immediately promulgated by Fr. General on July 13, 1965 (decree 9).

15.   On the Vows of Scholastics and Their Dismissal from the Society

(*From the Minutes,* Acta 37, 38)

Some postulata indicated that difficulties were to be found in the present regulations of vows after two years, and they proposed that this regulation either should be accommodated to the norms of the common law of the Church or should be changed in some other way. Other postulata saw a certain defect in fairness in the dismissal of scholastics and coadjutors according to the norms of the rescript of the Holy See of Aug. 10, 1959. Into both types of difficulties an appropriate subcommission looked carefully, and it prepared and distributed a report, but since this would touch the specific papal law of the Society, the question first was asked whether the Congregation even wished to discuss the matter. In both cases, the majority of the members of the Congregation voted negatively.

16.   The Third Probation

(From the Minutes, Acta 39, 40, 46)

The postulata which dealt with this central point of our Institute, rather than opposing the institution of the third probation itself, brought up instead questions of the concrete way in which in our times it is put into effect or pointed out difficulties in its external structure. The subcommission on the third probation, which was made up of eight tertian instructors, after looking at all of this very carefully, decided, first, that that external structure was neither necessary to obtain the purposes set down in the Constitutions and pontifical documents nor was it prescribed by the general congregations, but that it only came from the ordinances and instructions of previous Fathers General. The commission saw in addition that hardly anything could be set down for the whole Society before a careful investigation of the ways in which, for our times and conditions, other structures would better help obtain those same ends in various regions. So it proposed to the Congregation the draft of a decree in which it confirmed the importance of the tertianship and gave rather general norms for the way in which its external structure might be renewed. This renewal was to be effected after taking account of the appropriate experiments by which the General could see what ought to be set down for the whole Society. This the Congregation approved of in the first session on July 13, 1965 (decree 10).

17.   Admission to the Religious Vows

(From the Minutes, Acta 43, 55, 82-84, 104, 118, 121, 123)

1.   In accord with the will of the Congregation as it was made clear in both sessions (see above n. 10), the subcom-

mission on grades, with the help of certain experts, prepared a first report on the new norms to be observed in promotion to last vows. The tenor of that proposal was that, supposing a sufficient theological knowledge, the reason for admission to the solemn profession of four vows would consist especially in the outstanding apostolic capabilities of the candidate himself, which would be shown in the obvious evidence of his practice of virtue and in his uncommon aptitude, proven by experience, for one of the ministries of the Society. When the Congregation later decided that a decree on removing the distinction of grades was not to be passed, the question of the norms for promotion to last vows was taken up again. After the proposal of the subcommission had been examined and discussed in the usual way and finally after taking account of the comments and the amendments of the members of the Congregation, it was voted approval on November 3, 1966 (decree 11).

2. As to what pertains to the rite to be observed in the pronouncing of vows, the Congregation, in response to a particular postulate, committed to Father General on November 17, 1966, the task of preparing an ordination for the whole Society to be used on an experimental basis (decree 12).

18. The Religious Life

(From the Minutes, Acta 17, 33-38, 43, 44, 46-48, 77, 80, 81, 99-101, 105-123)

1. *Religious life in general*—The Congregation judged it opportune to start its decrees on the adaptive renovation of religious life in the Society by a preface "on the religious life in general." The Congregation excerpted that preface from a rather longer document on the teachings of the Council on religious life and their application to the Society, which the appropriate subcommission had prepared and which had undergone discussion. Later, with the approval

of the Congregation, the subcommission withdrew that document because there was still rather difficult work yet to be done on it which could not be done because of the imminent end of the Congregation. So this briefer introduction, after being discussed and amended in the usual way, was approved by the Congregation on November 16, 1966 (decree 13).

2. *On Prayer*—In the first session the particular subcommission prepared a report on spiritual life in the Society, which proposed solutions to the wishes expressed in the postulata. This report, revised according to the written comments of the delegates, was discussed in three sessions, but there was not time to finish the work. At the time of the interval between sessions, a large number of experts in history, spiritual theology, and psychology were questioned, and their written responses went out to all of the members of the Congregation. In the second session, it seemed opportune to separate the question of prayer from the other questions connected with it (spiritual formation, the vows, community life, and discipline . . .) which were going to be treated in other decrees. The subcommission on spiritual life again prepared the draft of a decree. On this draft there was discussion through almost five whole plenary sessions. After more than 80 speakers had been heard, the document went back to the subcommission which had been increased in size by two more members. However, since they were preparing a definitive text, it seemed best to know what the opinion of the majority of the members of the Congregation would be as to the rule of an hour of daily prayer. At the request of the subcommission, a secret written straw ballot or indicative vote was taken. In accord with the tenor of this ballot, the subcommission then revised the draft of the decree. Again public discussion ensued, so that the members of the Congregation could propose amendments. Finally, the revised draft and the amendments which had been proposed were voted on November 14, 1966. But on the following days three "intercessions" were made about n. 11 of the decree. Two of those "intercessions"

were rejected on November 17. The third, however, was agreed to by the Congregation. Finally, a further vote took place on the whole of section 11 which had been amended in accord with that third intercession, and it received approval by a large vote (decree 14).

3. *Devotion to the Sacred Heart of Jesus*—There were not a few postulata on this matter. Also, experts were consulted in the period between the two sessions. Nonetheless, because the desires expressed in the postulata would have entailed a long and difficult theological investigation which exceeded the scope of the labors of the Congregation, the subcommission on the spiritual life judged that a formal decree ought not to be passed, but rather that it ought to be recommended to Father General that he promote a theological and pastoral study of this devotion. However, in the general discussion it was clear that this was not satisfactory to many of the members of the Congregation, and finally when it came to a vote on November 17, 1966, in the very last meeting of the Congregation, it approved by a very large majority vote the text of the decree proposed in the course of an amendment (decree 15).

4. *Chastity*—The subcommission on vows, following in the steps of the Second Vatican Council and after consulting many other Fathers who are experts in moral theology, canon law, and psychology, prepared a report during the period between the two sessions of the Congregation and sent it to all the members. Once they had in hand their comments, the subcommission wrote a draft of the decree in the second session, and it was discussed in plenary meetings. The principal point of discussion was, whether in the brief amount of time available, a document could be prepared which would satisfy the demands of the Society. The greater part of the Congregation decided that a decree should be passed but that its general tenor should be completed by a study done by experts, and they committed to the care of Father General this study (decree 16).

5. *Obedience*—Not a few postulata complained of the crisis of obedience of the Society of today. Some of those postulata desired that the principles of Ignatian obedience should again be affirmed. Others asked that there should be an explanation of the relationship of those principles to the progress of biblical, psychological, and sociological scholarship. Others requested that a special commission be set up by Father General which would investigate the whole problem. The subcommission on vows already in the first session tried to prepare a report which in some way would respond to these desires. But after the conclusion of the Second Vatican Council, there was an obvious need for calling together a group of experts with whose help a draft of a decree might be prepared. So in the period between the two sessions, eleven experts of varying opinions and tendencies were consulted who, first of all, sent in written positions papers. Later, they met with the chairman and with the other members of the subcommission and prepared a second report which was sent to all the members of the Congregation. With these comments in hand, a final draft was written in accord with the comments. This draft was the object of discussion in plenary sessions. In the report, the chapter on the difficulties which might arise from the demands of conscience, as it was so-called, was omitted. However, it became clear in the discussion that this omission did not meet the approval of many of the members of the Congregation. Therefore, once the discussion was finished, the Congregation on November 11, 1966, voted on all the parts of the decree except for n. 10. Later, on the 16th of the same month, they approved paragraph 10 to which the subcommission had restored the paragraph on the difficulties of conscience (decree 17).

6. *Poverty*—Besides the work of the commissions which had been set up at the order of the 29th and 30th general congregations, there existed an abundant amount of explanatory material which had been prepared before the Congregation by a particular expert. With the help of these documents, the subcommission on poverty prepared eight

reports. They were as follows: the way of proceeding in this matter, the general principles of our poverty, the vow of not relaxing poverty, common life, collective poverty, remuneration for work, the gratuity of our ministries, foundations. After the members had commented, the draft of a decree was prepared which, after the usual discussion, the Congregation approved in the first session on July 10, 1965 (decree 18). On July 13, by majority vote the following were elected definitors: Fathers Antoine Delchard, delegate from the province of northern France; Jesus Diaz de Acebedo, delegate from the province of Loyola; Joseph Gallen, delegate from the province of Maryland; and Antonio Leite, delegate from the province of Portugal. According to n. 20 of the decree, they were to prepare a draft of an adaptive renewal and redoing of all of our law on poverty. Father General was later to promulgate this decree and put it into practice as an experiment until the next general congregation. Since, however, the decree would touch the Formula of the Institute as it was approved by the Holy See "in forma specifica", an account of what had been done was prepared and sent to the Supreme Pontiff. After consulting with the Sacred Congregation for Religious, he responded through a letter of His Eminence, the Cardinal Secretary of State, on June 6, 1966, kindly approving and confirming what had been done (see document 3).

7. *Common life and religious discipline*—The appropriate subcommission had prepared several documents. In the first session of the Congregation, the members received a first report, but they were unable to enter into discussion on it. In the interval between sessions, a second report was prepared and quite a few experts were consulted who sent in their written comments. After further remarks from the delegates of the Congregation had been received, the subcommission wrote a draft of the decree on which discussion took place in the second session in September, 1966, in the course of several meetings. Nonetheless, the Congregation thought that the whole draft ought to be more accurately

redone, and, for this reason, they sent it back to the sub-commission again. The subcommission, with an increase in membership, redid the whole draft, and, again, there was discussion on it in November. Finally, the decree was approved on November 17 in the two last meetings of the Congregation (decree 19).

8. *Reading at Table*—a. In some postulata, the pro-posal came up to revise the present norms for reading at table, but the subcommission on knowledge of the Institute, to whom the question was referred, after considering the nature of the proposal and the fact that it was rather a matter of Father General's power, as well as the difficulty of writing general laws for such a great variety of places, judged that the whole thing ought to be committed to him. This judgement the Congregation approved in the last ses-sion (decree 20, n. 1).

b. Father Janssens, in accord with the mind of the 30th general congregation, had changed the custom of reading the Summary of the Constitutions at table every month to the reading of it three times a year as long as rule n. 53 of the same Summary (about reading it monthly in private) still remained in force. Some complained in their postulata that because of this prescription knowledge of the Constitu-tions would decrease, and others proposed some remedies. Since, however, this pertained to the responsibility of Father General, and since besides, another decree had committed to him a revision of the rules (see decree 19, nn. 14-16), the subcommission on knowledge of the Institute thought that the whole thing should be referred to his prudent judgment and action. This proposition the Congregation also agreed to in the last session.

19. The Better Choice and Promotion of Ministries
(*From the Minutes,* Acta 23, 39-41, 48)

1. In the light of postulata which looked only to some aspects of our apostolates, the subcommission on the choice

of ministries judged that thought should be given to the adaptation of our total apostolate. Because of this, it proposed to the Congregation a general report on the apt choice and arrangement of ministries. Once it had received comments from the members of the Congregation, the subcommission prepared the text of a decree on which there was discussion in the first session and which was voted acceptance on July 14, 1965 (decree 21).

2. Many postulata asked that major superiors be helped in their better choice of ministries by commissions of experts, a situation which did not seem to have been provided for sufficiently in decree 50 of the 30th general congregation. The present Congregation, after the matter had been examined by a subcommission and, as usual, discussed in plenary sessions, thought it opportune to recommend the setting up of commissions on the choice and arrangement of ministries, not only for the individual provincials but also for regional gatherings of provincials. This, therefore, was decided on the same date, July 14, 1965 (decree 22).

20. Our Priestly Apostolate

(From the Minutes, Acta 66, 73-75, 87, 102, 108)

In this decree (decree 23), the Congregation wished to respond to many postulata. In some of them, the fear was expressed lest the present-day Society be too much given over to apostolic works of the temporal order which were rather the work of laity than of priests. Those postulata asked that our priests occupy themselves, especially in the ministry of the word of God and in the administration of the sacraments. Other postulata, on the contrary, expressed the desire that the Society declare that priesthood in the Society could be exercised not only in the direct care of souls but also in other works which were ordered to the good of the Church, for example, in scholarly research, in the education of youth, in the social apostolate. In the first session of the Congregation, the sixth commission prepared a report which, however, did not satisfy many of the participants in the Congregation. During the fourth session of the Second Vatican Council, a rather broad inquiry was made among the conciliar experts who were members of the Society and who were then at Rome. Later, a meeting with these experts was held in order that, among other things, this situation might be examined. With their help, some of the members of the Congregation prepared a second report which was sent to all of the members. After comments, a special subcommission was set up in the second session. It redid the whole text of the proposed draft before it went into discussion. Once the discussion was held, the Congregation approved this text with some amendments on October 19, 1966 (decree 23). There was later, however, a formal "intercession" which dealt with n. 6 of the decree, on the works which pertain to a priest by his very ordination. In order to avoid false interpretations, the Congregation corrected that number on November 7.

21. Mission Service

(From the Minutes, Acta 41, 61, 63-65, 92, 107)

1. To satisfy those who were asking either about the purpose and nature of our missionary work or about other questions of the missionary action of the present day Society, the Congregation preferred to pass a general decree rather than to give response to individual questions or wishes. With this in mind, toward the end of the first session, a draft was prepared and distributed to the members of the Congregation, but, because of the lack of time, there was no opportunity for discussion. After the first session of the Congregation, however, the conciliar decree, "Ad Gentes" and more recently the apostolic letter "Ecclesiae Sanctae" appeared, and several experts drawn from the whole Society were asked their counsel. Once having received their judg-

ments, the subcommission on foreign missions redid the whole draft. The members of the Congregation had their say in the discussion periods and proposed amendments. Finally, on October 22, 1966, the balloting took place, and the decree was approved in its latter form (decree 24).

2. There were seven postulata on the subject of more easily permitting journeys of missionaries back to the province of their origin. One of these postulata was sent and signed by all of the major superiors of East Asia. There was no obstacle to this in the decrees of preceding general congregations. Therefore, it seemed sufficient to the subcommission to declare that trips of this kind ought to be considered something normal for the benefit of the mission and of the missionaries and to recommend to Father General to set more specific norms in this matter. This judgment was approved by the Congregation on November 5, 1966 (decree 25).

22.   Ecumenism

(*From the Minutes,* Acta 77-79, 101, 102, 115)

Four postulata publicly expressed the wish that the spirit and work of ecumenism be promoted in the Society. In the first session of the Congregation, a report was prepared along with a very brief draft of a decree, but there was no time for discussion. Later, a certain number of the delegates, along with some experts on ecumenical and conciliar matters drafted another report which was sent to all of the members of the Congregation. At the beginning of the second session, a new subcommission was set up which, again, redid the text in the light of the comments of the delegates and of experts and in the light of the great diversity of circumstances in the various regions of the world. The draft was discussed in plenary session, and, once the discussion was over with, Augustin Cardinal Bea, the head of the Secretariat for the Union of Christians, who had been invited by Father General, gave a talk to all the members of the Congregation. Finally, on November 2, 1966, the decree was approved (decree 26).

23. Pastoral Institutions

(From the Minutes, Acta 43, 44, 95-97, 116)

In the first session of the Congregation, inquiry was undertaken and discussion took place in the plenary sessions about accepting the care of souls in parishes as was proposed in several postulata. There was no time, however, to come to a vote on this. In the period in between the sessions, two reports were prepared by the appropriate subcommission, one on pastoral institutions, especially on the Apostleship of Prayer and the Marian Congregations or Sodalities, the other on apostolic work in parishes. These reports were sent to the members of the Congregation and after their comments had come in and the Secretariats of the Apostleship of Prayer and the Sodality had been consulted, three separate chapters were written by three groups of delegates in the second session out of which the draft of the decree was fashioned. The usual general discussion took place and the definitive text of the decree was approved by the Congregation on November 14, 1966 (decree 27).

24. The Apostolate of Education

(From the Minutes, Acta 97-100, 115, 123)

There were not a few postulata which asked the Congregation to set forth accurately our task of teaching students in colleges in the light of the characteristics of our vocation and in the light of the theological doctrine on the character and office of the priest in the Church. These postulata were seriously considered in the first session of the Congregation. Later, at the end of January, 1966, some of the delegates met, and after examining the earlier work and the recommendations made by prefects of study and also listening to several experts, they prepared a report which was sent to all the members of the Congregation. Because of the importance of the matter, this report occasioned many comments; some called into doubt the very usefulness of this apostolate and others concerned themselves with particular problems in it. Therefore, a subcommission on education, after speaking of more general matters, decided to insert in the text of the decrees, along with norms appropriately adapted to our day, the norms also given in the decrees of previous congregations. This draft underwent quite a bit of discussion in the second session of the Congregation, in this instance using as an experiment simultaneous translations. About 40 of the members of the Congregation spoke and almost 60 amendments were proposed. Balloting took place on all of this on November 12, 1966, and the definitive text was then approved (decree 28). However, several "intercessions," were made which sought a somewhat more accurate way of expressing matters in two places in the decree, and the Congregation accepted these two "intercessions" on the 17th of the same month.

25. Scholarly Work and Research

(*From the Minutes*, Acta 65, 66, 68, 69, 103)

This question was touched upon in many postulata, either directly or indirectly. In the first session of the Congregation, the matter was looked into in the light of the office and the responsibilities of priest, and in that light a draft was prepared and distributed to the members of the Congregation. Many comments ensued and at the beginning of the second session a specific subcommission was set up which prepared a new report in two sections. The first of them set forth a sort of rationale for a decree, and the second gave the text of a decree in five chapters. After the usual discussion, the subcommission went back to revising the decree in the light of the amendments and proposals of the speakers, and, for this reason, the first chapter was divided into two paragraphs in order that more emphasis might be given to the question of the sacred sciences. The decree as thus revised was approved by the Congregation on November 2, 1966 (decree 29).

26. Cultivating the Arts in the Society

(From the Minutes, Acta 112-114, 119)

Some of the members of the Congregation asked that the Congregation acknowledge by a specific decree the apostolic values of the liberal arts. A subcommission, therefore, was set up which prepared a report. In the report it pointed out what place the arts of this type should have in the history of the Society and in the documents of the Church. In confirmation of the latter, the subcommission adduced the conciliar decree "Gaudium et Spes," n. 62. It also contended that those arts exercised a great influence in our day on the minds of men because of the prominent place which the communications media have in present day life. In these contents, it proposed the text of a decree, which after discussion in the general sessions, was agreed upon by the Congregation on November 15, 1966 (decree 30).

27. Interprovincial Houses in Rome

(From the Minutes, Acta 100, 102-104, 106, 118)

In order to respond to the postulata which asked that the houses in Rome which were immediately dependent upon the General might be more generously provided for, the subcommission on education already in the first session prepared a report on the nature and on the conditions of these houses, along with draft recommendations, and gave it to the members of the Congregation. In order to examine this matter more accurately, a special subcommission was set up in the second session, which prepared another draft decree. After the usual discussion, this draft was accepted by the Congregation on November 15, 1966 (decree 31).

28. The Social Apostolate

(From the Minutes, Acta 23, 24, 32)

Although the three previous general congregations, 28, 29 and 30, had occupied themselves with the social apostolate, nonetheless in order to repair certain defects in our legislation on social matters and to respond to postulata, the appropriate subcommission proposed to the Congregation that, presupposing and confirming antecedent decrees, it also pass a new decree in which certain aspects of the social apostolate would be more distinctly defined. This was done in the first session of the Congregation and in accord with the established procedural norms, the new decree was discussed and then approved on July 1, 1965 (decree 32).

29. Relations with the Laity

(From the Minutes, Acta 63-66, 82, 100-103, 112)

In several of the decrees of the Congregation mention is made of the laity and of their collaboration in our apostolate. In the light of the decisions and the teachings of the Second Vatican Council and of the wishes expressed by many Jesuits in their postulata, it seemed necessary to pass a specific decree, with this especially in mind, that Jesuits might appropriately adapt to the teachings of the Second Vatican Council the way in which they related to the laity. Toward the end of the first session, a subcommission on the laity was set up which in the interval between the sessions prepared the draft of a decree. At the beginning of the second session, after having received the comments of the members of the Congregation, the subcommission thought it appropriate to open to discussion two different decrees, the one, more general, on the relationship of the Society to laypersons and their apostolate, and the other on a closer juridical bond between the Society and certain laypersons. This second question touched not only upon the apostolate but also upon other aspects of our Institute.

The first decree after the usual discussion and amendments was approved on October 14, 1966 (decree 33).

With reference to the other problem, after discussion and in the light of the extraordinarily large variety of conditions in the various regions of the Society, it seemed more appropriate to leave the whole matter to the judgment and the prudence of the General. This was approved by the Congregation on November 10, 1966 (decree 34).

30. The Mass Media

(*From the Minutes,* Acta 18, 32)

1. In the light of some of the postulata and the ordinations of Very Rev. Father John B. Janssens, already in the first period of the Congregation it seemed opportune to pass a decree on this matter. It would bring together and arrange the norms which up to the present had been established and would strengthen them by a new declaration on the part of the Society (decree 35). To this, the Congregation added a special recommendation of the Vatican radio station which had been entrusted to the Society by the Supreme Pontiff (decree 36). Both of these decrees were approved on July 1, 1965.

2. Two postulata treated of the opportuneness of setting up at the curia of the General an information center for the purpose of collecting and disseminating news which would be useful for our apostolates. After the matter was considered and examined by the appropriate subcommis-

sion and discussed in full assembly, the Congregation decided that this proposition was to be recommended to Father General (decree 37).

31. The General Congregation

(From the Minutes, Acta 47, 52, 53, 55, 58-60, 75, 76, 108, 109, 120)

1. A certain number of postulata proposed that a general congregation be summoned at specifically stated times, for example, every six years. After the matter had been investigated by the subcommission on congregations, it seemed that the reasons which, at the time of St. Ignatius, held that a general congregation should not take place at specific times were still valid. The difficulties which had been set forth in several of the postulata could be sufficiently obviated by the congregations of procurators and by the provincial congregations, the functions of which had now been increased. Besides, the fuller communication between head and members could be brought about through the congregations of provincials, through the "relatores" elected in the provincial congregations, through the trips by Father General to the various provinces and the journeys of the provincials to Rome. After consideration of all of this, the Congregation decided on July 14, 1965, that the general congregations were not to be summoned at set intervals.

2. Quite a few postulata also dealt with restricting the number of members in a general congregation. They also dealt with a more equitable "representation" of the provinces, with granting to vice-provincials the right to come ex officio to general congregations either with or without an elected member. Even before the present Congregation, a particular expert had undertaken a full and accurate investigation of this matter. In the first session of the Congregation, the subcommission on congregations prepared a report and, after receiving comments, revised it. In it sev-

eral methods were thought up and elaborated upon to solve what is not an easy question. In the second session of the Congregation, the discussion went on through plenary meetings, but finally on September 22, 1966, the Congregation decided that in the next, i.e., the 32nd general congregation, the rules presently in force should be observed, namely, at that congregation there would be present from each of the provinces the provincial along with two elected members, but from the independent vice-provinces, the vice-provincial was not to come ex officio, neither with another delegate who had been elected in the congregation of the vice-province nor without such a delegate.

3. The experience of this present Congregation and many postulata were persuasive on the need of preparing more accurately the material to be dealt with in the congregation and on the need of having present at the congregation itself experts for all the more difficult matters. The appropriate subcommission studied this matter and prepared a report in the first session. The discussion on this was held on November 19, 1966. A decree, with certain amendments which had been proposed during the course of the discussion, was passed on November 16, 1966 (decree 38).

4. Since the apostolic letter "Ecclesiae Sanctae" which had been published by the Supreme Pontiff, Paul VI, on August 6, 1966, prescribed that in order to promote the adaptive renewal of each individual religious institute, a special general chapter should be held within two or at the most three years, whether this chapter be an ordinary or an extraordinary one, the question arose whether this present 31st General Congregation satisfied the prescription of the Holy Father or whether another general congregation had to be called. The question was examined in the usual way. Six special experts were consulted. A report was prepared by a subcommission. Members of the Congregation gave their written comments. Discussion took place in the plenary sessions. The Congregation, however, decided that it

was not its part to vote on this matter but rather that the Sacred Congregation for Religious ought to be asked about it. On November 12, 1966, the Sacred Congregation replied during the course of our second session that the present Congregation fulfilled those requisites which the apostolic letter, "Ecclesiae Sanctae," had set forth (see document 4).

32. Congregations of Procurators and Provincials

(From the Minutes, Acta 15, 16, 42, 85, 89, 90, 93)

Some postulata asked for the suppression of the congregation of procurators; others asked that it be more appropriately adapted. Already in the preparations for this General Congregation, Rev. Father Janssens had posed the question, and research had been undertaken by a expert. In the first session of the Congregation, the subcommission on congregations prepared a report and after the usual comments and the discussion in general sessions, the matter was proposed to the Congregation by stages. On July 9, 1965, the Congregation decreed the following: The congregation of procurators was not to be suppressed. It was, however, to be renewed or adapted in its purpose and in its members. (a) As for the purpose of the congregation, besides the vote on whether to call or not to call a general congregation, consultation was to be held under the leadership of Father General about the circumstances and the activities of the whole Society. (b) As far as the members go, alternatively to Rome were to come procurators who had been elected in provincial congregations, and provincial superiors (who, however, were obliged to follow the vote of their own provinces if that vote was to call a general congregation). When the provincials did thus meet, another member of the Society was to be elected who could be either a professed father or a spiritual coadjutor. He was to send a written report to Rome and, at the judgment of Father General, could be called to Rome. Finally, the Congregation extended all of these provisions to the independent vice-provinces. In the second session of the present Congregation, a subcommission, relying specifically upon certain historical facts which previously could not be considered, proposed that the whole question be reintroduced, but the Congregation did not approve of this. Therefore, certain added questions alone were considered. On October 24, 1966, it was decided that the meeting of provincials every six years with the General and his assistants and counselors was to be called the "Congregation of Provincials." It was also decided that the first meeting to be called after the present General Congregation would be a congregation of procurators elected in their own provincial congregations. Finally it was decided that if, after the "votes" of the provincial congregations and of the congregations of independent vice-provinces had been received in Rome, and it was certain from those votes that there was an affirmative majority for calling a general congregation, the congregation of provincials would de jure not be held (decree 39).

33. The Provincial Congregation

(From the Minutes, Acta 19-23, 42, 83, 85-88, 97-99, 114, 115, 119, 120, 123)

The rules presently in force on the make-up of the provincial congregations had for a long time displeased many Jesuits. Therefore, it is hardly to be wondered at if many postulata brought up this question. In the preparation for the General Congregation, Father Janssens had already proposed the problem and an expert had done research on it. In the first session of the present Congregation, three principal solutions were proposed by the subcommission on congregations: a limit on the age of those who were to be delegates, a proportionate representation from age levels, and an antecedent or previous election. Once the matter, as usual, had been examined and discussed, on July

9, 1965, the Congregation decided the following: (a) The legislation presently in effect was to be reformed and some limitation on the number of members to be called to the congregation was to be retained. (b) There was to be no age limit on the members, nor was there to be a distribution of delegates according to age; rather, preference was to be given to some kind of antecedent election. There were many further specifications to be determined; they were examined in the second session. After the preliminary vote had been taken which, according to the Formula of the General Congregation, defines those points for which a two-thirds majority vote is needed for passage, on October 22, 1966, the Congregation decided on the following specifications for the election to a provincial congregation: (a) Not only the professed of four vows but also the formed spiritual and temporal coadjutors would have the same right to active voice (the right to vote) in the election; however, the scholastics who were priests and who had finished theology were not to have this right to vote as some had proposed. (b) Not only the professed of four vows but also the spiritual coadjutors, would have passive voice (the right to be voted for), so that the number of spiritual coadjutors in a provincial congregation could be the same as but could not exceed the number of professed. On November 12, going yet further, the Congregation decided that even the formed temporal coadjutors would have passive voice, with the proviso that at the most five of them could be members of the congregation and that at least one of them had to be present as a member. Finally, there were a certain number of complementary questions which came up and on which the Congregation voted in the last session, November 17th (decree 40 and 51).

34. Governance in General

(From the Minutes, Acta 17-19)

The document on governance in general was prepared by the appropriate subcommission; written remarks were handed in and a discussion was held in several plenary sessions. From these discussions, it was evident that the questions dealt with there would better and more accurately be treated in the decrees on the religious life, especially the decree on obedience, and because of this, it seemed much less useful to pass a separate decree on governance in general.

35. Governance of the Whole Society

(*From the Minutes,* Acta 3-7, 12-16, 20-26, 30, 32-34, 41, 46, 49, 53, 55, 56, 58, 60, 66)

1. *The Superior General*—(a) On the question of the length of office of the Superior General of the Society—as was said above in number 3—there had already before his election been discussion in several sessions. After the election the Congregation confirmed the Constitutions, which state that the Superior General is to be elected for life. After the matter had been considered in the usual way by a subcommission and had been discussed in several plenary sessions, clearer norms were set down for his resignation from office, and decree 260 of the *Collectio Decretorum* was reworded. Both of these were approved on July 8 and 13, 1965, and the Congregation voted on the text of the decree on July 15, adding to it the right to promulgate it immediately (decree 41).

(b) Lest the General lack the help he needs for the complexity and amount of business with which he deals, after a certain number of postulata had been examined by a subcommission and after the discussion in the plenary sessions, the Congregation on July 8, 1965 approved the addition of a fourth paragraph to decree 262 of the *Collectio Decretorum* (retaining the third paragraph about a substitute vicar-general). By this, the General has the right to nominate a vicar-general as a helper as often as this seems necessary or convenient to him (decree 41, n. 3).

(c) Some postulata expressed the desire that Father General would visit various regions and provinces of the Society, at least when there would be more serious business at hand. After considering the advantages and disadvantages, the Congregation decided to recommend those journeys to the General (decree 42).

2. *The Vicar-General nominated at the death of the General*—With the necessity of preparing well for a general congregation, something which the members of this Congregation were much aware of, and with the number of general assistants now set at four, questions arose on the function of the vicar-general at the death of the general. These questions, which had been proposed in two postulata, were examined by the subcommission on universal governance during the period between sessions of the Congregation and after comments by the members of the Congregation, they underwent discussion in the second session. On October 17, 1966, the Congregation decided upon the changes which were to be introduced into the office of the vicar-general (decree 43).

3. *The General Assistants*—With the growth of the Society and the growth, therefore, in the number of assistants, not a few inconveniences followed from the usage which began right at the first general congregation that the same persons be assistants "ad providentiam" and "ad consilium." Father Janssens acted on this matter in preparation for the Congregation and a study was done by an expert. Besides, almost 70 postulata were sent to the Congregation. The subcommission on the governance of the whole Society, after it had examined attentively the Constitutions of the Society and its history, thought out several solutions and proposed them to the Congregation. After an antecedent straw ballot or indicative vote in order to ascertain the mind of the Congregation, the subcommission prepared a report, and, after the usual comments, submitted

for discussion its final judgment. Lengthy discussion took place on the question. Finally, on June 24, 1965, the Congregation decreed the following: (a) Only four assistants would be elected by the congregation; they would exercise the providence of the Society toward the General; they would be the consultors of the General in the canonical meaning of the term. The other counselors (general counselors, regional assistants and expert counselors) would be named by Father General. (b) The length of office of those four general assistants, in accord with the norms of the Constitutions, would not be limited; they would be elected to serve until the election of a new general, in such a way, however, that others could take their place in accord with the revised norm of decree 269 of the *Collectio Decretorum;* the general congregation, even one which would be called simply to deal with business, would always be able to elect new general assistants. (c) These provisions would explicitly be labeled "experimental" until the next general congregation. Once the vote had been taken, Father General declared that on this occasion he would name as general counselors those whom the congregation would elect general assistants. There was an "intercession" on the length of office of general assistants, but when the vote was taken, in neither case was there the two-thirds majority necessary to change the Constitutions. Finally, on June 28, 1965, the text of the decree on the general assistants was approved. The second session of the Congregation added a certain number of declarations in order to clear up some doubts: Decree 264 of the *Collectio Decretorum* was simply suspended until the next general congregation; the approval of the assistants and of the provincials in designating a new general assistant outside of the general congregation would be required for the validity of such a designation (decree 44, I).

4. *The other Counselors of Father General*—In the voting on the general assistants, the existence of other counselors had already been approved, but further specifications were necessary. The question was proposed and

discussed, and on July 1, 1965, the Congregation decided the following: (a) The General would have general counselors who would help him especially in those things which were of more universal moment to the Society; regional counselors who would help him especially on the affairs of a particular region; and expert counselors who would help him especially in specific or special questions. (b) The four assistants "ad providentiam" would be called "General Assistants." The counselors on matters of more universal moment to the Society would be called "General Counselors." The counselors on the affairs of individual regions would be called "Regional Assistants" and the rest would be called "Expert Counselors." (c) Regional assistants would be named after hearing the advice of the provincials of the region and, if they were to be named during a general congregation, upon hearing the advice also of the delegates of that region or assistancy (decree 41, n.2).

5. With a change in the situation of the assistants, a doubt arose about their right to attend the congregations of the Society. After the customary examination and discussion, the Congregation decided that the new norms were to be observed until the next general congregation could give a final judgment about this experiment (decree 44, III).

6. *Visitors*—(a) A particular postulatum proposed that decree 274 of the *Collectio Decretorum* should be revised in order to avoid doubts or difficulties which could come up. After the usual examination and discussion, the Congregation decided on September 17, 1966, to agree to this suggestion (decree 45, I).

(b) Some postulata dealt with the office itself of the visitor. Documents of the law and history of the Society were consulted in dealing with the question. However on July 8, 1965, the Congregation decided that nothing was to be changed in our legislation on visitors, but it recommended to the General that visitors should not keep their office too long nor should they enjoy indefinite authority or jurisdiction (decree 45, n.2).

36. The Election of the General Assistants and the Nomination of the Other Counselors of Father General

(*From the Minutes,* Acta 24, 27-30, 33, 41)

1. Once the question of general assistants had been solved, and after the four days of information gathering, and after the other prescriptions of the Formula had been carried out, in three sessions and by separate votes on June 29, 1965, the Congregation elected the following as general assistants: Father Paolo Dezza, elector of the province of Venice-Milan (second ballot); Father Vincent T. O'Keefe, elector of the province of New York (first ballot); Father John L. Swain, who had just recently fulfilled the office of assistant and of vicar-general (second ballot); and Father Andrew Varga, substitute for the provincial of Hungary (third ballot).

2. On June 30, with those members also present who could be part of the Congregation only for the business of the Congregation, on the third ballot Father John L. Swain was elected admonitor of the superior General.

3. Father General, as has been said, named as general consultors those whom the congregation had elected as general assistants. Afterwards, after he had heard the advice of the provincials and delegates of each of the assistancies, he named the following as regional assistants on July 8th: For Italy, Father Hyginus Ganzi, from the province of Turin; for Germany, Father Mario Schoenenberger, from the vice-province of Switzerland; for France, Father Maurice Giuliani, from the province of Paris; for Spain, Father Victor Blajot, from the vice-province of Bolivia; for the English assistancy, Father Andrew Snoeck, from the

province of northern Belgium; for the American Assistancy, Father Harold Small, from the province of Oregon; for the Slavic Assistancy, Father Anton Mruk, from the province of lesser Poland; for the southern Latin American Assistancy, Father Candido Gavina, from the province of Argentina; for India, Father Jerome D'Souza, from the province of Madurai; for the northern Latin American Assistancy, Father Emanuel Aceves, from the province of North Mexico; for the East Asian Assistancy, Father Herbert Dargan, from the province of Ireland.

37.   The Governance of Provinces and Houses

(*From the Minutes,* Acta 16-18, 24, 30, 44, 47, 77-81, 95, 103, 104, 112, 121, 123)

1.   *Provincials*—Many postulata dealt with provincials, either to give them greater power or to aid them in receiving more help from consultors and experts, or to encourage inter-provincial cooperation. Since it belonged to the office of the General to grant greater power to the provincials, the Congregation on July 12, 1965, took the following actions: (a) Certain decrees by which provincials were obliged to seek the consent of Father General it wanted revised. (b) It recommended to Father General that in accord with his prudence he give wider powers to the provincials, and that the provincials, after they had been in office for a certain time, should be called to Rome so that they could consult with Father General and be better prepared to rule the province in accord with the mind of St. Ignatius. (c) It recommended to the provincials that they make better use of commissions or committees of experts and of consultors meetings of the province in which other fathers and brothers could be of help according to the subject matter to be dealt with. (d) It recommended that regulation 825, paragraph 3, of the Epitome be changed so that the office of admonitor to the provincial need not necessarily be en-

trusted to his socius. (e) Finally, it proved the text of the decree on provincials (decree 46).

2. *Local superiors*—A report was prepared in the first session of the Congregation and comments on it came from the members of the Congregation. Later, however, it seemed preferable not to pass a separate decree about local superiors but rather to treat the subject in other decrees, specifically in the decree on the life of obedience in the Society.

3. *The selection of consultors*—In the Society, differently than in other religious institutes, the consent or the advice of consultors is generally not required for the validity of the actions of superiors. However, in order to adapt itself to the mind of the Holy See as expressed in the apostolic letter "Ecclesiae Sanctae," the Congregation passed a decree on November 10, 1966, defining the way in which members of the Society would have a truly effective part in the selection of consultors. After an "intercession" the words "truly effective" which had been removed from the decree were again put back into it (decree 47).

4. *Inter-provincial cooperation*—This matter was deliberated on at length. In the first session of the Congregation, the appropriate subcommission had prepared a report and received comments on it, and discussion had gone on in full assembly. But at that point nothing was decided on because, at the request of certain of the delegates, the Congregation judged that the matter was not yet mature and should be postponed until the second session. A new report was prepared in the interval and it was discussed through several meetings in the second session. Finally, on October 25, 1966, a decree was approved (decree 48).

38.   The Formulas of the Congregations

(From the Minutes, Acta 3, 7, 11, 12, 17, 20, 23-25, 48, 59, 60, 64, 89-91, 107, 114, 115)

1. After the usual deliberations, the Congregation decided on June 9, 1965, what was to be changed in numbers 25, 118, and 124 of the Formula of the General Congregation so that the procedures for maintaining secrecy and for deciding on certain changes in the Institute could be defined. On November 16, 1966, it also approved certain amendments to number 116 which dealt with sending postulata to a general congregation (decree 50).

There was also question of changing the ceremonies connected with the election of the general, as two postulata proposed. The subcommission drew up various suggestions for discussion. However, since the conditions in which future elections would take place were not at all clear, especially in the matter of liturgical laws which were then in process of change, the Congregation on September 27, 1966, decided that it was enough to drop chapter 6 in title 3 of the Formula of the General Congregation and to add in number 56, a paragraph according to which the order and procedure for the day of election would be proposed by the vicar and approved by the congregation (decree 50).

There was also deliberation on the power of a general congregation before the election of the General himself, but since the matter needed further investigation and there were more serious and pressing questions, no decision was taken.

2. *The Formula of the Provincial Congregation*—Besides those points which dealt with the composition of the congregation, which were treated in number 33 above, this Congregation introduced certain other changes as follows:

(a) On June 27, 1965, changes in numbers 3 and 92, lest the provinces which were undergoing persecution would be totally absent from the congregation.

(b) On November 16, 1966, changes in numbers 28, 74, 81, 86, dealing with postulata and the matters to be treated in a congregation.

(c) On November 5, 1966, changes in numbers 29, 39, 43, 55, and 76, defining minor questions (decree 51).

3. Toward the end of the Congregation, a committee of experts was set up which was to take care of revising the several formulas of the congregations. However, since, besides the changes prescribed by this Congregation itself, there would be others which would have to be introduced either as necessitated by the legislation of the Congregation or as requested by certain postulata, and since there was not enough time to examine and approve each and every one of them, the Congregation gave to the General the responsibility and the power to finish this work of revising the formulas, with the deliberative votes of those members of the general curia who by reason of their office had a right to attend a general congregation (decree 52).

39. The Catalog of Censures and Precepts

(*From the Minutes,* Acta 110, 111, 119)

It was asked that the catalog of censures and precepts imposed upon Jesuits should be revised (*Collectio Decretorum,* nn. 303-315). Since this was a question of rather complicated legal matters which would need some research, especially historical research, and since it was foreseen that in the new code of canon law the part dealing with penalties was being revised, the Congregation decided, after hearing the report of a committee of canonists and after discussion, that it was enough to delegate this power to Father General (decree 53).

40. The Censorship of Books

(*From the Minutes,* Acta 111, 119)

Some postulata proposed the revision of the norms on previous censorship of books. A committee of canonists prepared a report which was discussed in plenary session. Since the commission which was to deal with the Ratio Studiorum still had to do research on the norms dealing with doctrine to be held in the Society, and since we could not know what laws would be set down on this matter by the Church in the new code of canon law, the question could not at present be decided. In order to provide some remedy for current difficulties, the Congregation recommended this matter to Father General, and gave him the necessary power to adapt the particular norms of our law after he had consulted experts and the general assistants (decree 54).

41. The Abrogation or Revision of Certain Decrees

(*From the Minutes,* Acta 120, 121, 123)

The present Congregation, after the usual research and deliberation, revised certain decrees in the *Collectio Decretorum,* which had been approved in 1923. For example, on the preservation and renewal of the Institute, on the studies of our scholastics, on poverty. However, there were requests that still other decrees for various reasons be revised or be taken out of the collection. Agreeing with this request, the Congregation passed decree 55. Numbers 2 and 3 of that decree it approved on July 12, 1965. Number 1 it approved on November 17, 1966 (decree 55).

42. Powers Granted to Father General

(*From the Minutes,* Acta 49, 123)

The following were in addition to the powers and delegations which were set forth in other decrees:

1) At the end of the first session of the Congregation for this one time alone, the Congregation gave Father General the power to change provincials for a proportionately grave reason before the end of the Congregation. This carried the proviso, however, that anyone who had finished his term of office of provincial in that period would, none-

theless, still retain the right of coming to the General Congregation in the second session, and that anyone who was during that time newly appointed a provincial also had the right to come to the Congregation with the full and complete rights of a delegate.

2. Since the legislative work of the 31st Congregation was very very large and simply could not, therefore, always provide for all of the implications which these new decrees and the other dispositions relative to our law might entail, the Congregation gave Father General the power, with the deliberative vote of the members of the general curia who by reason of their office had a right to attend a general congregation, to abrogate or to modify decrees of prior general congregations which could not be reconciled with the decrees of this Congregation (decree 56, n.)

3. As previous general congregations had been in the custom of doing, so also at the end of each session this Congregation gave to the General under certain conditions the power to dissolve colleges and professed houses, the right to approve the Acta or minutes of some of the sessions, and the right to polish stylistically the statutes or decrees of the Congregation (decree 56, n.2).

43. Other Acts of the Congregation

(*From the Minutes,* Acta 11, 12, 20, 34, 43, 74, 81, 83, 92, 96, 104, 105, 109, 112)

1. Since colleges can be sold, dissolved, or transferred only by a general congregation (see the Formula of the Institute, 2, and the *Collectio Decretorum,* n. 281), the Congregation was asked for permission to suppress Beaumont College in the English province and the college of Livorno in the Roman province. But at the request of delegates from several assistancies, since these were individual instances and very complex ones, the Congregation com-

mitted the care of the affair to Father General with full power to decide in accord with his own prudent judgment.

2. In each of the sessions of the Congregation, permission was given to certain members to leave early, either because of serious business which they had on hand which could not brook delay or because of ill health. Those members were:

(a) In the first session: Fathers Emmanuel Antunes, delegate from Portugal (from the 20th meeting); Wenceslaus Feřt, procurator from Bohemia (from the 35th meeting); Aloysius del Zotto, delegate from Kerala (from the 44th meeting);

(b) In the second session: Fathers Pedro B. Velloso, delegate from Central Brazil (from the 73rd meeting); Josef Čurič, delegate from Croatia (from the 76th meeting); Emmanuel Antunes, delegate from Portugal (from the 89th meeting); Mauritio Eminyan, delegate from Malta (from the 92nd meeting); John Thomas, delegate from Wisconsin and Eusebio Garcia Manrique, delegate from Aragon (from the 102nd meeting); John Foley, former provincial of Wisconsin (from the 108th meeting); Jean LeBlond, delegate from Northern France and Daniele Villanova, provincial of Sicily (from the 112th meeting); Jose Arroyo, delegate from Toledo (from the 118th meeting).

To other of the delegates permission was granted to be absent from one or another session.

3. The cut-off day for proposing new postulata was set for June 9, 1965, for all of those who were not actually members of the Congregation, and November 13, 1966, as the end of the work of the Congregation approached, even for those who were members of the Congregation.

44. The Benevolence of the Supreme Pontiff Toward the Congregation

(From the Minutes, Acta 1, 11, 105, 110, 120)

The Supreme Pontiff, Paul VI, twice wished to speak personally to the members of the General Congregation. On the morning of May 7, 1965, before the sessions began, he invited the whole Congregation to the Vatican and expressed his best wishes and paternal hopes (see Document 1). Toward the end of the Congregation, on November 16, 1966, he graciously concelebrated Mass with Father General and five others of the members of the Congregation in the Sistine Chapel in the presence of all the other members of the Congregation. In his talk, sincerely and with great affection he expressed his anxieties and his confidence in the Society (see Document 2). Besides, several times in each session of the Congregation and in the period between the sessions he wanted to be informed by Father General about the course of its work and to look at the decrees of the Congregation. The Congregation, in a letter of November 16, 1966, expressed its thanks to him (see Document 5).

45.   The End of the Congregation

(From the Minutes, Acta 49, 123)

On November 17, 1966, the General Congregation came to an end. It had previously interrupted its meetings on July 15, 1965, and had taken them up again on September 8, 1966.

In the last meeting of each session, Father Severiano Azcona, who was previously been an assistant and who was oldest in order of profession, spoke in the name of all the members of the Congregation in offering thanks, first of all, to God, and then to our Father General and to all who had helped toward the successful outcome of the Congregation. Then Father General spoke, and, after he had briefly described the sum total of the work of the

Congregation, he gave encouragement to everyone to work effectively to put into practice the decrees and the ordinances of the Congregation so that the hoped for renewal of the Society might thereby take place.

Finally, the members were asked whether they wished to declare the Congregation ended, and after they had responded with a unanimous "yes," they recited the hymn, "Te Deum Laudamus," and all made their ways home.

Thus, at the end of the 123rd meeting, after 141 days of work (70 in the first session and 71 in the second session), after many meetings of commissions and experts held in the interval between the two sessions of the Congregation, at eight in the evening on November 17, 1966, the 31st General Congregation, the twelfth in the restored Society, came to an end. May God bless the labors of this Congregation for His greater glory.

B.

DECREES
OF THE
31st GENERAL CONGREGATION

I

INTRODUCTORY DECREES

1 THE MISSION OF THE SOCIETY
OF JESUS TODAY

1. *On the Life and Mission of the Society in This New Era*

In this "new age" in which the human race now finds **1**
itself,[1] the Society of Jesus, according to the spirit of the
whole Church, which is itself in process of renewal, recognizes the difficulties with regard to its goal and plan of life
which are arising from the changes that have taken place
in man's way of living and thinking. At the same time it
recognizes the opportunities which arise from the new developments in our world and those which flow from the
renewal of the Church that has been begun by the Council.
It intends, therefore, to take a very close look at its own
nature and mission in order that, faithful to its own vocation, it can renew itself and adapt its life and its activities to
the exigencies of the Church and the needs of contemporary
man.

The nature and the special grace of our vocation are to **2**
be discovered above all in the dynamic development of the
Society from its earliest historical beginnings.

2. *The Origin of the Society in the Experience of the Spiritual Exercises*

For this history has its beginnings in the Spiritual Exer- **3**
cises which our holy Father Ignatius and his companions
went through. Led by this spiritual experience, they formed
an apostolic group rooted in charity, and in which, after
they had taken the vows of chastity and poverty and had
been raised to the priesthood, they would offer themselves

1 GS 4.

67

as a holocaust to God for whose praise and honor they had given up all that they had.[2]

4   They had heard the invitation of Christ the King and had followed it; for that reason they not only dedicated themselves entirely to labor, but desiring to become outstanding in every service of their king, they made offerings of greater worth and importance;[3] so that they would be sent under the banner of Christ by Him into the entire world, spreading His teachings among all degrees and conditions of men.[4]

3. *The "Mission" under the Roman Pontiff*

5   In this spirit they had offered and dedicated themselves and their lives to Christ our Lord and to His true and legitimate vicar on earth; so that he as Vicar of Christ might dispose of them and might send them where he judged that they could bear greater fruit.

6   But the first mission entrusted to them by Pope Paul III was one that was likely to scatter the group of Fathers in all directions. Therefore, after many deliberations in which they tried to distinguish between various spiritual inspirations and weigh the reasons for each side carefully, these first Fathers decided that they should not break up "a society united in God," but rather gradually strengthen it and stabilize it by making themselves into a unified body. Indeed they judged it more expedient to give their obedience to one of their number that they might more successfully and perfectly carry out their first desire of fulfilling

---

2 See *Deliberatio primorum Patrum* (a. 1539), *Cons*MHSJ, I, 2.

3 See *SpEx,* The Kingdom of Christ (97).

4 See *SpEx,* The Two Standards (145). In the deliberation on poverty Ignatius listed among its advantages: "13. Esta (la pobreza) elegiendo todos diez, nemine discrepante, tomamos por cabeza al mismo Jesú nuestro Criador y Señor para yr debaxo de su bandera para predicar y exortar, que es nuestra profesión." *Cons*MHSJ, I, 80, No. 13.

the divine will in all things. Thus also the Society would be more securely preserved.[5]

4. *The "Missionary" Constitution of the Society of Jesus*

Thus it came about that the promise made to God of   7
obeying the Roman Pontiff with regard to all missions turned out to be "our beginning and first foundation."[6]

Such an offering expressed the consummation of that   8
knowledge of Christ which they had acquired in the Exercises, and united and drew that first apostolic band together in one body. It was in order to fulfill this offering more completely that the Society, as a mode of life, had its beginning under the Constitutions.

The first steps of the Society were directed by Ignatius   9
himself in the way of the Lord by his spiritual experience, in accordance with which he interpreted the course of events in the light of their relation to God. The result was that Ignatius founded the Society as an organization which would continually renew itself in the Church through the inner vigor of the Exercises and under the vitalizing impulse of the Spirit to fulfill those things which its vocation and its mission to promote the divine glory and the greater service of souls demanded.

5. *New Developments in the History of Man*

The history of four centuries, with its fluctuations be-   10

---

5 See *Deliberatio primorum Patrum, Cons*MHSJ, I, 7. In order that the true value of obedience in the Society may become more clear, this should be noted: in the beginning obedience was rather *ad intra* for the body of the Society, since "missions" came directly from the Holy Father. The power to send Jesuits to the Christian faithful was given to Father General by Pope Paul III in 1542, but the power to send them to infidels was not given until 1549 in the Bull *Licet Debitum.* And this was done even though some of the first members were opposed (see *ibid.,* p. 395). From that time on obedience in the Society acquired its full apostolic or "missionary" sense and consequently its supreme importance.

6 *Declarationes circa missiones* (1544-45), *Cons*MHSJ, I, 162.

tween honor and humiliation, has cast a rather penetrating light upon the nature of the Society and its originating idea. With whatever degree of fidelity to its vocation and mission the apostolic works of the Society were begun and carried on, nonetheless on the one hand they show an internal dynamism in the attitude of universality and flexibility, while on the other hand the limitations and deficiencies of its individual members stand revealed.

11   Today, however, our Society, along with the whole Church, finds the conditions of human history profoundly changed.[7] The members themselves share in the contemporary "social and cultural transformation," and the new ways of living which arise from socialization, urbanization, industrialization, and ever widening communication among men, and they do not fail to participate in the changed ways of thinking and feeling and weighing the values of human life. They experience also the fact that a keener sense of liberty has developed and that there is a more universal desire for the "full and free life"; they realize therefore at the same time that the conditions which affect religious life have been changed.[8]

12   For they are conscious on the one hand of that purifying of the religious life which, according to the Second Vatican Council, flows from the "more critical faculty of judging" which has grown up in our day.[9] They are conscious as well of the grave problems which can be found among many, even among Christians, arising from the crisis to which the Gospel itself and the Church's doctrine have been exposed because of modern criticism and contemporary philosophy. And they cannot avoid hearing the widespread criticism that the teaching and life of the Christian estrange him from the world and its struggles,[10] while at the same time great multitudes are still compelled to live a life unworthy

---

7 See GS 1.
8 See GS 4, 6, 7, 9.
9 See GS 7.
10 See GS 34.

of the human person and the human race itself remains without any true unity.

They are also acutely aware that they are surrounded by **13** various sorts of atheistic teachings and especially by that humanism which contends that "liberty consists in this, that man is to be an end unto himself, the sole artisan and creator of his own history" and that "this freedom cannot be reconciled with the affirmation of God."[11] Often, too, they feel in themselves also that ambivalent desire of their contemporaries to perfect themselves as men.

6. *The Need for Revitalizing the Mission of the Society*

But all the members of the Society, firmly grounded in **14** faith, in company with all other Christians, lift their eyes to Christ, in whom they find that absolute perfection of self-giving and undivided love which alone completely reconciles man to God and to himself. For unless men adhere to Christ and follow the way which He shows, they desire and seek in vain for that full realization of themselves which they long for in their undertakings.

From this love for Christ, the Society offers itself com- **15** pletely to the Church in these needs, so that the Supreme Pontiff, as the Vicar of Christ, may "send" all its members into the vineyard of the Lord.

Thus the Society will try to be of assistance to the Church **16** according to the measure of the grace of its vocation, while the Church itself is helping the world so that the kingdom of God may come and the salvation of the human race may be achieved. Our Lord, with whose name our Society has been signed and under the standard of whose cross it desires to serve the kingdom of His love, is Himself the goal of human history, the point to which the desires of history and civilization converge, the center of the human race, the joy of all hearts and the fulfillment of all seeking. "Enlivened

---

11 **GS** 20. See decree 3 (on atheism).

and united in His Spirit, we journey toward the consummation of human history, one which fully accords with the counsel of God's love: 'To re-establish all things in Christ, both those in the heavens and those on the earth' (Eph. 1.10)."[12]

7. *The Need of Renewal and Adaptation in the Society*

17   In order that our Society may more aptly fulfill in this new age its mission under the Roman Pontiff, the 31st General Congregation has striven with all its power so to promote a renewal that those things may be removed from our body which could constrict its life and hinder it from fully attaining its end, and that in this way its internal dynamic freedom may be made strong and vigorous, and ready for every form of the service of God.

---

12 GS 45.

2   THE RENEWAL OF OUR LAWS

1.   The adaptation and renewal of our way of living   **18**
and acting extends itself, as it should, even to the body of
laws which contain the spirit and end of the Society and
also describe its structures and govern its apostolic action.
Although the Council and the post-Conciliar documents
invite us to this renewal, they carefully and clearly distinguish between fundamental or permanent elements of
the Institute (whether this is understood as a way of living
or as a collection of laws), and elements which are contingent and therefore changeable in response to the circumstances and needs of various times.

2.   The former, since they flow either from the very   **19**
nature of the evangelical counsels,[1] or constitute the specific
nature of our Institute,[2] are to be conserved as having a
perennial value. At the same time, however, they are to be
renewed by a continuous return to the sources of all Christian life, to the spirit of the founder, and to the originating
inspiration of the Institute.[3] Contingent elements, however,
should be so skillfully adapted that the religious life is

---

1 See Paul VI, Address *Magno gaudio,* To the general chapters of
  some religious families, etc., May 23, 1964, *AAS* 56 (1964) 567;
  ActRSJ 14 (1964) 408.
2 These proper elements, as being specific and to be preserved, are
  described in various ways: "the integral mind of the founder,"
  (Paul VI, *ibid.,* p. 569), "the proper nature and discipline of the
  institute" *(loc. cit.),* "the integral spirit of the rules" *(loc. cit.),*
  "individual character" (PC 2, c), "the spirit of the founder, as
  also . . . the particular goals and wholesome traditions which constitute the heritage of each community" (PC 2, b); see ES II,
  12*a*; "the proper spirit" (ES II, 31); "the end, nature, and character of the institute should be preserved" (ES II, 6); see ES II,
  33 and 40; also PC 20; "the primitive spirit" (ES II, 16§3).
3 See PC 2.

purified of foreign elements and freed from those that are obsolete.[4] Indeed, with a view to this end experiments in matters at variance with our own law may be instituted prudently by legitimate authority, or even in matters at variance with the common law, insofar as the Holy See, in suitable cases, will permit.[5]

20   3.   The 31st General Congregation has approached the task of adapting and renewing the Society in this manner, called by our mother the Church and under her guidance, and in a certain continuing tension between the faithful desire of retaining what is permanent and ought to remain as fundamental, and the vital necessity of adapting the Institute to those circumstances in which its life is led and its mission is carried out.

21   Thus it has determined that the entire government of the Society must be adapted to modern necessities and ways of living; that our whole training in spirituality and in studies must be changed; that religious and apostolic life itself is to be renewed; that our ministries are to be weighed in relation to the pastoral spirit of the Council according to the criterion of the greater and more universal service of God in the modern world; and that the very spiritual heritage of our Institute, containing both new and old elements, is to be purified and enriched anew according to the necessities of our times.

22   4.   Finally, since every true law seeks to enunciate the will of God, and since this will can be manifested under the inspiration of the Holy Spirit through subjects as well as through superiors and congregations, the Holy See properly urges full and free consultation of all members as a means of helping and directing the work of the congregation.[6] Indeed, as much as time and the circumstances of its convo-

---

4 ES II, 16 §2.
5 ES II, 6, 7, 8.
6 ES II, 4.

cation permitted, our present Congregation has enjoyed this help.[7]

But since a suitable renovation cannot be made once and **23** for all but must be continually promoted,[8] consultation can be employed even more extensively in the future,[9] both with a view to the preparation of future general congregations, and in order that the Superior General together with his council may make use of it for carrying on the renewal of the Society in virtue of the faculties granted him by the Holy See until the next congregation.[10]

---

7 See Letter of Reverend Father Vicar-General, December 15, 1964, *ActRSJ* 14 (1964) 525-26.

8. ES II, 19.

9 See *Formula of the Provincial Congregation,* N. 28, §§ 1-2; *Formula of the General Congregation,* Nn. 116-17.

10 ES II, 7-8.

3   THE TASK OF THE SOCIETY
REGARDING ATHEISM

I.   THE SPREAD OF ATHEISM AND THE MANDATE
OF THE HOLY FATHER

24   1.   The glory of God, as the goal of all creation, and man's own good require that he acknowledge, reverence, and serve God. Hence, the danger of atheism which faces so many men today should greatly stimulate the companions of Jesus to offer a purer witness of religious life and a more zealous devotion to apostolic work. The denial of God is no longer, as in former centuries, an isolated phenomenon; it has become widespread, affecting entire social groups and nations. In some countries, atheism is systematically spread by public authority, thereby violating the rights of man to the free investigation of truth and the practice of religion. In many more regions, the denial of God or indifference to religion has directly or indirectly infected the cultural and social life. The Supreme Pontiff Paul VI, on the occasion of the gathering of the Fathers for the 31st General Congregation, committed to the Society, in view of its special vow of obedience, the task of resisting atheism "with forces united."[1] Each Jesuit, therefore, earnestly though humbly, should take part in this task by prayer and action, and each should be grateful that he can thus better serve "his Lord alone and the Church, His spouse, under the guidance of the Roman Pontiff, the Vicar of Christ on earth."[2]

II.   THE UNDERSTANDING OF ATHEISM AND ITS CAUSES
AND OF THE MOTIVES OF ATHEISTS

---

1 Paul VI, Address to members of 31st General Congregation, May 7, 1965.
2 *FI* Julius III, n. 2.

2.   All Jesuits, whatever their particular apostolic work,   **25**
should give more attention to atheists and try to reach a
better understanding of atheism and of indifference to
religion. They should examine the different kinds of atheism, both systematic and practical, and should understand
them as well as possible.

3.   They should also distinguish its causes, such as the   **26**
relationship which the modern denial of God has to all the
changes taking place in the material and social condition
of mankind; or those "complex and multiple" causes which
may exist "in the minds of atheists, so that one should be
cautious in passing judgment on them";[3] or those social
injustices which, especially in developing countries, incline
many men to accept the atheistic doctrines which are connected with programs of social revolution.

III.   SOME DIFFICULTIES URGED AGAINST BELIEF IN GOD AND HOW TO DEAL WITH THEM

4.   To overcome the difficulties which are raised against   **27**
faith, often even among believers, Jesuits should take appropriate action, not for any political reasons, but purely
from apostolic motives.

5.   Many difficulties arise from this, that "there is a   **28**
demand that the world of divine realities be presented in a
higher and purer way than has been the custom in some
imperfect forms of speech and worship."[4] Jesuits should
therefore try to purify the presentations of God and to promote a truly personal adherence to the faith among believers.

6.   There are also some atheists, "gifted with a greatness   **29**
of spirit," who are motivated by impatience with "the
mediocrity and desire of personal advantage which infect
so many parts of human society in our times."[5] Jesuits

---

3 ES, *AAS* 56 (1964) 652.

4 Ibid.

5 Ibid., 653.

therefore should make every effort to see that faith may always lead to a genuine love of neighbor, a love that is practical and social-minded.

30   7.   On the other hand, the legitimate aspiration toward the autonomy of the sciences and of human enterprise is often carried to such a point that it arouses objections against the acknowledgement of God; indeed, some men present abandonment of religion as man's path to freedom. Therefore, our aim must be to let faith penetrate the concrete totality of life. It should be made clear that the Christian life does not turn away from developing the world. In fact, human values, cultivated without pride, and the universe itself, cleansed of the corruption of sin, illuminated and transfigured, will have their place "in that eternal and universal kingdom" which Christ will restore to the Father at the end of time.[6]

IV.   THE CHARACTER OF OUR WAY OF LIFE

31   8.   These means should be applied by members of the Society first of all in their own lives. Each should constantly cultivate an awareness of God who is living, working, and loving, an awareness which the Exercises of St. Ignatius impart through the meditation on the Foundation and the Contemplation for Obtaining Love. And, as far as possible, what God is should be made evident in the entirety of the Jesuit way of living and acting, namely, by taking on that basic attitude which the incarnate Word of God revealed throughout His life and especially in His supreme sacrifice, the attitude which the Exercises aim at, beginning with the contemplation on the Kingdom of Christ.

32   9.   Because atheists, estranged as they are from the environment of the religious world, will mainly judge us by our lives and actions, our way of living and acting must be entirely sincere and free from all appearance of pride or pretense.

---

6 See I Cor. 15.24.

V.   THE FORMATION OF JESUITS

10.   The formation of Jesuits should be adapted so as to   **33**
establish and promote this kind of spiritual life and a sincere
and fraternal manner of acting. Scholastics should also be
trained to understand the mentality of atheists and their
theories, and they should be furnished with appropriate
information, especially in the scholarly disciplines dealing
with man, presented in modern terms. Care should also be
taken that, as far as this is possible, those especially who
come from an entirely Christian environment can, in good
time, have some personal contacts with atheists.

VI.   THE RIGHT ORDER OF OUR MINISTRIES
AND THEIR ADAPTATION
TO THE TASK COMMISSIONED BY THE HOLY FATHER

11.   The mandate of resisting atheism should permeate   **34**
all the accepted forms of our apostolate so that we may
cultivate among believers true faith and an authentic
awareness of God. But we must also direct a greater part
of our efforts, more than we have in the past, to nonbelievers, and we must search for and experiment with new
ways for coming into closer and more frequent contact with
atheists themselves, whether they belong to those parts of
society which are most in need or to those which are
culturally more advanced.

12.   With regard to the areas where atheism is being   **35**
spread, we should concentrate on aiding the developing
regions, where religious life is liable to greater and more
abrupt disturbances because of the faster rate of change.

13.   In the light of the principal causes of atheism, it is   **36**
clear that we must emphasize both the social and the
university apostolates, either at our own or in secular universities.

14.   The vigorous intellectual efforts of all our scientists,   **37**
philosophers, and theologians are also called for, and there
should be a continuing cooperation among Jesuit scholars

in various disciplines, especially the sciences dealing with man.

38   15.   In our schools, the modern atheistic positions should be explained and subjected to careful evaluation, not by indulging in empty polemics, but by promoting the most accurate critical understanding of the atheists' arguments and ways of thinking.

39   16.   Jesuits should approach atheists with the firm conviction that the divine law is written in the hearts of all men and with the belief that the Holy Spirit moves all men to the service they owe to God their creator. Both by a style of proclamation adapted to each person, combined with religious respect, and by a brotherly witness borne in the concrete details of living and acting, Jesuits should work to remove obstacles and to help atheists find and acknowledge God.

40   17.   All superiors should see to it that our apostolate is constantly adapted to this end. It is especially recommended to Father General that in conversation with the Holy Father he try to obtain a clear knowledge of his mind with regard to the task he has committed to us and that, with the advice of experts, he direct the entire apostolate of the Society in carrying out that mission as effectively as possible.

II

THE INSTITUTE IN GENERAL

4   THE PRESERVATION AND RENEWAL
OF THE INSTITUTE

1. *Introduction*

Since "the most important work to which the General **41**
Chapters should devote their chief attention consists in
carefully adapting the laws of their Institute to the changed
condition of the times . . . but in such wise . . . that the
specific nature and discipline of the Institute is preserved
intact,"[1] the General Congregation, heartily desiring to
open up the road, and provide the juridical principles for
the adaptation of our body of laws, as mentioned in the
Introductory Decree, determines and decrees the following
changes in the *Collection of Decrees.*

2. *On the Institute and its parts*

This new decree is to be inserted at the beginning of the **42**
Prooemium of the *Collection of Decrees.**

The term "Institute of the Society" means both our way **43**
of living and working,[2] and the written documents in which
this way is authentically and legitimately proposed.[3] Among

---

*The use of roman or italic type for textual changes in previous
decrees is different in the official Latin editions of the documents of
the 31st and 32nd General Congregations. This English translation has
followed the same usages as the official Latin texts.

1 Paul VI, Address *Magno gaudio,* to the general chapters of some
  religious families, etc., see *AAS* 56 (1964) 569. *ActRSJ* 14 (1964)
  410.
2 See Paul III, *Regimini Militantis;* Julius III, *Exposcit Debitum:
  Formula of the Institute* of Paul III, 1, 9; *Formula of the Institute*
  of Julius III, 1, 2, 9; *Cons* [134, 152, 186, 398, 686, 603]; etc.
3 See *CollDecr* 7.

these documents some are laws properly so called; others set forth the legitimate traditions of the Society.[4]

44   To maintain faithfully the grace of our vocation as described in the Institute, the Spiritual Exercises of our holy founder stand in first place, both as a perennial source of those interior gifts upon which depends our effectiveness in reaching the goal set before us,[5] and as the living expression of the Ignatian spirit which must temper and interpret all our laws.

45   §1. The *Formula of the Institute,* or fundamental Rule of the Society has primacy of dignity and authority in the Institute.[6] It was set down first by Paul III,[7] then more exactly and in greater detail by Julius III,[8] was approved *in forma specifica* by many of his successors, and has obtained in a special way the status of pontifical law.

46   §2. There are also other laws of the Institute which have obtained the status of pontifical law, but not all have been approved by the Holy See in the same way; hence they enjoy varying degrees of dignity and authority.

47   §3. Apostolic Letters, rescripts, and indults issued for the Society also pertain to the pontifical law specific to the Society.

3. *On the preservation and renewal of the Institute*

48   In the *Collection of Decrees* decrees 12-16 are to be changed in this way:

49   Decree 12—§1. The substantials, or fundamentals, of our Institute are, first, the matters contained in the *Formula* of Julius III.[9] For the *Formula* exhibits the fundamental

---

4 E.g., St. Ignatius, *Letter on Obedience;* see *CollDecr* 7 §1, 2°.
5 *Cons* [813].
6 *Formulas of the Institute* of Paul III and Julius III.
7 Paul III, *Regimini Militantis.*
8 Julius III, *Exposcit Debitum.*
9 GC5, D. 44, 58.

structure of the Society, based, with the help of grace, on Gospel principles and the experience and wisdom of our holy Father Ignatius and his companions.[10] Accordingly, as the *Formula* itself recommends, all Jesuits should strive to keep before their eyes this image of their Institute, which is a way to God, as long as life lasts.[11]

§2.   Secondly, among the substantials are included also those matters without which the substantials of the *Formula* can be preserved with great difficulty or not at all.[12] General congregations have the power to declare which matters are substantial, and have done so at times;[13] moreover the General has the same power, to be exercised in matters of practice on a temporary basis.   50

Decree 13 is abrogated.   51

Decree 14—§1. The general congregation can declare the meaning of the substantials of the Formula of the Institute, but cannot change them on its own authority.[14]   52

§2.   Let substantials outside the *Formula of the Institute* continue to have the same stability they have previously enjoyed, except perhaps where the general congregation shall have determined that the connection of any one of them with the *Formula* has been notably weakened.   53

§3.   In matters which are not substantial, the Constitutions can and sometimes should be changed by the general congregation, but such a change should not be decreed definitively without a previous experiment or without a very clear reason.[15]   54

§4.   Decrees of general congregations, as well as rules and ordinations drawn up by the generals, even if inserted in the *Collection of the Institute,* not only may be changed   55

---

10 See the beginning of the Bulls of Paul III and Julius III.
11 *Formula of the Institute* of Julius III, 1.
12 GC 5, D. 44, 45, 58.
13 GC 5, D. 58; GC 27, *Colldecr* 13, b.
14 *Formula of the Institute* of Julius III, 2. GC 1, D. 16.
15 GC 1, D. 16.

by the aforesaid authorities in accordance with the competence of each, but it is their duty to provide for the continuing adaptation of them to the needs of the times.[16]

56 §5. Every adaptation of the Institute should aim at always establishing whatever seems to contribute most, all things considered, to the knowledge, love, praise, and service of God, and to the salvation of souls. For our holy Father Ignatius laid down as the foundation, or first criterion, of all our laws the greater glory of God and the help of souls.[17]

57 Decree 15—§1. It is permitted to the provincial congregations to treat of the substantials of the Institute, provided there are serious reasons, and in accordance with the norms laid down in the Formula of the Provincial Congregation.

58 §2. In sending postulata to the general or provincial congregation, all Jesuits should bear in mind the above decrees; and let each, with due love of the patrimony of the Society and with due regard for his own responsibility, propose what he desires for the renewal and adaptation of the Institute, realizing, moreover, that the light necessary for making such postulata will be obtained not only from dialogue but most of all from prayer.

59 Decree 16—Customs contrary to our law are not permitted in the Society.

4. On censures and precepts pertaining to the preservation of the Institute

60 The 31st General Congregation abrogates the precept of holy obedience in No. 306 of the *Collection of Decrees;* and commissions Father General to petition the Holy See, insofar as this is necessary, to revoke the penalties in No. 305 of the *Collection of Decrees.* For it is the desire of the Congre-

---

16 *Cons, Prooemium in Declarationes et Annotationes Constitutionum* [136].
17 *GenExam* and *Cons, passim.*

gation that a love and longing for all perfection may lead all Jesuits to the genuine preservation and increase not only of the body but also of the spirit of the Society.[18]

---

18 See *Cons* [602, 813].

5   THE DISTINCTION OF GRADES

61   1. The General Congregation decrees that, immediately after the close of the 31st General Congregation, a commission should be set up which will study the whole matter of suppressing the grade of spiritual coadjutor, either in law or in practice, and which will report on it to the next congregation, either of provincials or of procurators, in order that it may decide whether a general congregation should be summoned to deal with this matter.

62   2. The General Congregation recommends that the commission which is to study the entire problem of the distinction of grades should extend its study to include the advantages and disadvantages involved in granting solemn profession also to the temporal coadjutors.

6   THE PERMANENT DIACONATE

1.   Gladly complying with the will of the Church which **63** orders the restoration of the permanent diaconate in Eastern Churches where it has fallen into disuse[1] and also in the Western Church, where, in the judgment of the bishops and with the approbation of the Holy See, such a restoration may tend to the good of souls,[2] the 31st General Congregation declares that there is no obstacle preventing our Society, as far as it depends on us, from being helped in the future by certain members who would work permanently in the sacred order of the diaconate for the service of the Church.

2.   But the General Congregation entrusts this matter of **64** permanent deacons to Father General for prudent experimentation, according to the mind of the Church, where it is needed for the good of souls, as, for example, in our houses of the eastern rites in which it is not permitted for a priest to exercise the functions of a deacon in the celebration of liturgical offices.

---

1 See OE 17.
2 See LG 29, AG 16.

65   1. Since it is of the greatest moment that all Jesuits truly understand the nature of the Jesuit brothers' vocation in order that they may be properly integrated into the life of the Society, it seemed clear to the 31st General Congregation that the principal task to be accomplished with respect to the brothers was clearly to state the nature of their vocation and the practical applications which flow from it. The result will be that all members of the Society, even at the cost of a complete change of mind,[1] may be truly of "one heart and one mind,"[2] and all, enjoying one and the same vocation apart from the priesthood, may together and in the spirit of our founder dedicate themselves totally to the mission of the Church.[3]

66   2. Since apostolic activity belongs to the very nature of the religious life in Institutes devoted to the apostolate,[4] the whole life of a brother must be called apostolic by reason of the specific consecration which they make to God through vows in the body of the Society. But beyond that, the brothers have a full share in the special apostolic nature of the Society, which pertains to all its members. For that reason their activity in the Society is to be defined by the same principles which define the apostolic service of the whole Society, namely, through its attention to the greater service of God and the universal good. Thus it is that, through various talents and activities—all its members being united in one spirit by the bonds of love and obedi-

---

1 See the letters of Fr. Janssens, October 30, 1959, *ActRSJ* 13 (1959) 628; and August 31, 1964, *ActRSJ* 14 (1964) 553 ff.

2 AA 4, 32 (cited in PC 15).

3 See PC 6.

4 See PC 8.

ence[5]—the Society is to enjoy the presence of Christ, perform His tasks, and manifest His coming.[6]

3. Those offices and functions of the brothers which are **67** described in the Institute have a true apostolic value and are to be performed in a spirit of cooperation. It is by works such as these that the religious intimacy and calm of the Society's houses, the fraternal union in the service of Christ,[7] the dedication of scholastics to their studies, and especially the mobility and freedom of priests in the ministries[8] are more perfectly maintained. Such offices are to be committed to the brothers with the fullest possible responsibility.

Furthermore, in the service of the Society,[9] administrative **68** offices may be given them, even in our communities and with respect to other Jesuits, always excluding, of course, the power of jurisdiction.

4. Moreover, following precedents in both the old and **69** the restored Society, in addition to the offices mentioned above and in accordance with the judgment of superiors, brothers properly undertake those other tasks for which they may have a God-given talent and in which they may be of assistance and example "for the help of souls."[10] Among such tasks are teaching, practicing the liberal and technical arts, laboring in the fields of science and in whatever other areas their work, according to circumstances and places, may prove more useful in attaining the end of the Society.

In all the above mentioned ways the brothers, as men **70** consecrated to God, show that only in the spirit of the beatitudes can the world be transfigured and offered to God;[11] and in the Society they make a great contribution to the good of the Church.

---

5 *Cons* [821].
6 See PC 15.
7 See LG 43.
8 *Cons* [149] ; ES II, 27.
9 *Cons* [148].
10 *Cons* IV, *Prooemium,* 1 and A [307-8].
11 See LG 31.

71   5.   Since the Society wishes that the brothers be brought closely into both the social and liturgical life of the community as well as into its works,[12] as befits companions who live the religious life in the same family, fraternal union and communication are to be fostered more and more among Jesuits by all the means which a discerning love may dictate.[13]

72   6.   To this end the following will also be conducive: (*a*) the avoidance of every social distinction in community life; (*b*) the sharing, on the part of all Jesuits, in common domestic tasks, always with consideration for the greater service of God and the help of souls; (*c*) progressive participation on the part of the brothers in consultations; (*d*) the observance of the decisions of the 31st General Congregation regarding their participation in congregations.[14]

73   7.   The formation of brothers is to be entrusted to men who are carefully selected and diligently prepared.[15] They are to be taught especially to devote their lives to the service of the Church in the following of Christ. In order, however, that they may fulfill their duties and perform their functions more perfectly in the circumstances of modern life, their formation is to be spiritual, doctrinal, and technical, even confirmed with suitable degrees. This formation is to be carried out in suitable houses and is to be continued throughout life in accordance with each one's abilities.[16] The diversity which can result from this will contribute greatly to all the varied and necessary ministries which are to be carried on with one and the same spirit, supposing, of course, the preservation of indifference and availability for any offices whatsoever. "There are varieties of graces but one and the same Spirit."[17]

---

12 See PC 15.
13 See what is said on this subject in decree 19, nn. 1-8, (Community Life).
14 See decree 40, nn. 2, 4; ES II 27.
15 See PC 18.
16 *Loc. cit.*
17 1 Cor. 12:4.

8.   In order that all this may be conveniently put into execution, Father General is to establish a commission of experts. It will be their function: (*a*) to study more profoundly and to propound the theology of the vocation of the religious who is not destined for the priesthood in the Society;[18] (*b*) to advise Father General on practical experiments to effect the application of this decree; (*c*) to propose general guidelines for the formation of brothers, which ought to be adapted by provincials for their respective areas; (*d*) to revise the rules and regulations concerning the brothers according to the spirit of this decree.

---

18 See ES II 16 § 2.

III

THE FORMATION OF JESUITS

III

THE FORMATION OF ISOTOPES

8 THE SPIRITUAL FORMATION OF JESUITS

To all Jesuits the General Congregation fraternally pro-   75
poses the following norms as a kind of spiritual pedagogy,
ardently desiring that each Jesuit may become that instrument joined to God which is demanded by our religious
and apostolic vocation.

I. GENERAL NORMS

1. Since all spiritual progress is the work of divine   76
grace, it is essential that each one should dispose himself to
implore that grace by humble prayer and to respond to it
with docile obedience in all his actions.

2. Spiritual formation will assist Jesuits, as they grow   77
in faith, hope, and love, to follow Christ ever more closely
and become ever more intimately conformed to him according to the grace of our vocation. But since, though called to
perfect love, we are still sinners, our following of Christ
must take the form of continual conversion to him.

This progressive conformity to Christ can take place only   78
on condition that we humbly listen to his word in Scripture,
continually draw life from his sacraments, and follow him
as present in the Church.

3. Our following of Christ will be more genuine and   79
intimate the more intent each Jesuit is on adopting that
manner of serving Christ peculiar to this Society, which
precisely "desires to be distinguished by the name of Jesus."[1]
Let all, then, learn to esteem this vocation as God's gift and
adhere to it loyally. And let those attitudes of mind be
cultivated which St. Ignatius held most dear: personal love

---

1 Formula of the Institute, n. 1.

for the poor and humble Christ, filial devotion to our Lady His mother, sincere zeal for souls, fortitude in undertaking even more difficult enterprises for God's glory, a readiness for service founded on obedience and self-denial, the ability to find God in all things, development of skill in the discernment of spirits, ease in initiating spiritual conversation with others, a concern for thinking with the Church . . .[2]

80   4.   The Society's apostolic objective is to be considered the principle which regulates the entire formation of our members. It should, therefore, inspire their formation in prayer, the aim of which is to fashion men who will seek God in everything, as well as that formation in the religious and apostolic life whereby Jesuits are trained to become "prompt and diligent" in sharing Christ's redemptive mission in the Church with a magnanimity that embraces ever greater tasks and bears every adversity with steady cheerfulness.[3]

81   5.   For the sake of each one's spiritual growth, we should all cooperate actively in a spirit of fraternal love, bearing one another's burdens according to the measure of each one's grace and the work entrusted to each one by the Society. All should therefore have high regard for the account of conscience to superiors, which has been held in such honor by the Society's long tradition, for conversation with the spiritual father, and also for fraternal gatherings which, if they promote a common seeking of God's will, bring spiritual joy, encouragement, and apostolic fruitfulness to all.

82   6.   It should not be forgotten that the process of formation, a progressive and never completed work, is to take the form of an organic development in the various stages of formation, such that the spiritual life is never split off from the affective, intellectual, or apostolic life. Let us rather be directed by that discerning charity which St.

---

2 See *SpEx* 146-47, 352-70; *Cons* [288, 547, 648, 729, 813].
3 See *SpEx* 91, 97-98; *Exam* [101-102] *Cons* [547, 621].

Ignatius teaches us and seek to be able to recognize and choose the will of God in every situation.

7.   Following the pedagogy of the Exercises, spiritual   83
formation should fashion men who have true freedom and
maturity of spirit, who feel themselves to be freer, the closer
they are dedicated through obedience to the will of God.
This divine will is concretely revealed to us especially by
the inner promptings of grace and the direction of superiors,
as well as by the example of our brothers, by the demands
of our apostolic work, of common life, and of our rules, and
by the contingencies of our own life and the spiritual needs
of our time.

This objective is unattainable apart from the constant   84
cultivation of a spirit of initiative and responsibility within
obedience, and of self-denial in working together at a common task. This, as St. Ignatius rightly perceived, can be
obtained only through experience, which makes it necessary
during the time of formation to provide opportunity for all
to advance in freedom and maturity.

8.   Since St. Ignatius so strongly recommends to us a   85
right intention,[4] Jesuits do well to cultivate sincerity, which
is not genuine unless it be combined with loyalty to those
norms given us by the Church and the Society in accordance with the promises we have freely made. Thus all
should be convinced that subjective sincerity must find its
complement in objective loyalty.

9.   Since conditions in the modern world demand firmer   86
foundations for the spiritual life, it is necessary that from
the very beginning the scholastics and brothers be educated
continually and progressively to a deeper knowledge of the
mystery of Christ based on Holy Scripture and the liturgy,
as well as on the Society's traditional devotion to the Sacred
Heart of Jesus, and on the teaching concerning the Church
and other theological themes, always with the same purpose

---

4 *Cons* [288, 360, 618, 813].

in view, that faith, hope, and love be together nourished and strengthened.[5]

87 In mission lands it will help to enlist their rich heritage of sound morality and ascetical and mystical aspiration for the spiritual formation of Jesuits.

88 10. Human virtues are to be held in high esteem because they make the apostolate more fruitful and religious life happier; among these virtues are "goodness of heart, sincerity, strength of mind and constancy, diligent care for justice, politeness, and other virtues which the Apostle Paul commends."[6]

89 11. As other general congregations have already declared, special care must be paid to the selection of superiors and those who serve as fathers and masters of the spiritual life, so that the most capable men may be chosen for these offices which are more important than any other whatsoever. It is vitally important to be sure that, over and above knowledge and virtue, they are especially endowed with those human and spiritual gifts whereby they can inspire communities, foster fraternal cooperation, and help all towards greater spiritual maturity in discerning God's ways. What must be looked for, therefore, is openness of spirit, ease in dialogue, and abundant talent in these men whose essential task is to stimulate and attract their brethren by means of new things and old.

90 12. For any spiritual pedagogy to be fruitful it has to be adapted to those for whom it is meant to be used. Hence it will be up to the superiors and those groups in provinces and regions which care for the formation of Jesuits to seek, under Father General's direction, those means which are better accommodated to different situations. Throughout the indications set forth in the following chapters, this continued quest for adaptation is always presupposed.

---

5 OT 8, 14; PC 2.
6 PO 3; see Phil. 4, 8.

II.   THE NOVITIATE

The content of this chapter pertains alike to the scho-   **91**
lastics' and the brothers' novitiate. It will only be necessary
to introduce such differences of method as are required by
the different modes of one and the same service to which
all are called. Whether the scholastics and brothers have
the same master or different ones, care must be had to
obtain a common formation.

This initial stage of formation is defined by its twofold   **92**
purpose: it is a time at once of probation and of formation,
during which the grace of vocation should be cultivated and
during which it should already manifest its fruitfulness.

13.   To this end, sufficient human maturity is a require-   **93**
ment for candidates. Experience has shown, however, that
in our own time affective maturity has become more difficult for adolescents. Deficiencies in this regard are difficult
to detect, especially in candidates who in other respects are
mature and intellectually gifted. According to circumstances,
opportune provision must be made for this serious difficulty:

—by instituting a more searching examination of candi-   **94**
dates, adapting the instructions given by St. Ignatius to our
own times and having recourse when necessary to the
recommendations of men skilled in psychology. The secrecy
of consultation, the candidate's freedom, and the norms
established by the Church are, however, to be strictly
safeguarded;

—by postponing, when it seems advisable, the time of   **95**
admission. In such cases the applicants can be recommended
to certain selected fathers who will help them towards
obtaining maturity in their vocation while they prepare for
entrance into the novitiate by means of studies and apostolic
experiments.

14.   A vocation is then to be tested by various experi-   **96**
ments which, in St. Ignatius' view, constitute the specific
characteristic of the Society's novitiate. To achieve their
purpose, however, these must place the novices in those

circumstances wherein they can give evidence of "what they really are"[7] and show how they have made their own the spiritual attitudes proper to our vocation. New experiments, therefore, which fulfill this purpose today, ought to be prudently and boldly pursued.

97   15.   The primacy in the novices' formation should be given to the Spiritual Exercises, since of all the experiments they are the chief and fundamental one. Let them, therefore, be well prepared for, made at the most advantageous time, and presented in all their force and spiritual vigor. For it is by means of them that the novices are introduced into the heart, as it were, of their vocation, so perceiving its distinctive grace that they are able to bear witness to it.

98   16.   Education towards familiarity with God in prayer should be carried out in the apostolic atmosphere of the Exercises. The daily exercises of piety should tend to arouse personal love for Christ and teach the seeking of familiar communion with God in all things. Care should also be taken that the novices clearly understand how the different means presented in the Constitutions themselves (examinations of conscience, prayer, meditation, reading . . . [277])[8] serve to complement one another. These modes of prayer ought to be nourished by assiduous reading of Sacred Scripture and participation in the sacred liturgy. The novices will thus be introduced more deeply into the common prayer of the People of God and each one's sacramental life will be more abundantly fruitful. Primacy in this sacramental life belongs to the Eucharist, which from the start should be made our life's vital center. The sacrament of penance, moreover, should be cultivated in such a way that it retains its theological and ecclesial value and exerts its full effect on spiritual progress in the way of the Lord.

99   17.   This familiarity with God depends on self-denial, a spirit of recollection, and peace of mind. In these times it

7 Gonçalves da Cámara, *Memoriale,* 257, MHSI, I, 678.
8 *Cons* [277].

not infrequently happens that conditions of life are such as to engender, even unconsciously, a certain disquiet or anxiety of mind which makes a life of prayer more difficult despite good will. All therefore need to understand how, in addition to a living faith, emotional balance, humble acceptance of oneself, trust in others, and freedom of mind constitute for each one virtually fundamental conditions for the enjoyment of true and familiar converse with God.

18.   The practice of community life should both develop   **100**
the brotherhood of our members and benefit the affective maturity of the novices. This supposes that the novitiate community is already a brotherhood in the Spirit, which imparts to true friendship that perfection of charity to which the vow of chastity is itself ordered. The more fraternal is community life, the more will the novices grasp its meaning and its demands and feel themselves to be a part of the whole Society.

In the same spirit a suitable sharing of life and work   **101**
should be fostered between the scholastic and coadjutor novices, whereby they can be familiarly known and helped in esteeming and realizing their own vocation. In external matters such as food, clothing, and lodging, there should be complete equality.

19.   Education towards a discerning charity by means of   **102**
spiritual direction and obedience supposes that complete trust and freedom prevail between Father Master and the novices. A further necessity is that the novitiate's way of life be not so rigidly determined that the novices, lacking in all initiative, can hardly ever practice spiritual discernment, or even obedience itself, except in the form of a passive and impersonal submission.

20.   Formation in self-denial will be more authentic the   **103**
more closely the novices follow in the footsteps of Christ who took the form of a servant. Self-denial will be exercised primarily, humbly and simply, in the everyday demands of our vocation. Particular mortifications should, however, be

undertaken, under the guidance of obedience, as indicated by the individual's requirements, the Church's call, and the world's needs. Let the novices learn, in theory and by practice, so to shape their life by austerity and sobriety that, being "really and spiritually poor," they may be that sign "highly esteemed today" which the Church desires.[9]

104　　21.　During the time of novitiate, the doctrinal elements referred to in No. 9 comprise both a deeper initiation into the mystery of Christ and a fuller knowledge of the sources of the Society's spiritual doctrine and manner of life, chiefly to be drawn from the Society's history and the examples of its saints. Faults and deficiencies should not, however, be systematically overlooked, in order that the novices may be more ready to follow in the footsteps of our better members and more aware of their responsibility to the Society.

105　　Instruction should be given from the outset to the scholastic novices concerning the priestly character of their vocation, and to the novice brothers concerning the religious and apostolic character of their vocation and the meaning and value of work in accordance with the decree on the brothers.

106　　22.　Although entrance into the novitiate should entail a real separation from the life previously led in the world, superiors should nevertheless provide that the novices, while consistently maintaining a spirit of recollection, should have sufficient social contact with their contemporaries (both within and outside the Society). Likewise the necessary separation from parents and friends should take place in such a way that genuine progress in affective balance and supernatural love is not impeded.

107　　For this purpose the novitiate should, as far as possible, be located in a place where the novices' probation can be conducted according to the manner of life proper to the Society.

---

9 PC 13.

23.   Since spiritual progress requires living conditions **108**
which stimulate rather than crush human virtues, care must
be taken to prevent the novitiate's being so remote from
reality that novices' difficulties are there overlooked rather
than solved. The more the novices are stimulated to assume
responsibilities with prudent and discerning charity, the
more successfully will they acquire spiritual maturity and
the more freely will they adhere to their vocation.

24.   Since human development does not proceed at the **109**
same pace in everyone, if, when the time of noviceship is
ended, some of the novices, well endowed with the qualities
requisite for this vocation, still have not shown sufficient
maturity, major superiors should not hesitate to use the
faculty given them by our law and postpone the taking
of first vows or even extend the noviceship for a time by
the introduction of some longer experiment.[10]

25.   It will benefit the spiritual, intellectual, and affec- **110**
tive formation of the novices if they are associated with
some other selected men besides Father Master who at certain times can assist him in his work, in order to provide
the novices with a richer and fuller image of the Ignatian
vocation.

26.   The master of novices is to be assisted in acquiring **111**
ever better knowledge of the mentality of the candidates, so
that he can adapt to it his spiritual pedagogy and the structural features of the novitiate. It is especially the provincial's
role to help him in this task, providing him with the collaboration of experts and fostering meetings between masters
of novices and those who, within or outside the Society, are
devoted to the formation of youth.

III.   THE BROTHERS' SPIRITUAL FORMATION AFTER THE
NOVITIATE

27.   After the completion of the noviceship, the brothers' **112**
formation should be continued until tertianship, both in the

---

10 See *Exam* [100] ; *Cons* [514].

juniorate[11] and afterwards with various experiments and assignments. Thus the technical, cultural, and doctrinal formation which renders them more apt for the service of God will be closely conjoined with spiritual development.

113   28.   Where it has not been done already there should be instituted during the time of juniorate a complete and well-adapted course in theology as a principal discipline. There should also be among the other disciplines suitable instruction concerning "ways and habits of thought and opinion in contemporary social life."[12]

114   29.   After the juniorate the brothers should be sent to those houses where their progressive spiritual training can be provided for more easily. The superior of the house should have the greatest care for their formation and should provide them with appropriate means for developing their personal spiritual life at the same time that he entrusts them with increasing responsibility. He should especially urge their active and conscious participation in liturgical celebrations, particularly of the Eucharist.[13]

115   They should have a qualified spiritual father who is seriously devoted to their care. Under his direction they should receive spiritual instruction by way of rather frequent conversations and private reading.

116   30.   A short course or program on spiritual and doctrinal formation should be set up each year especially for those brothers who have not yet completed tertianship. On such occasions, following a closely integrated program, lectures are to be offered on Sacred Scripture, liturgy, theology, or social doctrine.

IV.   THE SCHOLASTICS' SPIRITUAL FORMATION AFTER THE NOVITIATE

117   31.   The vocation tested and strengthened during the

11 See GC 30, D. 41.
12 PC 18.
13 See SC 7, 10.

novitiate should continue its growth throughout the whole time of formation. Accordingly it is necessary for there to be an appropriate transition and continuity between the noviceship and subsequent formation, and between various stages of the latter. Intellectual formation and the genuine integration of human values can assume full meaning and importance only if they are accompanied by deeper knowledge and love of Christ, so as to bring about a unification of the whole personality.

32.   All ought therefore to read carefully what is said of **118** formation in general in the decree on the training of scholastics especially in studies (Chapter I) and strive to put it faithfully into effect. Moreover, the scholastics should persuade themselves that the best way to union with God and the proper preparation for the priesthood are to be found in seriously striving to live the spirit of our vocation.

33.   Wise and competent spiritual fathers are to be **119** chosen, who can offer fraternal help to the scholastics during their time of study to achieve a true discernment of spirits.

All the fathers who reside in houses of formation should **120** also feel that each in proportion to his office shares in the task of providing for the scholastics' spiritual growth and their apostolic preparation.[14] Indeed, everyone in the province should be ready to offer generous help to the formation of our men.

It is further to be hoped that in particular regions meetings will be held, either independently or in collaboration **121** with groups concerned with intellectual and pastoral formation, to develop an organized survey of spiritual training for the whole program of formation.

34.   Throughout all of their formation the scholastics **122** should keep in view the priestly character of our vocation, with the result that study, prayer, and all other activities

---

14 See OT 5.

may be imbued with a desire of serving God and the Church with priestly love for men. Especially before they come to theology, they should be provided with opportunity to secure a deeper understanding of their priestly calling.

123   35.   A life of prayer should be cultivated which is suitable for a time of study. Each one should therefore earnestly seek, with the spiritual father's help, a way of prayer which has vitality for him. To this end they should carefully search out among the different ways of prayer proposed by the Exercises, namely, meditation, contemplation, *lectio divina,* liturgical and vocal prayer, those which best lead them to God. This personal effort, pursued with constancy, will be a great help to the scholastics in acquiring familiarity with God.

124   The annual Spiritual Exercises are to be regarded as the spirit which animates our formation and brings us to fuller awareness of our vocation. The scholastics should learn to apply the rules and principles of the Exercises to those difficulties which are likely to arise during the time of studies. The scholastics should be permitted on occasion during their formation to make the Spiritual Exercises alone under the direction of an experienced spiritual father so as to have freer and more fruitful communion with God and respond with fuller and more ready availability to the promptings of the Holy Spirit.

125   36.   The scholastics should recall that the virtues required by intellectual labor, such as attention, humility, readiness to serve, constancy, patience and tolerance of adversity, and love of truth, open up to them a most fitting way of finding God in studies.

126   It should also be kept in mind that the time of studies, undertaken according to the spirit of our vocation, provides valuable opportunities for obedience joined to personal initiative, for affective maturity and charity, and for a life that is poor and devoted to labor. The life of a scholastic should, therefore, be so arranged that occasions are not lacking for the truly responsible exercise of these virtues, so that Jesuits may personally experience the meaning of the evangelical counsels.[15]

37.   At the same time that the scholastics, impelled by an apostolic spirit, seek to know the world with its aspirations and values, which today are so often alien to faith, let them earnestly nourish their own faith and each day shape their intellect more to the mystery of Christ, lest otherwise there should gradually develop a most serious divorce of human wisdom from faith. "Above all, let Sacred Scripture be daily in their hands, so that from reading and meditating the divine Scriptures they may learn 'the surpassing knowledge of Jesus Christ' (Phil. 3:8)."[16]

127

38.   Finally, scholastics, who are greatly affected by the aspirations and movements of our time, must respond to them as spiritual men, with humble loyalty to the Society. Thus by their vigor and alertness they will make a much desired contribution to the Society's renewal and adaptation.

128

39.   During the time of teaching or experiments, treated in the decree on the training of scholastics especially in studies (No. 30), care is to be taken that the scholastics' spiritual life not only does not thereby suffer damage, but on the contrary that it derive therefrom a proper growth. For inasmuch as such experiments represent at once testing and formation, their particular circumstances should contribute to that full apostolic and religious maturity to which the entire education of Jesuits is directed.

129

40.   The scholastics should therefore be seriously concerned to seek their own spiritual growth and to adapt it more closely to the particular conditions of an apostolic life. If in the process they experience greater difficulties in prayer and work, let them learn to overcome these with magnanimity and patience in the Lord.

130

---

15 See OT 9.
16 PC 6.

131   41.   Superiors should take care that only those apostolic works are entrusted to the scholastics which are consistent with their spiritual progress. Let them provide the spiritual help which such a time most requires. Thus superiors should see to it that the scholastics are accepted in a brotherly spirit into the community of members already formed, and that they are assisted by some suitable spiritual father so that these experiments strengthen them in their vocation.

132   Scholastics are not, however, to be sent to such experiments before they have acquired the doctrinal formation which will enable them to fulfill them profitably. Special care should be taken of those destined for secular studies that they may secure a doctrinal formation adapted to their particular studies and requirements.

V.   TERTIANSHIP

133   Since the General Congregation has already promulgated a decree on tertianship, urging instructors to undertake experiments with a view to rendering it more profitable, only its place and importance in the organic process of the fathers' and brothers' formation are treated here.

134   42.   Tertianship aims at perfecting the formation of the affections[17] and testing whether the tertian, imbued with the Society's spirit, shows promise of continuing to make progress himself and of helping others in the Lord.

135   43.   The expression *school of affection*[18] characterizes that institution in which members of the Society are so "filled with love of the true doctrine of Christ"[19] that they "progress in the Spirit and seriously follow Christ our Lord" and "love and ardently desire to put on the Lord's own clothing and insignia for his love and reverence."[20] This

---

17 See *Cons* [516] ; see *Polanci Complementa,* II, Industria 5 [Ser. 1]. 744.
18 *Cons* [516].
19 *SpEx* 164
20 *GenExam* [101].

schooling consists in concrete and personal contact with the things of the Society, consisting on the one hand in a vital confrontation with the Institute both in documents and in religious and community life itself, and on the other hand in actively participating in various experiments, first in the Spiritual Exercises, so as to develop a deeper practice of prayer (and in it "to seek God and direct all their affection towards the Creator"[21]), and then in other experiments, which in the case of the priests should be of a pastoral nature, so that they may be practiced in the discernment of spirits while working in the varied circumstances of the world.

44.   To bring this about it will help most if the tertians have an instructor who is in the first place a genuine spiritual teacher and who will examine the experiences undergone in the course of formation and help each one by means of the rules of the discernment of spirits to find his own way to greater progress. **136**

45.   The greatest benefit is rightly expected from this final probation, namely, for each one to bring to completion the desired synthesis of spiritual, apostolic, and intellectual formation which makes for the fuller integration in the Lord of the whole personality, in keeping with the Society's objective as St. Ignatius described it: "that, since they themselves have made progress, they may better help others to make spiritual progress to the glory of God and of our Lord."[22] **137**

VI.   CONTINUING FORMATION

46.   Closely following the Church, which, in liturgical renewal, biblical and theological reflection, and attention to the changing conditions of the times, is led by the Holy Spirit to complement the wisdom of antiquity by means of new developments, all, even those who have already com- **138**

---

21 *Cons* [288].
22 *Cons* [516].

pleted their formation, should strive constantly to draw from these sources renewal for their own spiritual lives. Their apostolic activity will thus be enabled to answer more effectively the needs of the Church and of men.

139   47.   The means commended by our Institute are therefore to be carefully preserved (the annual Exercises, recollections, etc.). Prudently adapted to the requirements of age or spiritual condition, these means are purged of all taint of formalism and exert their proper effect. Those new means should also be adopted (special courses, meetings, etc.) which commonly serve to promote renewal in the contemporary Church. It will be up to superiors to provide opportunities for these, especially for those men who are usually kept from them by duties and occupations.

140   48.   It is likewise desirable that for the Society as a whole as well as for its particular regions, the tools necessary for spiritual formation may be made available also in vernacular languages, as, for example, St. Ignatius' works and the texts of our spiritual tradition, theological writings of outstanding worth, news about enterprises undertaken in other regions, etc. Thus will the whole Society be enabled to accomplish in common the study and discernment of the will of God, which is the principle and goal of all spiritual growth, so that all "may learn to live in close and familiar fellowship with the Father through his Son Jesus Christ in the Holy Spirit."[23]

---

23 OT 8.

9   THE TRAINING OF SCHOLASTICS
ESPECIALLY IN STUDIES

I.   TRAINING IN GENERAL

1. The training of the scholastics should be apostolic in **141** its orientation; namely, that Jesuits may be able "with the help of God to benefit both their own souls and those of their neighbor."[1] Therefore, the scholastics, called by Christ our Lord to serve the universal Church as future priests, should prepare themselves, with the help of divine grace, "for the defense and propagation of the faith and the growth of souls in Christian life and doctrine."[2] The result should be that, living in close familiarity with God, through a profound understanding of the faith and a vital knowledge of men, they will become true ministers of Christ, who make the presence of God felt in the modern world.

2. There should be an organic unity in the whole train- **142** ing of the scholastics. Thus, beginning with the novitiate and throughout the entire course of studies there should be a close integration of spiritual formation, the work of study, and apostolic activity. All who have charge of the training of Jesuits, either in government or in teaching, should diligently and harmoniously work together for this integration.

3. The scholastics should base their lives on the princi- **143** ples of the spirituality of the Society, as explained in the decrees on the spiritual life. They should strive for the fullness of Christian life in charity. They should practice a true self-denial, especially in faithful application to study, should come to an intimate knowledge and a generous observance

---

1 *Cons* [351].
2 Formula of the Institute, n. 1.

of the Constitutions, and should continuously foster, in intimate prayer and the mysteries of the sacred liturgy, a personal union with Christ their Lord, who calls them to share in his priesthood.

144   4.   In the whole course of training, apostolic experiments of a suitable nature should be undertaken. These experiments should be carefully directed by experts, who are themselves so filled with the priestly and pastoral spirit that the training, both spiritual and intellectual, will be filled with that same spirit. An additional help to this end will be frequent meetings with those who are already working in the apostolate.

145   5.   Provision should be made in each stage of the training for personal maturity, especially of the emotions; the advice of trained psychologists should be used when it is necessary. In this way, the balanced development of the spiritual, intellectual and affective life will be secured, and the true maturity of the whole person will be achieved.

146   6.   The scholastics, in their whole course of studies, should try to develop a sense of genuine and sober responsibility, rejecting every form of immaturity which would make them unable to face the difficulties of life. Therefore, frequent occasions should be given them for exercising responsibility, in leading the spiritual and intellectual life more actively and spontaneously, in doing some work in the house, and in vigorously carrying on various apostolic experiments as well.

147   7.   Great care should be taken that each scholastic be directed according to his own gifts, both natural and supernatural. At the same time a sense of solidarity and collaboration should be fostered in the whole period of training, so that every trace of that egoism which is rightly criticized may be removed from our training.

148   8.   The discipline of common life is to be embraced from the inner law of love, as a necessary element in our training; namely, to follow the divine will faithfully in daily

life, to promote solid personal maturity, to practice the duties of charity toward fellow religious. Let the practice of this discipline be such that the scholastics, following Christ their Lord and Master in humble reverence and obedience, may enjoy the true freedom of the children of God in the Holy Spirit.

9. Care is to be taken that the number of scholastics in the houses of formation be not too large, so that mutual relations can be spiritual and fraternal, the discipline may be that of a family, and the government truly paternal. **149**

10. True dialogue should exist between superiors, professors, and scholastics. It should be possible for all to express opinions and make suggestions with openness and candor. Thus in the final decision, which belongs to the superior, there will be closer consensus and obedience, and a filial spirit and fraternal communion of mind will grow continuously within the community. **150**

11. The scholastics should have suitable contacts with outside university groups, with clerics and religious, and also with laymen both of their own and of other nations. This, of course, should be arranged with prudence. In this way, ridding themselves of nationalism and every other form of particularism, they will acquire the universality of mind and openness toward different forms of culture and diverse civilizations and mentalities which our apostolic vocation demands. **151**

12. The entire training of the scholastics should be inspired by the spirit of the Second Vatican Council as manifested in its constitutions and decrees, namely in the constitutions on the Church and the Sacred Liturgy and in the decrees on priestly formation, on the appropriate renewal of the religious life and on ecumenism.[3] **152**

II. ON STUDIES

13. The purpose of studies in the Society is apostolic, **153**

3 See LG, SC, OT, PC, UR.

as is the purpose of the entire training. Through their studies the scholastics should acquire that breadth and excellence in learning which are required for our vocation to achieve its end.

154   14.   The education given through our studies is both general and special: the general education which is necessary for all priests in the Society; the special education which is daily more necesary for the various tasks for which Jesuits are to be prepared. Their general education should give to the minds of the scholastics that Christian vision which will illuminate the entire field of future special study and work, and also bring light to others with whom they work.

155   15.   To insure that the intellectual formation of Jesuits is ordered to meet the needs of the times, the entire *Ratio Studiorum* shall be revised. Considering the great diversity of regions and circumstances, this *Ratio* shall determine only general norms. It should have due regard both for the laws of the Church (those now in force as well as those to be passed by the Council or after the Council) and for the laws passed by the present General Congregation. The new *Ratio Studiorum* can depart from the decrees of preceding general congregations as this is opportune, until the next general congregation makes a final decision. In the meantime, some definite experiments, with the approval of Father General, can be carried on; the results of these experiments are to be accurately reported to the commission on the *Ratio Studiorum*.

156   16.   In the different regions, it will be the task of the (group of) provincials to have a special *Ordo Studiorum* drawn up, which will adapt and fill out the general norms, considering the special circumstances of each region. These special Ordinations, which must be approved by Father General, are to be regularly revised, so that the training of Jesuits may always correspond to the apostolic needs of each region.

A.   The General Curriculum of Studies

17.   Before they begin philosophy and theology, the **157**
scholastics should have completed that training in letters
and sciences which in each nation is required before specialization is begun. Their knowledge of Latin should be
sufficient for them to understand and use with ease the
sources of the sacred sciences and the documents of the
Church. This training in letters and sciences, if it has not
been completed before entrance into the Society, shall be
completed in the novitiate; and, if necessary, in the juniorate.

18.   In those provinces in which, according to their **158**
special Ordinations, higher studies are pursued in the
juniorate, they should be capable of developing in the
juniors a well-balanced religious and human maturity, and
they should give them as well a vital knowledge of man and
of the modern world. This humanistic training is to be
achieved by the study of ancient and modern literature,
and also of history and the sciences. Furthermore, the juniors should endeavor early to develop their aesthetic sense.
It is urgently desired that the scholastics early in their studies
learn one or more modern languages in addition to their
own. Finally, in the entire course of studies, but especially
in the juniorate, the scholastics should practice those means
of expression which are suited to the people of our age.
Skilled in the arts of writing and speaking, they can become
better preachers of the Gospel of Christ.

19.   Since in modern civilization, the audio-visual media **159**
are most effective in moving the souls of every class of
people, the scholastics shall have suitable opportunities for
access to them, and also of learning how they can be used
succesfully in the apostolate.

20.   In the novitiate or the juniorate or at least in the **160**
beginning of the course of philosophy, the scholastics shall
receive an appropriate introduction to the mystery of Christ
and the history of salvation; this should give them a vision

of the meaning, order, and apostolic purpose of all their studies; it should likewise help to ground their own religious life in faith, and strengthen them in their vocation. The methodical reading of Holy Scripture shall be begun with a gradual initiation in the novitiate. Likewise, throughout the whole course of training they shall learn to take an active part in the lturgy, and come to understand it more deeply.

161   21.   The courses in philosophy and theology shall be so fitted to each other, and the disciplines shall be so arranged, that all of them harmoniously work together to attain the apostolic end of our studies. This end will not be obtained in the Society unless apostolic men trained as well as possible in these studies are prepared. Therefore, as a general rule, our scholastics should work for those academic degrees in philosophy and especially in theology, which can be obtained in our course of studies and help towards our apostolic purpose.

162   22.   All scholastics shall study philosophy for at least two years. The introduction to the mystery of Christ is to be their guiding light; the patrimony of a perennially valid philosophy is to be the foundation of their thinking. Thus they can be brought to a personal and truly philosophical reflection on human existence, and especially on Christian existence. This reflection should take account of the progress of both philosophy and science, and try to respond to the vital problems of contemporary men, especially of those who have a greater influence in the territory. Through this reflection they should gain an insight into the whole of reality according to its metaphysical structure; it should lead to a knowledge of God, and in this way prepare the way for theology.

163   23.   The instruction in theology for all scholastics shall be given for four years. This instruction shall be pastoral, in the sense that by an accurate study of the sources and by an investigation of the meaning of the faith, the scholastics shall so deeply penetrate the richness of divine revelation,

118

that the word of God will nourish their own personal spiritual life and will be able to be effectively communicated in the priestly ministry to the people of their own time. They shall seriously study Sacred Scripture, so that it will be the very soul of all the other disciplines, by means of accurate exegesis and a suitable doctrinal synthesis. To reach this deeper understanding of the faith, so necessary for our times, they shall reverently, without preconceived opinions, study the relation of the mysteries among themselves as well as their relation to the urgent philosophical questions of their time. In all this they shall loyally follow in the footsteps of the Fathers both of the East and of the West and of the great Doctors of the Church.

24.   Separate classes for long and short course are not **164** required in theology. Nonetheless, individual care should be given to the scholastics so that they will be better trained according to their individual aptitudes and their special future assignments.

25.   The programs of the entire philosophical and theo- **165** logical curriculum shall be revised, so that disciplines can be taken in their entirety, the matter be distributed more systematically, unnecessary repetitions can be avoided, obsolete questions can be omitted, and those which have an influence at the present time can be treated more profoundly. New disciplines should not be lightly introduced, but rather new questions should be taken up in the appropriate places in already existing disciplines. For the social formation of the scholastics, in addition to special courses, care is to be taken that in other philosophical and theological disciplines their social aspect and dimension be developed more fully.

26.   The methods of teaching shall be revised. The **166** hours of class shall be reduced when circumstances require it; correspondingly, the active participation of the scholastics shall be increased, and encouragement shall be given to their mutual cooperation, under the personal direction of

the professors, in seminars, written papers, private study, and small groups.

167   27.   It is also desirable that each scholastic, under the direction of the prefect of studies, find some field of specialization according to his individual talent; he should work on this in the time left over from the ordinary studies; he should foster a personal interest in studies, and prepare himself remotely for his own future apostolate in the modern world.

168   28.   Examinations should be genuine tests. According to the norms to be determined in the *Ratio Studiorum*, they can be both oral and written; but in a principal discipline they may not be merely written. The examiners shall make a personal and free judgment; it is permissible for them to consult together after the examination. Examinations can be repeated once; but those who do not pass the second examination in a principal discipline lose the right both to a licentiate and to the profession in the Society.

169   29.   The matter for the *examen ad gradum* is the whole of theology. Philosophical questions are to be included insofar as they are related to theological ones. The examination will last one hour and a half, and the candidate shall be examined by each examiner for about twenty minutes. This examination also can be repeated once. It is permissible, however, for the examiners to consult together; they can make their judgment also from knowledge they have outside the examination and can take account of the grades given through the entire course; therefore these grades should be available to the examiners.

170   30.   Regency can be made after philosophy, or, where it seems better, deferred until after theology, or omitted, or joined with special studies. But when it is omitted, care should be taken to secure the purpose of the regency by various apostolic works. These works should be set up during the entire period of training (see No. 4), especially during the annual vacation, arranged with prudence, without harm to studies, and under the direction of a man of experience.

31.   Ordination to the priesthood, especially when regency does not take place before theology, can suitably be deferred, according to the special norms to be approved by Father General for the needs of a particular region.   **171**

32.   In the houses of study there should not be too many scholastics for the reasons given in No. 9. But since a sufficient number of professors, a good library and other scholarly helps are necessary for intellectual training, schools and faculties should not be multiplied; but, where this can be conveniently done, let there be several religious communities, the scholastic members of which attend the same school or faculty. Indeed, let there be concern, as far as it is possible, that our houses of study be built near university centers, so that the scholastics can also have the advantage of other professors and libraries; care should be taken, however, that their training, far from being injured thereby, become better.   **172**

B.   Special Studies

33.   Since it is daily more necessary that not only those who are destined to teach, but also those who exercise other ministries of the Society, have special preparation, the provincials should provide for the training of an ample number of competent men for the various tasks, keeping in mind both the needs of the apostolate and the talents and preference of the scholastics.   **173**

34.   Those who are to have special studies should be chosen carefully and in good time; they should be directed by a special prefect of studies even during the period in which they are still following the general curriculum; they should devote themselves to their specialization generously and exclusively, and continue in it so that, as far as possible, they become outstanding.   **174**

175   35.   Likewise, those who are destined for administrative functions in large houses, especially in houses of study, should have some advance preparation. This may include special studies, and, in any case, it presupposes the natural and supernatural gifts required for such offices. This is especially true for treasurers of large houses or provinces.

176   36.   Special care should be given to the preparation of spiritual fathers of Jesuits and of externs. This can be done in special courses in Rome or elsewhere, or privately, under the direction of a trained, experienced man, or with some other suitable preparation, according to decree 40 of the 30th General Congregation. This is especially true of those destined to be masters of novices and instructors of tertians.

177   37.   Those who are to teach the sacred sciences in major seminaries and especially in Jesuit faculties, should take special studies either in the international institutes in Rome or in other universities, as the provincial, with the advice of experts, shall think best. They are to obtain the appropriate academic degrees, especially ecclesiastical ones, and to be well prepared for teaching.

178   38.   Scientific and technical advancement is a major factor in our times. The positive sciences exert an ever increasing influence on the mentality of men and on the very structure of our daily lives. Hence those who are destined for scientific research and for teaching the secular sciences should have special training to fit them for the scientific apostolate which is so very important. In fact, the Society should have men with doctoral degrees who become truly eminent in these fields.

179   39.   Men skilled in pastoral work should also be trained with special studies. This will enable them to promote the proper arrangement of our ministries and their adaptation to modern times and special circumstances.

180   40.   Those who are destined for other regions, in addition to the general preparation, should, where it is necessary, have a specialization before they go to that region, with a view to the circumstances of that region.

C. Doctrine and Teaching

41.   The purpose of our studies is to train Jesuits to   **181** proclaim and transmit the truth revealed in Christ and entrusted to the Church. Our teaching therefore should faithfully adhere to what "was once given to the holy men of the faith,"[4] and should be such that, accommodating itself to changing ways of speaking and thinking, and adapting itself to the diverse cultures of the whole world, it can continually revivify that faith in the hearts of men.

42.   Let Jesuits put their trust in the strength of the   **182** divine truth, and in that inner unction of the Holy Spirit which leads the Church of Christ to all truth. Therefore let them join to their studies a close familiarity with God, and in this secure way they will be safe from timidity as well as from thoughtless innovation. Let them in all matters see that their knowledge is well-grounded, according to the norms which the Holy See has given us.

43.   Professors should bear in mind that they do not   **183** teach in their own name, but that their mission is in the Church and from the Church, and that they are joined in charity in the Society of Jesus. Hence they should let themselves be guided by the mind and will of the Church, show proper respect for the teaching authority of the Church, and have regard for the building up of the faith in their students and in all the faithful. At the same time they should keep in mind those who are separated from us.

44.   Let both professors and scholastics faithfully adhere   **184** to and diligently study the word of God in Scripture and Tradition. Let them also have high regard for the holy Fathers and other Doctors, and for those authors of the Society who are highly regarded in the Church. Let them

---

4 Jud. 3.

follow principally the mind and principles of St. Thomas; his works should be well known to them.

185 45. Professors should clearly distinguish between matters of faith to be held by all and teachings approved by the consent of theologians. Probable, new, and merely personal explanations are to be proposed modestly.

186 46. For more secure and profitable progress in doctrine, it will be very helpful if the professors freely and sincerely communicate to their colleagues their new ideas, even before they are published. Thus, if necessary, they can be corrected, and can perhaps also be of benefit to others.

187 47. The scholastics during their course of studies should learn, under the direction of their teachers, to read critically and use prudently the works even of non-Catholics, especially of those who have great influence on the modern mind. Thus they should learn how to retain what is good, and correct what is unacceptable.

1.   The 31st General Congregation, having a high re-   **188**
gard for the institution of the third probation, which is
defined by our holy Father St. Ignatius in the Constitutions
and praised in apostolic letters and the documents of the
Society, and yet at the same time aware of the difficulties
which beset the third probation, seeks its adaptation and
renewal. This renewal, which should help to achieve more
efficaciously the purposes intended by the founder himself,
should be carried out according to the norms of the Second
Vatican Council, the principles of the religious life, and the
apostolic goal of the Society, which are proposed in other
documents of this Congregation.

2.   This renewal will be especially brought about by the   **189**
particular care taken to acquire an interior knowledge and
personal experience of the spirit of the Spiritual Exercises
and the Constitutions,[1] and to put this spirit into one's own
prayer and apostolic action.

3.   But since many modern difficulties concern the con-   **190**
crete ways in which the practice of this institution of the
third probation is carried out, the Congregation, considering the different circumstances in different countries, con-
cludes that for the present new experiments are to be
attempted with regard to the structure of the third probation before anything is definitively decided for the whole
Society.

4.   Therefore, in the different regions it shall be the   **191**
duty of the provincials and instructors to try new methods
and suitable experiments, with the approbation of Father

---

1 *CollDecr* 156.

General, so that the purposes set down in the Constitutions[2] and in the Bull *Ascendente Domino* may be achieved again in our time. It is understood, moreover, that these purposes are to be renewed and adapted, in the light of the principles enunciated by this Congregation, to the circumstances of different regions.

192   5. These experiments should be carried on for three years, or longer if Father General sees fit. When this period is finished, there shall be a meeting, which will be able to judge about the results of these experiments and shall be a help to Father General in writing a new Instruction and in revising the rules of the instructor.

---

2 *Cons* [514, 516].

11 NORMS FOR PROMOTION TO FINAL VOWS

193 The General Congregation, desiring to meet requests of very many postulata that the claim to profession of four vows should be based more on the overall religious and apostolic capability of a man, supposing of course that he has suitable knowledge of theology, lays down by way of experiment the following revision of the norms for profession of four vows:

194 1. Decree 158 of the *Collection of Decrees* shall be revised to read:

All who are to be advanced to final vows must be outstanding in that following of Christ proposed to us in the gospels since this is the ultimate norm of religious life;[1] such men are those who:

1° regularly and for the most part, in ordinary matters, act according to the demands of virtue that is rooted in love of Christ, and are expected to do the same under more difficult circumstances if they occur;

2° humbly accept corrections concerning faults they have committed in religious life and generously strive to improve;

3° driven on by love, live more and more for Christ and His Body which is the Church,[2] and in the daily practice of virtue bear witness both to their fellow Jesuits and to others of the new life that is had through the redemption of Christ.[3]

---

1 See PC 2, a.
2 See PC 1.
3 See LG 44.

195   2. Decree 160 of the *Collection of Decrees* shall be revised to read:

In order that a man may be admitted to the solemn profession of four vows the following are required:

1° a high level of virtue in conformity with decree 158, one that is positively proved and evident to the extent that it stands out as a good example to others.[4] A deficiency in this regard cannot be supplied by any other endowments.

2° sound judgment and prudence in action,[5] as well as tested and basic strength of character;

3° a more than ordinary talent for our ministries;[6]

4° a high level of learning in conformity with decree 118 (of which § 3 has been abrogated) or other outstanding endowments in conformity with Nos. 3 and 4 below;

5° the priesthood;[7]

6° at least thirty-three years of age;[8]

7° at least ten full years in the Society in addition to the years spent in initial studies of philosophy and theology in the Society;[9]

8° at least three full years, after the completion of the course in theology and in addition to tertianship and to special studies, if any were made, spent in carrying out ministries or offices.

196   3. Decrees 161 and 162 of the *Collection of Decrees* and decree 36 of the 28th General Congregation are abrogated, and in their place a new decree is enacted which reads:

§1. Provided always that the requirements contained in No. 2 are kept, those men can be admitted to the solemn profession of four vows without an examination *ad gradum*

---

4 See *GenExam* [12]; *Cons* [819].

5 See *Formula of the Institute* of Julius III, 9.

6 See *ibid; GenExam* [12]; *Cons* [308, 819].

7 See *GenExam* [12].

8 See GC 8, D. 7, 33.

9 See GC 9, D. 42; GC 13, D. 9; GC 16, D. 20.

who have a doctorate or licentiate or some other equivalent degree in the sacred sciences, or who have engaged in these sciences with success either in teaching or writing.[10]

§2.   In each individual case it is necessary that the provincial and his consultors have proof of the candidate's high level of learning.

4.   Decree 163 of the *Collection of Decrees* shall be revised to read: **197**

§1.   Provided always that the requirements contained above in No. 2 are kept, those men can be admitted to solemn profession without an examination *ad gradum* who show outstanding apostolic or ministerial capability. Such are:

1° those who have shown noteworthy talent in governing or preaching or writing;[11]

2° men who are proficient in literature or the sciences and who have received higher academic degrees or who have taught successfully at an advanced level;[12]

3° those who have filled any post or ministry proper to the Society in an outstanding way that has won general acclaim.

§2.   In each individual case it is necessary that the provincial and his consultors have proof of the outstanding apostolic and ministerial capability of the candidate, in addition to his adequate theological learning.

5.   A new decree is enacted which reads: **198**

Provincials and their consultors, when they are treating of those to be advanced to final vows, should inquire whether some spiritual coadjutors or approved scholastics deserve to be proposed to the General for the grade of the professed in conformity with Nn. 3 and 4 above. If any such are discovered, evidence of the sort specified in §2 of these decrees should be gathered, as well as all other person-

---

10 See GC 7, D. 96; GC 30, D. 68.
11 See GC 7, D. 33; GC 13, D. 19.
12 See GC 6, D. 15; GC 7, D. 33, n. 6; GC 29, D. 33.

nel reports, so that they can be sent to the General. This can be done not only once but repeatedly.

199   6.   Decree 165 of the *Collection of Decree*s shall be revised to read:

No men should be admitted to the grade of formed coadjutor, whether spiritual or temporal, unless:

1° they have risen above mediocrity in virtue in conformity with decree 158;

2° they have shown sufficient talent for the works and ministries that are proper to the Society;[13]

3° if they are brothers, they have completed ten years of religious life and thirty-three years of age; if they are approved scholastics, they have completed the time in the Society and are of the age specified in No. 2, 6°, 7° and 8° above.

200   7.   The General Congregation recommends that:

1° the whole process for gathering personnel reports, whether for admission to theology, or for advancement to holy orders, or to final vows, or to an office of government should be thoroughly studied and reviewed;

2° the provincial and his consultors, when they are to pass on someone for advancement to the grade of professed, should have available:

a)   a complete transcript of grades received in examinations throughout the course of philosophy as well as theology;

b)   full information on other advanced studies, whether made in the Society or outside of it;

c)   an accurate report of the ministries and works in which the candidate has engaged, along with judgments on his success, etc.

---

13 *Cons* [522].

The 31st General Congregation entrusts to Father General the task of drafting an Ordination for the whole Society, at least for the purpose of experimentation, concerning: **201**

a)   concelebration at the pronouncing of last vows;

b)   the use of the vernacular in the pronouncing of first vows;

c)   the presence of at least close relatives at the pronouncing of first vows, and similar details.

IV

RELIGIOUS LIFE

13   RELIGIOUS LIFE IN GENERAL

1.   The Second Vatican Council profoundly investigated **202**
the mystery of the Church in relation to the conditions of
our times. In that investigation it cast a special light upon
the religious profession of the evangelical counsels both as a
means of attaining sanctity by special grace and as a way
of fulfilling service to God and man.

2.   Inserted by baptism into the Mystical Body of Christ, **203**
strengthened by confirmation with the power of the Holy
Spirit, and consecrated into a royal priesthood and a holy
people,[1] we receive a more special consecration for the
divine service in the Society of Jesus by the profession of
the evangelical counsels, so that we may be able to bring
forth richer fruits from the grace of baptism.[2]

3.   Since the goal to which the Society directly tends is **204**
"to help our own souls and the souls of our neighbor to
attain the ultimate end for which they were created,"[3] it is
necessary that our life—of priests as well as scholastics and
brothers—be undividedly apostolic and religious. This intimate connection between the religious and apostolic aspects
in the Society ought to animate our whole way of living,
praying, and working, and impress on it an apostolic
character.

4.   To attain this end which the Society places before **205**
itself and "for the conservation and growth not only of the
body . . . but also of the spirit of the Society . . . those means
which join the instrument with God and dispose it to be

---

1 See AA 3.
2 See LG 44.
3 *Cons* [307].

rightly governed by the divine hand are more efficacious than those which dispose it towards men."[4]

206   5.   For the spiritual life is a participation in the life of the most holy Trinity dwelling within us so that we may be made conformed to the image of the Son of God "so that He may be the firstborn among many brethren,"[5] for the glory of God.

207   This life involves the whole man and all his activities, by which he as a Christian corresponds to every impulse received from God. It does not consist only in individual acts of devotion, but ought to animate and direct our whole life, individual and community, together with all our relations to other persons and things. It is nourished and fostered by every grace by which God turns to us and communicates Himself to us, especially by His word and the sacraments of Christ.

208   We for our part respond by the obedience of faith in which we give ourselves freely to God, "offering the full submission of intellect and will to God who reveals,"[6] celebrating as the high point of our life the sacred liturgy of the Lord's Eucharist, participating in the sacraments of Christ, and offering ourselves through love in all our actions, especially those which are apostolic, and all our hardships and joys.

209   6.   In order to promote the adaptation and renewal of religious life among all Jesuits, the 31st General Congregation has made these decrees in the spirit of the Second Vatican Council.

---

4 *Cons* [813].
5 Rom. 8. 29.
6 DV 5.

14 PRAYER

Introduction

210

1.   The Second Vatican Council, encouraging the work of renewal in the Church, wishes every Christian, and particularly all priests and religious, earnestly to advance in the spirit of prayer and in prayer itself.[1] At the same time, difficulties and doubts, both theoretical and practical, are raised against prayer and these cause no little harm to the Society. Hence the General Congregation considers that it must recall the importance of prayer and propose specific orientations on the manner and conditions of prayer in the Society so that superiors and each individual member may be able to weigh their responsibilities in God's presence.

211

2.   Our entire spiritual life is in Christ Jesus. We share, of course, the adoptive sonship of God which all the faithful have through faith and baptism, but belong in a special way to God through our consecration as religious in the Society which our founder wished to bear the name of Jesus. We desire to know only Christ Jesus who, sent forth from the Father, consummated the work of saving creation by His life, death, and resurrection. Risen now and exalted by the Father, He draws all things to Himself through the Holy Spirit whom He has sent into the world, so that in Him all may be one as He and the Father are one. Thus, through the grace of our vocation, at once both religious and apostolic, we share in the salvific work of Christ, partaking more fully and intimately of Christ's own love for the Father and for all men, for He loved us unto the end and gave Himself as a ransom for all. Here, then, is our vocation, to love the Father and His children, to work with

---

1 See PC 5-6; PO 18; OT 8; ES II, 21.

Christ in His Church for the life of the world that the Father may receive greater glory, to strive towards our goal in the Spirit—this is the everflowing font of the joy of our charity and the offering of our strength.

212   3.   The Spiritual Exercises of our father St. Ignatius are both the heritage of our spirituality and the school of our prayer. They indeed open the way through which we may penetrate ever deeper into the mystery of salvation which in turn feeds our lives as apostles in the world. For it is faith, progressively encompassing all reality, that must permeate us as persons if we are to give authentic witness to the living presence of Christ the Lord. The witness is what we seek in mental prayer as we enjoy God's presence and try, with the aid of His grace, to see all things in the light of Christ. Through mental prayer our individual lives receive clarity and meaning from the history of salvation, are set against the background of God's speaking to us, and hopefully are enriched with that freedom and spiritual discernment so necessary for the ministry of the Gospel. These reasons apply to all religious involved in the world of today, which far too often ignores its God. For these religious, formal prayer is a precious chance to see the unity of creation and to refer creation to the Father. Our own men, conscious of our special task of challenging atheism, find further apostolic significance in prayer as it fosters in us a sense of the living God and an encouragement of our faith.

213   4.   The Jesuit apostle goes from the Exercises, at once a school of prayer and of the apostolate, a man called by his vocation to be a contemplative in action. For the closer and more firmly we bind ourselves to Christ, denying self-love in our association with His salvific work, the more fully do we adore the Father in spirit and truth and the more effectively do we bring salvation to men. Witnesses to Christ in our apostolate, we see Him praying always to the Father, often alone through the night or in the desert. We, too, must enjoy familiar conversation with Him in continuous and in formal prayer. This very intimacy with Christ forges

a union of our life of prayer and our life of apostolic work. Far from living two separate lives, we are strengthened and guided towards action in our prayer while our action in turn urges us to pray. Bringing salvation to men in word and deed through faith, hope, and love, we pray as we work and are invited to formal prayer that we may toil as true servants of God. In this interplay, praise, petition, thanksgiving, self-offering, spiritual joy, and peace join prayer and work to bring a fundamental unity into our lives. Truly this is our characteristic way of prayer, experienced by St. Ignatius through God's special gift nourished by his own generous abnegation, fiery zeal for souls, and watchful care of his heart and senses. He found God in every thing, every word, and every deed. He relished God's omnipresence. If the Jesuit apostle is to live this intimate marriage of prayer and action in today's world, he must return each year to the school of the Exercises, so that, spiritually renewed, he may take up his work again with deeper faith and love.

5. The People of God, in whom Christ shows us the **214** way to the Father, are our people. Hence the prayer of every Christian is rooted in the prayer of the Church and flowers into liturgical action. Thus the celebration of the Eucharist is the center of the life of the apostolic religious community, bringing fraternal union to its perfection and blessing every apostolic endeavor with the waters of holiness.

6. Since it has pleased the Father to speak to men both **215** in His Son, the Word Incarnate, and in many ways in Scripture, the Bible, a treasure bestowed by the Spouse on His Church to nourish and guide all men, is truly the ever-flowing font of prayer and renewal of religious life. In each of us, as the whole tradition of the Church attests, Holy Scripture becomes our saving word only when heard in prayer that leads to the submission of faith.[2] *Lectio divina,* a practice dating back to the earliest days of religious life in the Church, supposes that the reader surrenders to God

---

2 See DV 25.

who is speaking and granting him a change of heart under the action of the two-edged sword of Scripture continually challenging to conversion. Truly we can expect from prayerful reading of Scripture a renewal of our ministry of the word and of the Spiritual Exercises, both of which derive their vigor from our familiarity with the Gospel. And, since the word of God comes to us in the living tradition of the Church, our scriptural reading can never be improved apart from revived interest in the Fathers and the outstanding spiritual writers, especially those of the Society. Nor can we ever forget that spiritual reading played a key role in the conversion of St. Ignatius. Similarly, our theological studies, which ought to be continued through our entire apostolic life, should be united to prayer to lead us to an ever deeper experience of the Lord.

216   7.   Those means which unite us to God and aid us in helping souls are mentioned in the Constitutions as "integrity and virtue, especially love, purity of intention in serving God, familiarity with God in spiritual exercises of devotion, and sincere zeal for souls for the glory of Him who created and redeemed them."[3] Hence our father St. Ignatius urges us to advance "in zeal for solid and perfect virtue and spiritual matters,"[4] pointing out how vital it is for each of his men to seek that manner and kind of prayer which will better aid him progressively to find God and to treat intimately with Him. With brotherly union, each Jesuit and his superior must collaborate in this humble and oft-repeated search for the divine will.

217   Every one of us, therefore, must keep some time sacred in which, leaving all else aside, he strives to find God. Through prayer he must seek to develop his spiritual life. In his dialogue with God he will grow in knowledge of God's ways with him, of the choices God desires him to make, of the apostolate God has for him, of the height and manner

---

3 *Cons* [813].
4 *Loc. cit.*

of perfection to which God lovingly invites him. His prayer thus becomes a truly vital activity whose progressive growth evidences increasingly the action and presence of God in him. His prayer teaches him and tries him in faith, hope, and charity through which we seek, love, and serve God progressively in all things.

Prayer, then, becomes not only a matter of obeying our religious rule, acceptable as that is to God, but also a personal reply to a divine call. Prayer is thus a faithful response to the law of charity towards God and men which the Holy Spirit has written in our hearts. The charity of Christ urges us to personal prayer and no human person can dispense us from that urgency. **218**

8.   To live his life of prayer, which in the Society is never separated from apostolic action, each of us must first deny himself so that, shedding his own personal inclinations, he may have that mind which is in Christ Jesus. For while on the one hand, prayer brings forth abnegation, since it is God who purifies man's heart by His presence, on the other, abnegation itself prepares the way for prayer, because only the pure of heart will see God. Progress in prayer is possible for those alone who continually try to put off their misguided affections to ready themselves to receive the light and grace of God. This continual conversion of heart "to the love of the Father of mercies" is intimately related to the repeated sacramental act of penance.[5] **219**

Self-denial, which disposes us for prayer and is one of its fruits, is not genuine unless amid the confusion of the world we try to keep our hearts at peace, our minds tranquil, and our desires restrained. Abnegation for us will consist chiefly in fidelity as we daily live our first consecration to God and remain faithful to Him even in insignificant details. Growth in prayer and abnegation necessarily implies spiritual discernment by which a man is willing to learn from God, so **220**

---

5 See PO 18.

that these gifts appear more clearly externally while they strike deeper roots into his inner life.

221   Though modern living seems to make it hard for us to provide these conditions for true prayer, with trust in God we must try courageously to actualize these aids to prayer in our own lives. Then we can truly serve our neighbor better.

222   9.   Superiors must actually lead the way in this matter of growth in prayer, inspiring by their example, helping their men, encouraging them, and aiding their progress. If their leadership is to be truly spiritual, they must understand the consciences of their men and get to know them through dialogue which is based on mutual trust. Further, it is the superior's function to promote the prayer life of the entire community as well as the individual's and to provide those conditions which favor prayer. He should see that the daily order and house discipline give each enough time for his customary prayer and its preparation and aid him to pray better.

223   Spiritual fathers, as well as superiors, show the true charity of Christ towards those placed in their charge when they guide them and aid them in this art of prayer, at once most difficult and divine.

Decree

224   10.   Liturgical celebrations, especially those in which the community worships as a group, and above all the celebration of the Eucharist, should mean much to us. For it is the Eucharistic sacrifice, the highest exercise of the priesthood, that continually carries out the work of our redemption, and for this reason, priests are strongly urged to celebrate Mass every day,[6] for even if the faithful are unable to be present, it is an act of Christ and of the Church.[7]

---

6 See PO 13.
7 See PO 13.

Concelebration, by which the unity of the priesthood is appropriately manifested, is encouraged in our houses when allowed by the proper authority, while each priest shall always retain his right to celebrate Mass individually.[8] Priests themselves extend to the different hours of the day the praise and thanksgiving of the Eucharistic celebration by reciting the divine office.[9] Hence our priests should try to pray attentively[10] and at a suitable time[11] that wonderful song of praise[12] which is truly the prayer of Christ and that of His Body to the Father.[13]

11.   The General Congregation wishes to remind every   **225**
Jesuit that personal daily prayer is an absolute necessity.

But the Congregation, recognizing the value of current de-   **226**
velopments in the spiritual life, does not intend to impose upon all indiscriminately a precisely defined universal norm for the manner and length of prayer.

Our rule of an hour's prayer is therefore to be adapted   **227**
so that each Jesuit, guided by his superior, takes into account his particular circumstances and needs, in the light of that discerning love which St. Ignatius clearly presupposed in the Constitutions.

The Society counts on her men after their formation to   **228**
be truly "spiritual men who have advanced in the way of Christ our Lord so as to run along this way," men who in this matter of prayer are led chiefly by that "rule . . . which discerning love gives to each one," guided by the advice of his spiritual father and the approval of his superior.[14]

All should recall that the prayer in which God com-   **229**
municates Himself more intimately is the better prayer,

---

8 See SC 57.
9 See PO 5.
10 See SC 90.
11 See SC 94.
12 See SC 84.
13 See SC 84.
14 *Cons* [582].

whether mental or even vocal, whether it be in meditative reading or in an intense feeling of love and self-giving.

230 12. As for what concerns the approved scholastics and brothers in particular, account should be taken of the following:

1° During the entire time of their formation they should be carefully helped to grow in prayer and a sense of spiritual responsibility towards a mature interior life, in which they will know how to apply the rule of discerning love which St. Ignatius prescribed for his sons after the period of their formation.

231 2° To foster this growth, the Society retains the practice of an hour and a half as the time for prayer, Mass, and thanksgiving. Each man should be guided by his spiritual father as he seeks that form of prayer in which he can best advance in the Lord.[15] The judgment of superiors is normative for each.[16]

232 3° In the communities in which they live, since these are ordinarily more tightly structured and larger in numbers, the daily order should always indicate clearly a portion of the day fixed by superiors, within which prayer and preparation for it may have their time securely established.

233 13. The exercise of prayer known as examination of conscience, aptly designated by St. Ignatius to develop purity of heart, spiritual discernment, and union with God in the active life, should be made twice daily. The Society, following its approved tradition, recommends that it last a quarter of an hour.

234 14. The prayerful reading of Scripture is a spiritual exercise that all should highly esteem and faithfully perform. As we read, we should try to deepen our familiarity with the word of God, to listen carefully to His voice, to sharpen our perception of salvation history in which the mystery of Christ is foretold, fulfilled, and continued in His

---

15 See decree 8 (spiritual formation of Jesuits), 35 § 1.
16 See *Cons* [342].

Church. We should truly seek and find Christ in the pages of the Fathers and of all Christian writers, especially Jesuits.

15. Insofar as their apostolic character permits it, Jesuit **235** communities should be united daily for some brief common prayer. The particular form should be approved by the provincial according to norms to be established by Father General. The prayer should take into account the greater needs of the whole world, the Church, the Society, and the community itself. Moreover, for the faithful fulfillment of their apostolic vocation both communities and individuals should cherish daily converse with Christ the Lord in visiting the Blessed Sacrament.[17]

16. The Spiritual Exercises should be made yearly by **236** all, according to the method of St. Ignatius,[18] for eight successive days.[19] Adaptations may be allowed because of particular circumstances; the provincial is to be the judge of the merits of each case. More general adaptations which affect an entire province or assistancy are to be submitted to Father General for approval. The circumstances of the annual retreat (such as silence, recollection, a location removed from ordinary work) should be managed in such a way that the Jesuit is able truly to renew his spiritual life through frequent and uninterrupted familiar conversation with God.

17. Decrees 52, 55, 81 of the *Collection of Decrees* are **237** to be modified according to Nos. 10 to 16 of the above.

---

17 See PO 18.
18 See *CollDecr* 55 § 3.
19 *CollDecr* 55 § 1.

15 DEVOTION TO
THE SACRED HEART OF JESUS

238   1. The Second Vatican Council has shed a brilliant new light upon the mystery of the Church, but this mystery is perceptible only to eyes directed in faith to the eternal love of the Incarnate Word. For Christ, who "thought with a human mind, acted by human choice, and loved with a human heart,"[1] sacrificed Himself in human love that He might win as His bride the Church which was born from His side as He slept on the cross.

239   2. The Church finds a splendid symbol for this love, at once human and divine, in the wounded heart of Christ, for the blood and water which flowed from it aptly represent the inauguration and growth of the Church[2] and solicit our response of love. Devotion to the Sacred Heart, as proposed by the Church, pays tribute to "that love which God has shown us through Jesus, and is also the exercise of the love we have for God and for our fellow-men,"[3] effecting that interpersonal exchange of love which is the essence of Christian and religious life. This is why devotion to the Sacred Heart is regarded as an excellent and tested form of that dedication "to Christ Jesus, king and center of all hearts, which our age urgently needs, as Vatican II has insisted."[4] This should be the concern of the Society above all, both among its own members and in its apostolic ministry, not only because of our long and venerable tradition but also because of the very recent recommendation of the Roman Pontiff.

---

1 GS 22.
2 See LG 3.
3 Pius XII, *Haurietis Aquas, AAS* 48 (1956) 345.
4 Paul VI, *Investigabiles Divitias, AAS* 57 (1965) 300.

3. For these reasons the General Congregation readily **240** embraces the wishes of the Supreme Pontiff; it recalls the decrees of earlier congregations concerning devotion to the heart of Christ[5] and urges all members of the Society to "spread ever more widely a love for the Sacred Heart of Jesus and to show all men by word and example that the renewal of minds and morals, as well as the increased vitality and effectiveness of all religious institutes in the Church, which are called for by the Second Vatican Council, ought to draw their chief inspiration and vigor from this source."[6] In this way we shall more effectively make the love of Christ, which finds its symbol in the devotion to the Sacred Heart of Jesus, the center of our own spiritual lives, proclaim with greater effect before all men the unfathomable riches of Christ, and foster the primacy of love in the Christian life.

4. It is no secret, however, that devotion to the Sacred **241** Heart, at least in some places, is today less appealing to Jesuits and to the faithful in general. The reason for this is perhaps to be found in outmoded devotional practices. Therefore our theologians, men experienced in spirituality and pastoral theology, and promoters of the apostolate of the Sacred Heart of Jesus are urgently asked to search out ways of presenting this devotion that are better suited to various regions and persons. For, while preserving the essential nature of the devotion, it would seem imperative to set aside unnecessary accretions and adapt it to contemporary needs, making it more intelligible to the men of our time and more attuned to their sensibilities.

5. The General Congregation also recommends that **242** Father General encourage these studies. He will then be in a position to assist the whole Society to a better renewal of its religious and apostolic spirit.

---

5 See *CollDecr* 223, 286 § 1; GC 23, D. 46, n. 1; GC 26, D. 21; GC 28, D. 20; GC 30, D. 32.

6 Paul VI, *Disserti Interpretes, ActRSJ* 14 (1965) 585.

16 CHASTITY IN THE SOCIETY OF JESUS

243   The mental attitude of men today and the new ways in which our ministry must be fitted into their lives give rise to new problems which touch upon our consecration to God through the vow of chastity. But since these problems are not yet mature enough for a fully balanced and wise solution, the 31st General Congregation recommends to Father General that, as soon as he deems it opportune, he entrust to experts a study on the apt assimilation of advances in the fields of theology, psychology, and pedagogy, and on their application to the direction of Jesuits, so that they may ever more surely persevere in perfect chastity.

244   Moreover, the Congregation, after attentive study of the documents of the Second Vatican Council, and mindful of its own decrees on the spiritual life and the formation of Jesuits, proposes and enacts the following declarations and norms.

245   1.   God, pouring forth his charity in our hearts through the Holy Spirit, confers upon some in the Church the gift of consecrated chastity,[1] a sign of charity and likewise a stimulus to it, whereby they may more easily devote themselves with an undivided heart to Him alone and to the service of His kingdom.[2] Therefore, chastity "for the sake of the kingdom of heaven,"[3] to which by both His example and His calling Christ invites us, and which we as religious profess,[4] following the lead of so many saints, should, as the Church repeatedly urges and as our founder expressly declares, be "perfectly observed" by us.[5]

---

1 See Rom. 5.5; Matt. 19.11; 1 Cor. 7.7.
2 See LG 42.
3 Matt. 19:12.
4 See LG 46; PC 12.
5 *Cons* [547].

2.   Our contemporaries, to whom we are sent[6] and with   **246**
whom we deal in fraternal fashion,[7] are freshly pondering
the meaning and value of human love and of the entire
sexual life. To them we wish to offer the sincere, simple,
and prudent[8] testimony of our consecrated chastity.

3.   For the vow of chastity, inspired by charity, in a new   **247**
and wonderful way consecrates us to God, and engages us
in a new and eminently human state of life, which renders
the heart singularly free and inflames it with charity towards
God and all men. The life of chastity consecrated to God
is, moreover, a living sign of that future world in which the
children of the resurrection "will neither marry nor take
wives,"[9] and likewise a most suitable means "for religious
to spend themselves readily in God's service and in works of
the apostolate."[10]

4.   Accordingly, in our Society, not only poverty and   **248**
obedience, but chastity also is essentially apostolic. It is not
at all to be understood as directed exclusively to our
personal sanctification. For, according to the whole intent
of our Institute, we embrace chastity as a special source of
spiritual fruitfulness in the world.[11] Through it, full dominion of our energies, both bodily[12] and spiritual,[13] is
retained for a prompter love and a more total apostolic
availability towards all men.[14] Moreover, the profession of
chastity for the sake of the kingdom of heaven is of itself
a true preaching of the Gospel, for it reveals to all men how
the kingdom of God prevails over every other earthly consideration, and it shows wonderfully at work in the Church

---

6 See *Cons* [163, 603] ; see PO 16; GS *passim*.
7 See PO 3.
8 See Matt. 10.16.
9 Luke 20.35.
10 PC 12, PO 16.
11 See LG 42.
12 See 1 Cor. 7.4.
13 See 1 Cor. 7.32-33.
14 See PC 12.

the surpassing greatness of the force of Christ the King and the boundless power of the Holy Spirit.[15]

249   5.   On the other hand, chastity vowed to God through celibacy implies and requires of us a sacrifice by which we knowingly and willingly forego entrance into that family relationship wherein husband and wife, parents and children, can in many ways, even psychologically, attain mutual fulfillment. Hence, our consecration to Christ involves a certain affective renuntiation and a solitude of heart which form part of the cross offered to us by Jesus as we follow His footsteps, and which closely associate us with His paschal mystery and render us sharers of the spiritual fertility which flows from it. The vow of chastity, then, on the indispensable condition that it be accepted with a humble, joyous, and firm spirit as a gift from God, and be offered as a sacrifice to God, not only does not diminish our personality[16] nor hamper human contacts and dialogue, but rather expands affectively, unites men fraternally, and brings them to a fuller charity.[17]

250   6.   However, that a man may dare to enter upon this vocation of love in the Church, he will necessarily require:

a)   lively faith, for only with the help of faith can the meaning and worth of that higher love be understood which, through consecration, takes up the affections of the personality of a man or woman and transcends its natural expression;

b)   a sound balance in affective life, constantly becoming more perfect, whereby the conscious and subconscious impulses and motivations of the entire personality are integrated to pave the way for a fully human commitment;

c)   and finally, in our days particularly, an informed choice, freely, explicitly, and magnanimously made, of the properly understood excellence and worth of chastity consecrated to Christ. For through chastity a man, by the obla-

15 See LG 44.
16 See LG 46, see GS 41.
17 See LG 44, PO 16, OT 10.

tion of his whole body and soul, devotes himself to the Lord,[18] and by a genuine act of assent takes up the gift of a vocation to establish a relationship of the love of friendship and charity which goes beyond the fullness of Christian marriage.

7. Besides, in order that perseverance in one's vocation **251** throughout life may be obtained, and that the love once consecrated may grow unceasingly, it is necessary:

a) continually to nourish that original lively faith through familiar converse with God, though contemplation of Christ's mysteries, and through vital assimilation to Him in the sacraments, both of penance, whereby we are made progessively more pure and at peace, and of the Eucharist, whereby we come to form one heart and one spirit with the people of God;

b) to sustain the initial resolve of persevering and growing in love, by fostering charity and the ready union of souls which flourish "when in common life true fraternal love thrives among its members";[19]

c) to strengthen the pristine desires of serving God in this vocation through truly responsible apostolic labor, which in the course of years should be adapted constantly, as far as possible, to the progressive development of one's personality;

d) to protect constancy of will, both by a vigorous prudence, which leads individuals and communities "not to presume on their own resources, but to practice mortification and custody of the senses,"[20] and by mutual confidence between subjects and superiors, which contributes wonderfully to renewal of the account of conscience, so much recommended;[21]

e) to renew incessantly the strong desire of persevering, through humble and simple devotion to the Blessed Virgin

---

18 See OT 10.
19 PC 12; see LG 43.
20 PC 12; see PO 16
21 See *Cons* [551].

Mary, who by her chaste assent obtained divine fecundity and became the mother of beautiful love.

252   8.   Therefore, the 31st General Congregation proposes and commends the following.

a)   All should cultivate close friendship with Christ and familiarity with God, for in this world, no one lives without love. But when our contemporaries question or fail to understand what our love is, we should offer them a fitting reply through the witness of a life of consecrated chastity, and at the same time with humble and persevering prayer we should beg for ourselves and our confreres the grace of personal love for Christ.

253   For our Father Ignatius experienced this grace, so permeating his entire personality that he bound his brethren to himself as friends and by his personal affability led countless men and women to God.

254   In the Spiritual Exercises he wished to urge the imploring of this grace, so that throughout the meditations and contemplations on the mysteries of the life, death, and resurrection of our Lord Jesus Christ, and in the application of the senses to them he would have us beg to know interiorly the Lord "who for me was made man, so that I may love Him the more, and follow Him more closely."[22]

255   *b*)   Still, all should keep in mind that love consecrated by chastity should constantly grow and approach the mature measure of the fullness of Christ.[23] It is, consequently, not a gift bestowed once and for all, mature and complete, at the beginning of one's spiritual life, but such as by repeated decisions, perhaps serious ones, should steadily increase and become more perfect. Thus the heart is more and more cleansed of affections not yet sufficiently understood, until the man adheres totally to Christ through love.

256   Such love of Jesus our Lord impels a person likewise to genuine human love for men and to true friendship. For

---

22 *SpEx* 104.
23 See Eph. 4.13.

chastity for the sake of the kingdom of heaven is safeguarded by fraternal friendship and in turn flowers forth
in it. Hence also, we should regard as the precious apostolic
fruit of ever more perfect love of friendship that mature,
simple, anxiety-free dealing with the men and women with
whom and for whom we exercise our ministry for the building up of the body of Christ.[24]

c)   But to attain the perfect liberty of chaste love, be-   **257**
sides the familiarity with God mentioned above, all the supernatural and natural helps available should be used.[25]
Among these, however, those contribute more to the faithful fulfillment of one's oblation of chastity which are positive, such as probity of life, generous dedication to one's
assigned task, great desire for the glory of God, zeal for
solid virtues and spiritual concerns,[26] openness and simplicity
in activity and in consulting with superiors, rich cultural
attainments, spiritual joy, and above all true charity. For
all these things will of their nature more easily bring a man
to the really full and pure love for God and men which we
earnestly desire.

d)   Nevertheless, mindful of the above-mentioned soli-   **258**
tude of heart which constitutes part of the cross embraced
through our vocation to follow Christ, and of our frailty
which from youth to old age necessarily accompanies the
development of chaste love,[27] we cannot forget the ascetical
norms which the Church and the Society in their wide experience maintain and which dangers against chastity require today no less than in the past.[28] So we should diligently stand firm against desires which might lessen a just
and wholesome dominion over our senses and affections.

e)   Finally, sustained by the grace of God and mortified   **259**
at all times,[29] we should generously and strenuously devote

---

24 See Eph. 4.12.
25 See PO 16.
26 See *Cons* [813], PO 11.
27 See 2 Cor. 4.7.
28 See PO 16, PC 12.
29 See 2 Cor. 4.7 f.; 6.3 f.; Col. 3.1 f.; *GenExam* [103].

ourselves to apostolic labor and know how to participate with moderation in the human contacts which our ministry involves, our visits and recreations, our reading and study of problems, our attendance at shows, and use of what is pleasurable, so that the testimony of our consecration to God will shine forth inviolate.

260 9. As for superiors: a) Let them know first of all that no one is to be admitted to the Society whom they consider ill-suited for consecrated chastity.[30] Accordingly, they should study and faithfully fulfill what the Church tirelessly enjoins in this respect.[31] Therefore, they should carefully inquire "about the free consent of the candidates, their moral fitness, physical and psychic health, and tendencies which might have been transmitted from their family."[32] And especially, "since the observance of total continence intimately involves the deeper inclinations of human nature, candidates should not undertake the profession of chastity nor be admitted to its profession except after a truly adequate testing period, and only if they have the needed degree of psychological and emotional maturity."[33] Proof of this is to be found particularly in a certain stability of spirit, in an ability to make considered decisions, and in an accurate manner of passing judgment on events and people.[34]

261 b) The superiors, together with spiritual fathers thoroughly trained for their task, should see to it that Jesuits in the course of their formation be educated in the matter of sex in a suitable, positive, and prudent manner, so that they may properly know and esteem not only the meaning

---

30 *Cons* [163, 179].
31 CIC 571 § 2; 575 § 1; 973 §3; OT 6; see *Cons* [205, 819]; *Instruction of the Sacred Congregation of Religious,* February 2, 1961, Nos. 29-31; GC 28, D. 24; Rev. Fr. Ledochowski, in *ActRSJ* 12 (1951) 127-28; Rev. Fr. Janssens, *De indole votorum, ActRSJ* 13 (1959) 623-625; *De perseverantia, ActRSJ* 14 (1965) 445-451.
32 See QT 6.
33 See PC 12.
34 See OT 11.

and superiority of virginity consecrated to Christ, but also the duties and dignity of Christian marriage.[35] Moreover, they should be manfully armed in advance, so as to be able vigorously to surmount the various crises of maturation.

c) Likewise, superiors and spiritual fathers alike should **262** manifest the utmost solicitude for the spiritual life of each individual, aware that they must give an account of all of them before God. Hence they should try to see fully and, as it were, to anticipate the psychological problems, the fatigue and difficulties, the wavering, weaknesses, and temptations which Jesuits, either in conversation or in any sort of contact, manifest more or less clearly. These they should perceive and evaluate accurately; what is more, they should show themselves ready to re-examine a man's aptitude for our vocation before permitting that further steps in it be made.

d) Let superiors, exercising due firmness and putting **263** aside a kindness which might better be called cruelty, take care that those who are unfit or doubtfully suitable be not advanced to vows or to orders. Thus, for example, someone who so lives separated from the others in the community that he raises a positive doubt about his aptitude for ready companionship with Jesuits or for apostolic contacts with his neighbors, should be directed to some other way of serving God.

And in our times, those who hold fast to a firm doubt **264** regarding the value and worth of the vow of chastity and of celibacy are not to be judged fit for religious life and the priesthood.

e) Solicitous, attentive, and with much trust, superiors **265** should be at the service of the recently ordained priests and brothers who are beginning to work in the vineyard of the Lord, as also of those who for a long time engage in arduous special studies, so as to make them conscious that they form a true part of their communities.

---

35 See OT 10.

266   Superiors should lovingly endeavor to lead back those whom they see or sense to be drawing away from the community. And all Jesuits should be prepared to cooperate with superiors in their solicitude, discreetly but in good time making known to them the difficulties and temptations of their confreres.[36]

Conclusion

267   10.   Finally, with superiors taking the lead, whose duty it is to be present and available, to encourage their brethren, and to offer them solicitous care, and with the cooperation of subjects, there will reign in the community through the wholehearted efforts of everyone the fraternal charity which, with participation in the same Eucharist, will make us all one united body. That charity, moreover, purifies our hearts of all feeling of envy, hostility, or bitterness. It so disposes us to bear each other's burdens and to treat one another with reverence that we may feel a generous love for one and all in the community and at the same time conduct with all a profitable and fruitful dialogue.

---

36 See *GenExam* [63].

17 THE LIFE OF OBEDIENCE

I. INTRODUCTION

1.   The General Congregation, solicitous to take into ac-   **268**
count the signs of the times according to the mind of the
Church,[1] and conscious of the social change in our day
which gives rise to a new awareness of the brotherhood of
men and a keener sense of liberty and personal responsibility, along with an excessively critical attitude and an
overly naturalistic view of the world, has thought it necessary to express its mind on obedience, which is a hallmark
of the Society and her principle of vitality. The Congregation considers this new situation "not in the spirit of fear,
but of power and of love and of prudence"[2] as a fitting occasion and challenge for the Society's renewal in the spirit
and practice of obedience. It is convinced, moreover, that
the way to the grace of our vocation will be opened not by
natural means alone, whether philosophical, psychological,
or sociological, but ultimately under the light of faith alone,
"with the eyes of the mind enlightened."[3]

II. OBEDIENCE IN THE SOCIETY APOSTOLIC BY NATURE

2.   Impelled by love of Christ, we embrace obedience as   **269**
a distinctive grace conferred by God on the Society through
its founder, whereby we may be united the more surely and
constantly with God's salvific will,[4] and at the same time
be made one in Christ among ourselves. For the Society of
Jesus is a group of men who seek close union with Christ

---

1 See GS 4, 11.
2 2 Tim. 1.7.
3 Eph. 1.18.
4 See PC 14.

and a share in the saving mission which He realized through obedience unto death. Christ invited us to take part in such a mission when, bearing His cross, He told St. Ignatius at La Storta, "I will that you serve Us." Through obedience, then, strengthened by vow, we follow "Jesus Christ still carrying His cross in the Church militant, to whom the eternal Father gave us as servants and friends, that we may follow Him with our cross"[5] and be made His companions in glory. We render service to Christ as He lives and works in the Church. Nor could our Society be sealed with the name of Jesus were it not fully committed to the service of the Church, which is the society of the Son of God, Christ Jesus our Lord.[6] Now through the vow of obedience our Society becomes a more fit instrument of Christ in His Church, unto the assistance of souls for God's greater glory. Hence, neither our religious life nor our apostolic action can survive or be renewed unless we hold firmly to sincere obedience.

III. THE SUPERIOR AS REPRESENTING CHRIST

270   3. The first Fathers of the Society held the unshaken conviction that "they had no other head than Christ Jesus, whom alone they hoped to serve,"[7] and they solemnly sanctioned this fact in the Formula of the Institute, affirming that they wanted "to serve the Lord alone."[8] In the same Formula, however, they already expressly declared that "they are serving the Lord alone and the Church His spouse, under the Roman Pontiff," understanding that they offer obedience to Christ Himself when they obey the visible head of the Church. Moreover, in the deliberations of the first Fathers, all decided unanimously that they should obey not only the Vicar of Christ, but also the superior chosen from among them, "so that we can more sincerely and with

---

5 *Monumenta Patris Nadal* (in MHSJ), IV, 678; see V, 296.
6 See 1 Cor. 1.9.
7 *Fontes narrativi de S. Ignatio* (in MHSJ), I, 204.
8 See *Formula of the Institute*, 1.

greater praise and merit fulfill through all things the will of God."[9] St. Ignatius repeatedly states this, that every superior is to be obeyed "in the place of Christ and for the love of Christ."[10] For Christ, as head and shepherd of the Church, is truly present in lawful superiors. The Church is the sacrament of salvation and unity,[11] i.e., the visible sign of His invisible presence and power. Therefore He is present in him who is Vicar of Christ "presides over the universal Church,"[12] and by whose ministry "the whole multitude of believers . . . is maintained in unity."[13] He is likewise present in a special way in religious superiors, who under the Roman Pontiff lawfully govern the community of their brethren, and by whose ministry "the community is gathered as a true family in the name of the Lord."[14] For them also, then, the promise of the Lord holds good: "He who hears you, hears me,"[15] so that in faith we can hear in their commands the voice of Christ commanding. Rightly, therefore, are we said to serve the Lord alone when we obey superiors in the Church.[16]

IV.   AUTHORITY TO BE EXERCISED IN THE SPIRIT OF
SERVICE AND OF DISCERNING LOVE

4.   After the example of Christ, whose place he holds,   **271** the superior should exercise his authority in a spirit of service, desiring not to be ministered unto, but to serve;[17] he should be the servant of all, set over a family of fellow servants, in order to serve by his governing. Resplendent in his ruling should be the kindness, meekness, and charity of Christ,[18] who, bearing the likeness and authority of the

---

9 *Deliberatio primorum Patrum,* 4, *Cons*MHSJ, I, 4.
10 See *GenExam* [83, 85] ; *Cons* [286, 424, 547, 551].
11 See LG 1, 48.
12 First Vatican Council, DS 3063.
13 First Vatican Council, DS 3051.
14 PC 14.
15 Luke 10.16
16 See *Formula of the Institute,* 1.
17 See Matt. 20.28.
18 See *Formula of the Institute,* 6.

Father, became the brother and companion of us all to live among us and labor with us. While he maintains sincere interior reverence, he should exercise simplicity in his way of speaking, so that the friendly concord of Christ with His apostles may come to view. And yet superiors should learn how to blend necessary rectitude and strictness with kindness and meekness,[19] desiring more to serve their brethren than to please them. Hence government in the Society should always be spiritual, conscious before God of personal responsibility and of the obligation to rule one's subjects as sons of God and with regard for the human personality,[20] strong where it needs to be, open and sincere. Superiors should reckon their direction of Jesuits, both as a community and as individuals, more important than any other tasks to be done. Superiors should be appointed who, as far as possible, are gifted with true personal authority, so that they can stir subjects to voluntary obedience, and so that the subjects may willingly agree to be guided by them.

272   5.   In the exercise of authority, however, the gift of discretion or of discerning love is most desirable.[21] To acquire this virtue, so necessary for good government, the superior should first of all be free from ill-ordered affections[22] and be closely united and familiar with God,[23] so that he will be docile to the will of Christ, which he should seek out with his subjects and authoritatively make manifest to them. Besides, he ought to know thoroughly our ways of acting, according to our Institute. Keeping in view, then, our end, which is none other than the greater service of God and the good of those who engage in this course of life,[24] he should command the things which he believes will contribute

---

19 See *Cons* [727].
20 See PC 14.
21 See *Cons* [161, 219, 269, 423, 624, 729].
22 See *Cons* [222, 726].
23 See *Cons* [723].
24 See *Cons* [746].

towards attaining the end proposed by God and the Society,[25] maintaining withal due respect for persons, places, times, and other circumstances.[26]

6.   But in order that he may more easily discover the **273** will of God, the superior should have at hand able advisers and should often consult them. He should also use the services of experts in reaching decisions on complex matters. This will the more easily enable members of the Society to be convinced that their superior knows how, wants, and is able, to govern them well in the Lord.[27] Besides, since all who work together in God's service are under the influence of the Holy Spirit and His grace, it will be well in the Lord to use their ideas and advice so as to understand God's will better. Superiors in the Society should readily and often ask for and listen to the counsel of their brethren, of a few or of many,[28] or even of all gathered together, according to the importance and nature of the matter. Superiors should gratefully welcome suggestions which their fellow Jesuits offer spontaneously, with a single desire of greater spiritual good and the better service of God, but the duty of the superior himself to decide and enjoin what ought to be done remains intact.[29]

7.   It is also advantageous to the Society that the su- **274** perior leave much in his orders to the prudence of his confreres, making liberal use of the principle of subsidiarity. To the extent that they make the spirit of the Society their own, especially if they are men long proven in humility and self-denial, individuals are to be allowed suitable freedom in the Lord. And finally, the universal good itself will sometimes demand that, in the manner of urging what has been commanded, account be taken also of human frailty.

---

25 See *Formula of the Institute*, 6.
26 See *Cons* [746].
27 See *Cons* [667].
28 See *Cons* [221, 810] ; *Cons*MHSJ, I, 218-219.
29 See PC 14.

275   8.   This truly spiritual government, whereby Jesuits are
directed by superiors with discerning love rather than
through external laws, supposes communication between
the two which is as far as possible plain and open. The
superior should endeavor to make his mind clearly known
to his confreres and understood by them; and he should
take care that they, according to the nature and importance
of the matter and as their own talents and duties require,
share more fully in his knowledge and concern both for the
personal and community life of Jesuits and for their apostolic labors. The religious, for his part, should try to make
himself known, with his gifts and limitations, his desires,
difficulties, and ideas, through a confiding, familiar and
candid colloquy, about which the superior is held to strict
secrecy. In this way an account of conscience is obtained
which is sincere and open in form, and not reduced to a
formal, periodic inquiry about actions already performed.[30]
That kind of friendly and confidential conversation, one
that is frankly spiritual and aims at promoting the apostolic
objective of our vocation and the religious sanctification of
the apostle, will constitute the dialogue that is fundamental
and essential for the wholesome progress of our Society.
Hence it is the mind of the Congregation that the account
of conscience in its proper sense should remain and be
strengthened as a general practice. But it is charity which
should inspire it, as St. Ignatius wished, with any obligation
under pain of sin always precluded.

V.   OBEDIENCE TO BE OFFERED WITH COMPLETE AVAILABILITY IN A PERSONAL, RESPONSIBLE WAY

276   9.   The Society's members, as the Constitutions provide,
should show respect and inward reverence for their superiors, and in the Lord should love them from the heart.[31]
To them they should leave the full and completely free disposal of themselves, desiring to be guided not by their own

---

30 See *Cons* [551].
31 See *Cons* [284, 551]; PC 14.

judgment and will,[32] but by that indication of the divine will which is offered to us through obedience. Jesuits, mindful that they are part of a Society which is wholly dedicated to Christ and His Church, should for their part primarily direct their labors under the guidance of the Holy Spirit for the service of the whole Church and Society.

277 Obedience is to be offered by all promptly, cheerfully,[33] and in a supernatural spirit, as to Christ. In this spirit, all should make their own the superior's command in a personal, responsible way, and with all diligence "bring to the execution of commands and the discharge of assignments entrusted to them the resources of their minds and wills, and their gifts of nature and grace," "realizing that they are giving service to the upbuilding of Christ's body according to God's design."[34] Hence, not just any sort of obedience is expected of us, but an obedience full and generous, of the intellect, too, insofar as possible, rendered in a spirit of faith, humility, and modesty.

278 10.   Our holy Father St. Ignatius desired that we should all excel in the virtue of obedience.[35] Accordingly, with all our force and energy we should strive to obey, first, the Sovereign Pontiff, and then the superiors of the Society, "not only in matters of obligation, but also in others, even at the mere hint of the superior's will, apart from any express command."[36] We are to respond with perfect obedience in all things where there is not manifestly any sin.[37] Nor may a subject refuse to obey because he thinks it would be better to do other things, or because he believes he is led along lines by the inspiration of the Holy Spirit.

279 It happens more often nowadays that a member of the Society will sincerely consider that by a dictate of con-

32 See Cons [618-619].
33 See *Cons* [547] ; *Letter on Obedience,* 12.
34 PC 14.
35 See *Cons* [547] ; *Letter on Obedience,* 2-3.
36 *Cons* [547].
37 See *Cons* [284, 549].

science he is forbidden to follow the superior's will, for he thinks that in a given case he is morally obliged to the contrary. Now it is true that no one may act against the certain dictates of his conscience. Still, conscience itself requires that in its formation attention be paid to all the factors which merit consideration in judging the morality of a decision, such as the universal good of the Church and the Society, which may be at stake, as well as the rights of others and the special obligations and values of religious life, which were freely assumed. Only a consideration of the whole reality can bring about a well-formed conscience. A member of the Society, therefore, should sincerely ponder the matter before the Lord, and present his reasons to his immediate or higher superior. It will then be the duty of the superior to weigh these reasons with an open mind, to review the case, and finally urge or withdraw the command.[38] But if the subject cannot be induced in this way to accept with a good conscience the decision of the superior, he may request that the whole question be referred to the judgment of certain persons, even non-Jesuits, to be chosen by common consent.[39] If after such a decision, however, no solution is reached which the Jesuit thinks he can follow without sinning, the superior, having consulted higher superiors as the case may merit, should provide for the course of action which seems more advisable in view of both the good of the whole Society and the good of the individual Jesuit's conscience. But a man who, time after time, is unable to obey with a good conscience, should take thought regarding some other path of life in which he can serve God with greater tranquility.

280   11.   Obedience is the ordinary means by which God's will is made clear to the members of the Society. However, it does not take away, but rather by its very nature and perfection supposes in the subject the obligation of personal responsibility and the spirit of ever seeking what is better.

---

38 See *Cons* [543, 627] ; *Letter on Obedience,* 19.
39 See *GenExam* [48-49] ; MHSJ, XII, 680.

Consequently the subject can, and sometimes should,[40] set forth his own reasons and proposals to the superior. Such a way of acting is not opposed to perfect obedience, but is reasonably required by it, in order that by an effort common to both superior and subject the divine will may more easily and surely be found. For obedience of judgment does not mean that our intellect is bereft of its proper role, and that one should assent to the superior's will against reason, rejecting the evidence of truth. For the Jesuit, employing his own intelligence, confirmed by the unction of the Holy Spirit, makes his own the will and judgment of superiors, and with his intellect endeavors to see their orders as more conformed to the will of God.[41] He diverts his attention from a fretful consideration of the opposite reasons, and directs it solely to positive reasons intrinsic to the matter or to motives which transcend this order, namely, values of faith and charity. For practical matters are at issue, in which almost always there remains some doubt as to what is most fitting and more pleasing to God. Theoretical certitude or very high probability about the objective superiority of a given solution is not to be awaited before a superior can authoritatively impose it; nor are the reasons for a course of action always and everywhere to be given the subject that he may devote himself wholeheartedly to the goals and works assigned to him. For the final reason for religious obedience is the authority of the superior. Trust is to be placed in Christ, who by means of obedience wishes to lead the Church and the Society to the ends He proposes.

12. Thus understood, obedience is not opposed to the **281** dignity of the human person who obeys, nor to his maturity and liberty,[42] but rather strengthens such liberty[43] and admirably fosters the progress of the human person by purification of heart and assimilation to Christ and His mother.[44]

---

40 See PO 15; *GenExam* [92, 131]; *Cons* [543, 627].
41 See *Cons* [284, 550, 619].
42 See PC 14.
43 See LG 43.
44 See LG 46.

For sons of the Society in the light of faith find the foundation of obedience in the example of Christ. Just as the Son of God "emptied himself, taking the form of a servant, being born in the likeness of men;" just as He humbled himself and became obedient unto death, even death on a cross,"[45] so also do members of the Society from love for Christ and to gain souls, "offer the full dedication of their own will as a sacrifice of self to God."[46] Thus they bind themselves entirely to God, beloved above all, and by a new and special title dedicate and consecrate themselves to His service and honor, bearing witness to the new freedom whereby Christ has made us free.[47]

VI. OBEDIENCE AS A BOND OF UNION

282
13. The Society "can neither be preserved nor governed, and so it cannot attain the end to which it aspires for God's glory, unless its members be united to each other and with their head."[48] This will be effected mainly by "the bond of obedience, which unites individuals with their superiors, and these among themselves and with the provincials, and all with Father General."[49] But union and obedience are founded on charity, for "if the superior and his subjects are strongly united with God's sovereign goodness, they will easily be united with one another."[50]

Impelled by the same charity, all "should show reverence and render obedience in accord with Church law to bishops because of their pastoral authority in the particular churches and for the union and harmony necessary in apostolic labor."[51] In this way Jesuits are proven to be true sons of the Church and contribute to the building up of the Body of Christ.[52]

---

45 Phil. 1.7-8.
46 PC 14.
47 See Gal. 4.31.
48 *Cons* [655].
49 *Cons* [821].
50 *Cons* [671].
51 LG 45.
52 See Eph. 4.12.

18 POVERTY

I. INTRODUCTION

1. The 31st General Congregation, having carefully **283** considered the need of adaptation and renewal of the Institute in regard to poverty, has decreed by its own authority that it be undertaken according to the norms defined below.

II. DIRECTIVE NORMS ON EVANGELICAL AND RELIGIOUS POVERTY IN THE SOCIETY OF JESUS

2. Since the Church of the Second Vatican Council, in **284** its desire to be "the Church of all, but in a special way the Church of the poor,"[1] calls on all the faithful to give an authentic testimony of poverty, and since the world, infected with atheism and closed to the heavenly goods of the kingdom of God, desperately needs this sign, the Society of Jesus, avowing at the same time poverty and the apostolate, in the Church, will try to give this witness of poverty in a more perfect way.

The Society of Jesus is also impelled to this by the innate **285** force of its vocation. For it is a community of disciples of the poor Christ, which has taken up an "apostolic life" to lead men to the kingdom of the Father by the path of poverty of spirit.

To bring about this renewal of our way of poverty, the **286** following declarations are made.

3. The spirit of poverty has an essential value in our **287** evangelical and religious life. For it is the spirit of Christ,

---

1 John **XXIII**, Address. *La grande aspettazione,* Sept. 11, 1962, AAS 54 (1962) 682.

who "though He was rich, became poor for your sake, to make you rich out of His poverty."[2] Imbued with this spirit, the companions of Jesus in a true consecration "more closely follow and more clearly show the Savior's self-emptying by embracing poverty with the free choice of God's sons."[3] At the same time, they manifest the wealth of the kingdom of God, in that they give up earthly goods and practice charity for the needy, knowing that "our Lord Jesus Christ will provide the necessities of life and dress for his servants who are seeking solely the kingdom of God."[4]

288   4.   Our poverty in the Society is apostolic: our Lord has sent us "to preach in poverty."[5] Therefore our poverty is measured by our apostolic end, so that our entire apostolate is informed with the spirit of poverty.

289   5.   In order that this poverty may flourish the more, the Society seeks its adaptation and renewal both by a return to the true doctrine of the Gospel and the original inspiration of the Society and by the adaptation of our law to the changed conditions of the times, in such a way that, insofar as it may be necessary, the letter of the norms may be changed, but not the spirit, which must continue undiminished.[6]

290   6.   This adaptation and renewal must affect the forms of our poverty as well as the juridical norms, so that these forms may truly suit the mentality, life, and apostolate of our times and give a visible witness to the Gospel. Therefore our contemporary poverty must be especially characterized by these qualities: sincerity, by which our lives are really poor; devotion to work, by which we resemble workers in the world; and charity, by which we freely devote ourselves and all we have for the service of the neighbor.

---

2 2 Cor 8.9.
3 LG 42.
4 *Formula of the Institute*, 7.
5 *S. Ignatii Epistolae et Instructiones* (in MHSJ), I, 96.
6 Paul VI, Address *Magno Gaudio*, May 23, 1964, *ActRSJ* 14 (1964) 410.

7.   Our profession of poverty should be sincere, so that **291**
the manner of our life corresponds to this profession. St.
Ignatius wanted us to take the criterion for the poverty of
our life both from our apostolic end and from the principles
of the Gospel, for we are apostles of the Gospel. But since
we are apostles of this age, we must pay special attention
to the social circumstances of time and place.

If, following in the footsteps of our predecessors, we **292**
would wish to give—or repeat—more concisely defined
norms, assuming discernment in their application, we
should have to say that the character of our poverty in
regard to our way of life must be adapted to people of
modest means so that our food, clothing, dwelling, and
travels are such as are suited to the poor.[7] Where we must
make use of larger buildings, travel, or instruments for our
work, these should really be, and as far as possible clearly
appear to be, necessary instruments intended solely for our
apostolate which we use in adherence to our poverty.[8]

The Society really intends to answer the demands of this **293**
real, not pretended, poverty.

8.   The witness of our poverty today most aptly shines **294**
forth in our practice and spirit of work undertaken for the
kingdom of God and not for temporal gain. This poverty
should be filled with activity, by which we resemble men
who must earn their daily bread; it should be equitable and
just, ordered in the first place to giving each one his due;
finally, it should be generous, so that by our labor we may
help our poorer houses, our works, and the poor.

9.   Our poverty, then, should become a sign of our **295**
charity in that by our lack we enrich others. Nothing should
be our own so that all things may be common in Christ.
Communities themselves, renouncing their own advantage,
should be united to each other by the bond of solidarity.

---

7 See *GenExam* [81]; GC 30, D. 46, 4°.
8 See GC 30, D. 46, nn. 2, 4.

Finally, the parts of the Society should freely become poorer so that they may serve the whole body of the Society. And the bond of charity should not be restricted only to Jesuits, for all men are related to the Mystical Body of Christ. Charity should always crown the obligations of justice by which we are bound in a special way to those who are poorer and to the common good.

296   10.   All should remember, however, that no community form of poverty nor any outward profession of it will be genuinely Christian unless it is inspired by a highly personal sentiment of the heart, that is, by a spiritual poverty, drawn from a close and constant union with the incarnate Word of God. Therefore, there is a broad field of personal responsibility in which each can more perfectly live his calling to poverty and, within the limits of the common good, express it with discerning love by living more frugally, under the guidance of superiors.

297   11.   The Society, facing a world in which a large part of mankind lies wounded and despoiled, moved by the love of the Good Samaritan, and conscious of its universal vocation, should subject its apostolate to examination, to see how it may more fully turn itself to those who are abandoned, "to evangelize the poor, to heal the crushed in heart."[9]

III.   DIRECTIVE NORMS CONCERNING COMMON LIFE IN THE SOCIETY OF JESUS

298   12.   The General Congregation, in its concern about the obligation of religious life and the evangelical witness given by that life in all our apostolic activity, has set itself to define what "common life" means as applied to the Society's poverty so that our communities and individual members may be more accurately guided in really practicing in an always more perfect way personal poverty and communal or collective poverty.

---

9 Luke 4.18; see *SpEx* 167.

13.   Our community poverty includes two aspects: that **299**
"common life" which St. Ignatius derived from a centuries-
old tradition and current Church law still sanctions as an
essential element for all religious families; and that mode of
living which, in the following of Christ as He preached with
the apostles, bears the mark of the special calling that ought
to characterize the Society's efforts as it works among men
for the redemption of the world. Moreover, it is of the utmost importance that an apostle, always following the poor
Christ, somehow accommodate himself to the manner of
life of those whom he helps, becoming all things to all
men.[10] Therefore our every use of material things should be
such that by the sharing of these goods in common we not
only express and strengthen the unity of heart and mind of
all members of the Society, but also, by the tenor of our
life, signify to the world our will, both common and personal, to give a witness of evangelical poverty, humbly and
fraternally serving all, especially the poor, so that we may
gain all for Christ, living as poor men and in externals in a
manner common to all.

IV.   THE MATTER OF THE VOW NOT TO RELAX POVERTY

14.   The General Congregation authentically declares **300**
the matter of the vow not to relax poverty to be completely
defined in this statement: "To bring about an innovation
in regard to poverty means to relax it by admitting any
revenues or assets for the use of the community, whether
with a view to the sacristy, maintenance, or any other purpose, apart from the case of the colleges and houses of
probation."[11] Therefore, in virtue of the vow the solemnly
professed are obliged only to this: not to grant a stable
income to professed houses and independent residences,
notwithstanding other more general expressions which are
found in the same Declaration.

---

10 See 1 Cor 9.22.
11 *Cons* [554].

V. THE FRUIT OF LABOR

301   15.   The General Congregation declares, that in addition to the alms and income admitted by the Constitutions, gain from or remuneration for work done according to the Institute is a legitimate source of material goods which are necessary for the life and apostolate of Jesuits. But we are to select these labors according to the obligations of obedience and the nature of our ministries, avoiding every desire of monetary gain or temporal advantage.

VI. THE GRATUITY OF MINISTRIES

302   16.   The General Congregation interprets the gratuity of ministries in the Society in the following way:

a)   The nature of gratuity is to be explained in the first instance from its purpose, which is both inner freedom (absence from seeking one's own temporal advantage), outer freedom (independence from the bonds of undue obligation), and the edification of the neighbor which arises from this freedom and from the love of Christ and men.

303   b)   This gratuity is not opposed to the acceptance of Mass stipends or alms according to the current law of the Church. But in practice account must be taken of edification and of charity to the poor both in and outside of the Society, according to norms to be established by Father General.

304   c)   Exception being made of the special norms for parishes and for a legitimate recompense for travel and other expenses, including sustenance, Jesuits may demand no stipend for their work in spiritual ministries, especially for those mentioned in the beginning of the Formula of the Institute of Julius III; they may accept only those which are offered to them. It belongs to Father General to define the norms for this in practice.

305   d)   The General Congregation declares that the rights of authors, emoluments, honoraria, grants, and other gifts which are considered to be the fruit of the talents and industry of Jesuits may be accepted; however, in the choice of ministries or works, let Jesuits not be influenced by the intention of making profits.

e) Tuition charges for education do not of themselves **306** go against gratuity. Nonetheless, from the very apostolic intention of the Society in the ministry of the teaching and formation of youth and according to the mind of St. Ignatius, we are to try our best, as far as is possible according to the circumstances of time and place, to devise means by which we can return to the practice of teaching without the help of tuition.[12]

VII. FOUNDATIONS IN THE LAW OF THE SOCIETY

17. The General Congregation modifies decree 188, § 1, **307** in the *Collection of Decrees* thus: "It is to be understood that those revenues which, according to the Constitutions, may be accepted by a 'house' if they are offered by founders 'in such a way that their disposition is not in the hands of the Society and that the Society is incompetent to institute civil action in their regard,' may be received—either from founders of houses or churches, or from any other benefactor—not only for the purpose of maintenance but also for other similar purposes, such as for the sacristy, for the library, or even for living expenses."[13]

18. The General Congregation believes that it is expedi- **308** ent to request from the Holy See in favor of the Society the power by which Father General can establish, define, administrate, suppress, and assign non-collegiate foundations, notwithstanding the fact that the common law gives the right and duty to local ordinaries to establish and visit such foundations.

19. The General Congregation gives a mandate to **309** Father General that, when this power has been obtained, he will by an Ordination establish the norms for setting up foundations for the good of some houses or works, and for

---

12 See *CollDecr* 193 §§ 3, 4.

13 See GC 24, D. 16.

a more precise definition of the nature and purpose of some funds which are necessary for the financial life of the Society.

VIII. PROCEDURES

310   20.   The General Congregation decrees that a commission shall be set up, according to the Constitutions VIII, 7, 3 [715], and the Formula of the General Congregation (Nos. 125-27), adding some prescriptions which seem appropriate, even though contrary to some of the statutes of the Formula of the General Congregation; this commission shall consist of Father General, who has the right to preside, and four *definitores,* on these conditions:

a)   The four *definitores* shall be chosen by the General Congregation by a majority of secret votes, each one by a distinct vote, or, if some names shall be proposed by Father General, by a vote (or votes) containing several names; moreover, it shall be in the power of Father General, for a good reason and with the advice of the General Assistants, to accept or even to ask for the dismissal of one of the *definitores* and to replace him with another.

b)   The *definitores* with Father General shall determine matters only with that power which the General Congregation gives to them.

c)   Their task will be to prepare in stages a schema of adaptation and renewal, and revision of our entire law concerning poverty.

d)   The schema definitively worked out by the commission of *definitores* shall be promulgated by Father General for use and experiment for the whole Society until the General Congregation immediately following this one.

IX.   APPLYING TO THE HOLY SEE

21.   The General Congregation decides that numbers **311**
IV, V, and VI of this decree be submitted to the Holy Father for confirmation, or at least for the purpose of inform-
ing him.[14]

---

14 See the letter of Cardinal Cicognani, June 6, 1966, to Fr. General
   (communicating the papal approval of the Congregation's decrees
   on religious poverty and the gratuity of ministries).

I.   COMMUNITY LIFE

A.   The Nature of Community Life in the Society of Jesus

312   1.   The sense of community evolved gradually in the infant Society. The first members, "friends in the Lord,"[1] after they had offered themselves and their lives to Christ the Lord and given themselves to His vicar on earth that he might send them where they could bear more fruit,[2] decided to associate themselves into one body so that they might make stronger and more stable every day their union and association which was begun by God, "making ourselves into one body, caring for and understanding one another for the greater good of souls."[3] Similarly they agreed later to give their obedience to some superior "so that they might better and more carefully fulfill their first desires to do the divine will in all things,"[4] and gain greater internal cohesion, stability, and apostolic efficacy.

313   2.   And so community in the Society of Jesus takes its origin from the will of the Father joining us into one, and is constituted by the active, personal, united striving of all members to fulfill the divine will, with the Holy Spirit impelling and guiding us individually through responsible obedience to a life which is apostolic in many ways. It is a community of men who are called by Christ to live with Christ, to be conformed to Christ, to fulfill the work of

---

1 *S. Ignatii Epistolae et Instructiones* (in MHSJ), I, 119.
2 B. Petri Faber, Ad D. de Gouvea (in MHSJ) I, 132; *Cons* [605].
3 *Deliberatio primorum Patrum,* 3, *Cons*MHSJ, I, 3 (a. 1539).
4 *Deliberatio primorum Patrum,* 8, *Cons*MHSJ, I, 7.

Christ in themselves and among men. This is the foundation and aim of community life in the Society of Jesus.

3. The union of minds of the members among themselves and with their head, leading to personal holiness and at the same time to apostolic activity, flows from a love for our God and Lord, Jesus Christ,[5] and is sustained and governed by the same love. When it is strengthened by mutual understanding, this love gives a community a way of finding God's will for it with certainty. For this dialogue between superiors and subjects or between the members of the Society, whether it takes place man to man or as a community effort, becomes supernaturally meaningful when it is directed towards finding the divine will, cultivating fraternal love and promoting our work as apostles.

314

B. The Importance of Community Life for Religious Life

4. When community life flourishes, the whole religious life is sound. Obedience, for instance, is a very clear expression of our cooperation toward common ends, and it becomes more perfect to the extent that superiors and subjects are bound to one another in trust and service. Chastity is more safely preserved, "when there is a true brotherly love in community life between the members."[6] Poverty, finally, means that we have made ourselves poor by surrendering ourselves and our possessions to follow the Lord.[7] Community life aids and assists us in this surrender in a great variety of ways, and in its own unique way is the support of poverty.[8] When the religious life is thus strengthened, unity and flexibility, universality, full personal dedication, and the freedom of the Gospels, are also strengthened for the assistance of souls in every way. And this was the intention of the first companions.

315

---

5 See *Cons* [671].

6 PC 12.

7 See Luke 18.28.

8 See *Cons* [570].

316   In addition, community life itself is a manifold testimony for our contemporaries, especially since by it brotherly love and unity are fostered, by which all will know that we are disciples of Christ.[9]

C.   Conditions for Community Life

317   5.   a)   The principal bond of community life is love,[10] by which our Lord and those to whom He has entrusted His mission of salvation are loved in a single act. By this love, which contains a real offering of one's self to others, a true brotherhood in the Lord is formed, which constantly finds human expression in personal relationships and mutual regard, service, trust, counsel, edification, and encouragement of every kind.

318   More concretely, the following are increasingly necessary for community life in the Society of Jesus:

b)   Exchange of information in the community,[11] by which superiors and subjects are kept informed about common works and plans, and help each other with advice.

319   c)   Frequent consultation with experts, to share their insights, and frequent consultation among the members of the community, aimed at actively engaging everyone in the process of coordinating and promoting the apostolate, and in other things which pertain to the good of the community.

320   d)   Delegation, by which the superior willingly gives the members greater responsibility for special missions and projects, and makes use of the principle of subsidiarity. When responsibility of this kind grows, a common burden is carried by many, and the sense of community is increased.

321   e)   Collaboration of every kind, transcending every sort of individualism, which is more necessary in contemporary circumstances than ever before for the apostolate of the Society and a more intimate way of living together.

---

9 See John 13.35; PC 15.

10 See *Cons* [671].

11 See *Cons* [673].

f) A certain order of life which is determined by the **322** conditions of life and work proper to each community. For this is a very apt means for making more efficacious both individual and community work, for making mutual interchange among members easier, and for creating those exterior and interior conditions of silence, recollection, and peace of mind, which are so useful for personal study, reflection, and especially prayer. In addition, it is a complement of charity itself and its realistic expression, as well as a sign of religious consecration and union in the service of Christ.

g) A feeling for the whole Society on the part of the **323** members, which transcends local and personal limits, and in many ways helps community life itself, for each individual is included "as a member of one and the same body of the Society."[12] Therefore, the more clearly the members recognize that they are connected with the whole life and apostolate of the Society, the more community life will become psychologically and spiritually richer.

D. More Concrete Applications

6. a) In relation to the whole Society: The sense of **324** belonging and responsibility of each individual toward the whole Society, which was mentioned in No. 5g, is manifested in a knowledge of our history, our saints, our works, and our men, especially of those who are facing difficulties for the sake of Christ; in maintaining Ignatian mobility and flexibility with a view to helping any region of the Society whatsoever; in the practice of a generous hospitality towards all Jesuits.[13]

b) In relation to neighboring houses and provinces: **325** There should be more association between the fathers and brothers of different houses and provinces, so that they can help each other by this association and by the way their experiences complement one another. They should meet

---

12 *Cons* [510].
13 See *CollDecr* 74.

more frequently to discuss the apostolate, the religious life, the teaching of the Council, and new questions of theology, in order to improve their knowledge and enable them to act in basic unity. And one house should share with another material goods "so that those which have more may help those which are in need."[14]

326   7.   In the houses of those who have final vows: a) Since common prayer, especially the celebration of Mass and devotion to the Eucharist, is very helpful for tightening the bonds of community, all should faithfully fulfill the prescriptions of No. 15 of the Decree on Prayer.

327   b)   Our community life should at the same time be improved by our common apostolic work. So we must promote the closest possible cooperation among Jesuits, both by having all or very many in a community devoted to the same work and by making use of small groups, to whom the superior can grant the powers he judges to be helpful for meeting the needs of the apostolate (see No. 5, d). Cooperation in work begins and is sustained by previous exchange of information on the community level, by encouraging one another's efforts, and by various forms of consultation (see No. 5, b-c) beyond those prescribed in our law.

328   c)   Priests, brothers, and scholastics should all associate with one another easily, in sincerity, evangelical simplicity, and courtesy, as is appropriate for a real family gathered together in the name of the Lord.[15] As far as apostolic work or other occupations for the greater glory of God permit it, all of us, "esteeming the others in their hearts as better than themselves,"[16] should be ready to help out in the common household chores.[17]

329   d)   The standard of living with regard to food, clothing, and furniture should be common to all so that, poor in fact

---

14 See PC 13; D. 18, n. 9.
15 See PC 15; ES II, 25.
16 *Cons* [250].
17 See D. 7, nn. 5-6.

and in spirit, differences may be avoided as far as possible. This does not prevent each one from having what is necessary for his work with the permission of the superior. But while he applies himself intensely to his own work, let each one also recognize his responsibility for the spiritual help and material sustenance of other members of the community.

e) Customs which are more suitable for monastic life **330** shall not be introduced into our community life, nor those which are proper to seculars; much less, those which manifest a worldly spirit.

Let our relationship with all other men be such as can **331** rightly be expected from a man consecrated to God and seeking the good of souls above all things; and it should include a proper regard for genuine fellowship with all other Jesuits.

Our houses should be open in genuine hospitality even **332** to persons not members of the Society, especially to religious and to those who work with us.

f) Keeping in mind apostolic poverty and our witness **333** to those among whom we must live, our houses should be made suitable for apostolic work, study, prayer, relaxation of mind and a friendly spirit, so that Jesuits will feel at home in their own house.

It can be a great help to the simplicity and intimacy of **334** community life as well as to poverty if the house or place where we live and the house or place where we work or even where we study can be conveniently separated.

g) After consultation a simple daily order should be **335** established which will suit our apostolic activities and the common good of the members, and which can be adjusted by the superior for good reason.

h) Those norms of community life which are to be **336** observed uniformly in the houses of any region should be proposed at a meeting of the provincials, and after the approval of Father General are to be maintained with equal vigor by all the provincials.

337   8.   In the houses of formation: a) Our younger members, both scholastics and brothers, are to be prepared for that community life which has been proposed in the preceding numbers as proper to those living in the apostolate. But the pedagogical nature of the years of formation, the nature of the studies or activities in these houses, and the number of members, make some suitable adaptations of community life necessary.

338   b)   In houses of formation there should be more room for common participation in some forms of prayer, especially for active and varied participation in a community celebration of the Eucharist, and for some short common prayer every day, to symbolize and deepen the religious bond which unites us in our Lord and by our Lord with the Society, the Church, and the world.

339   c)   Each one's sense of community, as a necesary prerequisite for the apostolic life of the Society, should be seriously tested and formed during these years. Candidates and those in the course of training should be examined with special attention to their ability to get along with people; it is to be considered as one of the signs of vocation to the Society.

340   d)   The scholastics and brothers should in suitable ways be initiated into their community of work, whether it be in studies or other duties or in the apostolate, maintaining a suitable balance with individual work in depth, especially in studies, a balance which modern conditions seem to make rather difficult to preserve.

341   At the same time attention must be paid to education for dialogue among themselves and with superiors, for cooperation and obedience, in line with the suggestions made in other decrees of this Congregation,[19] all of which tend to form men who are capable of making the best possible choices, with the help of supernatural illumination and sufficient advice from others.

---

18 See PC 15. [This footnote appears in the Latin original without a specific reference indication in the text itself.]
19 See D. 8 and D. 9.

e) A communal life, which according to No. 7, *b-d,* is **342** based on the evangelical spirit of service, work, and authentic poverty, is to be made more perfect by a gradual participation of the young men in offices and consultations. This will help to develop their responsibility and a realistic sense of their vocation, while it shows "who they really are."

f) The order of the day, mentioned in No. 5, *f* and No. **343** 7, *g,* is to be faithfully observed particularly in houses of training, in order that due regard may be had for these values: the interior spiritual life which is to be fostered even by external helps; charity, or responsibility for those conditions of silence, recollection, etc., which aid the work, quiet, and prayer of others; the efficacy of personal and community work as well as our living together; the intrinsic and formative value of a well considered rule,[20] and the formative value of fidelity in carrying out those things God entrusts to us by obedience.

g) In due proportion and under direction, we should **344** foster relationships between the younger members of different nations, either for the sake of higher studies or to learn modern languages, or for apostolic experiments. This will greatly increase understanding and unity in the Society in the future.

II. RELIGIOUS DISCIPLINE

9. The life of the Society, its activity, and more con- **345** cretely community life in it, is a cooperation of all members flowing from love.[21] But according to the mind of our founder and the desires of the Church, it ought to be defined and ordered by rules. Rules are a safeguard for charity and a sign of the union of members, and they also constitute a real help for human weakness, a stimulus to individual responsibility; and a means of coordinating activities for the common good.

---

20 See OT 11; *Cons* [294-295 and 435-436].
21 See *Cons* [671].

346   10. These rules pertain to the whole vital spiritual range of religious obedience, and their application to individuals is subject to the living rule of the direction of a superior. Therefore what this General Congregation has said about obedience, especially in No. 8 of the Decree on the Life of Obedience in the Society, should be recalled again here, since religious discipline in the Society of Jesus ought to be marked with the characteristics of Ignatian obedience. According to the will of the Church and the Vicar of Christ, again manifested to us,[22] rules were written and are to be written to make clear the will of God "in order to make better progress in the way of divine service upon which we have entered."[23] They show us a way of loving which is concrete, constant, and personal, and they give us an externally uniform way of serving others. For the rule prepares us for a closer union with Christ and the Church. It leads us to Christ like a guardian, and therefore it ought to be accepted with that filial love with which it was given[24] and which leads to the liberty of sons.

347   11. Understanding the observance of rules in this way, as a movement from love to love, we must say that it is a means of sanctification for everyone,[25] a sanctification indeed ordered toward more fruitful apostolic action.

348   In addition, it is a way to human perfection, for this kind of observance of rule is neither an empty formalism nor a so-called self-alienation. In fact, since it sometimes requires a renunciation and denial of real values, by which denial we are associated with Christ, it leads to solid personal maturity.[26]

349   12. Therefore religious discipline in the Society sup-

---

22 See *Cons Prooemium* [134]; Pius XII, *ActRSJ* 13 (1957) 293; LG 45; PC 4; Paul VI, *AAS* 56 (1964) 565-571; *ActRSJ* 14 (1964) 409-410; ES 12-14.

23 *Cons Prooemium* [134].

24 See *Cons* [602].

25 See GC 28, D. 22, 3°.

26 See LG 46, OT 11, PC 14.

poses and produces superiors and subjects who are obedient
men, mature in a Christian way.

For it is the task of superiors to seek diligently the will of **350**
God even with the help of advice from others about the
most suitable means, and to decide what is to be done,[27]
and then to express their decisions clearly. It is also their
duty to foster the observance of rules and to adapt them to
individuals as circumstances require. The most efficacious
means of obtaining this is that they stand before their
subjects as living examples who will continually draw the
rest to fidelity and generosity in the service of the Lord.

But their greatest duty is to lead their subjects, especially **351**
the younger ones, to an ever increasing formation in responsibility and freedom, so that they observe rules not in
the spirit of fear[28] but from an intimate personal conviction
rooted in faith and charity.

Subjects, for their part, should foster a love for the rules **352**
by constant reading and meditation on the Constitutions,
from which they can draw the genuine spirit which should
pervade our way of life. In fact, from a familiarity with the
text of our founder we can gather what importance many
of the rules have for the perfection of our own vocation
and for the apostolic mission of the Society, so that with
hearts full of love we may set ourselves to observe them.

13.   Discipline, however, is not to be sought in itself and **353**
for itself. Its purpose is "to enable us to accomplish God's
will in all things more honestly and with greater praise and
merit."[29] A dynamic resolve to accomplish this when faced
with the variety of constantly new challenges which face
the Church should make all, superiors and subjects alike,
attentive to the signs of the times. They must read these
signs with God's help and be ready to propose in due time

---

27 See PC 14.
28 See *Cons* [547, 602].
29 *Deliberatio primorum Patrum,* 4, *Cons*MHSJ, I, 4.

suitable revisions of the rules, which will remove things which are obsolete and out of place, strengthen what is still vital, and open up paths which are perhaps new and more likely to lead us to our goal.[30]

354 Rules, however, remain in force until they are revoked or changed by competent authority.

III. REVISION OF THE RULES

355 14. A revision of the rules is entrusted to Father General for completion as soon as possible, according to the principles of the Church,[31] so that some common norms may be established for the whole Society. These will of necessity be few in number, rather general, brief, as far as possible expressed in a positive way and organically ordered, and solidly based in theology, so as to signify and bring about the union of the members. It should be left to the provincials to determine with the approbation of Father General more particular norms for individual provinces.[32]

356 15. The rules of the Summary and the Common Rules are to be within the competence of the General. Therefore, in the *Collection of Decrees,* decree 3, § 2, 3°, the words "Summary of the Constitutions" and "Common Rules" are now deleted.

357 16. The General is commissioned to issue Ordinations dealing with the matters presently contained in the *Collection of Decrees,* decrees 48; 52, § 2; 61; 65-72. The power is also given to him to suspend, from the day on which he promulgates each Ordination of this sort, the related decrees, until the next congregation, with the consent of the General Assistants.

---

30 See ES II, 14, 17.
31 See ES II, 12-14.
32 See *Cons Prooemium* [136].

1. After careful consideration of the reasons advanced 358
for introducing changes in the present directives for reading
at table and in light of the variety of circumstances prevail-
ing in various parts of the Society, the General Congregation turns over to Father General the task of making prudent arrangements for the practice in each province or
region.

2. To prevent a decline in knowledge of the Constitu- 359
tions as a consequence of discontinuing the monthly reading
of the Summary of the Constitutions at table, the General
Congregation recommends to Father General that he take
measures effectively to preserve and foster this knowledge,
either by restoring the monthly reading of the Summary, or
by determining that key paragraphs of these Constitutions
should be read in order at table, or by some other more
suitable method.

V

THE APOSTOLATE

21 THE BETTER CHOICE AND PROMOTION
OF MINISTRIES

1.   While the 31st General Congregation recognized the **360**
hard work that our Society puts into its apostolic ministries,
at the same time it notes that our labors have not produced
all the results that we could rightly expect, if one considers
the proportion between the efforts and the results achieved.

Part of the reason for this is our failure at times continu-   **361**
ally to renew our apostolic or missionary spirit and to maintain the union which the instrument should have with God,[1]
or our neglect of "moderation in labors of soul and body"[2]
or a too great scattering of our forces;[3] but the principal
reason is our failure adequately to adapt our ministries to
the changed conditions of our times.

2.   Hence, not a few doubts are being raised whether   **362**
some of our works have become obsolete or are in need of
a profound renewal at least in regard to the way in which
they are carried on. On the other hand, new fields of
apostolic labor invite us, fields which seem to be of very
great importance for spreading the faith and imbuing the
world with the spirit of Christ and are at the same time
entirely in harmony with the particular spirit of our Society.
Likewise, other apostolic forces are frequently found in the
Church today which in a special way cultivate this or that
field of the apostolate, so that our work in almost the same
field has lost its note of urgency. Finally, we need to be
more available to take on those ministries which answer the

---

1 See *Cons* [813].
2 See *Cons* [822].
3 See GC 30, D. 50, § 1.

urgent pastoral needs of the modern church and the special missions of the Roman Pontiff. For these missions, in keeping with our distinctive spirit, we should be particularly ready.

363   3.   Weighing all these points, the General Congregation judges that the Society still retains a capacity for renewal and adaptation to our time. This capacity comes from the unique flexibility given to our Institute by the Holy Spirit and from the varied and widespread experience of our men in so many fields of the apostolate. Renewal and adaptation require a continual revision of the choice and promotion of our ministries. Such a revision moreover answers the express wishes of the Fathers of Vatican II for renewal and adaptation in the religious life.

364   Therefore, it seems that certain more general orientations should be set down in this matter.

A.   THE NORMS FOR RENEWAL

365   4.   All Jesuits, especially superiors, to whom the choice of ministries belongs "as the most important task of all,"[4] must work very hard at bringing about this renewal of our ministries. The norms for renewal are found in the Constitutions themselves. Much light is shed on these norms by the decrees of the general congregations and the Instructions of the Fathers General. While retaining their perennial validity, these norms must always be rightly applied to historical circumstances. But it is especially from a renewed and profound study of our spiritual heritage that this renewal must be drawn. The Spiritual Exercises of St. Ignatius can pour into us the spirit of magnanimity and indifference, of firm decision and reformation, a renewal, that is to say, of our activity or of the means for reaching our goal more successfully through the light of those well known principles: the greater service of God, the more

---

4 Fr. Janssens, Letter on Our Ministries, *ActRSJ* 11 (1947) 299-336.

universal good, the more pressing need, the great importance of a future good and special care of those significant ministries for which we have special talent.

B. CERTAIN DISPOSITIONS REQUIRED
FOR THIS ADAPTATION

5. In order to use these norms correctly and effectively, **366** there is especially needed that union of the instrument with God which comes from faith and charity. From this union, above all else, comes the efficacy of our apostolate; and this union cannot be supplied for by other gifts of the merely natural order.

6. This familiarity with God, moreover, because of the **367** union of our apostolate with the mission of the Incarnate Word, calls for not less, but closer involvement in this world. This demands certain dispositions of soul which will better serve this purpose.

a) The contemporary world, shaken by such rapid and **368** profound changes, demands of us the capacity to recognize this process. This ability to recognize change is, as it were, the humility that befits us as creatures, a humility that makes us open and faithful to all creation so that, discovering the will of God in these processes, we may bring about a continual renewal and adaptation of our apostolate.

b) Besides, the closer social relations now being formed **369** among men and nations, in a world that is on its way to becoming unified, demand of us the spirit of fraternal dialogue, mutual reverence and a sense of complementarity and collaboration in action.

c) A livelier awareness of human progress and of **370** temporal values, the abuse of which frequently leads to a denial of religion and of God Himself, is a consideration also of great importance in the apostolate. For in apostolic work, whose true goal is to announce to men the mystery of Christ who is at work in us and in the world, it is man in his entire life and concrete existence who must be reached.

C. OUR COOPERATION WITH OTHERS IN THE APOSTOLATE

371   7. In keeping with the mind of Vatican II in its theological and pastoral teaching, the provincials are invited to a close collaboration with those whom the Holy Spirit has placed to rule the church of God.[5] Keeping ourselves available in the first place to the Holy See, let all Jesuits and especially superiors propose to themselves "to follow the plans, judgments and works of the hierarchy and to bring them to completion and be animated by the dynamic spirit of fellowship."[6] Therefore, let our works be harmonized with the pastoral programs of the bishops, especially by means of our collaboration as religious with the conferences of bishops. Let us be eager to render apostolic service to priests and to those aspiring to the priesthood.

372   8. Collaboration with other religious is also to be commended, keeping intact, however, the character of each order. Spiritual helps which are asked for by other religious societies are to be gladly supplied. For this purpose the conferences of major superiors will be of great service.

373   9. An extensive and sincere collaboration with the laity is likewise to be commended. For in the works of our Society, our own responsibility for their inspiration, orientation and direction must be shared in a certain definite way by the laity. In the expanse, moreover, of the whole Church, serious care must be fostered to help the laity to grow and become true men and Christians, fully conscious of their own responsibility toward the Church and the world. This is especially true of those lay persons (men and women) who, because of their greater importance for the universal good of the Church, deserve special spiritual attention. Finally, contacts of true friendship with the laity in secular associations and in the multiple circumstances of daily life

---

5 See Acts 20.28.

6 Paul VI, Address *Sincero animo* to the Fathers of the 31st General Congregation (May 7, 1965); Document 1 in this volume and *AAS* 57 (1965) 511-15.

manifest our attentive presence to the concrete existence of man, express a form of charity and constitute a real beginning of the apostolate; at the same time they will enrich us interiorly and make us more human in exercising our apostolic work.

10.   With regard to the universal Church, lastly, let the   **374** Society provide cooperation in the same spirit of service, through centers that organize apostolic action.

D.   SOME FIELDS OF THE APOSTOLATE WHICH TODAY DESERVE SPECIAL ATTENTION

11.   The world of our day is marked by certain charac-   **375** teristics, namely, the progress of higher education, the advance of professional life, the increasing proportion of younger people, international organizations and the serious needs of some parts of the world. Hence it comes about that certain fields of modern life have acquired a special urgency, fields that must be considered among the other works laudably carried on by our Society:

a)   the field, namely, of higher education, especially in the positive sciences through which scientific research and the technical arts are advanced;

b)   the field of labor and professional groups, especially those in greater need;

c)   the education of youth, especially that part which, it is foreseen, will have greater influence in the life of the Church and the world;

d)   international organizations which aim at bringing together organically every sector of the world, an activity whose importance for the whole of mankind can scarcely be exaggerated;

e)   certain geographical regions where the very great increase in population, the rapid evolution in social, economic and political life, hunger and many other miseries of every sort, as well as the bitter struggle between the Christian conception of life and opposed ideologies, demand strong apostolic efforts without delay;

f) in addition, in regions which are traditionally Christian, we must expend a great deal of effort on behalf of those who are called "neopagans," those namely who are infected with either theoretical or practical atheism.

376   12.   With great eagerness, let all Jesuits undertake those apostolic works which are calculated to implement the constitutions and decrees of Vatican II, always keeping in mind the proper character of our Institute. Missions, moreover, which the Supreme Pontiff may wish to entrust to our Society at any time and in any part of the world, we are to place in the category of the highest priority. Hence, the commission to oppose atheism which Paul VI has given to us, we should accept with grateful eagerness.

377   13.   Let our entire Society renew its missionary spirit in keeping with the Decree on the Missionary Activity of the Church *(Ad Gentes)*, since our Society was founded to spread the faith.

378   14.   In developing the apostolate of the Society in the world of today, the use and vitalization of the means of social communication should be promoted more every day. These mass media go far toward shaping the modern mind, and they lead us to a manner of expression which is adapted to the temper of present-day man.

379   15.   Since experience shows that we have not lacked well-ordered norms admirably composed by the Fathers General nor the sincere wish of the whole Society nor decrees calling for an adaptation, we must now use the means that will more effectively put all these forces into operation. For this purpose, besides the awareness which must of necessity be made more sensitive in the whole Society to the urgency of renewal and adaptation in the choice and promotion of our ministries, the setting up of special commissions will be of great service to the Fathers Provincial and even to Father General in the choice of ministries and in organizing our apostolate.

22 THE COMMISSION FOR PROMOTING
THE BETTER CHOICE OF MINISTRIES

1.   To promote the better choice of ministries and some **380** long-range planning, a commission should be set up as an aid to the provincial and under his authority.

2.   The task of this commission will be, after careful **381** study, to advise on an overall review of ministries. This will involve making suggestions as to which ought to be kept or dropped and which ought to be renewed or begun for the first time. We should always keep in mind social conditions and pastoral programs, the supply of apostolic forces that is at hand or hoped for, the more pressing needs, and the help which ought to be given Father General for more universal works.

3.   The provincial should appoint to such a commission **382** those Jesuits who have sufficient experience in the ministries of the Society, and also experts in those special disciplines (e.g., pastoral theology and the sociology of religion) that are of greater importance for a reconsideration of the matter. If it is necessary, experts from outside the Society, even lay persons, should be called in at the right moment.

4.   When the commission has in due time gathered its **383** information, it should place before the provincial the conclusions of its investigation and deliberate on them in a meeting together with the consultors of the province at least once a year.

5.   After everything has been considered in this fashion, **384** it will be the task of the provincial to decide on the reorganization and promotion of ministries and to determine whether or not, if conditions have perhaps changed, further studies by the commission are needed.

385 6. In order to achieve a more effective coordination of the apostolate in a given region, boards of provincials, where they already exist or where it might seem good to set them up, can be greatly helped by a similar inter-provincial commission linked with the provincial commissions. In regions that are sufficienty homogeneous, a single interprovincial commission can be instituted in place of commissions for the individual provinces.

23   THE JESUIT PRIESTLY APOSTOLATE

I.   INTRODUCTION

1.   From the Society's beginning and throughout its   **386**
history, Jesuit priests have always given themselves to the
ministry of God's word and Christ's sacraments and to
other works as well for the sake of churches and nations.
Today, too, as members of a single body they are at work
in many different fields.

But the manifold changes that mark the present age de-   **387**
mand that the Society reassess its works, adapting them to
present and, as far as possible, to future circumstances. For
relationships within the Church are being profoundly transformed: the laity is assuming its proper active role; the
union of priests with each other and with their bishops is
coming to the fore; all are being stirred to a sense of responsibility for the good of the Church as a whole. Relationships between the Church and the world, too, are being
transformed: for while the lawful autonomy of earthly
values is being more expressly recognized,[1] at the same
time the intimate connection between the Gospel and the
earthly progress and service of the human family is being
more vividly perceived.[2] Finally, the proportion of priests
to a growing population and its increased needs is being
lessened, so that a better distribution of priests is demanded.

Due to these changes, the place and role of the priest is   **388**
being variously envisioned by many today. Some think the
Jesuit priest should be engaged solely in directly pastoral
work; others desire that he should be more fully present in

---

1 See GS 36.
2 See GS 38.

the areas where man's secular efforts are being expended. Some hope that the early vigor of the Society will be recaptured if the priestly ministry is purified of all so-called accidental forms; others believe a more universal good will emerge if no limits are placed on the scope of priestly activity.

389   It is not for the General Congregation to settle theological differences on the priestly role and ministry. We intend, however, to recall some principles of the Catholic faith and of the Jesuit Institute and to draw from them several criteria which may help the Society and its members to determine, according to the talent given each by the Lord of the vineyard and according to their vocation in the Church, what works our priests ought to engage in principally, and what works ought rather to be left to others.

390   2.   Some principles pertinent to the matter under dispute and drawn from the teaching of Vatican II will help us resolve this problem.

391   All members of the People of God share in Christ's priesthood and in the one mission of the Church; but different degrees or states bring different functions, though these are ordered to and complement each other.[3]

392   Priests "by the power of the sacrament of orders, and in the image of Christ the eternal High Priest . . . are considered to preach the Gospel, shepherd the faithful, and celebrate divine worship . . . They exercise this sacred function of Christ most of all in the Eucharistic liturgy . . . For the penitent or ailing among the faithful, priests exercise fully the ministry of reconciliation and alleviation . . . Exercising within the limits of their authority the function of Christ as Shepherd and Head, they gather together God's family as a brotherhood all of one mind and lead them in the Spirit, through Christ, to God the Father."[4]

---

3 See LG 10, PO 2.
4 LG 28..

This priestly ministry, within the unity of the presbyteral 393
order, embraces various functions: evangelization of nonbelievers, catechesis, parochial or supraparochial ministry,
scientific research or teaching, participation in the life and
toil of workers, and many other activities that are apostolic
or ordered to the apostolate.[5]

It is indeed characteristic of laymen, passing their lives 394
as they do in the midst of the world and amid secular tasks,
that they be led by the spirit of the Gospel to "work for the
sanctification of the world from within, in the manner of
leaven. In this way they can make Christ known to others
especially by the testimony of a life resplendent in faith,
hope, and charity."[6] Yet such an apostolate is not theirs
alone;[7] priests, too, in their own way, share it, and must,
moreover, effectively help laymen in their apostolic task in
the Church and the world.[8]

Religious, finally, are called from both the clerical and 395
the lay state to be consecrated and entirely dedicated to
loving God above all, and by their special charism within
the Church's life to bear witness that "the world cannot be
transfigured and offered to God without the spirit of the
beatitudes,"[9] and thus each in his own way will forward the
saving mission of the Church.[10]

3.   The overall guiding norm for our own apostolate, as 396
is clear from our holy founder's special charism,[11] from the
Formula of the Institute[12] and the Constitutions,[13] and from
the Society's living tradition, is the greater service of God
and the more universal good of souls, to be striven for in
the greatest possible docility to God's will as manifested to

5 See PO 4, 8.
6 LG 31; AA 2, 5.
7 See LG 31, GS 43.
8 See AA 25.
9 LG 31.
10 See LG 43.
11 See *SpEx* 23, 98.
12 See *Formula of the Institute,* 1, 2.
13 *Cons* [603, 622].

us in the Church and the circumstances of each age, but especially through the Roman Pontiff.

397   The Society itself is made up of various members; "according to the grace imparted to them by the Holy Spirit and the specific quality of their vocation,"[14] some are priests, some not. Yet all with one mind strive for the single apostolic end set before the whole body of the Society.

398   As for priestly functions, both the Formula of the Institute and the Constitutions clearly state that the Society's priests are destined "above all . . . for every form of ministry of the word"[15] and for the administration of the sacraments.[16] Yet other works are not only not excluded but expressly commended to priests,[17] "as shall be judged best for God's glory and the common good."[18]

399   In defining more accurately the supreme norm of our apostolate, Ignatius says: "Those of the Society may devote their energies to spiritual objectives and also to corporal ones, in which, too, mercy and charity are practiced . . .; if both cannot be achieved simultaneously, then, other things being equal, the former are always to be preferred to the latter."[19] With the words "other things being equal," St. Ignatius instructs us that the principle of the pre-eminence of spiritual works is itself subordinate to his supreme and fundamental norm.

400   4.   If criteria for our activity are to be derived correctly from the principles given, the following distinctions must be kept in mind.

401   In dealing with the priesthood, careful distinction must be made between its essential nature as grounded in Christ's institution, and the concrete historical forms in which that

---

14 *Formula of the Institute,* 1.
15 Loc. cit.; see *GenExam* [30] ; *Cons* [308, 603, 645] and passim.
16 See *Formula of the Institute* 1; *Cons* [406-407, 642-643].
17 See *Formula of the Institute* 1; *Cons* [623, 650].
18 *Formula of the Institute* 1; *Cons* [591-593, 650, 793].
19 *Cons* [623].

nature is, as it were, variously incarnated in divergent cultures, social structures, and patterns of custom. The nature of Christian priesthood is a matter of dogma and thus unchangeable; concrete forms, on the other hand, are to be adapted to the specific contemporary situation, under the inspiration of the Holy Spirit, the guidance of the hierarchy, and according to the standards of prudence.[20]

All Jesuits, scholastics and brothers included (in schools, **402** for instance, and in other communal works), share together in the one total apostolate exercised by the Society as a priestly body. Each priest, however, is called by God through his ordination to exercise his priesthood in the concrete circumstances of his life.

To grasp this priestly vocation more fully, other distinc- **403** tions must be made. A priest of the Society is a man created by God and placed amid a certain people. He is a man baptized and confirmed and therefore, as a "brother among brothers,"[21] he shares in the priesthood common to all the faithful. Furthermore, he is a religious, and a religious of the Society: as a religious he has by vow consecrated himself to God in the Church to be "an admirable sign of the heavenly kingdom";[22] as a member of the Society, he lives his religious consecration in an apostolic body. He is, in addition, a priest, taken into the presbyteral order, which is in hierarchical communion with the episcopal order at whose head is Peter's successor.

Each priest must integrate all these aspects of his life into **404** a unified, personal, concrete spirituality; he must, with the interior help of the Holy Spirit and under the guidance of superiors, bring them to fulfillment in an organic and vital unity. In priestly activity and spirituality, then, we need to avoid all one-sided solutions and tendencies; for then some single aspect, be it humanistic, religious, or priestly, is

---

20 See PO 22.
21 See PO 9.
22 PC 1.

so stressed that the others fade into the background because of this stress.

405   The 31st General Congregation, with the foregoing exposition of principles in mind, establishes the following.

II. DECREE

406   5.   The manifold activity of priests in the Society flows from the nature and mission of the priesthood and from the distinctive grace and overall guiding norm of our Institute.

407   6.   Since priests by their ordination as assistants, of subordinate rank, to the episcopal order, are consecrated for the manifold ministry of the word, for the administration of the sacraments, and for the pastoral rule of the family of God, these forms of ministerial apostolate are deservedly to be held in special esteem.

408   7.   Since, however, Christ, Head of the Church, is integrating the whole world into a kingdom for the Father, it is for the priest, as sign and minister of the Lord's active presence, to be present in or to collaborate with all human efforts which help in establishing the kingdom.

409   8.   Since today such collaboration is urgently needed in preparing the way for the Gospel and in establishing or extending the Church's presence by scholarly research and teaching, especially in the sacred sciences, by social work and work in communications media, this type of collaboration ought to be regarded as a genuine apostolate for the Society's priests. Especially indeed ought we be concerned with areas critical for the human person as a whole, such as the sciences of man and the education of youth.

410   9.   Although the General Congregation intends to offer brothers greater opportunity for all such apostolic works and responsibilities as suit their state, and while, on the other hand, it also desires a greater collaboration with laymen in the apostolate, this does not at all imply—as is clear from what has already been said—that the Society's priests

are to be diverted from fields more proper to laymen or the brothers.

10. The choice of one or other apostolate is to be made **411** according to the criteria set down in the Decree on the Better Choice and Promotion of Ministries, where the Ignatian guiding norm is applied to the contemporary situation with a view to reaching the best possible balance in our ministries.

11. In assigning priests to various ministries, superiors **412** should look, as our founder did, not only to existing apostolic needs, but also to the call and particular gifts of those to be assigned. All, however, should cultivate the greatest possible docility to the divine will and thus be ready to meet the more pressing and universal needs of the Church, expressed to them through superiors.

12. Priests of the Society whose apostolate lies primarily **413** in areas of temporal concern, united with all other priests in one total priestly ministry for the sake of men,[23] should bring their priesthood to bear upon all their activity, especially through prayer, though the witness of their lives, and through the Holy Eucharist, which "contains the Church's entire spiritual wealth, that is, Christ Himself,"[24] and through which men and all created reality are brought to the Father.

---

23 See PO 8.
24 See PO 5.

414   1. From the "fountain of love" which is God the Father, mankind has been freely created and graciously called to form a community of sons in the Son; for by the mission of the Son, God "determined to intervene in human history in a way both new and definitive."[1]

415   The only-begotten Son has been sent by the Father to save what was lost, and through the Holy Spirit, to unite men who were redeemed by Him into one Mystical Body which is the Church.

416   As the Son was sent by the Father, He in turn sent the apostles[2] as heralds of saving charity, giving them this solemn command: "Go, therefore, and make disciples of all nations, baptizing them . . . and behold, I am with you all days, even unto the consummation of the world."[3]

417   Heeding the mandate of Christ, the Church "continues unceasingly to send heralds of the Gospel until such time as the infant churches are fully established and can themselves carry on the work of evangelizing."[4] Thus, "the specific purpose of this missionary activity is evangelization and the planting of the Church among those peoples and groups where she has not yet taken root."[5]

418   2. It was for this task of announcing the Gospel that God in His providence called, along with other heralds of the Gospel, our holy Father Ignatius and his companions. God set their hearts on fire with a zeal which made them

1 AG 2-3.
2 See John 20.21.
3 Matt. 28.19-20.
4 LG 17.
5 AG 6.

desire at first to go to Jerusalem to help nonbelievers.[6] And when this project proved impossible, this same zeal urged them to offer themselves without reservation to the Vicar of Christ so that he might show them what part of the Lord's vineyard stood most in need of their labors.[7]

And so the new-born Society, by this commitment to **419** Christ's Vicar, was established as an apostolic order for work "among believers and nonbelievers"[8] and was made an intimate sharer in the mission mandate of the entire Church.

As part of the pilgrim Church, therefore, the Society has **420** embraced as strongly as it can the Church's universal mission, and is so alive with this missionary spirit that it necessarily communicates to its members a zeal for souls great enough to make both the defense of the faith and its propagation one and the same vocation. The Formula of the Institute approved by Julius III described this quite aptly: "Whoever wishes to fight under the banner of the cross in our Society . . . should seriously consider himself part of the Society established chiefly for this, that it especially labor for the defense and propagation of the faith . . ."[9]

3. The 31st General Congregation keeps before its eyes **421** those serious words of the Second Vatican Council: "The present historical situation is leading humanity into a new stage. As the salt of the earth and the light of the world, the Church is summoned with special urgency to save and renew every creature."[10] It is also aware of the large segment of mankind that is not yet Christian. Accordingly, this Congregation establishes that the following means be earnestly employed in order that Jesuits may better respond to their own mission calling and to the desires of the Church.

---

6 *Chronicon Societatis Iesu, auctore Joanne Alphonso de Polanco* (in **MHSJ**), I, 26, 50.

7 *Cons* [618].

8 *Cons* [618]; and the *Formulas of the Institute* approved by Paul III (1540) and Julius III (1550).

9 Julius III, *Exposcit Debitum* (July 21, 1550).

10 AG 1.

422   4. Jesuits should be convinced that activity aimed at spreading the Church among those groups and peoples where it is not yet fully established is not a work reserved merely for some Jesuits who may have received a kind of second vocation. Rather, all Jesuits, with the same zeal and for the same basic reason, should strive to respond to this mission vocation with largeness of spirit. Every Jesuit, therefore, and not only those who so petition, may be sent to the missions by reason of his vocation to the Society. Those of the Society, moreover, who were born in mission lands ought to be clearly aware of their serious responsibility for planting the Church with deep roots in their own countries. But even these men should be prepared to undertake mission service among other peoples.[11]

423   Superiors, however, ought to select for the missions those who are men of solid virtue, who are clearly flexible, and who are capable not only of learning languags, but also of fitting into a new culture. Among those chosen there should be some who have the intellectual capacity to become outstanding in the intellectual apostolate, and in scientific, cultural and religious research.[12]

424   All Jesuits dedicated to missionary activity, according to the spirit of the Second Vatican Council, should try to walk "the same road which Christ walked: a road of poverty and obedience, of service and self-sacrifice to the death, from which death He came forth a victor by His resurrection. For thus did all the apostles walk in hope."[13]

425   5. In order that the Society may respond more fully both to the contemporary needs of the Church and to its own essential vocation, every effort should be made to increase the proportion of members in mission work. It is especially desirable that this increase in the missionary ac-

---

11 See AG 20.
12 See AG 34; ES III, 22.
13 AG 5; see *SpEx,* 95, 98, 167.

tivity of the Society develop out of the fostering of vocations in mission lands themselves. Superiors must be convinced, therefore, that this formation of members who come from the newly-established churches themselves is the most important contribution to mission work that the Society can make.

6. In order to achieve fully the genuine goal of mission **426** activity, Jesuits engaged in this work should be aware of the following:

a) It is according to the spirit of the Second Vatican Council that "the young churches, rooted in Christ and built upon the foundation of the apostles, take to themselves in a wonderful exchange all the riches of the nations which were given to Christ as an inheritance."[14] All Jesuits, therefore, who work among other peoples, should not only treat individual persons with charity, and the positive elements of their religions with reverence,[15] but in everything which does not run counter to Christian faith and sensibility, they should highly esteem the culture, customs and traditions of these peoples.[16]

b) The principal means for the work of planting the **427** Church, and the one recommended above all others, is the preaching of the Gospel. But where the direct preaching of the Gospel is for the time being impossible, Jesuits must strive in every other method they use "to bear witness to Christ by charity and by works of mercy."[17]

c) The work of education "by means of different kinds **428** of schools, which should be considered not only as an outstanding means for forming and developing Christian youth, but also as a service of supreme value to men, especially in the developing nations,"[18] should be ranked very high. Education can, in this way, become an excellent form of preaching whereby all the human values found in the

---

14 **AG** 22
15 See **NA** 2.
16 See **AG** 9, 11, 15-16, 18-22, 25-26; **GC** 30, **D.** 54.
17 **AG** 6.
18 **AG** 12; see **GE** 9.

culture of those people who are not yet Christian are embraced, raised up, and offered to God the Father through the Church.

429   For the same reason, students who leave their native land to study abroad and who are very often in need of spiritual assistance should receive brotherly care and attention. Young people of this kind—and others too, whether they be workers or members of other classes—should be helped to fit into the social and Catholic life of the people among whom they dwell. In areas, therefore, where foreigners such as these are found, it recommended that provincials be ready and willing to assign some Jesuits to this kind of work.[19]

430   d)   Although no type of ministry is foreign to the Society, nevertheless, those works should be chosen first which are more urgent or more universal. Among these, special mention ought to be made of cooperation in the formation of diocesan clergy, cooperation in the formation of religious men and women, the formation of the laity for the apostolate, the use of communications media, the social apostolate, ecumenical work, by which the reason for scandal arising from the division among Christians is removed, and dialogue with non-Christian religions.[20]

431   e)   "For building up of the body of Christ,"[21] cooperation with bishops is important, as is collaboration in a fraternal spirit with both diocesan and religious clergy, and participation in conferences of religious.[22]

432   7.   All Jesuits applied to the missions should be thoroughly prepared and sent as soon as possible, although the proper time will depend on the qualities of individuals and the conditions of the regions.

433   This preparation, for those who are assigned abroad or

---

19 See AG 38; ES III, 23.
20 See AG 15, 34.
21 Eph. 4.12.
22 See AG 33; ES III, 21.

for those who come from the young churches themselves, should include, according to the needs of each one, a sufficient knowledge of the language, history, culture and religion of the people. All of these are to be kept in mind throughout their entire formation, but especially during the time of philosophy and theology.

Moreover, all Jesuits the world over should be sufficiently **434** instructed in the theology of the missions and should try to nourish their zeal for souls by means of constant communication from the missions.

8.   The missionary character of the whole Society should **435** make itself evident in its works. For this reason:

1° a)   Provinces should consider the mission works that are entrusted to them as an integral part of the province, on the same level as the other works of the province. They should help these mission works with money and men, and with a greater enthusiasm where the needs are more pressing. This applies as well to those areas that have already been erected as independent vice-provinces and provinces.

b)   After assuming office, provincials should visit the **436** mission works that are under their care in order to acquaint themselves with their needs, and they are to be liberal in extending help to these missions.

c)   It is recommended that in provinces responsible for **437** mission works there be a father who is knowledgeable in mission affairs and has the missions as his particular responsibility. He will furnish needed advice to the provincial and to the consultors in planning the apostolic works of the province.

2°   Let Jesuits diligently promote the work of the missions among all the faithful, and foster missionary vocations. **438**

3°   It is very important that knowledge of the missions **439** be more and more widely circulated by mission periodicals or even other types of periodicals.

4°   Each Jesuit, according to his own ability, should help **440** to encourage and fulfill the aspirations of those lay people who wish to be of service to the developing nations. The

Society throughout the world has the opportunity to instill Christian inspiration into the social and economic endeavors undertaken by various other institutions for the good of those nations.

441 5° For better information, coordination, and cooperation among Jesuits and for the benefit of those engaged in mission service, the Mission Secretariat should be enlarged.

442 9. The 31st General Congregation desires that the Society for its part offer itself to the service of the Church in its worldwide mission, so that "the splendor of God which brightens the face of Jesus Christ may shine upon all men through the Holy Spirit."[23]

---

23 AG 42.

A return to the province of origin is considered some-   **443**
thing normal for the benefit both of the missions and of the
missionaries. With regard to its frequency, the general
norms to be established by Father General must be observed, their application according to the situation being
left to the provincials.

I. INTRODUCTION

444   1.   Together with all the faithful the Society of Jesus welcomes with filial devotion the Decree on Ecumenism *(Unitatis Redintegratio)*, the Decree on Eastern Catholic Churches *(Orientalium Ecclesiarum)*, and the Declaration on Religious Freedom *(Dignitatis Humanae)* as they come from the Second Vatican Council. The 31st General Congregation urges that through their prayer and study all members of the Society make the spirit and teaching of these decrees their own. They are to be mindful that the ecumenical frame of mind itself, as well as all ecumenical activity, is founded on the spirit of truth and sincerity, a spirit of progressive interior renewal and especially the spirit of love. They are to pursue with their holy desires and prayers that full unity which the Father Himself is preparing through the Holy Spirit for the Church of Christ, His Son. Let them be aware that they are now being gathered together with other Christians in a genuine form of communion, and together with them they are to realize that they are brothers as well of all who believe in God and adore Him.

445   2.   The 31st General Congregation, humbly acknowledging the sins against unity committed by members of the Society, whether in the past or in more recent times, joins with the Council itself in recalling the witness of John: "To say that we have never sinned is to call God a liar and to show that His word is not in us."[1] "Thus, in humble prayer, we beg pardon of God and of our separated brethren, just as we forgive those who trespass against us."[2]

---

1 1 John 1.10.
2 UR 7.

3.   Therefore the 31st General Congregation proposes to   **446**
offer certain practical directives to Jesuits. These should be
applied with due account being taken of each one's training, of local circumstances, and particularly of the directives of the hierarchy.

II.   THE ECUMENICAL EDUCATION OF JESUITS

4.   For a suitable training of Jesuits in the matter of   **447**
ecumenism the following recommendations are offered.
During the time of their studies, scholastics are to acquire
a solid knowledge of the history of the separated churches
and communities and of their spirituality. The course in
sacred theology provided for the theologians should be in
harmony with the ecumenical spirit. Where for various con-
siderations it seems opportune, special courses are to be
given in Eastern theology and in that of the Reformation.
In the lectures on pastoral theology attention is also to be
given to the sometimes very difficult problems which can
arise in certain regions from contacts with other religions.
Professors are to be sure that the facts of history and of doctrine also are interpreted with calm objectivity.[3] And finally, all are to avoid prejudices and offensive modes of
speech, and they are to eliminate entirely "words, judgments and actions which do not truly correspond with the
situation of our separated brethren, since they are neither
true nor fair, and thus make our relations with them more
strained."[4]

5.   An education in ecumenism is not a matter of the   **448**
intellect alone, but must be part of one's spiritual formation
as well, since a truly ecumenical spirit cannot be had without a change of heart.[5]

6.   All are to be mindful that personal contact with the   **449**
separated brethren is of the highest value in wiping out age-

---

3 See UR 10.
4 See UR 4.
5 See UR 7.

old prejudices, in coming to a better knowledge of their faith, their love of Christ, and their spiritual life, as well as the difficulties, even of conscience, which they experience in regard to the Catholic Church.

450　　For this reason, where it can be done fruitfully, professors or ministers of other confessions are, on appropriate occasions, to be invited to give lectures. They are to be received fraternally and Jesuits are to accept their invitations willingly in return.

451　　If, moreover, there is a seminary of another confession near our scholasticate, it can be helpful to provide for the scholastics some opportunity for contacts with their colleagues.

452　　7. Due consideration being had for their religious formation and the offices they hold, brothers are to be informed in the matter of ecumenism so that by prayer, suitable understanding, and such personal contacts as fall to them, they too may participate in this activity of the Society.

453　　8. Provision is to be made that some of our men are prepared as experts in ecumenical matters according to the requirements of different regions. They are to learn to grasp fully the doctrine and the spiritual life both of Catholics and of separated brethren. Thus they will be equipped to give accurate instruction to our scholastics; to be available with their counsel and collaboration for the works of the province, in the colleges, in the parishes, and the like; to take competent part in ecumenical meetings and, finally, by study and writing, to foster ecumenical theology and contribute to its advance.

III. THE PRACTICE OF ECUMENISM

454　　9. A dignified and reverent celebration of the liturgy, both of the Eucharist and of the other sacraments, often contributes more to the elimination of prejudice than learned argument. Moreover, where the local bishop permits it, Jesuits are to take part with our separated brethren in some public forms of common prayer, especially prayer for the grace of union. The octave of prayer for Church unity, which is customarily celebrated annually in many places, is warmly recommended to Jesuits.

10. The study and use of Sacred Scripture is to be en- 455 couraged. Of itself this is a great contribution to the unity of Catholics with other Christians.[6] The greater the influence of Sacred Scripture on our spirituality, liturgical worship, and theology, the closer will be the union of all believers in Christ. For then they will be drawing the water of salvation from a common spring.

11. The Society should stand ready to offer whole- 456 hearted assistance to others within the Church who are engaged in this same work of ecumenism and likewise to receive help from them. Such collaboration is itself a sign of the unity present in the Church and at the same time a source of inspiration for promoting it further.

12. Ecumenical contacts, whether indirect, through 457 books and periodicals, or direct and personal are to be fostered by Jesuits according to the special circumstances of a locality, a province, or a house.

a) Those who work in education are to imbue their 458 students with the ecumenical spirit by their teaching and example. They should make efforts to establish dialogue between their students and those of the separated brethren and to initiate cooperation with them on the institutional level.

In setting up our university programs of scientific re- 459 search in biblical exegesis, dogmatic theology, Church history, religious sociology, and the like, cooperation with separated brethren is to be sought wherever it seems especially profitable.

b) Those who engage in social work or dedicate them- 460

---

6 See UR 21.

selves to works of mercy, or who collaborate in international organizations for peace and unity among nations and for the conquest of world poverty, ought to keep before their minds what a lively sense of justice and sincere love of their neighbor our separated brethren have developed out of their faith in Christ. Cooperation should be sought with them and where it already exists it is to be even further promoted.

461   c)   Those who are occupied in the pastoral ministries through work in the parishes, in giving the Spiritual Exercises, etc., should seek to discuss parallel or mutual problems with their counterparts in other churches and communities, and to undertake cooperation with them, even where more difficult questions, such as mixed marriages or the like, are involved.

462   d)   Mindful of the scandal given non-Christian peoples by our divisions, those who labor in the missions should foster an ecumenical spirit and cooperation so that insofar as possible, through the common witness of all believers, the light of Christ may shine more brightly among non-Christians and the scandal of division may be lessened by the sincerity of our mutual esteem and charity. On the other hand, vigilant care must be taken that the faithful not be exposed to the danger of syncretism or indifferentism. However, particularly in the case of the cultivated, such danger is to be avoided by means of a solid education in doctrine and in a training directed to a deeper love of the Church rather than through a timorous isolation from other Christians.

463   13.   Lest they hinder rather than advance the progress of unity, Jesuits must remember that ecumenical work is no easy task and that it is not to be left to the indiscreet zeal of private individuals. "Nothing is so foreign to the spirit of ecumenism as a false conciliatory approach which harms the purity of Catholic doctrine and obscures its assured genuine meaning."[7]

---

7 See UR 11.

Therefore in ecumenical activity Jesuits are faithfully to 464
observe all the prescriptions and directives of the Holy See
and of those whose duty it is to direct the ecumenical movement.

IV. RECOMMENDATIONS TO FATHER GENERAL

14. Moreover, the 31st General Congregation makes 465
the following recommendations to Father General so that
in his prudence he may see to it:

1° that there be established a council on ecumenical affairs composed of experts from various nations, and at the
same time appoint one of the Assistants or expert advisors
as delegate for fostering the ecumenical movement;

2° that insofar as it can serve the purpose of the promo- 466
tion of the ecumenical movement, there be established,
either by Jesuits alone or in collaboration with others, institutes or houses of study for experts and students, and this
in centers renowned for ecumenical studies;

3° that liturgical texts pertaining to the Society, or 467
other official documents, such as the *Ratio Studiorum* and
the like, be revised according to the ecumenical spirit, and
in particular that all offensive expressions be eliminated.

I.   PASTORAL SERVICES

468   1. Under present circumstances in the Church, those pastoral works or services that have been begun for the greater service of God and the more effective welfare of souls in accordance with the spirit of our vocation are to be renewed and energetically promoted, provided that they still fulfill the end for which they were intended and are approved by the hierarchy. Those should be dropped that cannot be adapted. In arriving at this decision the judgment of the bishops and of lay directors should be taken into account. Jesuits should diligently look for new forms of pastoral services, according to the tradition and spirit of the Society, that answer contemporary needs. For the teaching of the Second Vatican Council on the pastoral apostolate does not imply uniformity, but rather proposes a harmonious plurality of all pastoral undertakings, according to the diversity of the Spirit's gifts.[1]

469   2. So that in this adaptation the spirit of our distinctive calling may flourish in its entirety:

1° Jesuits themselves especially are to be trained to give the Spiritual Exercises in the true and correct way, and others among the diocesan and religious priests are to be helped to do the same, so that the faithful may be led to an intimate knowledge of the Lord, to love and follow Him more.[2]

470   2° All should have a high esteem for, and be keenly

---

1 See PC 20

2 See *SpEx* 104; *Cons* [408-409].

mindful of, the mystery of the heart of Christ in the life of the Church. It should be so much a part of their own lives that they can promote the knowledge of it among others in their apostolic activity. In this way the results of different ministries may be daily increased, "for from the side of Christ asleep on the cross there has arisen the wonderful sacrament of the entire Church."[3]

They should also trust in the patronage of the Blessed **471** Virgin Mary in their assigned tasks and activities, and everywhere show more and more clearly the role of the mother of the Savior in the economy of salvation.[4] For in holy Church and in our tradition the Virgin Mary "holds a place which is the highest after Christ and yet very close to us."[5]

3° In all their apostolate, our men in pastoral work, in **472** accordance with the desires of the Second Vatican Council, should share with a generous and open mind in the spirit of liturgical, ecumenical and pastoral renewal as well as the introduction to the faith, and with all their strength propagate this spirit.

4° Our works should begin and be carried on under the **473** guidance of superiors, and not in an individualistic and scattered way. Cooperation should be stressed, both among Jesuits who are working amicably and most eagerly for the same apostolic goal, and with others, religious and diocesan priests and the laity. Jesuits should willingly take part in the pastoral planning proposed by the bishops and collaborate with it in a humble and sincere desire of serving the Church.[6]

5° In the selection and planning of ministries and pas- **474** toral services of Jesuits as well as in the determination of the places where such ministries are to be exercised, careful attention should be given to what is contained in the Decree

---

3 SC 5.
4 See LG 55.
5 See LG 54.
6 See LG 45; CD 33-35; PC 23, 25; GC 31, D. 48.

on the Better Choice and Promotion of Ministries. In order that Jesuits may be better integrated into pastoral work today, it is necessary that men working in this field be really suitable and competent, and thus they should be trained:

475   a) on the one hand, by the general training in the course of studies, provision for which has already been made in the Decree on the Training of Scholastics Especially in Studies;

476   b) on the other hand, by special training, so that the Jesuits who are to be assigned to these ministries have a sufficient skill in some pastoral work (e.g., in preaching the word of God, in giving the Exercises, in catechetics, in spiritual guidance, in ecumenical activity, in spiritual theology, in family counseling and dealing with working men, and the like);

477   c) and also by institutes that are to be conducted at regular intervals in their regions, so that the priests who are already working in the ministries may be continually kept up to date in regard to new aids.

II. RESIDENCES

478   3.   In this decree, "residences" are understood to be communities destined for pastoral work,[7] or for any other apostolic work other than the education of youth, which according to the Constitutions belongs to another class of houses.[8]

479   4.   Though these residences are generically of one kind, they can have different names, structures, and ministries, according to the needs of men, times, and circumstances.[9] In them, not only the ministries that are strictly priestly works are carried on, but also all those that, according to our situation[10] and according to the needs of the Church of Christ in the modern world, ought to be accepted, as is set forth in the Pastoral Constitution *Gaudium et Spes.*

---

7 See *Epit* 29 § 1, 5°.
8 See *Cons* [289].
9 See *Epit* 29 § 1, 2°, 5°-7°.
10 See LG 31; *Cons* [591].

5.   Residences should be "living communities," in which   **480**
the members feel that they are working for the same goal,
and, moved by a common spirit, share with each other their
worries and successes. So that this can be done more easily,
these communities should not be too large, and should be
set up, as far as possible, according to natural grouping by
works.

The community should be gathered together at regular   **481**
intervals under the direction of the superior or of some expert designated by him, to review their work, to investigate
in common both their methods and their results, and to
study contemporary problems.

The tools needed for their labors should be found in the   **482**
house, such as books, specialized periodicals, and the like.

Young men engaged in this work should be introduced   **483**
to their pastoral ministries by experienced priests in a brotherly way.

6.   The whole house should be so set up that the mem-   **484**
bers can pray, work, and rest according to the demands of
their apostolate.[11] Under the direction of the superior, the
house discipline should be adapted with the needed flexibility, in accordance with the Decree on Community Life
and Religious Discipline.

7.   According to our Constitutions[12] and also according   **485**
to the new dispositions of the Council,[13] a house destined
for the apostolate ought to be outstanding as a "collective"
and "more effective" witness to poverty.

The members who live in the residences can live off the   **486**
income from their work, in accordance with the Decree on
Poverty of the 31st General Congregation, but "they should
avoid every appearance of luxury, of excessive wealth and

---

11 See PC 15; ES II, 26.
12 See *Cons* [555-60].
13 See PC 13; ES II, 23.

accumulation of possessions;"[14] they should cherish the free rendering of ministries,[15] and place their confidence in God alone.[16] They should look for new forms of poverty with diligence and in a concrete way, each according to his fashion, and insist[17] that there be, e.g., a more extensive practice of hospitality, a fraternal sharing of possessions,[18] support of the poor, and so on.

487   8.   In accordance with the spirit of the Society, and especially in accordance with the repeated wish of the Church, the General Congregation urgently requests the provincials to establish and promote residences among working men and among the more neglected groups. There, Jesuits in a special way should carry on their apostolate, in various manners, while living their life with the poor Christ.[19]

III.   PARISHES

488   9.   Decree 233 in the *Collection of Decrees* is abrogated.

489   10.   A new decree should be entered in a suitable place to this effect:

1° Our Society freely embraces the wish of the Church expressed by the Second Vatican Council, that the religious who are called on by bishops in accordance with their needs "should lend helpful efforts in various pastoral ministries," no exception being made of parishes.[20]

490   2° The care of souls in a parish, in general, is no longer to be said to be contrary to the principles of the Constitutions, now that the discipline of the Church in regard to parishes committed to religious has been changed. But be-

---

14 PC 13; see *GenExam* [81]; GC 31, D. 18, n. 7.
15 See *GenExam* [4]; *Cons* [565].
16 See *Cons* [555].
17 See PC 13; ES II, 23.
18 See PC 13.
19 See GC 28, D. 29, n. 8; GC 29, D. 29, n. 5.
20 CD 35 § 1.

cause of the seriousness of the matter, it belongs to Father
General to judge, all things considered, whether a particular parish is to be accepted or given back. The texts of
agreements with local ordinaries about parishes are to be
approved by Father General.

IV.   RECOMMENDATIONS TO SUPERIORS

11.   Superiors, with the approval of Father General,   **491**
should insist:

1° that the apostolic services of the province and the
region be reviewed by the commission on the review of ministries,[21] so that Jesuits may serve the hierarchy of the
Church with greater freedom;

2° that the directors of works sincerely adapt themselves   **492**
to contemporary pastoral practice, for example, in giving
the Exercises, in popular missions, in the cooperation of
Jesuits with a program of renewal of the sodalities or the
Apostleship of Prayer in those regions where the bishops
and major superiors, having first listened to the lay directors, decide in fraternal harmony to renew them so that
they may be more effectively promoted;

3° that Jesuits have a high esteem for the teaching of   **493**
Christian doctrine to children and the uneducated, either
by themselves or by others, as occasion may offer, in accordance with the tradition of the Society and the vows they
have taken; for the promotion of new forms of modern
catechetics and introduction to the faith by suitable means;
for the giving of spiritual aid in hospitals and prisons;

4° that there be set up institutes for the training of di-   **494**
rectors of the Exercises as soon as possible, because of their
importance and their necessity for the renewal of our ministries; in these institutes there should be research into the
"genuine meaning of the Ignatian text;" indeed, there
should be a real "reworking" "of the Spiritual Exercises

---

21 See GC 31, D. 22.

themselves to unfold their spiritual riches to modern man, and to express them in the concepts of the theology of the Second Vatican Council."[22]

---

22 See Paul VI, Address of December 29, 1965; Letter to Cardinal Cushing, August 25, 1966 (both documents appear in the *Annuarium S. I. 1966-67*).

28 THE APOSTOLATE OF EDUCATION

I. INTRODUCTION

1. Throughout the world today, whether in the advanced or in the evolving nations, there is clear recognition of the importance of education for the formation of society and particularly for the initiating of youth into life in the human community. Nothing is more esteemed by political leaders than this education of the citizenry, for without it no nation or state can develop or progress and meet the national and international responsibilities imposed by the needs of this age.

495

2. The Church has, therefore, reflected upon "the paramount importance of education in the life of man, and its ever-mounting influence on the social progress of this era"[1] and once again affirmed its own role in the development and extension of education. To fulfill this function the Church wishes to employ all appropriate means. Yet it recognizes that schools are educational agencies of "special importance,"[2] for in these institutions Christian teachers are to promote the renewal of the Church and maintain and intensify her beneficent and salutary presence in the contemporary and, particularly, the intellectual world.[3]

496

3. In our day we are witnessing everywhere the rapid emergence of new social forms and the society of the future. When new ideas are so widely sown, it is not hard to discern the birth of new patterns of thought and action in the modern world. The promoters of these new ideas, especially when they work out of centers of higher culture and re-

497

---

1 GE introduction.
2 GE 5.
3 GE conclusion.

search, are exercising a mounting influence upon the whole of social culture through highly effective modern means of popularization. But since this influence inclines ever more toward an atheistic and agnostic ideology and makes itself felt particularly in educational centers, the presence of Christians in those centers is of the highest moment if the Church is indeed to make an opportune contribution to the society of the future by forming and educating its mind to reverence for God and in the fullness of Christ.

498   4.   For many centuries the Society of Jesus, in accordance with its Institute, has diligently exercised its teaching function almost uninterruptedly throughout the world. Now, impelled and inspired by the Second Vatican Council, the Society, through its 31st General Congregation, wishes to confirm the high regard it has for this apostolate of education and earnestly to exhort its members that they maintain unflaggingly their esteem for this significant apostolate.

499   There are some members of the Society, however, who think that our educational institutions in certain parts of the world have become practically useless and should therefore be given up. There are others who recognize the continued effectiveness of these institutions but believe that there are other ministries in which we could perhaps be even more effective. Hence they conclude that it is necessary, or at least appropriate, to leave the work of formal education to laymen or to religious whose institutes dedicate them exclusively to this apostolate. This Congregation judges that there is no uniform solution for this very real and pressing problem. The solution it requires will necessarily vary according to differences of circumstances. Therefore, it must be determined by superiors, with the aid of their brethren and according to the norms for the choice of ministries as applied to the needs of each province or region.

500   The intention of this present decree, however, is, in the first place, that the Society may think with the Church con-

cerning the paramount importance and effectiveness of the educational apostolate, particularly in our times. Secondly, it is intended that our schools be outstanding not so much for number and size as for teaching, for the quality of the instruction, and the service rendered to the people of God. Thirdly, we should be receptive toward new forms of this apostolate, particularly adapted to the present age, and we should energetically investigate or fashion these new forms either in our own schools or elsewhere. Finally, for those laymen who generously spend themselves with us in this apostolate, the way should be opened to a wider collaboration with us, whether this be in teaching, administration, or on the board of directors itself.

5. It is evident that we can exercise the apostolate of **501** education in various ways either in our own institutions or **502** by collaborating with others. There is an extensive variety today, whether one is speaking of colleges and universities, or vocational schools, or the so-called normal schools for the training of teachers. Which forms of the apostolate of education the Society should take up is a matter for superiors to decide according to the norms for the selection of ministries. But in making this selection, we should consider the new means of social communication, particularly radio and television. For these are highly effective instruments for new kinds of educational organization and pedagogy since they extend to the widest possible audience and reach those who would otherwise be deprived of schooling. Besides, they are very much in line with the present day "culture of the image."

The Society should have its own educational institutions **503** where resources and circumstances permit and a greater service of God and the Church can be thereby expected. For these schools constitute at least one effective instrument for the promotion of our educational purpose, i.e., the synthesizing of faith and culture. Through these schools a firmer and more lasting social presence in the community is achieved, both because they are a corporate effort and because through the students families are influenced. Thus the school becomes an apostolic center within the community.

504   If, indeed, there is question of closing schools or of handing them over to others, superiors are to work out the best way of doing this in consultation with the local Ordinary and with the approbation of Father General.

II.   DECREE

505   6.   Let Jesuits have a high regard for the apostolate of education as one of the primary ministries of the Society, commended in a special way by the Church in our time. For the transmission of human culture and its integration in Christ significantly contribute to realization of the goal set by our Lord "that God may be all in all things."[4]

506   7.   This apostolate aims to provide a service of love for mankind redeemed by Christ. On the one hand, it aims so to educate believers as to make them not only cultured but, in both private and public lives, men who are authentically Christian and able and willing to work for the modern apostolate.

On the other hand, it aims to provide non-Christians with a humanistic formation directed towards the welfare of their own nation and, at the same time, to conduct them by degrees to the knowledge and love of God or at least to the acceptance of moral, and even religious values.[5]

507   8.   Let the provincials see to it that the apostolate of education, along with other ministries, be really and continually adapted to the circumstances of men, time, and place, making use in this of the advice both of experts and of the committee on the choice of ministries. Let the pro-

---

4 I Cor 15.28; see GE introduction; *CollDecr* 131; GC 28, D. 31, n. 1.
5 *CollDecr* 136; GC 28, D. 31, n. 1.

vincials also see to it that really competent men are prepared in education.

9. In collaboration with the bishops, other religious, **508**
and their fellow citizens, let Jesuits be alert to correlate the Society's activity with the complex of pastoral and educational work in the whole region or nation. Since, moreover, dialogue in this pluralistic world is both possible and desirable, let them also willingly cooperate with other organizations, even if these do not depend either on the Church or the Society. Let Jesuits therefore keep in mind the special importance of collaborating with those international organizations which promote education, especially in the less developed countries.

10. a) Let students be selected, as far as possible, of **509**
whom we can expect a greater progress and a greater influence on society, no matter to what social class they belong.

b) In order that this criterion of selection may be **510**
equitably applied, Jesuits should firmly advance the claims of distributive justice, so that public aid will provide parents with the real liberty of choosing schools for their children according to their conscience.[6]

c) However, until such rights have been vindicated, **511**
the Society, in accordance with its Constitutions[7] and traditional practice, must make it easy for talented young people, particularly in the emerging nations, to attend our schools. Therefore, let all Jesuits try to obtain public or private endowments, with the help of our alumni, or of those who are bound to the Society through special friendship or apostolic zeal.[8]

11. Our educational institutions should be established **512**
only when and where they show promise of contributing significantly to the welfare of the Church, and can be fur-

6 See GE 6.
7 See *Cons* [478].
8 See GC 28, D. 31, n. 3.

nished besides with an adequate supply of competent Jesuits without harm to the training or studies of our own members.[9] Let superiors inquire whether it is more suitable to open or to retain schools of our own or whether it would be better in some circumstances to teach in public schools, or in schools directed by others.

513 12. a) The first care of Jesuits should be that Christian students acquire that knowledge and character which are worthy of Christians, along with the letters and sciences. To this end, it will help very much if, in addition to the suitable amount of time given to the teaching of Christian doctrine and religion according to modern methods, Jesuits also offer to the students a good example of hard work and dedication as well as of religious life.[10]

514 b) We should try in a special way to imbue our students with the true charity of Christ, according to the social doctrine of the Church. Let them learn to honor and be grateful to laboring men; let them learn to hunger and thirst for that justice which aims to provide all men with an adequate recompense for new work, that the distribution of wealth be more equitable, that the sharing of spiritual goods be fuller and more universal.[11]

515 c) Let youth be progressively formed to liturgical and personal prayer. As they come to be more mature, exercises of piety should be proposed to them rather than imposed.

516 d) Selected spiritual and apostolic activities which will really be an efficacious means of character formation, for example the sodalities, should be properly established and directed and esteemed by us all. For they serve to introduce and educate our students in apostolic activities step by step.

517 e) Special importance should be attributed to the spiritual direction of students. For this is an effective way of nourishing a person's sense of responsibility both for the

---

9 See *CollDecr* 133.

10 See *CollDecr* 136 § 1.

11 John XXIII, Mater et Magistra *AAS* 53 (1961) 401-464; GS 29; Fr. Janssens, *ActRSJ* 11 (1949) 720-721.

ordering of his spiritual life and for the choosing of an adult vocation in accordance with the divine will. In addition, every effort should be made for a fresh increase of priestly and religious vocations so as to help the Church in its present needs.

f) Regarding non-Christian students, care must be **518** taken throughout the whole course of studies and especially in ethics courses that men be formed who are endowed with a sound moral judgment and solid virtues. Therefore in their training, the first rank of importance must be given to the formation of a true and right moral conscience, and at the same time of a firm will to act according to it. For in this way they will be best prepared to have a saving effect on family life and society, and in addition to serve their country and to obtain the reward of eternal life.

13. a) Let Jesuits remember that the task of teaching **519** is not restricted to some hours nor only to some persons.[12] Let all give a witness of religious and apostolic life; let all be convinced that the common task is more important than individual success; and let them try continually to renew themselves in spirit and understanding. To this end, superiors should favor research, experiments, the discovery of new methods of teaching, and see to it that the members have libraries, audio-visual aids, conferences by experts, possibilities of attending meetings, and other helps.

b) Scholastics and younger brothers who are sent to the **520** colleges should be watched over with special care by superiors and spiritual fathers.[13] They should remember that regency is established for their own growth, and so that their virtue may develop, their character be trained, their gifts manifested, and they themselves may make progress in studies. But the real assistance they provide for the work of education should also be considered, and so they should share in the common responsibility for and the discussion of plans concerning the school, according to its statutes.

---

12 See *CollDecr* 142.

13 See *CollDecr* 145.

521   14.   For its part, the Society should help those many children of the Church who are being educated in non-Catholic schools. Superiors should be mindful of the Church's solicitude in this matter. In their concern for the spiritual formation of all youth, superiors should attentively and willingly listen to bishops who ask for the collaboration of the Society in this ministry, especially in directing Catholic centers for students, in the office of chaplains, and also in teaching in non-Catholic schools.[14]

522   15.   a)   Young people who travel abroad for their education, as often happens nowadays, should be attentively helped. This is especially important in the case of those, whether Catholic or not, who are outstanding and can be expected to become leaders when they return to their own country.[15]

523   b)   We should maintain a relationship with our former students, the products of our whole educational effort, so that they may take their place in society in a Christian and apostolic way and help one another in their respective tasks. The bond which they have with the Society ought to become closer as time goes on so that their influence assists its work.[16]

524   16.   Elementary schools may be founded and directed where it is necessary. For they are very important and not contrary to our Institute. Nonetheless they should not be accepted without a real and great need, lest on account of the lack of men a greater good would be hindered. Where they are accepted, so far as possible our priests should have only the teaching of religion.[17]

525   17.   It is during the period of secondary education that many young people (twelve to eighteen years old) either synthesize religion and culture in themselves or fail to do

---

14 See GE 7, 10.

15 See *CollDecr* 418.

16 See *CollDecr* 144.

17 See *CollDecr* 132.

so and are strongly oriented towards good or away from it. Hence, having weighed the objections often made nowadays against secondary schools by those who would rather restrict themselves to pastoral ministries, the Society again asserts that the teaching of youth according to the principles of our Institute, even in the so-called profane disciplines, is entirely conformed to our vocation and to our sacerdotal character. Indeed, it is the ministry to which the Society up to the present owes most of its growth.[18]

18.   Secondary schools, be they old ones retained or new **526** ones founded, should improve continually. They should be educationally effective as well as centers of culture and faith for lay cooperators and the families of students and alumni. Thereby they will help the whole community of the region. Let Jesuits also foster a closer cooperation with the parents of students, upon whom the primary responsibility of education rests.[19]

19.   a)   Each province should have its own *ordina-* **527** *tiones* for secondary schools, in harmony with its own needs.[20]

b)   As far as subject matter is concerned, the education **528** of our students should be in conformity with the genuine cultural tradition of each nation or region, in so-called classical literature, or modern literature, or in science.

c)   Moreover, other schools, such as technical and agri- **529** cultural schools may well be opened where need or great utility suggest it.[21]

20.   a)   Subjects should be so taught that the mind of **530** the young is not overwhelmed with a multiplicity of details, and that all their powers may be suitably developed and they may be prepared for higher studies. In addition, our students should be helped so that they can make progress

---

18 See *CollDecr* 131.
19 See GE 3.
20 See *CollDecr* 139.
21 See *CollDecr* 140 § 1.

by themselves, and so that there may grow in them firmness of mind, uprightness of judgment and sensibility, aesthetic sense, a capacity to express themselves orally and in writing, a sense of community and of civil and social duty, and depth of understanding.[22]

531   b)   Regarding the method of teaching, let there be kept in all fields, as far as is possible, the proper method of the Society which is commended in the *Ratio Studiorum*. Therefore let all be familiar with those principles of sound pedagogy which are set down by our holy father in the Constitutions, Part IV, developed in the *Ratio Studiorum,* and clearly explained by many writers of the Society.[23]

532   21.   After they have consulted Father General, provincials should decide in light of the circumstances of persons and place, whether daily Mass should be obligatory in our residential secondary schools.[24]

533   22.   So-called apostolic schools can be kept and, established where, all things considered, they seem to be for the greater glory of God.[25] What is said primarily concerning secondary schools is to be applied also to them.

534   23.   Coeducation in secondary schools is not to be allowed except with the approval of Father General.[26]

535   24.   a)   On account of the ever-growing importance of universities and institutions of higher learning for the formation of the whole human community, we must see to it that the Society and its priests are present to this work. Let there be, therefore, an ever greater number of professors prepared for such institutions, whether directed by the Society or by others. These profesors should be able not only to teach advanced courses, but also to contribute to scholarly

---

22 See *CollDecr* 140 § 2.
23 See *CollDecr* 140 § 3.
24 See GC 30, D. hist. 17, n. 3.
25 See *CollDecr* 135.
26 See GC 30, D. hist. 17, n. 1.

progress by their own research and that of their talented students whom they have trained.[27]

b) Among the faculties belonging to our institutions of higher education, theology and philosophy should especially have their proper place to whatever extent they contribute, in various places, to the greater service of God.[28] **536**

c) The prohibition in the Constitutions, according to which that part of canon law which serves for contesting suits is not to be touched by Jesuits, is to be thus understood: "unless the General judges that something else is good."[29] **537**

25. The education of priests, as a work of the highest value, is to be considered one of the chief ministries of the Society. Therefore, the seminarians who attend our universities are to be watched over with special attention, and directors and teachers chosen from among our best men are to be assigned to those clerical seminaries whose direction is accepted by the Society.[30] But if there is question of diocesan seminaries, a definite contract shall be made with the bishop and approved by the Holy See.[31] **538**

26. Not only youth but adults are to be educated, both for the advancement of their professional lives and for the efforts which make their conjugal, family, and social life more human and Christian, and develop a better understanding of the faith.[32] **539**

27. a) According to the mind of the Second Vatican Council, a close collaboration with the laity is recommended. On the one hand we can give them help in their formation by schools, conferences, spiritual exercises and other suitable works, and by our friendly dealing with them and the testimony of our life. On the other hand, let Jesuits **540**

---

27 See GC 30, D. 51, § 1.
28 See *CollDecr* 137 § 1.
29 See *CollDecr* 137 § 2.
30 See OT 5; *CollDecr* 134
31 See ES I, 30 § 1; *CollDecr* 134.
32 See GE introduction, 9.

consider the importance for the Society itself of such collaboration with lay people, who will always be the natural interpreters for us of the modern world, and so will always give us effective help in this apostolate. Therefore, we should consider handing over to them the roles they are prepared to assume in the work of education, whether these be in teaching, in academic and business administration, or even on the board of directors.[33]

541   b)   It will also be advantageous to consider whether it would not be helpful to establish in some of our institutions of higher education a board of trustees which is composed partly of Jesuits and partly of lay people; the responsibility both of ownership and of direction would pertain to this board.

542   28.   Men of our time are very interested in new and more adequate intercommunication, by which international union and progress are fostered. Therefore Jesuits should be concerned to promote among their students and alumni and other members of the social community those efforts and means which can lead to a greater and more efficacious collaboration among nations.

543   29.   Prefects or directors of education should be named who will help the provincials in directing the whole effort of education; they can be so united that the whole Society can enjoy the benefits of the studies and the experiments which are being carried on in various regions of the world.

544   30.   In each province or region there should be a permanent committee of experts who will help superiors in this apostolate, drawing up and continually adapting regulations concerning our schools, in harmony with each one's needs.[34]

545   31.   To help Father General in fostering the whole work of education, a secretariat of education should be estab-

---

33 See GC 31, D. 33.
34 See *CollDecr* 139; GC 28, D. 31, n. 2.

lished. Its task will be to collect and distribute information about the apostolate of education carried on by Jesuits and also to promote alumni associations and periodic conventions.

32.   Decree 141 of the *Collection of Decrees* is abrogated.   **546**

29   SCHOLARLY WORK AND RESEARCH

547   1. a)   Jesuits should have a high regard for scholarly activity, especially scientific research properly so called, and they are to view this as one of the most necessary works of the Society. It is a very effective apostolate, entirely in accord with the age-old tradition of the Society from its earliest times.[1] It is a generous response to recommendations that the popes have often repeated, especially during the past hundred years.[2] It is more suited to the needs of the men of our times and an excellent means for opening up and carrying on dialogue with them, including nonbelievers, for establishing confidence in the Church, and for elaborating and teaching a synthesis of faith and life.

548   b)   All of this applies first of all to the sacred sciences and those connected with them, which have the first claim on the scholarly potential of the Society. It applies also to those sciences which are called positive, both those which look to man and society and the mathematical-natural sci-

---

1 *Discourse of Father Christopher Clavius* ("De modo et via qua Societas Iesu ad maiorem Dei honorem, et animarum profectum augere hominum de se opinionem, omnemque haereticorum in litteris aestimationem, qua illi multum nituntur, convellere brevissime et facillime possit"), (Archivum Romanum Societatis Iesu, Hist. Soc. 5c, fol. 185-87); *Ordination on Training Mathematics Teachers,* by Father Robert Bellarmine, promulgated in 1593 by the authority of Father Claudius Aquaviva, (Archivum Romanum Societatis Iesu, *Epp. NN.* 113, fol 184); V. Carrafa, Ad Praep. Prov. Austriae, Aug 17, 1647 (Archivum Romanum Societatis Iesu, *Austr.* 5, fol. 1116).

2 See Leo XII, *Quod divina Sapientia,* Aug. 28, 1824; Bull. Rom. Cont., VIII (Prati, 1854), 95-117; Leo XIII, *Ut mysticam Sponsam,* Mar. 14, 1891; Leonis XIII P.M. Acta, XI, 60-66; Pius XI, Address, *Ecco dilettissimi,* Mar. 12, 1934; *ActRSJ* 7 (1934), 643-648; Pius XII, Address, *Siamo particolarmente,* Sept. 29, 1935; *ActRSJ* 8 (1935), 84-86.

ences, as well as the technical sciences proceeding from them, which profoundly affect the mentality of our times.

2.   Those Jesuits, therefore, who are assigned to this **549** work by superiors are to give themselves entirely and with a strong and self-denying spirit to this work, which, in one way or another, makes demands upon the whole man. They are to be on guard against the illusion that they will serve God better in other occupations which can seem more pastoral, and they are to offer their whole life as a holocaust to God. At the same time they should do this in such a way that they do not lose touch with the other apostolic activities of the Society. Finally they are to strive earnestly to show themselves truly religious and priestly men in this scholarly work. They should remember that in undertaking this work, they are enlisted in the cause of Christian truth and are serving the people of God either by showing forth the presence of the Church among the men of the scientific community or by enriching the understanding of revelation itself through the progress of human knowledge.

3.   Provincials, for their part, must not be deterred by **550** the demands of other works of the province from applying to this scholarly work, definitively and in good time, men whom they find inclined and in the judgment of experts truly suited, yet well proven in the spiritual life. Once assigned to this work, they are not to be taken away from it without grave reason, especially when they have finished their studies, even post-doctoral work, and have begun to produce. Since many of the positive sciences often require youthfulness for their study if one is to become really outstanding in them, provincials are not to hesitate to propose to Father General suitable changes in the ordinary course of study for the young Jesuits engaged in them as need may dictate, according to the Decree on the Training of Scholastics Especially in Studies. Priests who are applied to these studies are to be mindful that, the more advanced they are in any discipline, the more careful they should be that their knowledge of theology is broad and sound, in order that

they may be able to exercise their scholarly apostolate with greater authority and profit.

551   4.   Superiors, especially higher superiors, are to take care that those applied to work in the scholarly disciplines give themselves primarily to the work of research, study, and writing, and that the necessary leisure and helps are provided for this work. They are to acknowledge that scholars have "a lawful freedom of inquiry and thought and the freedom to express their minds humbly and courageously about those matters in which they enjoy competence."[3] Superiors are to permit them to join national and international professional organizations and to attend their meetings when it seems expedient. Finally they are to encourage Jesuits to work not only in our own centers but also in public universities and scholarly institutions according to the various opportunities and necessities of the region. In this way they will cooperate more closely with laymen in penetrating the whole human culture with the Christian spirit and better ordering the world to God, its ultimate end.

552   5.   Small periodic meetings of Jesuits who are expert in the different scholarly disciplines, especially those closely related, are recommended to provincials. These should promote interdisciplinary communication from time to time and, after careful study of the condition of the scientific apostolate in each region, procure among themselves greater collaboration of all who are working in the sciences. They should also help superiors with their advice in planning, coordinating, preparing, promoting, and also abandoning scholarly works, in such a way that the effort expended in this apostolate may be directed more efficiently to its end.

------

3 GS 62.

30   CULTIVATING THE ARTS
IN THE SOCIETY

I.   INTRODUCTION

1. The Church, which has at all times given most **553**
generous encouragement to the arts, today again hails their
importance.[1] Indeed, in our day especially works of art can
exert a vast influence, whether it be with respect to the
growth and unfolding of human personality, or to the development of civil society, or to the mutual union of men,
a union that paves the way to union with God.

For the arts provide a special pathway to the human **554**
heart. As a result, men are often stirred not only by rational
arguments but also by artistic works.

2. In times past under the patronage of the Society **555**
many outstanding artists, not a few of them members of
the Society itself, have achieved greatness in poetry, music,
the theater, and architecture. In both the Western world
and mission areas, all these arts were eagerly pursued by
sons of the Society for the greater glory of God and the
welfare of souls. This tradition lives on even in the Society
of today. Many modern Jesuits who are themselves artists
of repute not only pursue the arts but promote an understanding and deeper appreciation of the Gospel message by
this activity.

II.   DECREE

3. The 31st General Congregation, taking into con- **556**
sideration both the tradition of the Society and the signs of

---

1 See GS 62.

the times, and aware of the importance of the arts for building up the kingdom of God, wishes to encourage the activity of its members who toil in this field for the greater glory of God.

557   4.   During their training Jesuits should be given opportunities to become acquainted with and to appreciate the arts as part of their general education so that all may be better prepared for the apostolate in today's world. The arts can be a genuine help in this apostolate.

558   5.   Measures should be taken to permit those who manifest outstanding talents in this field to develop them and to learn how they can integrate their artistic activity into the context of priestly and religious life. In the missions Jesuits should endeavor to make full use of these arts in the apostolic work of spreading Christ's message.

559   6.   In addition, mutual communication is recommended among members of the Society who are engaged in artistic activity.

31 INTERPROVINCIAL HOUSES IN ROME

1. The 31st General Congregation, in view of the spe- **560**
cial importance for the service of the Church of the
Pontifical Gregorian University and of its associated Biblical and Oriental Institutes as well, joins with previous
Congregations[1] in recommending that the whole Society
furnish effective help to these common works through
subsidies and especially by training professors for them.

2. The 31st General Congregation also recommends to **561**
all provincials those other works or houses in Rome that
either are entrusted to the whole Society, such as the Vatican Radio, the Vatican Observatory, and the Russian College, or render a service to the entire Society, such as the
Historical Institute or the College of St. Robert Bellarmine.

3. All provinces ought to share, according to their re- **562**
sources, in the responsibility for those works which become
a concern and charge of the whole Society through the person of Father General. Provincials should keep this obligation in mind and, at fixed times, should give thought to
assigning one or other of their men to these works.

4. Recommendations to Father General: **563**
a) The 31st General Congregation recommends to
Father General that he provide for the drawing up of a list,
to be sent out to the provincials, of professors and other
personnel for whom a need may be foreseen over the next
three, five or ten years in these houses in Rome.

b) It is recommended to Father General that he set up **564**
a permanent administrative council to assist him, particularly with regard to needed funds and personnel, in ad-

---

1 See GC 29, D. hist. 17, n. 2; D. 32; GC 30, D. 18, n. 1.

ministering these works placed under his care by the Holy See. This council should include, in addition to the directors of these works, some provincials from different regions.

565   c)   It is also recommended to Father General that he set up a council for academic planning, one that will be concerned with reviewing broad academic policies in the light of the needs of the times and that will in this way aid him in directing these works entrusted to him by the Holy See, namely, the Pontifical Gregorian University and its associated Institutes. This council should be made up of members of the University itself and of the Institutes as well as of other Jesuit or non-Jesuit experts. The function of this council will be to advise Father General on academic policy and planning for these works, within the framework of the statutes of the Gregorian University and the Institutes.

566   d)   The General Congregation further recommends to Father General that the statutes of the academic institutions of the Society in Rome be revised with the help of the faculty. At the same time a study ought to be made as to whether the faculty should have a consultative role, and even a deliberative vote in decisions on some matters, so as to play a greater part in the academic government.

567   5.   Those other houses in Rome that depend directly on Father General but are under the charge of only some provinces, such as the national or regional colleges and the *Civilta Cattolica,* are likewise recommended to the attention of the General and those provincials who have a concern in the matter.

568   6.   Proper care should be shown for the language training and the psychological and spiritual adjustment of those brothers who come to Rome from provinces elsewhere. Moreover, if they are to return again to their own provinces, after having rendered excellent service at Rome, superiors ought to see to it that this return takes place at a suitable time and that they are helped to make a psychological readjustment and to continue to contribute to the work of the apostolate.

1.   The 31st General Congregation wishes to recall to all **569** members of the Society that the aim of the social apostolate is "to provide most men, and indeed all of them insofar as earthly conditions allow, with that abundance or at least sufficiency of goods, both temporal and spiritual, even of the natural order, that man needs lest he feel himself depressed and despised."[1] The scope of the social apostolate is broader, therefore, than the task of exercising our ministries or maintaining social works among workmen or other groups of the same sort that are especially needy. These works, indeed, according to the mind of the 28th General Congregation, decree 29, and the 30th General Congregation, decree 52, are to promoted with great diligence, especially in those regions that are economically less developed. But the social apostolate strives directly by every endeavor to build a fuller expression of justice and charity into the structures of human life in common. Its goal in this is that every man may be able to exercise a personal sense of participation, skill, and responsibility in all areas of community life.[2]

From this it is clear that the social apostolate is fully in **570** harmony with the apostolic end of the Society of Jesus according, namely, to that distinctly Ignatian criterion by which we should always keep before our eyes the more universal and more enduring good. For social structures, above all today, exert an influence on the life of man, even on his moral and religious life. The "humanization" of

---

1 Father Janssens, *Instruction on the Social Apostolate* (October 10, 1949), No. 7, *ActRSJ* 11 (1949) 714.
2 See John XXIII, *Mater et Magistra* and *Pacem in Terris, passim.*

social life is, moreover, particularly effective as a way of bearing evangelical witness in our times.

571   2.   These things are all the more true because in our day the focal point of the social problem goes beyond the inequality between different social groups to "global" inequalities between sectors of economic life, between regions of one nation, between nations themselves or classes of nations. Again, the social problem today is also a matter of inequalities between different racial groups. And people today are not troubled only by particular questions, for example, about wages or working conditions, about family and social security. They are especially concerned with the massive worldwide problems of malnutrition, illiteracy, underemployment, overpopulation. Thus it is that social action looks more and more to the development of economic and social progress that will be truly human.

572   The Society of Jesus, which has its home "in every corner of the world," seems suited in a special way to entertain this universal or "catholic" vision of the social apostolate by endeavoring with all its might to see that the less developed regions of the world are helped "in deed and in truth" by the more advanced and that the whole world movement of economic progress is imbued with a Christian spirit. It can do this by contributing as well to establishing the presence of the Church in the great national and international associations and congresses that attempt to bring about such progress.

573   3.   Since, finally, every form of the apostolate of the Society of Jesus flows from its mission "for the defense and propagation of the faith and the progress of souls in Christian life and learning," we must be very careful lest the social apostolate be reduced merely to temporal activity. This is all the more necessary because in these activities men are often affected by one-sided "ideologies" and violent passions. Never more than in our day is it necessary, therefore, that that "universal love which embraces in our Lord

all parties, even though they are at odds with one another,"[3] should shine forth among the companions of Jesus. Our men should be looking only to this, that they are trying to restore "peace on earth," a peace that is "based on truth, on justice, on love, on freedom." We are not forbidden, therefore, to undertake those things "which tend to infuse Christian principles into public life, provided that means in keeping with our Institute are employed,"[4] in the light of the Church's teaching and with proper respect for the sacred hierarchy.[5]

4. In order that those prescriptions concerning the so- **574** cial apostolate already laid down in the decrees of general congregations and in the Instruction on this subject may be more effectively carried out, the 31st General Congregation earnestly recommends that:

a) in the planning of apostolic activities, the social **575** apostolate should take its place among those having priority;[6]

b) in the entire course of Jesuit training, both theo- **576** retical and practical, the social dimension of our whole modern apostolate must be taken into account;

c) members who are to be specifically destined for this **577** apostolate should be chosen in good time; provincials should not hesitate to assign some men among them who are endowed with truly outstanding gifts both of mind and judgment and of virtue, and train them in the best universities;

d) social centers should be promoted by provinces or **578** regions according to a plan that will seem better suited to the concrete circumstances of each region and time; these centers should carry on research, social education, both doctrinal and practical, and also social action itself in brotherly collaboration with the laity;

---

3 *Cons* [823].
4 *CollDecr* 239 § 2.
5 See GC 28, D. 29, n. 16.
6 See GC 28, D. 29, n. 5.

579   e)   centers of this kind should be in close contact with one another both for the sake of information and for every kind of practical collaboration. Such collaboration should also be encouraged between centers in developed regions and those in regions which are less developed.

33 THE RELATIONSHIP OF THE SOCIETY
TO THE LAITY AND THEIR APOSTOLATE

1. In its teaching and decrees the Second Vatican **580**
Council stressed the just autonomy of earthly affairs, the
secular character which is proper and peculiar to the laity,[1]
the active part they ought to take in the entire life of the
Church, and their duty and right to the exercise of the
apostolate.[2] These demand that our Society examine the
relationship it has to laymen and their apostolate and that
it bring this relationship into greater harmony with the
norms and spirit of the Council itself.

2. Jesuits should be more keenly aware of the impor- **581**
tance of the state and vocation of laymen and their apostolate since in many areas of human activity and in many
places the Church can be present to the world only through
laymen. Let them strive not only to recognize the place
which the laity have in the mission of the Church but also
to promote it, and to hold in high esteem their just liberty.

The laity help us to understand more fully the world and **582**
Christian truth itself, and give us a more vivid sense of our
mission "for the defense and propagation of the faith." At
the same time they are a stimulus to our own continual
conversion.

3. Therefore we should make efforts to understand bet- **583**
ter their life, their ways of thinking and feeling, their aspirations and their religious mentality, by means of fraternal
dialogue. Jesuits can be present to and serve all men, including unbelievers, by taking an appropriate part in vari-

---

1 See GS 36, LG 31.
2 See AA 3, GS 43.

ous associations and organizations even on the national and international scale.

584   4.   Whenever and wherever we are associated with laymen, whether they are young people or adults, we must give an example of lively faith, charity, and a genuine fidelity to the Church, always testifying to the high value of religious life.

585   5.   There are many ways in which we can be of assistance to the laity. It is especially necessary that we bend all our efforts to forming both youth and adults for the Christian life and apostolate so that they may be able to fulfill their mission and assume their proper responsibility according to the Church's expectations.

586   By means of special instruction and spiritual direction we should communicate to those who can profit by it a fuller understanding of the evangelical life according to the Exercises of St. Ignatius, which are also very well suited to the lay state. Thus they may be able to direct all the acts of their daily professional, familial, and social life with a sincere mind and increased liberty to the greater glory of God, and may be able to discover and fulfill the divine will in all things and in this way devote themselves entirely to the service of their brothers as well. This direction is expected of us especially by the rejuvenated sodalities and the various other associations of laymen who are trying to cultivate an intense Christian and apostolic life according to this spirit.

587   6.   On the other hand, we ought to help the laity in their apostolate. Jesuits should be prepared to offer their cooperation as counselors, assistants, or helpers in the works which the laity themselves promote and direct.

588   We should also foster the collaboration of the laity in our own apostolic works. We must not only fully observe the demands of justice toward those who work with us but also establish a cordial cooperation based on love. We must open

up to them in various ways a wide participation in as well as responsibility for the direction, administration, and even government of our works, keeping of course the power of ultimate decision in the hands of the Society where it has the ultimate responsibility.

In the same spirit, in order that a greater respect may be had for the responsibility of laymen in the Church, let the Society examine whether some works begun by us might be turned over to competent laymen for the greater good of the Church. In all things we should promote an apostolic brotherhood with the laity, based on the unity of the Church's mission. **589**

7. Since a closer communion and association exists between us and those laymen who have shared more intimately our spirituality and way of feeling and acting, Jesuits, while maintaining our apostolic freedom, should show their close relationship by carefully preserving our loyalty to them and cultivating a sincere friendship with them, and also by actively showing fraternal hospitality toward them. **590**

34 LAYMEN LINKED TO THE SOCIETY BY A CLOSER BOND

591   Since in some regions of the world there are laymen who desire that the Society of Jesus join them to itself by a tighter bond in order that they may be better able to fulfill their own proper lay vocation in the Church;

592   And since the Society of Jesus, in fulfillment of the Second Vatican Council, seeks a renewal and adaptation which is at once spiritual and apostolic, making a judicious evaluation of the varieties of vocations for the service of the Church and souls;

593   The 31st General Congregation urges Father General to study the ways by which such bonds and a more stable and intimate collaboration can be achieved, taking into consideration the experiences of different parts of the world.

1.   The presence and influence of the new mass media **594** (radio, films, television) daily grow in intensity and extent in the modern world.

On the one hand, they are for our age the most important **595** means of expression and therefore provide us with very suitable aids to our apostolate in many ministries of the Society.

On the other hand, the spread of these media to the **596** entire human family so reaches the minds and hearts of men of every age and situation that they have a truly universal influence. As a result, they determine to a great extent what modern men think, even what they do.

2.   It follows, therefore, that these media can no longer **597** be looked on as something directed primarily to the relaxation of the spirit, but rather as the means of expression and mass communication in today's state of men and affairs, one which can to some extent be called a "culture of the image."

3.   The General Congregation, reviewing earlier direc- **598** tives in the light of the Second Vatican Council's decree on the Instruments of social communication,[1] wishes to recommend the following with respect to an apostolate of these new means of communication:

1° These mass media should be employed as very effec- **599** tive tools in many of our ministries, especially in preaching the word of God and in the training of youth.

2° Consideration should also be given to the specific **600** opportunity afforded by these media to have an impact,

---

1 See Vatican II, *Decree on the Instruments of Social Communication.*

whether with regard to treating questions or to influencing people, where one could not easily be had by other means and forms of the apostolate.

601   3° Provision should be made in our formation program for a training in the mass media that is adapted to each period of formation.

602   4° Provincials should in good time choose some men who are endowed with a religious spirit and other gifts, so that, after they have become expert at various levels of specialization and have acquired academic degrees, they may become competent in the practice of this apostolate and in directing others in it. Where it might seem useful, a center should be set up as a help in the acquiring of this specialization.

603   5° What Father Janssens decreed concerning secretariats on the international, regional and provincial levels should be faithfully carried out, since this is a necessary and effective means of stressing and promoting this kind of apostolate.

36   THE VATICAN RADIO STATION

Since the operation of the Vatican Radio Station was en- **604**
trusted to the Society in a particular way by the Holy
Father, it should be helped with the most suitable personnel
and means so that it can achieve its special objective. The
General Congregation asks Father General to undertake
such studies as seem useful in order that he may take
prompt and effective care of the matter.

605   The 31st General Congregation recognizes how important it is for the Society and especially for Father General to be informed about all that goes on in the Society or outside of it which in any way affects its life. It recommends that Father General examine the entire question of an information service, both in the General Curia and in the whole Society, and that he take care to have some specialists trained who will be able at a suitable time to set up effective information centers. In addition, the *Memorabilia Societatis Iesu* should be revised. It should be edited in a modern language and contain not only "what makes for edification"[1] but everything that is "worthy of note,"[2] including the problems and difficulties that confront the Society in different parts of the world.

---

1 *Cons* [675].
2 *Loc. cit.*

VI

CONGREGATIONS

38 PREPARATION FOR A
GENERAL CONGREGATION

1. Father General together with the General Assistants **606** should take care of all long term questions and problems that refer to a future general congregation.

2. It will help if the province congregations that pre- **607** cede a congregation of procurators or of provincials send to Father General not only the postulata and the reasons for or against calling a general congregation, but also questions and problems to be proposed to the future general congregation.

3. It is the duty of Father General and the General **608** Assistants to see to it that these questions and problems (mentioned above in Nos. 1 and 2) are put in suitable order and carefully studied and prepared, with the assistance of experts, for the future general congregation. When the time has been fixed for the general congregation, these questions and problems, together with the studies made of them, should be sent to all the provincials for communication in a suitable way to the province congregation.

4. In a congregation of procurators or of provincials, **609** when Father General makes his report on the state of the Society, he should also take into account these problems.

5. There should be a sufficiently long interval between **610** all the province congregations and the start of the general congregation.

6. All postulata sent by province congregations or by **611** private individuals should arrive in Rome several months (at least two months) before the start of the general con-

gregation, as far as circumstances permit and Father General or the Vicar decide. It is allowed, however, for the fathers of the congregation to bring their own postulata in keeping with the Formula of the General Congregation, No. 116, §2, and No. 101, §6.

612   7.   To Father General or the Vicar is entrusted the task of calling experts to Rome as soon as possible after the date of the general congregation has been officially announced and of setting up preliminary committees to gather together and put in order the postulata and to prepare the order of the agenda for the general congregation. These preliminary committees should be filled out, immediately after the province congregations, with electors chosen from the various assistancies.

613   8.   When the province congregations are concluded, care should be taken to send information to the preliminary committees about each elector's competence and knowledge of questions to be treated, and the same information should be communicated to all the electors. The purpose of this will be to make it easier to set up the commissions for handling the business of the general congregation.

614   9.   Father General or the Vicar should see to it that the studies and works of the preliminary committees are organized in proper order and communicated to the provincials and electors.

615   10.   Since the help of experts is of great importance, when the general congregation has assembled, Father General or the Vicar should see to it that a sufficient number of experts are on hand in Rome who can help the commissions in handling their assignments.

39 CONGREGATIONS OF PROCURATORS
AND OF PROVINCIALS

1. Every other third year, in place of procurators **616** elected in the province congregations, all the provincials should meet in Rome in a congregation to be called the Congregation of Provincials; the three-year periods are to be calculated in such a way that the first congregation after the General Congregation will be a congregation of procurators, the second, that of provincials. The congregation of provincials, however, is omitted in that third year in which from the number of "votes" of province congregations in favor of summoning a general congregation, it is already certainly clear that a general congregation must indeed be called.

2. The purpose of each of these congregations is two-**617** fold:

1° To cast a deliberative vote as to whether or not a **618** general congregation should be called;

2° To consult with Father General about the state and **619** affairs of the Society as a whole, especially about the more universal undertakings of the apostolate and, when it is a question of provincials, to set up those talks and meetings with Father General that are so important for good government. These congregations have, however, no legislative power.

3. In casting their vote as to whether a general congre-**620** gation should be called:

1° The provincials are bound to follow the opinion which was approved by their province's congregation in an instance where that opinion was affirmative, i.e., for calling the congregation, but not if it was negative.

621   2° Procurators are never bound to follow the opinion of their province, but they should adopt as their own that opinion which, after considering all the information they received, seems better in the Lord.

622   4.   In province congregations that precede a congregation of provincials, one *relator* is to be elected from the professed and spiritual coadjutors, other than the provincial, who will inform Father General by letter of the state of the province. It is left to the prudence of Father General to judge whether, besides this written report, the *relator* himself should be called to Rome.

623   5.   What is said here of provinces and provincials is to be understood also of independent vice-provinces and their provincials.

1. The following have a right to attend a province **624** congregation by reason of office (maintaining also decree 44, n. 11, of the present General Congregation and nn. 21-26 of the Formula of the Provincial Congregation):

1° the provincial;

2° all local superiors, whatever their title, who are normally named by Father General;

3° the vice-provincial and vice-superiors in accordance with the Formula of the Province Congregation;

4° the treasurer of the province;

5° the consultors of the province.

2. Besides those who enter by reason of office and those **625** who are summoned by the provincial in keeping with the following number, forty fathers or brothers will assemble for the province congregation who were previously elected in accordance with the rules that follow:

a) In this prior election, all the solemnly professed and formed spiritual and temporal coadjutors who are members of the province have active voice, and unless they are already attending the congregation by reason of office, they also have passive voice.

b) The election takes place by means of a form sent to **626** the provincial "soli" in which each elector can write the names of twenty-five candidates. The votes should be personal, that is, based on one's own conscience and knowledge and after mature consideration in prayer before God; it is permitted, however, to ask one or other prudent man in secret for information. The electors should look to the good of the whole province and Society rather than the advantage of some house or some part of the province.

c) The counting of the ballots, after the names of the **627** voters have been removed from them, is done by the provincial with the consultors of the province.

628   3.   The provincial, with the deliberative vote of the group that counts the ballots, can summon to the congregation three other fathers or brothers, and these attend in addition to the fixed number of forty (*supra numerum*).

629   4.   At least half of the members of the congregation, including those who enter *supra numerum,* should be professed of four solemn vows. The formed temporal coadjutors should not number more than five, but at least one of them should be present in the congregation.

630   5.   In a vice-province congregation, the number of members is twenty, in addition to those who enter by reason of office or by nomination by the vice-provincial. Each elector can write on his form the names of twelve candidates.

VII

GOVERNMENT

41   THE OFFICE OF THE GENERAL

1.   The 31st General Congregation, after a protracted **631**
and full discussion of both sides of the question, reaffirms
the prescription of the Constitutions that the General is to
be elected for life and not for some fixed term;[1] it has made
provision, however, for resignation from this office according to norms in the revised version of decree 260 of the
Collection of Decrees.

2.   Decree 260 of the *Collection of Decrees* shall be **632**
revised to read:
§1.   Father General may in good conscience and by law
resign from his office for a grave reason that would render
him permanently incapable of the labors of his post.

§2.   The obligation rests especially on the Fathers Pro-   **633**
vincial in the sight of God to consider and do what they
ought to do for the universal good of the whole Society in
those matters that concern Father General;[2] generally,
however, unless the matter should be extremely urgent,
they will fulfill this duty through the General Assistants.[3]

§3.   If at least a majority of the General Assistants, out   **634**
of their knowledge and love of the Society, shall have
decided that Father General ought for a grave reason to
resign his office, they should advise him of this through the
admonitor.

§4.   When Father General, either of his own accord but   **635**
after consultation with the General Assistants, or after having been so advised by them, shall have judged that it is
proper to resign his office, he should ask for a secret vote of
the General Assistants and the provincials of the whole So-

---

1 See *Cons* [719-722] ; see Paul V, *Quantum Religio.*
2 See *Cons* [778].
3 See *Cons* [782].

ciety on the seriousness of the causes. These votes should all be counted in the presence of the General Assistants and the Secretary of the Society. If a majority judges that a general congregation ought to be convoked for the purpose of making provision for the supreme government of the Society, Father General ought then to summon it.

636 §5. Father General's resignation from office does not take effect until it has been accepted by the Society in a General Congregation.[4]

637 §6. If, after he has been duly advised by the General Assistants, Father General either cannot or is unwilling to resign his office, and if a majority of the same Assistants judge that the welfare of the Society might suffer great harm from quite serious causes, such as very grave illness or senility where there is no hope of improvement in the case:[5]

638 1° A congregation for electing a temporary Vicar should be summoned in accordance with the Formula for such a congregation;

639 2° The temporary Vicar thus elected, after consultation with the General Assistants, should as soon as possible, under secrecy, inform the provincials and the two superiors or rectors of each province who are oldest in order of solemn profession of four vows, and ask their votes and those of the General Assistants in order to find out what they think should be done for the welfare of the Society;

640 3° When all the votes have been counted in the presence of the General Assistants and the Secretary of the Society, if a majority judges that a general congregation should be convoked, the Vicar ought to summon it; in the meantime, however, he should govern the Society in accordance with the norms of the office of Vicar.[6]

641 3. In decree 262 of the *Collection of Decrees,* §4 should be added in these words:

---

4 See CIC 186-87.
5 See *Cons* [773].
6 See *Cons* [766-777]; GC 8, DD. 28-29; GC 12, D. 55.

Father General has the right to appoint a Vicar-General to assist him as often as it may seem to him to be necessary or helpful to do so.

42   JOURNEYS BY FATHER GENERAL

642   Since trips by Father General to the Society in various parts of the world truly help union of hearts in the Society and are helpful in giving him a fuller knowledge of affairs, such trips from time to time are recommended to him by the General Congregation so that personal and fatherly contact with members of the Society may be fostered.

43 THE VICAR-GENERAL
AFTER THE DEATH OF THE GENERAL

1. The right and duty of the Vicar-General, after the **643** death of the General, to convoke and prepare for a General Congregation in accordance with norms laid down by the General Congregation is explicitly asserted.

2. The rules for the office of the Vicar-General are to **644** be revised so that, where mention is made of a vote of the Assistants, this is to be understood to refer to the General Assistants.

3. In the rules for the office of the Vicar-General, No. 7 **645** is to be revised to state that the Vicar-General must have four consultors (in the strict sense, i.e., the General Assistants) appointed by the Society; if one of them is lacking, a substitute shall be designated according to the norm of No. 12 in the rules for the office of Vicar-General.

4. The last clause of decree 274 in the *Collection of* **646** *Decrees* is to be revised to state that the office of Visitors, after a General dies, continues until such time as either the Vicar-General, after consultation with the General Assistants, or the new General shall have decided otherwise.

5. Concerning the deliberative vote of the General **647** Assistants (No. 12) and affairs which are not to be brought to a conclusion (Nos. 8-9), it seems better to make no change, especially since (see No. 3 above) a Substitute Assistant can now be appointed in place of that General Assistant who might be named or elected as Vicar.

648   In order that the Society may better exercise its providence with respect to the General according to the norms of our Constitutions, and that the General may be better aided by the advice he needs in directing and deciding the grave matters that come before him,[1] the 31st General Congregation has made the following arrangements which are by way of experiment only and are to be submitted to the judgment of the next General Congregation.

I.   GENERAL ASSISTANTS

649   1.   Four General Assistants only are elected to carry out the Society's providence with respect to the General.[2]

650   2.   These four General Assistants have a deliberative or consultative vote in those cases in which the common law requires, even in the Society, that the General must act with the consent of his consultors or listen to their advice.

651   3.   The General has the right and duty to replace them with others, if, after consultation with the other General Assistants, he judges that, either because of notably impaired strength or for another reason, they are so unequal to their task that it can be foreseen that the Society may thereby be in danger of serious harm.[3]

652   The General ought, however, immediately to seek the approval of the General Assistants and the provincials after he has passed on to them suitable information about the man he has chosen.

---

1 See *Cons* [776-777, 803].
2 See *Cons* [779].
3 See *CollDecr* 269 § 2, 3°.

Approval of a majority of the General Assistants and **653** provincials is needed for validity. Therefore, until such time as this majority is established, the new General Assistant does not have the right to cast a vote on matters in which the Institute gives a deliberative vote to Assistants, nor does he have a right to attend congregations, whether a general congregation, a congregation of procurators or provincials, or a congregation to elect a temporary Vicar-General.

4. If a general congregation convoked *ad negotia* de- **654** clares its intention of proceeding to the election of new General Assistants, the incumbent Assistants ipso facto leave office, but can be reelected to the same office.

5. The following is to be added in No. 136 of the **655** Formula of the General Congregation: The first two Assistants are to be elected individually by separate, successive ballots in the same session, the third in the following session, the fourth in the third session.

6. All provisions to the contrary, whether in the *Col-* **656** *lection of Decrees,* or in the norms of the Formula of the General Congregation, or in the rules of the Assistants, and specifically in decrees 263; 268, §2; 269, §2, 3° and §§4, 5; and in No. 130 of the Formula, are suspended until the next general congregation shall have passed judgment on the present provision, which is introduced as an experiment. Decree 264, however, is for the time being simply suspended.

II.   OTHER CONSULTORS OF THE GENERAL

7. These will aid in advising the General: **657**
1° General Consultors, especially in considering matters pertaining to the whole Society;
2° Regional Assistants, especially in considering matters pertaining to different regions of the Society;
3° Expert Consultors, in considering matters, whether pertaining to the whole Society or to principal works of the Society, in which they are experts.

658   All these can give their advice either individually or gathered in a common consultation, as the General shall ask it of them.

659   8. The General Consultors, the Regional Assistants and the Expert Consultors are named by the General; before he names a Regional Assistant, however, he should hear the views of the provincials of that region or assistancy, and if the appointment is made while a general congregation is in session, also of all the other electors of the same region or assistancy.

660   9. All provisions to the contrary in the decrees of previous general congregations are suspended until the next general congregation shall have laid down a definitive judgment.

III. RIGHTS OF ASSISTANTS AND CONSULTORS OF THE GENERAL RESPECTING CONGREGATIONS OF THE SOCIETY

661   10. General Assistants, General Consultors and Regional Assistants have the right to attend a general congregation, congregations of procurators or provincials, and a congregation for the election of a temporary Vicar-General. General Assistants, however, attend a general congregation with full rights, i.e., as electors, with the right to vote in the election of the General and General Assistants; while General Consultors and Regional Assistants, attend only *ad negotia*. If any at all of these assistants and consultors are changed or cease functioning in their office during a general congregation, both former and new men keep the same right.

662   11. General Consultors and Regional Assistants by reason of their office have active voice in the congregation of their own provinces.

663   12. Expert Consultors have no right, by virtue of their office, respecting congregations of the Society.

1.   Decree 274 of the *Collection of Decrees* is revised as   **664**
follows:

Father General has the power to send Visitors to provinces
when it shall seem good to him and for the length of time
and with the authority and jurisdiction that seem good.
When a General dies, the office of Visitor continues until
such time as the Vicar-General, after consultation with the
General Assistants, or the new General shall decide otherwise.

2.   The General Congregation recommends to Father   **665**
General that, while our law with regard to Visitors is to
remain unchanged, they should not stay in office too long
nor enjoy undefined authority or jurisdiction.

666   1. The General Congregation calls to mind that our holy father Ignatius wished indeed that "Father General have all authority for the greater benefit of the Society,"[1] and that from him "as from the head, all power of the provincials should proceed, and descend through them to local superiors and through them down to individual persons."[2] He wished that "for the same reason, in each province Father General should have provincials of demonstrated trustworthiness, since he realizes that the good government of the Society to a great extent depends on them,"[3] and "they should be men of the sort to whom a great deal of power can be entrusted."[4] The power that is given to them either by common law or the Society's law in virtue of their office is "ordinary power."

667   2. In this way Father General, "by sharing his work with them as far as the business permits," can have more leisure and time to attend to more universal matters, and more light to see what must be done about them.[5] Subordination under holy obedience will be better preserved in the whole body of the Society, the more clearly inferiors understand that they depend immediately on their superiors and that it will be very proper for them, and even necessary, to be subject to them in all things for Christ our Lord's sake,"[6] having persuaded themselves that "their superior possesses the knowledge, the will, and the ability to govern them well

---

1 *Cons* [736].
2 *Cons* [666].
3 *Cons* [797].
4 *Cons* [791].
5 *Cons* [797].
6 *Cons* [206].

in the Lord."[7] Provincials themselves and other superiors should devote themselves with a greater sense of responsibility to the task of government entrusted to them, not seeking to avoid making plans or decisions by themselves, but with a courageous spirit embarking on great undertakings for the divine service and remaining constant in carrying them out.[8]

3. On this account, provincials should carefully listen **668** to their subjects and direct them in the Lord, taking into consideration the internal knowledge which they have of them.[9] This is especially so with regard to rectors and local superiors whom they ought diligently to aid in carrying out their own function, showing them confidence and sharing broad power with them as the matter may demand.[10] They should also foster in the province religious life, the training of our men, and apostolic ministries, seeking always in all things the greater service of Christ's Church. Moreover, although provincials are appointed to rule their particular provinces, "they should turn their attention to the needs of the whole Society and look on interprovincial and international houses and works as part of their duty and responsibility, and willingly help them according to the measure and proportion worked out by Father General for each of the individual provinces."[11]

4. In addition, the obligation rests "especially on the **669** Fathers Provincial in the sight of God to consider and do what they ought to do for the general welfare of the Society" in those matters that concern Father General;[12] as a rule, however, they will fulfill this duty through the General Assistants, unless the matter should be extremely urgent.[13]

---

7 *Cons* [667].
8 See *Cons* [728].
9 See *GenExam* [97].
10 *Cons* [423-425, 662]; *Epit* 822.
11 GC 30, D. 49, n. 2; see *Cons* [778].
12 *Cons* [778].
13 See *Cons* [767, 782].

670   5.   The participation of the provincials in the government of the Society demands that there be "a more frequent personal communication" between the general and the provincials[14] and that Father General "know well, as far as can be, the consciences of the Fathers Provincial,"[15] so that from this intimate knowledge and mutual communication the "necessary" influence of the head may more easily "descend" to the provincials "for the sake of the goal that is set for the Society".[16]

671   6.   Therefore, the General Congregation:

a)   recommends that the personal communication of Father General with the provincials be increased, not only by calling them to Rome some time after they have taken office so that they may discuss things with him, but also by calling together all the provincials of a region or even of the whole Society as he shall judge it to be useful;

b)   has revised some decrees of general congregations in which the necessity of seeking the consent of the General was laid down as a requirement;

c)   hands over to the prudent judgment of Father General the matter of his habitually sharing broader faculties with the provincials in some affairs.

---

14 *Cons* [791] ; see *Cons* [662].
15 *Cons* [764].
16 *Cons* [666].

47   SELECTING HOUSE AND PROVINCE CONSULTORS

In order that the members of the Society may take a **672** truly effective part in the selection[1] of those who make up councils, the General Congregation decrees that:

1° With regard to the consultors of a house: the provincial should inquire into the opinion of members of the community concerning the current or prospective consultors (this can, as a rule, be done readily during the visitation of a house), and in naming consultors he should give proper weight to the members' judgment.

2° With regard to the consultors of the province: in **673** their official letters to the general, local superiors, having heard the views of the members of their community, to whom they shall offer a clear opportunity of expressing their minds, shall submit their opinion of the province consultors. They shall state whether these consultors are satisfactory or not, and if they are not, they should indicate others who may seem to them to be suited for this post. The consultors of each house, in their official letters to the general, shall submit a similar opinion.

---

1 See ES II, 18.

48   INTERPROVINCIAL COOPERATION

I.   INTERPROVINCIAL COOPERATION

A.   Interprovincial Cooperation in General

674   1.   That open and complete cooperation which is more and more a requisite for apostolic action today and which the Second Vatican Council strongly recommends to religious everywhere, should be promoted among all the Society's members, whatever their province.[1] Wherefore, the 31st General Congregation, in accordance with the 30th General Congregation, which already expressed the same earnest desire in its decree 49, again even more vigorously urges all members to bring about by concrete deeds that cooperation of all the provinces.

675   2.   Therefore, among us from the very start of our training encouragement should be given to a spirit of union and charity that boldly rejects every brand of particularism and egoism, even of a collective kind, and reaches out readily and generously to the universal good of the Society in the service of God's Church.

676   3.   The organization and planning of all apostolic labors, whether of a province or a region, or the whole Society, can contribute greatly to cooperation among undertakings, especially those of a similar nature, of the same province, or region, or the whole Society.

677   4.   Moreover, lest we be satisfied with empty words, each provincial should not look solely to the advantages of

---

1 See CD 6, PC 23, AG 33, ES I, 2, II, 42, 43, III, 21.

his own province, but give as much support as possible to the needs of the weaker provinces and missions that unfortunately lack both the means and instruments of the apostolate, and the resources and funds and especially the men. In addition, each meeting of all the provincials, when it is assembled under the presidency of Father General, is asked especially to treat explicitly of this interprovincial cooperation.

5.   Thus generously observing its primitive tradition and **678** eagerly following the prescriptions of the Second Vatican Council, our Society, like a body that is one and apostolic, will pursue more effectively under the standard of Jesus the one and same end, namely, the fraternal reconciliation and salvation of all men in Christ.

B.   Economic Cooperation

6.   The 31st General Congregation, in view of the need **679** for this economic cooperation, asks the *definitores* on poverty to render this cooperation more complete by a new and truly appropriate law so that the fraternal charity of the provincials, which has been demonstrated in different ways (e.g., in supporting scholastics and other ways), may be expressed more easily and more universally. Economic cooperation should not be restricted to offering money and resources; for it can also find fulfillment through collaboration in methods of obtaining help from externs and in ways of using money and resources.

C.   Cooperation Among Neighboring Provinces

7.   In view of the great importance, urgency, and com- **680** plexity of interprovincial cooperation, the 31st General Congregation does not wish to impede its progress and establishment by rigid or abstract regulations and recommendations, but strongly endorses the idea that various experiments in different regions be approved by Father General with a view to achieving specific, well-adapted, and

effective regional cooperation on the basis of which more suitable laws can be formulated at a later time.

D. Principles to be Observed in Introducing Experiments

681   8. Nevertheless, it seems good that certain principles should be observed so that the development of interprovincial cooperation corresponds completely with the method of governing that is proper to the Society, and that certain experiments, among those that are possible, should receive special recommendation.

1° The provincials:

682   a) Progress in interprovincial cooperation should not so overburden the provincials with a multiplicity of difficult transactions that they abdicate their responsibility toward persons. One of the chief duties of their office is to become well acquainted with all who are ascribed or applied to their province, and competently, sincerely and honestly to adopt decisions that affect these persons and their ministries. For this is a fundamental principle of all government in the Society, which is above all a "Society of love." This government does not consist in administration alone, however effective that may be.

683   b) Whatever these laws for interprovincial cooperation are, they will become useless unless the provincials themselves possess the qualities and endowments so absolutely necessary for the establishment of true and productive collaboration among themselves, that is, that intelligence of mind that can grasp the broader and more profound problems, and those special gifts of character that make for easy and sincere relationships among equals. Father General should, moreover, have these qualities in mind when naming provincials.

2° The board of provincials:

684   a) Meetings of provincials should take place as soon as interprovincial cooperation is begun, whatever form this cooperation may take. For these meetings greatly foster mutual understanding and are a good way by which each pro-

vincial can grasp the problems of other provincials and at the same time all can comprehend common problems. By such a method the common good of the whole region can be determined and similarly advanced.

b) At times, at least, because of his comprehensive **685** knowledge of the whole region, the presence of the Regional Assistant at these meetings can be profitable in that the meeting may be helped in pursuing its own objectives by the counsels and judgment of the Assistant and the Assistant himself may be in a position to obtain fuller information for Father General.

c) The chairman of the board of provincials can be one **686** of the provincials who fills this office for a brief time, e.g., for a year, and with the help of a secretary also attends to the preparation and summoning of the meetings and the execution of their decisions according to the objective goals or prescriptions determined by the board.

d) The designation of certain experts to investigate and **687** prepare different questions, e.g., on apostolic planning, social, educational, pastoral affairs, etc., can greatly aid in promoting better interprovincial cooperation. These men may be assembled in some interprovincial commissions and can be called to the provincials' meeting or send in a written report. In this way, interprovincial decisions, which are often of rather great importance, may be made in a more objective fashion and be more suited to the needs.

e) A board of provincials has no juridical authority in **688** the Society. Even if the provincials agree on a certain decision, this agreement has no force except from the authority of each provincial, and even here the approval of Father General may be required according to the nature and importance of the question. However, if the provincials do not agree among themselves, the affair should be referred to Father General or to the person mentioned in No. 3° who has the power of decision from either his own or from delegated jurisdiction.

3° Delegations of authority made by Father General:

a) Father General, either by himself or through a dele- **689** gate, solves interprovincial problems insofar as they exceed the power of the provincials.

690   b)   To solve a particular problem, Father General can delegate authority to one of the provincials or another father. Such authority, however, should not be delegated too frequently to those whose own office is to serve as an adviser to Father General.

691   c)   When interprovincial affairs are so multiplied that their resolution by the means mentioned above becomes increasingly difficult, it is necessary to go further and to initiate more radical and even novel experiments, e.g., through delegation of authority, conferred and determined by Father General, either to different fathers according to the diversity, importance, and urgency of the problems or to only one father, so that the common good of the whole region may be provided for in a more organized fashion.

692   d)   However, these or various other methods of further extending interprovincial cooperation should be always so arranged that the common good of the region and unity of action are fittingly achieved, that provincials receive effective assistance, and that the rights of all members are fully safeguarded (namely, those mentioned above in No. 1°, *a*).

II.   COMMON HOUSES

693   9.   The decisions necessary for the organization of common houses are entrusted to Father General so that norms may be formulated gradually from concrete experience with that flexibility and adaptation demanded by the purposes of those houses.

III.   ESTABLISHING HOUSES IN THE TERRITORY OF ANOTHER PROVINCE

694   10.   Decree 275 § 2 of the *Collection of Decrees* should be revised to read:

Several provinces cannot be established in the same territory according to a difference in language or nationality, nor as a rule can houses of different provinces be established in the same territory. Father General can, however, after hearing the opinions of the provincials concerned, permit the establishment of houses of one province in the territory of another province under conditions approved by him and in favor of those who are suffering persecution on behalf of Christ or for other serious reasons.

VIII

APPENDIX

49 THE SECOND SESSION OR PERIOD OF THE 31st GENERAL CONGREGATION

695   1. The General Congregation decided the following about the second session of the Congregation:

1° July 15th is set as the last day of the first session;

2° The second session will begin in the month of September, 1966.

696   2. § 1 – The commissions which have already been set up will remain the same.

697   § 2 – At Rome a coordinating commission is set up, the members of which are Father General, the general assistants, the chairmen of the commissions and the secretary of the General Congregation.

698   § 3 – Father General, after consulting with the members of the coordinating commission, will set up a special commission to prepare the rules of procedure for the second session.

699   § 4 – The modus agendi of the commissions in the interval between the sessions will be substantially the same as it was in the first session and the small groups convoked in the meantime will complete their business by letter.

700   § 5 – A special commission will be set up composed of 12 or 15 members which will convene at stated times in order to complete reports, collect and elaborate upon comments received and prepare definitive position papers.

701   3. § 1 – Father General has the power to change provincials for proportionately grave causes before the end of the General Congregation.

702   § 2 – Provincials who in between the two sessions have completed their term of office retain their right of membership at the second session.

703   § 3 – Provincials who have been appointed in the time in between sessions are to be summoned to the second session as delegates with full power, that is as "Electors."

§ 4 – Prescriptions §§ 1-3 of this third article are to be understood as applying only at this particular Congregation. **704**

4. Those provinces which will find the expenses of the second session extremely burdensome will be helped by the General Treasurer of the Society in an appropriate way. **705**

50 CHANGES IN THE FORMULA OF THE GENERAL CONGREGATION IN ACCORD WITH THE DECISIONS OF THE PRESENT CONGREGATION

706   n. 7. – § 1. For the business of the congregation, that is ordinarily after the election of the General has been completed, the following are to be admitted to the congregation and they have from then on the right of voting in everything except the election of the general assistants:

1° the general counselors;

2° the regional assistants;

3° the secretary of the Society;

4° the procurator general of the Society;

5° the treasurer general of the Society;

6° the provincials of the vice-provinces and the superiors of missions which have the right to send electors in which a congregation could not be held, if perhaps they are not solemnly professed of the four vows.

7° Procurators who have been called to the congregation by the general in order to provide more ample information on affairs, or who have been sent by their own provincials with the approval of the general given at least after they have been sent.

707   § 2. If during the general congregation some or all of the general counselors or the regional assistants are changed, those who have newly been named immediately acquire the right mentioned above in § 1, 1° and 2°; those however who have left office do not lose that right for that particular congregation.

708   n. 25. – § 3. No one should communicate to others outside of the congregation the things which are done in the congregation except according to regulations which the general or the vicar-general have set down and the congregation has approved.

n. 56. – § 2, *(addenda)*. Then the order of business **709** and the manner of proceeding on the day of election are proposed to the congregation for its approval according to what the vicar-general has set down with the advice of the general assistants taking into account the norms of the Constitutions, the traditions of the Society and the circumstances of the times.

nn. 71 – 88: *omitted*.

n. 116. – § 1. Not only provincial congregations but **710** also all members of the Society can send postulata to the general congregation. The provincial congregation should not be bypassed without a proportionate reason expressed in the postulatum itself.

§ 2. A postulatum which touches on some law ought **711** to point out the detriments which have followed or which will follow from the observance of the law and only after that should seek some remedy or propose some solution.

§ 3. Those who are not members of the congregation **712** should in no wise embroil themselves in the affairs which the congregation is treating nor should they force memoranda or informatory material on the members of the congregation nor urge them to follow this or that opinion.

n. 116 bis. – § 1. The members of the congregation **713** are not bound to sign their postulata as long as they give them either to the secretary of the congregation or to one of the deputies for screening the postulata. Otherwise they are bound to sign them just as those members of the Society who are not members of the congregation.

§ 2. In all postulata the following is required: **714**

1° that they be written in Latin;

2° that they exhibit due seriousness and reverence toward the Institute. For this end it will much help if those who are less knowledgeable about the Institute seek the advice of experts;[1]

---

1 See GC 31, D. 4, n. 3 (D. 12 § 1 and D. 15 § 2).

3° that each postulatum be set out on a separate page adding concisely and clearly the principal reasons for the postulatum. It is by no means prohibited, however, for the position taken in the postulatum to be further and more fully developed in other additional pages.

715   no. 118. – § 1. Those prescriptions of the Institute which pertain to pontifical law, either the common law or law proper to the Society, cannot be changed by a congregation unless power to change them has been given to the Society by the Holy See. It will however be lawful to treat of them if the congregation has so decided by a prior majority vote. Before such a prior vote, it is appropriate for the commissions to set forth the meaning of and the reasons for the postulata. Once a formal discussion has been finished, the congregation should not go to the Holy See for a change in one of those prescriptions unless two-thirds of the members of the congregation agree to this.

716   § 2. The Constitutions of our holy founder can be changed by the congregation in those matters which are not among the substantials.[2] We are not to treat of changing them except after the congregation has decided that they are to be treated of by a majority vote. Commissions, however, may before this vote set forth the meaning of and the reasons for the postulata. A decree introducing such a change is not valid unless it has been approved by two-thirds of the votes.

717   n. 124. – All decrees are to be passed by a majority vote, keeping the prescriptions of n. 118 intact.

---

2 See GC 31, D. 4, n. 3 (D. 14 § 3).

51 CHANGES IN THE FORMULA OF THE PROVINCIAL CONGREGATION IN ACCORD WITH THE DECISIONS OF THE PRESENT CONGREGATION

n. 3. – § 7 *(addenda)*. If, because of religious persecution or similar adverse circumstances, a provincial congregation cannot be held nor can a provincial send someone from his province in his place to a general congregation or designate someone to fulfill the function of relator, the general, with advice of the general assistants or the vicar-general in the same circumstances, will name some member of the Society from that province who is professed of the four vows, either as elector who will then become a member of the general congregation with full rights in place of the provincial, or as procurator in a congregation of procurators. **718**

n. 6. – § 1. The right to attend a provincial congregation belongs by reason of their office to the following: **719**

1° the provincial;

2° all local superiors no matter what they are called who ordinarily are named by Father General;

3° the vice-provincial and vice-superiors but only according to the norms of n. 24-26;

4° the treasurer of the province;

5° the consultors of the province.

§ 2. The following do not have a right to membership by reason of their office: **720**

1° the socius to the provincial;

2° the instructor of the tertianship;

3° the master of novices.

n. 7. – § 1. Besides those who by reason of their of- **721** fice are members of the congregation and those who according to norm n. 6 may have been designated by the provincial, there should be in the congregation forty previously elected fathers or brothers.

722 § 2. In this preliminary election:

1° All the solemnly professed and the spiritual and temporal formed coadjutors who are members of that province have active voice, according to the norm of n. 7 bis.

723 2° The same members have passive voice unless they already are coming to the congregation by reason of their office, keeping intact the prescriptions of n. 113.

724 3° The election is to be carried out by written ballot sent to the provincial "soli" in two envelopes. The name of the person doing the voting is to be written on the inner envelope but not on the ballot itself.

725 4° Each member of the province who is voting can write on the ballot the names of 25 candidates. If someone, however, should know only a few members of the province, it will be enough to write only a certain number of names even if he does not fill out the total number of 25.

726 5° The electors ought to look to the good of the whole province and of the Society rather than to obtaining some benefit for a particular house or some other part of the province.

727 6° The votes are to be personal, that is, to be cast in accord with one's own conscience and knowledge and seriously thought about in prayer before the Lord. Secrecy is to be observed. However it is licit for the person voting to seek information under the seal of confidentiality from one or another prudent man.

728 7° No one is to volunteer information to someone who does not ask for it.

729 § 3. For the validity of this preliminary election it is not required that each and every person who has active voice respond, nor that two-thirds of the electors send in a ballot as long as suitably in advance they have received news of the fact the election is to held.

730 § 4. The counting of the ballots, with the names of the voters removed, is to be done by the provincial with the four consultors of the province. This election commission has the right to resolve doubts on the validity of the whole balloting and of each and every ballot.

§ 5.   After the counting of the ballots, a list should be **731** drawn up of those above who have been elected by the whole province, with no indication of the house to which each belongs.

§ 6.   The provincial may, with the deliberative vote of **732** the election commission, summon to the congregation three other professed fathers or spiritual or temporal coadjutors who are to be designated in the list as "named by the provincial." The provincial is however not so bound to name three people. Those so designated become members of the congregation "supra numerum." However they have the right not only to deal with the affairs of the congregation but also to participate in the elections which take place in the congregation.

§ 7.   At least half the members of the congregation in- **733** cluding those who are there "supra numerum" will be professed of the four solemn vows. The formed temporal coadjutors shall not exceed the number of five but there must be at least one of them at the congregation.

N.B.   It is further to be determined, according to the **734** norm of decree 52, what is to be done when the number of those who have been elected is not sufficient to complete the set number of 40 Jesuits who are to be members of the congregation.

n. 7 bis *(previously §§ 2-5 no. 7)*.   **735**

n. 8. – *§§ 1-2 are omitted.*   **736**

n. 10 *is omitted.*   **737**

n. 16. – § 1.   With reference to impediments which **738** might exist in those elected to the congregation, before the congregation begins the provincial, together with four of the members who are to come to that congregation by right of that office and who can conveniently be called together, will judge them.

739   n. 21. – The Jesuits who are members of the General's curia retain active and passive voice in their own province as do also those who are assigned to a house or a work immediately dependent upon the General. In addition, the secretary of the Society, the general counselors, the regional assistants, the procurator general and the treasurer general as well as the superior of the curia have a right to membership in the congregation of their own province by reason of their office. All of these, however, can be dispensed by Father General from the obligation of attending the congregation.

740   n. 28. – § 2.   All members of the Society may in their private capacity offer whatever information they wish to the consultors, to the superior or to anyone who is elected to the congregation, or they can send this material to the congregation itself, keeping however the prescriptions of n. 74 §§ 2-7.

741   n. 29. – § 2.   This is so to be made up that after the name of the provincial are listed all those who have taken final vows, according to the calendar order in which they have made their definitive incorporation into the Society. There is to be no precedence by grade or office. If several have pronounced their final vows on the same day, the earlier place on the list is to be given to the one who has been longest in religious life, and then to the one who is older. If there are some who have all of these characteristics identically, then before each provincial congregation the matter is to be decided by lot by the provincial in the presence of the consultors of the province. Scholastics, if there should be some on this list, are to be ranked in order of length of time in religious life.

742   n. 3. – § 2. *is omitted (keeping the prescriptions of n. 86).*

743   n. 43. – § 3.   No one should communicate to others outside of the congregation except to those who have been elected or to their substitutes who may have perhaps been absent from the congregation the things which are done in the congregation except according to the norms laid down at the immediately previous general congregation. However, the General or the Vicar-General has the power to further adapt these norms to the particular conditions of a provincial congregation.

n. 55. – Eighth, immediately after the two deputies **744** have been elected, the day will be set by a public majority vote on which the election of those to be sent is held. If it seems better to postpone that election, there is no impediment to conducting the affairs of the congregation before the election.

n. 74. – § 1 *(remains the same)*. **745**

§ 2.   These postulata: **746**

1° If they are destined for the General Congregation should be appropriate to preserving, promoting and adapting the Institute.

2° *(remains the same)*. **747**

§ 3.   It is not the prerogative of the provincial congre- **748** gation to deal with persons. If, however, in the course of business persons have to be dealt with indirectly, this is to be done with appropriate and religious modesty.

§ 4.   The provincial congregation may act: **749**

1° On the substantials or the fundamentals of the Institute whenever there are serious reasons to do so,[1] and those reasons ought to be the more serious insofar as the affair more intimately touches our way of life and acting;[2]

2° On other of our laws, observing the same proportion.[3]

§ 5.   A postulatum which touches on some law ought **750** to point out the detriments which have followed or which will follow from the observance of the law and only after that should it seek some remedy or propose some solution.

§ 6.   The members of the congregation are not bound **751** to sign their postulata as long as they give them either to the secretary of the congregation or to one of the deputies for screening the postulata. Otherwise they are bound to

---

1 See GC 31, D. 4, n. 3 (D. 15 § 1).

2 See *Ibid.* (D. 12 § 1 and D. 15 § 2).

3 See *Ibid.* (D. 14 §§ 3-5).

sign them just as those who are not members of the congregation.[4]

752   In all postulata the following is required:

1° that they be written in Latin unless they have been submitted by temporal coadjutors; to the Latin should be added a vernacular translation of the postulatum itself and of at least a summary of the whole proposition or argument.

2° that they exhibit due seriousness and reverence toward the Institute. For this it will help much if those who are less knowledgeable about the Institute seek the advice of experts.[5]

3° that each postulatum be set out on a separate page adding concisely and clearly the principal reasons for the postulatum. It is by no means prohibited, however, for the position taken in the postulatum to be further and more fully developed in other additional pages.

753   § 7.   Those who are not members of the congregation should in no wise embroil themselves in the affairs which the congregation is treating nor should they force memoranda or informatory material on the members of the congregation or urge them to follow this or that opinion.[6]

754   n. 76. – All the postulata which have been sent to the congregation are to be given to the members of the congregation along with the reasons added by the author of the postulatum; it is to be noted which of the postulata the deputation has admitted to consideration and which ones it has rejected.

755   n. 81. – § 2.   In order for a postulatum to be considered approved by the congregation when it deals with changing the substantials or the fundamentals of the Institute or the pontifical law proper to the Society or the Constitutions, a two-fold vote is required: the first ballot by majority vote is to decide whether the matter should be dealt with; the second ballot by a two-thirds majority vote whether the proposal is approved. It is, however, allowable

---

4 See GC 29, D. 38, n. 28 § 1.
5 See GC 31, D. 4, n. 3 (D. 12 § 1 and D. 15 § 2).
6 See GC 29, D. 38, n. 28 § 2.

before the first ballot to set forth the meaning and the reasons for the postulata.

n. 86 bis. — The provincial should take care that those **756** who have sent postulata to the provincial congregation learn in good time what happened to their requests, at least if a postulatum was rejected.

n. 92. — §. *(To be added at the end):* a) If neither **757** a congregation of a vice-province or mission can be held nor the vice-provincial or superior of a mission can send some professed father in his place, because of religious persecution or other unfavorable conditions, the norm of n. 3 § 7 is to observed.

§ 4. *(To be added at the end):* 3° If neither the con- **758** gregation of a vice province or a mission can be held nor the vice-provincial or superior of a mission can send some other priest in his place, because of religious persecution or similar unfavorable circumstances, the norm of n. 3 § 7, is to be observed.

n. 93. — § 1 *(remains the same).* **759**

§ 2. Besides those who come to the congregation by **760** reason of office and those who may have been designated by the vice-provincial or the superior of a mission in accord with the norm of § 3, the congregation will be made up of 20 fathers or brothers previously elected according to the norm of n. 7, §§ 2-5, except that each of the Jesuits voting can write on his ballot the names of only 12 candidates.

§ 3. The vice-provincial or superior of the mission can **761** call to the congregation three other fathers or brothers in accord with norm n. 7 § 6.

§ 4. At least half the members of the congregation in- **762** cluding those who are there "supra numerum" will be professed of the four solemn vows. The formed temporal coadjutors shall not exceed the number of five, but there must be at least one of them at the congregation.

52 COMPLETING WORK ON THE
FORMULAS OF THE CONGREGATIONS

763   With respect to the *Formulas* of congregations, the 31st General Congregation:

1° Orders and empowers Father General, with a deliberative vote of those fathers of the general curia who have a right to attend a general congregation by reason of their office:

a) to give an authoritative answer to questions that will of necessity arise concerning the next province congregations and congregations of procurators and of provincials by adapting the Formulas of these congregations and, where necessary, even changing them;

b) either to give provisional answers to juridical questions respecting the next general congregation and its Formula, or prepare the questions in such a way that the 32nd General Congregation can itself settle them at its outset.

764   2° Recommends also to the General that he communicate to the fathers of the 32nd General Congregation, in good time before the start of the congregation, the decisions so made and the questions to be settled.

53 THE CATALOG OF CENSURES
AND PRECEPTS

The General Congregation desires that the universal laws **765** of the Society be observed, but that they be observed according to the spirit and aim proposed by St. Ignatius. This means that "in place of fear of offense there be love and desire of all perfection, and that the greater glory and praise of Christ, our Creator and Lord, be achieved.[1] For this reason the Congregation has decided to review the canonical penalties and precepts in virtue of obedience in the "Catalogue of Censures and Precepts Imposed on Jesuits."[2] Therefore, by this decree it delegates to Father General the following powers:

1° that according to his prudent judgment, with the deliberative vote of those fathers of the general curia who by reason of their office have a right to participate in the general congregation, and having taken the advice of experts, he can abrogate the canonical penalties and those precepts that are imposed by the Society's own law;

2° that under the same conditions he has the power of abrogating penalties laid down by the Constitutions,[3] as well as permission to enable him to petition the Holy See in the name of the Society for the abrogation of penalties established by particular pontifical law.[4]

---

1 *Cons* [602].
2 See *CollDecr* 303-315.
3 See *Cons* [695-96]; *CollDecr* 303 § 2.
4 See S. Pius V. *Aequum Reputamus;* Gregory XIII, *Ascendente Domino; CollDecr* 307 § 1; GC 31, D. 4, n. 4.

54 PRIOR CENSORSHIP OF BOOKS

766   1. In order that more effective provision be made for Jesuits to engage with congruous freedom and responsibility in the intellectual apostolate of the press and other forms of mass communications, due consideration being given at the same time to security of doctrine and the interests of the Church and of the Society, the 31st General Congregation recommends and, insofar as necessary, communicates to Father General the power, without prejudice to the general principle of the Constitutions regarding previous censorship of writings, to adapt the particular norms of our own law in this respect, by way of experiment. This he may do according to his own prudent judgment, after consultation with experts and with the general assistants.

767   2. With a view to the same end, it is desirable that the boards of provincials, either of an assistancy or of a region or country, having heard the advice of experts, propose to Father General those adaptations which appear to be more appropriate to their own particular situations and problems.

55   ABROGATION AND REVISION OF
CERTAIN DECREES

1. In the *Collection of Decrees* decrees 21; 75, §3; 78, **768**
§1; 231; 232; 290; 293 are abrogated to this extent, that
norms contained in them shall continue to stay in force with
the authority of Ordinations of the Fathers General,[1] until
the General shall decide otherwise.

2. Decree 75, §3 of the *Collection of Decrees* should be **769**
revised as follows:

Letters written or received by the admonitor of a provincial are not subject to the censorship of the same provincial.

3. In decree 212 of the *Collection of Decrees,* the fol- **770**
lowing words should be added:

The General can, however, communicate to provincials
the faculty of approving specifications for construction of
a new building.

---

1 See *CollDecr* 4.

771   1. For the proper completion of the legislative work of the 31st General Congregation, Father General is empowered, after obtaining the deliberative vote of those fathers of the general curia who have a right *ex officio* to attend a general congregation, and without prejudice to the powers given him in other decrees, to abrogate or modify decrees of past general congregations which are seen to be not in accord with the decrees of this 31st General Congregation.

772   2. Moreover, the 31st General Congregation grants to Father General the following:

1° That he himself, if it should be a matter of necessity, can suppress colleges and professed houses, with the deliberative votes, however, of those fathers of the general curia who have the right *ex officio* to attend a general congregation and of the provincial of the province in whose territory the house to be suppressed is located.

773   2° That the minutes of some sessions that could not be distributed to the Fathers of the Congregation should be approved by Father General and the general assistants.

774   3° That with respect to decrees that must be promulgated after the close of the Congregation, it should be permitted to Father General:

a) to make whatever corrections seem obviously needed;

b) to reconcile contradictions, if any are detected, according to the mind of the Congregation, but after having ascertained the deliberative vote of those fathers of the general curia who have a right *ex officio* to attend a general congregation;

c) to edit the decrees with regard to style;

d) where necessary, to combine different decrees into one, while preserving the meaning and intent of each;

e) to fix a *vacatio legis* or delay with respect to enforcement, in the light of circumstances, when promulgating the decrees, especially the decree on new norms for advancement to final vows.

C.

DOCUMENTS PERTAINING
TO THE GENERAL CONGREGATION

1. Address of His Holiness, Pope Paul VI, to the Members of the 31st General Congregation, May 7, 1965

2. Address of His Holiness Pope Paul VI, to the Members of the General Congregation, November 16, 1966

3. Approval by the Supreme Pontiff of the Decrees of the 31st General Congregation on Religious Poverty and on the Gratuity of Our Ministries

4. Letter of Cardinal I. Antoniutti

5. Letter of the 31st General Congregation to the Supreme Pontiff

1. ADDRESS OF HIS HOLINESS POPE PAUL VI, TO THE MEMBERS OF THE 31st GENERAL CONGREGATION MAY 7, 1965

Beloved Sons:

We are happy to receive you today, dear members of the Society of Jesus, and We greet you with Our warm and heartfelt good wishes.

You have gathered in Rome in accordance with the original law of your Society to form the General Congregation which will choose the succcessor of Father John Janssens, your Superior General, whose loss We mourn with you. The task before you is a difficult and momentous one, for on it depend the well-being and success, the vigor and progress of your religious Institute.

Weigh with sound and well-informed judgment, with the steady wisdom that comes from true prudence, every element that has a bearing on your decision, and, before all else, invoke the light and guidance of the Holy Spirit in pure and fervent prayer, that your voting may conform to the will of God: "Show us the one whom You have chosen."[1]

For Our part, as We greatly share your concern and unite Our prayers with yours, We earnestly wish that the one to be chosen will meet the highest expectations and fully satisfy the needs of your religious family.

Everyone knows that Ignatius, your holy father and lawmaker, wanted your Society to be marked by a distinctive characteristic and to achieve results by a zeal rooted in virtue. Founded as the result of his unselfish and heavensent inspiration, the Society of Jesus was to be, in his plan,

---

1 Act 1.24.

outstanding as the solid bulwark of the Church, the pledged protector of the Apostolic See, the militia trained in the practice of virtue.

Your glorious mark of distinction, the great claim to renown, with which you are endowed, is "to fight for God under the standard of the Cross, and to serve God alone and the Church, His spouse, under the Roman Pontiff, the Vicar of Christ on earth."[2] If, in the fulfillment of this pledge of service, other religious have the duty of serving with loyalty, courage and distinction, you ought to possess these qualities in the highest degree.

The glorious pages of your history proclaim that the ambitions and lives of the sons have matched the ideals of their holy father, and that you have deserved the reputation and glory of being the legion ever faithful to the task of protecting the Catholic faith and the Apostolic See.

Like the heavens with their stars, your Order has gained brilliance from your holy martyrs and confessors, from the Doctors of the Church, Peter Canisius and Robert Bellarmine, and from a countless throng of devout, learned, and zealous men. By word and work, they have taught the lesson of fidelity, and have left to their successors as an imperishable example and a spur the path which they have blazed.

The tenor of your lives, as befits valiant soldiers of Christ, tireless workers beyond reproach, should be based solidly on the holiness of behavior which is characteristic of you, on an asceticism of the gospels, which is austere and noteworthy for its virility and strength. It should be permeated by an unwavering discipline which does not give way before individual inclinations, but instead is prompt and ready, reasonable and constant in all its ways and undertakings. In an army, if a line or unit does not keep to its assigned place, it is like an instrument or a voice out of tune. Your new General will take every care to ensure that your harmony be not disrupted by discordant voices, but rather that

---

2 Formula of the Institute of Julius III, 1.

you deserve full credit for fidelity and devotion. We are happy to see that most of you partake of this fitting unanimity, and We congratulate you for it.

Therefore, all should take care in their thinking, their teaching, their writing, their way of acting, not to conform to the spirit of the world, nor to let themselves be buffeted by every wind of doctrine[3] and not to give in to unreasonable novelties by following personal judgment beyond measure.

Instead, let each one of you consider it his chief honor to serve the Church, our Mother and Teacher; to follow not his own, but the counsel, the judgments, the projects of the hierarchy and to bring them to fruition; to be animated more by the spirit of cooperation than by that of privilege. The Church recognizes that you are most devoted sons, she especially cherishes you, honors you, and if We may use a bold expression, she reveres you. Now when more than ever, as a result of the decrees of the Second Vatican Council, the extent and the possibilities of the apostolate are seen to be so vast, the holy Church of God needs your holiness of life, your wisdom, your understanding of affairs, your dedication to labor, and she asks of you that, holding on most tenaciously to the faith of old, you bring forth from the treasure of your heart new things and old for the increase of God's world-wide glory and for the salvation of the human race, in the name of Our Lord Jesus Christ whom God has glorified and to whom He has given a name which is above every name.[4]

Hold fast at all times to the safe protection of this Holy Name, your name too and your special glory. Strive eagerly to make it more widely loved and honored since it is the true, never-failing source of salvation: "For there is no other name under heaven given to men, whereby we must be saved."[5]

---

3 See Eph. 4.14.

4 See Phil. 2.9.

5 Act 4.12.

We gladly take this opportunity to lay serious stress, however briefly, on a matter of grave importance: We mean the fearful danger of atheism threatening human society. Needless to say it does not always show itself in the same manner but advances and spreads under many forms. Of these, the anti-God movement is clearly to be reckoned the most pernicious: not content with a thoroughgoing denial of God's existence, this violent movement against God attacks theism, aiming at the extirpation of the sense of religion and all that is good and holy. There is also philosophical atheism that denies God's existence or maintains that God is unknowable, hedonistic atheism, atheism that rejects all religious worship or honor, reckoning it superstitious, profitless and irksome to reverence and serve the Creator of us all or to obey His law. Their adherents live without Christ, having no hope of the promise, and without God in this world.[6] This is the atheism spreading today, openly or covertly, frequently masquerading as cultural, scientific or social progress.

It is the special characteristic of the Society of Jesus to be champion of the Church and holy religion in adversity. To it We give the charge of making a stout, united stand against atheism, under the leadership, and with the help of St. Michael, prince of the heavenly host. His very name is the thunder-peal or token of victory.

We bid the companions of Ignatius to muster all their courage and fight this good fight, making all the necessary plans for a well-organized and successful campaign. It will be their task to do research, to gather information of all kinds, to publish material, to hold discussions among themselves, to prepare specialists in the field, to pray, to be shining examples of justice and holiness, skilled and well-versed in an eloquence of word and example made bright by heavenly grace, illustrating the words of St. Paul: "My message and my preachings had none of the persuasive

---

6 See Eph. 2.12.

force of 'wise' argumentation, but the convincing power of the Spirit."[7]

You will carry it out with greater readiness and enthusiasm if you keep in mind that this work in which you are now engaged and to which you will apply yourselves in the future with renewed vigor is not something arbitrarily taken up by you, but a task solemnly entrusted to you by the Church and by the Supreme Pontiff.

Hence in the laws and regulations of your Society, ratified by Paul III and Julius III, there is the following declaration: "All who make the profession in this Society should understand at the time, and furthermore keep in mind as long as they live, that this entire Society and the individual members who make their profession in it are campaigning for God under faithful obedience to His Holiness Pope Paul III and his successors in the Roman pontificate. The Gospel does indeed teach us, and we know from the orthodox faith and firmly hold, that all of Christ's faithful are subject to the Roman pontiff as their head and as the vicar of Jesus Christ. But we have judged nevertheless that the following procedure will be supremely profitable to each of us and to any others who will pronounce the same profession in the future, for the sake of our greater devotion in obedience to the Apostolic See, of greater abnegation of our own wills, and of surer direction from the Holy Spirit. In addition to that ordinary bond of the three vows, we are to be obliged by a special vow to carry out whatever the present and future Roman pontiffs may order which pertains to the progress of souls and the propagation of the faith; and to go without subterfuge or excuse, as far as in us lies, to whatsoever provinces they may choose to send us."[8]

It should be considered fully consistent with this vow and its characteristic obligation that it is not merely a matter binding in conscience, but one that must also shine forth through actions and become known to all.

---

7 I Cor. 2.4.
8 *Formula of the Institute of Julius III*, 3.

St. Ignatius, your holy Founder, wanted you to be so; We too want you to be so, being sure that the trust We place in you will be entirely fulfilled. We are confident also that the fulfillment of these wishes of Ours shall yield to the Society of Jesus, in all parts of the world where it struggles, prays and labors, a plentiful harvest of renewed life and excellent merits which God will fittingly reward.

With these heartfelt greetings to you all, members of the Society of Jesus, the festive and happy group that surrounds us today, We impart our apostolic blessing on all of you, on all your undertakings, and on the great hope which sets your hearts on fire for pure and lofty aims to be achieved.

2. ADDRESS OF HIS HOLINESS, POPE PAUL VI, TO THE MEMBERS OF THE GENERAL CONGREGATION, NOVEMBER 16, 1966

Beloved sons:

It was Our desire that you concelebrate and share with us in the Eucharistic Sacrifice before departing, each to his own land, at the conclusion of your General Congregation and before setting out from Rome, the center of Catholic unity, for the four corners of the world. We wanted to greet each and every one of you cordially, to hearten and encourage you, and to bless each of you, your entire Society and your various works which you undertake for the glory of God and in the service of Holy Church. We desire to renew in your hearts in an almost palpable and solemn way the sense of the apostolic mandate that characterizes and strengthens your mission, as though it were conferred and renewed by your blessed Father Ignatius, a most faithful soldier of the Church of Christ; or as though Christ Himself, whose vicar We are here on earth in this Apostolic See, unworthily but truly, confirmed and mysteriously aided and extended your mission.

For that reason, We have chosen this place that is sacred and awe-inspiring in its beauty, its majesty and especially in the significance of its paintings. This is a place especially venerable by reason of our prayer pronounced here, a most humble prayer but a Pope's prayer, a prayer which gathers together not only the praise and longing of our spirit but also of the whole Church throughout the world and even of all mankind, which We represent before God through our ministry and to which We bring the message of Him Who is most high. We have chosen this place where, as you know, the destinies of the Church are discerned and decided upon at certain periods of history, destinies which we duly believe are ruled over not by the will of men but by the mysterious and most loving assistance of the Holy Spirit. Here, today, when this most holy rite has been finished We shall invoke that same Holy Spirit for our Holy Church which is summed up, as it were, and represented in our apostolic office, as well as for you, the members and superiors endowed with the authority of your and our Society of Jesus.

By this prayer in which we shall implore the Holy Spirit together, all those things which you have so carefully done during this most important period will receive a special approval. You have subjected your Society and all its works to a critical examination, as though concluding four centuries of its history just after the close of the Second Vatican Council, and beginning a new age of your religious life with a fresh outlook and with new proposals.

This meeting therefore, my brothers and most beloved sons, takes on a particular historical significance in that it is given to you and to us to define by means of reciprocal clarification the relationship which exists and which should exist between Holy Church and the Society of Jesus. Through divine mandate We exercise the pastoral guidance of this Church and sum up in ourselves and represent it. What is this relationship? It is up to you and to us to furnish a reply, which will follow a twofold division:

1) Do you, sons of St. Ignatius, soldiers of the Society of Jesus, want even today and tomorrow and always to be what you were from your beginnings right up to today, for the service of the Catholic Church and of this Apostolic See? There would be no reason for asking this question had not certain reports and rumors come to our attention about your Society just as about other religious families as well, which—and We cannot remain silent on this—have caused us amazement and in some cases, sorrow.

What strange and evil suggestions have caused a doubt to arise in certain parts of your widespread Society whether it should continue to be the Society conceived and founded by that holy man, and built on very wise and very firm norms? The tradition of several centuries ripened by most careful experience and confirmed by authoritative approvals has shaped the Society for the glory of God, the defence of the Church and the admiration of men. In the minds of some of your members, has the opinion really prevailed to the effect that all human things, which are generated in time and inexorably used up in time, are subject to an absolute law of history as though in Catholicism there were no charism of permanent truth and of invincible stability? This rock of the Apostolic See is the symbol and foundation of this charism.

Did it appear to the apostolic ardor which animates the whole Society that your activities could be made more effective by renouncing many praiseworthy customs pertaining to spiritual, ascetical and disciplinary matters, as though they no longer helped but rather impeded you in expressing your pastoral zeal more freely and with more personal involvement? And so it seemed that the austere and manly obedience which had always characterized your Society, which made its structure evangelical, exemplary and very strong, should be relaxed as though opposed to the human person and an obstacle to alacrity of action. This is to forget what Christ, the Church, and your own school of spirituality have taught in so outstanding a way about this virtue. And so there might have been someone who judged that it was no longer necessary to impose spiritual practices on his own soul, that is, the assiduous and intense practice of prayer, a humble and fervent discipline of the interior life, examination of conscience, intimate conversation with Christ, as though the exterior action were enough to keep the soul wise, strong and pure, and as though such activity could achieve by itself a union of the mind with God. It would be as though this abundance of spiritual resources were fitting only for the monk and not rather the indispensable armor for the soldier of Christ.

Perhaps some have been deceived into thinking that in order to spread the Gospel of Christ they must take on the ways of the world, its manner of thinking and acting, and its worldly view of life. On the basis of naturalistic norms they judged the customs of this age and thus forgot that the rightful and apostolic approach of the hearald of Christ to men, who brings God's message to men, cannot be such an assimilation as to make the salt lose its tang and the apostle his own virtue.

These were clouds on the horizon, but they have been dispersed in large measure by the conclusions of your Congregation! It was with great joy that we learned that you, in the strong rectitude which has always inspired your will, after a careful and sincere study of your history, of your vocation, and of your experience, have decreed to hold fast to your fundamental constitutions and not to abandon your tradition which in your keeping has had a continual effectiveness and vitality.

By introducing certain modifications to your rule—this renewal of religious life which was proposed by the Council not only was permissible but recommended—you in no way violated that sacred law by which you are Religious and also members of the Society of Jesus. Rather you remedied your circumstances insofar as they showed the wear of time, and you brought new strength to all the undertakings you will assume in the future so that this happy result will stand forth among all the others which you have decided upon in your laborious discussions; this happy result We say which has brought about not only a real conservation and positive increase of the body but also of the spirit of your Society. And, in this regard, We fervently exhort you that also in the future you give pride of place in your program of life to prayer, not turning away from the wise directives which you received from your forebears. From where, if not from divine grace, which flows to us as living water through the humble channels of prayer, of dialog with God, and especially of the sacred liturgy, from where will the Religious draw heavenly counsel and strength for bringing about his supernatural sanctification? From where will the apostle receive the drive, guidance, strength, wisdom and perseverance in his struggle against the devil, the flesh and the world? From where will he draw the love by which he loves souls for their salvation and builds a Church along with the workers who have been entrusted with and are responsible for this mystical building, the Church? Rejoice, dearest sons, this is the way, old and new, of the Christian dispensation; this is the form which produces the true religious disciple of Christ, the apostle in His Church, and teacher of His brothers whether believers or not. Rejoice; our good will, indeed our very being, joined in communion with you, comforts and accompanies you.

And thus We should receive your particular deliberations—on the formation of your scholastics, on respect for the teaching and the authority of the Church, on the criteria of religious perfection, on the norms by which your apostolic activity and pastoral works are properly directed, on the correct interpretation of the decree of the Ecumenical Council, on the way by which they are to be put into effect, and on other matters of this kind—as the replies to the question We asked above. Yes, to be sure; the sons of St. Ignatius who are honored by the name of members of the Society of Jesus are still today faithful to themselves and to the Church! They are ready and strong! Arms that are used up and less efficient have been cast aside and they have new ones in their hands along with the same obedience, with the same spirit of dedication, with the same desire for spiritual victories.

2) And now the second question arises, that of determining the relationship of your Society to the Church and in a special way to the Holy See. There is a second question which We can almost read on your lips: does the Church, does the successor of St. Peter, think that the Society of Jesus is still their special and most faithful militia? Do they think this is the religious family which has proposed as its particular purpose not so much one or other Gospel virtue to be cherished, but rather has set out, as a guardian and stronghold to defend and promote the Catholic Church itself and the Apostolic See? Are the goodwill, trust, protec-

tion which it has always enjoyed still assured? Does the Church assert through the mouth of him who speaks to you now that it still needs and is honored by the militant ministry of the Society of Jesus? Is the Society still strong and suitable for the work of such widespread and such diverse apostolate of today? Here, my dear sons, is our reply: Yes! We have faith and we retain our faith in you; and thus We give you a mandate for your apostolic works; We show you our affection and gratitude; and We give you our blessing.

In this solemn and historic hour you have confirmed with your new proposals that you wish to cling very closely to your Institute, which, when the restorative work of the Council of Trent burned bright, put itself at the service of the Catholic Church. Thus it is easy and enjoyable for us to repeat the words and acts of our predecessors at this time which is different but no less a time of renewal of the life of the Church, following the Second Vatican Council. It is a joy for us to assure you that as long as your Society will be intent on striving for excellence in sound doctrine and in holiness of religious life and will offer itself as a most effective instrument for the defense and spread of the Catholic Faith, this Apostolic See, and with it, certainly the whole Church, will hold it most dear.

If you continue to be what you have been, our esteem, and our confidence in you will not be lacking.

And the people of God will feel the same about you. For what was the mysterious cause that carried your Society to such great growth and success if not your particular spiritual formation and your canonical structure? And if this formation and structure remain the same and flourish in ever-new strength, virtues and works, the hope for your progressive increase and perennial effectiveness in preaching the Gospel and building modern society is not in vain. Are not the structure of your evangelical and religious life, your history and your character, by which you have been an example to others, your best argument and the most persuasive note of credit to your apostolate? And is it not on this spiritual, moral and ecclesiastical firmness that confidence in your work and also in your collaboration is founded? Permit us to say toward the close of this address that We place great hope in you. The Church needs your help, and is happy and proud to receive it from sincere and dedicated sons as you are. The Church accepts the promise of your work and the offer of your life; and since you are soldiers of Christ, it calls you and commits you to difficult and sacred struggles in His name, today, more than ever.

Do you not see how much support the faith needs today, what open adherence, what clear exposition, what tireless preaching, what erudite explanation, how much testimony full of love and generosity?

Do you not see what opportunities are furnished by modern ecumenism to the servant and apostle of the holy Catholic Church for happily creating close relationships with others, for entering prudently into discussions, for patiently proposing explanations, for enlarging the field of charity?

Who is better suited than you to devote study and effort in order that our separated brethren may know and understand us, may listen to us and with us share the glory, the joy, and the service of the mystery of unity in Christ our Lord?

As for the infusion of Christian principles in the modern world as described in the now celebrated pastoral constitution *Gaudium et Spes,* will it not find among you able, prudent and strong specialists? And will not the devotion which you show to the Sacred Heart be still a most effective instrument in contributing to the spiritual and moral renewal of this world that the Second Vatican Council has urged, and to accomplishing fruitfully the mission entrusted to you to confront atheism?

Will you not dedicate yourselves with new zeal to the education of youth in secondary schools and universities, whether ecclesiastical or civil, something which has always been for you a cause of high praise and eminent merit? You should keep in mind that you have been entrusted with many young persons who one day will be able to render precious service to the Church and to human society, if they have received a sound formation.

And what shall we say of the missions? These missions where so many of your members labor admirably, bend every effort, put up with hardships and strive to make the name of Jesus shine forth like the sun of salvation, are they not entrusted to you by this apostolic see as they were once to Francis Xavier, in the assurance of having in you heralds of the faith sure and daring, full of the charity that your interior life renders inexhaustible, comforting and beyond expression.

And finally, what about the world? This ambivalent world which has two faces: the one is that of the compact entered into by all who turn from light and grace; the other, that of the vast human family for which the Father sent His Son and for which the Son sacrificed Himself. This world of today is so powerful and so weak, so hostile and so well disposed; does not this world call you and us to itself, imploring and urging us to a task to be fulfilled? Does not this world, groaning and trembling in this place, in the sight of Christ, now cry out to all of you: "Come, come; the longing and the hunger of Christ await you; come, for it is time."

Yes it is time, my dear sons; Go forth in faith and ardor; Christ chooses you, the Church sends you, the Pope blesses you.

3. APPROVAL BY THE SUPREME PONTIFF OF THE DECREES OF THE 31st GENERAL CONGREGATION ON RELIGIOUS POVERTY AND ON THE GRATUITY OF OUR MINISTRIES

June 6, 1966

Secretariat of State of His Holiness

N. 73533

The Vatican

June 6, 1966

Most Reverend Father:

After the 31st General Congregation of the Society of Jesus, you sent to the Holy Father on July 10 of last year a very gracious letter containing the text of the decrees on religious poverty and on the gratuity of ministries which had been passed by an almost unanimous consent. In that letter you recounted the whole matter and in the name of your members you asked that the Holy Father approve those decrees by his favorable consent.

Since—as you wrote—the norms contained in the "Formula of the Institute" and approved by Julius III of venerated memory in the apostolic letter "Exposcit Debitum" on July 21, 1550, needed to be adapted to current circumstances, your General Congregation, desirous of declaring the meaning of the aforementioned Formula, decreed that it was allowable for the members of the Society of Jesus to accept Mass stipends (n.2), to receive honoraria which might be offered on the occasion of spiritual ministries but that they could not demand them (n.3), and that for other works undertaken by them (which were not considered strictly spiritual ministries) they could earn a recompense as a fruit of their abilities and their labor. (nn. 4-5).

The General Congregation wanted to submit these decrees to His Holiness, since these new regulations approved by the Congregation seemed to depart from the letter of the aforementioned Formula or to exceed the power of the General Congregation, by reason of the Formula, to declare the meaning of "what could be doubtful in . . . the Institute, including this Formula."

After carefully considering the matter, and after taking into account those conditions which in our times the nature of the ministry and the difficulties of providing for sustenance have brought on, with the advice of His Eminence, Ildebrando Cardinal Antoniutti, Prefect of the Sacred Congregation of Religious, His Holiness approves and confirms the decrees which you proposed for his examination, abrogating all prescriptions, even if they be worthy of special mention, which are contrary to those decrees. Therefore the "Formula of the Institute" will in this matter in the future be interpreted according to the intention of those decrees which were passed by the General Congregations and approved by Pope Paul VI.

As I gladly take care to let you know of this, so also I inform you that the Holy Father very lovingly imparts to you and to the whole Society of Jesus the apostolic blessing as a token of the gifts of God and as a sign of his good will.

I wish also to take the opportunity to acknowledge myself, as is appropriate,

Devotedly yours:

A. G. Cardinal Cicognani

4. LETTER OF CARDINAL I. ANTONIUTTI

Sacred Congregation of Religious

Prot.N. 6995/66   Rome, November 12, 1966

Most Reverend Father:

This Sacred Congregation has carefully considered the request which your reverence sent to us in your letter of October 30 on the question of whether the General Congregation of the Society of Jesus whose second session is now going on fulfills those requirements which in the apostolic letter "Ecclesiae Sanctae" are set down regarding the special Chapter demanded by the Norms (II.3) The response to the question is:

AFFIRMATIVE, since the second session of the General Congregation is being held after October 11, 1966, on which date the norms began to go into effect which were to carry out the decree "Perfectae Caritatis" of the Second Vatican Council.

This session fully complies with the requirements that a special Chapter be held in accord with the aforementioned norms.

As I inform you of this, I also express my deepest hopes that the decisions and the proposals of the members of the General Congregation will turn out to the good of the Church and of the renowned Society of Jesus, to the greater glory of God.

Devotedly yours in Christ,

Cardinal Antoniutti, Prefect.

5. LETTER OF THE 31st GENERAL CONGREGATION TO THE SUPREME PONTIFF

Most Holy Father:

Our 31st General Congregation, happily bringing to an end its two sessions of hard work, rejoices in this opportunity to express to you its deepest feelings and to give you heart-felt thanks for the good will which you showed to us when, as we began our work, you received us in audience and inspired us with a fatherly address and when now, after you have followed our labors with your counsel and your prayers, you wished to bring them to a climax with today's concelebration as a sacred seal.

We well know that we can do nothing more pleasing to you than to offer to you the decrees which we have passed in our General Congregation, religiously following the prescriptions of the Second Vatican Council. We want the Society of Jesus in our age most faithfully to carry out that mission which Ignatius took on among the people of God, eagerly to serve the Church of Christ under the Roman Pontiff. The Society will carefully adapt its apostolic ministries both to the wishes of the Holy See and to today's needs, fulfilling in the first place that responsibility to resist atheism with united force which you have in a special way wished to ask of us.

To this end we have taken care to adapt our laws to the new needs of our times. But at the same time, mindful that the effectiveness of our apostolate intimately depends upon our union with Christ, we have tried to renew and encourage the religious life of the Society.

May God grant that we fully put into practice our proposals and that the Society always be for you, Most Holy Father, and for the whole Catholic hierarchy, a strong support in the works of the apostolate. We do not deny that because of human weakness we have sometimes failed in that fidelity which we have promised to the Church and to the Roman Pontiff, and we are sincerely sorry that even from our members have come causes of anguish to you. But your apostolic blessing will ask for us from the Lord the abundant graces by which we shall be able to work better, in a more holy way, more effectively for the glory of God and the good of souls.

Rome, November 16, 1966.

D.

MEMBERS OF THE
31st GENERAL CONGREGATION

President:

To May 22, 1965: Rev. Fr. John L. Swain

From May 22, 1965: Very Rev. Fr. Pedro Arrupe

ASSISTANTS AND PROVINCIALS

SURNAME AND NAME	TITLE TO MEMBERSHIP
1. P. Severianus Azcona	*Assist. Hispaniae*
2. P. Albertus Moreno	*Assist. Am. Lat. Sept.*
3. P. Franciscus a B. Vizmanos	*Prov. Castell.*
4. P. Petrus van Gestel	*Assist. Germaniae*
5. P. Leo Rosa	*Prov. Ven. Med.*
6. P. Ioannes B. Rocha	*Assist. Am. Lat. Mer.*
7. P. Hieronymus G. D'Souza	*Assist. Indiae*
8. P. Iacobus Martegani	*Assist. Italiae*
9. P. Nicolaus Junk	*Prov. Germ. Inf.*
10. P. Ioannes Richard	*Prov. Mont. Reg.*
11. P. Ioannes R. Boylen	*Prov. Austral.*
12. P. Haroldus O. Small	*Assist. Americae*
13. P. Ioannes J. Foley	*Prov. Wiscon.*
14. P. Ioannes L. Swain	*Vic. Gen., Assist. Angliae*
15. P. Carolus O'Conor	*Prov. Hib.*
16. P. Antonius Kušmierz	*Prov. Polon. Min.*
17. P. Petrus Arrupe	*Prov. Iaponiae*
18. P. Iosephus Oñate	*Assist. Asiae Orient.*
19. P. Carolus Fank	*Prov. Germ. Sup.*
20. P. Iacobus I. Shanahan	*Prov. Buffal.*
21. P. Franciscus Burkhardt	*Prov. Extr. Or.*
22. P. Caecilius E. Lang	*Prov. Neo-Aurel.*
23. P. Stephanus Pillain	*Assist. Galliae*
24. P. Ioannes B. Sehnem	*Prov. Bras. Mer.*
25. P. Ioannes A. McGrail	*Prov. Detr.*
26. P. Iosephus A. de Sobrino	*Prov. Baet.*
27. P. Lucius Craveiro da Silva	*Prov. Lusit.*
28. P. Iosephus Emman. Vélaz	*Prov. Loyol.*
29. P. Ioannes Terpstra	*Prov. Neerl.*
30. P. Carolus Guaschetti	*Prov. Taur.*
31. P. Ludovicus De Genova	*Prov. Patn.*
32. P. Stephanus Dzierżek	*Prov. Pol. Mai.*

33.	P. Victor Mertens	*Prov. Afr. Centr.*
34.	P. Eduardus Briceño	*Prov. Colomb. Or.*
35.	P. Ioannes R. Connery	*Prov. Chicag.*
36.	P. Eduardus Mann	*Prov. Bombay.*
37.	P. Vitus Fortier	*Prov. Quebec.*
38.	P. Linus I. Thro	*Prov. Missour.*
39.	P. Ioannes V. O'Connor	*Prov. Novae Angl.*
40.	P. Ioannes F. X. Connolly	*Prov. Calif.*
41.	P. Ludovicus González	*Prov. Tolet.*
42.	P. Eduardus Ramírez	*Prov. Colomb. Occid.*
43.	P. Iosephus Aldunate	*Prov. Chil.*
44.	P. Ioannes I. Kelley	*Prov. Oregon.*
45.	P. Horatius de la Costa	*Prov. Philipp.*
46.	P. Ioannes I. McGinty	*Prov. Neo Ebor.*
47.	P. Armandus Gargiulo	*Prov. Neapol.*
48.	P. Franciscus Lacourt	*Prov. Gall. Sept.*
49.	P. Iulius Caesar Federici	*Prov. Rom.*
50.	P. Eugenius d'Oncieu	*Prov. Gall. Medit.*
51.	P. Georgius Ducoin	*Prov. Gall. Atlant.*
52.	P. Andreas Varga	*Subst. Prov. Hungar.*
53.	P. Ioannes M. Daley	*Prov. Maryl.*
54.	P. Daniel Villanova	*Prov. Siculae*
55.	P. Iosephus Hoing	*Prov. Belg. Sept.*
56.	P. Philippus Laurent	*Prov. Paris.*
57.	P. Ignatius Rentería	*Prov. Mex. Sept.*
58.	P. Gunterus Soballa	*V. Prov. Germ. Or.*
59.	P. Ioannes Schasching	*Prov. Austr.*
60.	P. Franciscus Crick	*Prov. Ranch.*
61.	P. Angelus Tejerina	*Prov. Legion.*
62.	P. Raphael Gómez Pérez	*Prov. Mex. Mer.*
63.	P. Hippolytus Salvo	*Prov. Argent.*
64.	P. Angus I. MacDougall	*Prov. Can. Super.*
65.	P. Antonius Aquino	*Prov. Bras. Centr.*
66.	P. Ioannes Mª Varaprasadam	*Prov. Madur.*
67.	P. Philippus Franchimont	*Prov. Belg. Mcr.*
68.	P. Petrus Ribas	*Prov. Tarrac.*
69.	P. Ioannes Gualb. Fuček	*Prov. Croat.*
70.	P. Marianus Madurga	*Prov. Aragon.*
71.	P. Terentius Corrigan	*Prov. Angliae*

ELECTORS

72.	P. Franciscus Robinson	*Elect. Mex. Sept.*
73.	P. Ioachimus Salaverri	*Elect. Legion.*
74.	P. Ioannes B. Kozèlj	*Elect. Croat.*
75.	P. Victor Iriarte	*Elect. Venezol.*
76.	P. Gulielmus I. Murphy	*Elect. Novae Angl.*
77.	P. Andreas C. Smith	*Elect. Neo-Aurel.*

78.	P. Melchior M. Balaguer	*Elect. Bombay.*
79.	P. Iosephus D. O'Brien	*Elect. Californ.*
80.	P. Isidorus Gríful	*Elect. Uruquar.*
81.	P. Antonius Romañá	*Elect. Tarrac.*
82.	P. Emmanuel Crowther	*Elect. Ceylon.*
83.	P. Paulus Dezza	*Elect. Ven.-Med.*
84.	P. Eduardus Bulanda	*Elect. Polon. Mai.*
85.	P. Iosephus Ant. de Aldama	*Elect. Baeticae*
86.	P. Ioannes Murray	*Elect. Angliae*
87.	P. Aemilius Ugarte	*Elect. Madur.*
88.	P. Ioannes-Mª Le Blond	*Elect. Gall. Sept .*
89.	P. Franciscus Xav. Baeza	*Elect. Castell.*
90.	P. Leo A. Cullum	*Elect. Philipp.*
91.	P. Henricus Klein	*Elect. Germ. Orient.*
92.	P. Aemilius Sogni	*Elect. Taurin.*
93.	P. Antonius Messineo	*Elect. Siculae*
94.	P. Ioannes C. Ford	*Elect. Novae Angl.*
95.	P. Petrus Abellán	*Elect. Tolet.*
96.	P. Emmanuel González	*Elect. Iapon.*
97.	P. Aloisius Renard	*Elect. Belg. Merid.*
98.	P. Iosephus F. Gallen	*Elect. Maryl.*
99.	P. Ferdinandus Barón	*Elect. Colomb. Or.*
100.	P. Iacobus Goussault	*Elect. Gall. Atlant.*
101.	P. Aloysius Del Zotto	*Elect. Keral.*
102.	P. Ieremias Hogan	*Elect. Austral.*
103.	P. Armandus Cardoso	*Elect. Bras. Centr.*
104.	P. Franciscus Xav. Mejía	*Elect. Colomb. Occ.*
105.	P. Ioannes Laramée	*Elect. Mont. Reg.*
106.	P. Candidus Mazón	*Elect. Aragon.*
107.	P. Iosephus Ridruejo	*Elect. Peruv.*
108.	P. Iacobus I. McQuade	*Elect. Detroit.*
109.	P. Georgius E. Ganss	*Elect. Missour.*
110.	P. Iosephus M. Riaza	*Elect. Castell.*
111.	P. Albertus A. Lemieux	*Elect. Oregon.*
112.	P. Iacobus Alf	*Elect. Buffal.*
113.	P. Georgius Mirewicz	*Subst. Pol. Mai.*
114.	P. Dionysius T. Tobin	*Elect. Iamaic.*
115.	P. Laurentius Van Roey	*Elect. Ranchien.*
116.	P. Ioannes I. McMahon	*Elect. Neo-Ebor.*
117.	P. Clemens Pujol	*Elect. Tarrac.*
118.	P. Antonius Pinsker	*Elect. Austriae*
119.	P. Ioannes Hirschmann	*Elect. Germ. Infer.*
120.	P. Vincentius Monachino	*Elect. Roman.*
121.	P. Carolus Gomes	*Elect. Goa-Poonen.*
122.	P. Gulielmus P. Le Saint	*Elect. Chicag.*
123.	P. Gulielmus A. Crandell	*Elect. Neo-Aurel.*
124.	P. Albertus Giampieri	*Elect. Neapol.*

SURNAME AND NAME	TITLE TO MEMBERSHIP
125. P. Iesus Iturrioz	*Elect. Loyolen.*
126. P. Antonius Leite	*Elect. Lusitan.*
127. P. Victorius Marcozzi	*Elect. Ven.-Mediol.*
128. P. Gulielmus González	*Elect. Colomb. Or.*
129. P. Laurentius Fernandes	*Elect. Maduren.*
130. P. Rodericus Mackenzie	*Elect. Can. Super.*
131. P. Ansgarius Mueller	*Elect. Bras. Merid.*
132. P. Antonius Delchard	*Elect. Gall. Sept.*
133. P. Iesus Díaz de Acebedo	*Elect. Loyolen.*
134. P. Carolus McCarthy	*Elect. Extr. Orient.*
135. P. Victor Blajot	*Elect. Bolivian.*
136. P. Ioannes Bru	*Elect. Gall. Atlant.*
137. P. Paulus L. O'Connor	*Elect. Chicag.*
138. P. Arthurus F. Shea	*Elect. Philippin.*
139. P. Petrus Smulders	*Elect. Neerland.*
140. P. Simon Maas	*Elect. Neerland.*
141. P. Ioannes Colli	*Elect. Taurinen.*
142. P. Petrus Fransen	*Elect. Belg. Sept.*
143. P. Michael Elizondo	*Elect. Argentin.*
144. P. Emmanuel Acévez	*Elect. Mex. Sept.*
145. P. Franciscus I. Silva	*Elect. Calif.*
146. P. Ioannes I. Reed	*Elect. Buffalen.*
147. P. Fridericus Buuck	*Elect. Germ. Infer.*
148. P. Ignatius Gordon	*Elect. Baeticae*
149. P. Georgius P. Klubertanz	*Elect. Wiscons.*
150. P. Franciscus L. Martinsek	*Elect. Patnen.*
151. P. Gustavus Voss	*Elect. Iapon.*
152. P. Franc. von Tattenbach	*Elect. Germ. Sup.*
153. P. Augustinus Fimmers	*Elect. Belg. Sept.*
154. P. Eduardus Sheridan	*Elect. Can. Super.*
155. P. Henricus F. Birkenhauer	*Elect. Detroit.*
156. P. Ricardus Arès	*Elect. Mont. Reg.*
157. P. Petrus B. Velloso	*Elect. Bras. Centr.*
158. P. Miecislaus Bednarz	*Elect. Polon. Min.*
159. P. Sylvester Monteiro,	*Elect. Kanarien.*
160. P. Ansgarius Simmel	*Subst. Elect. Germ. S.*
161. P. Rogerius Troisfontaines	*Elect. Belg. Mer.*
162. P. Henricus Gutiérrez M.	*Elect. Mex. Mer.*
163. P. Gulielmus Maher	*Elect. Angliae*
164. P. Eduardus A. Sponga	*Elect. Maryland.*
165. P. Alphonsus Villalba	*Elect. Aequator.*
166. P. Mauritius Giuliani	*Elect. Parisien.*
167. P. Blasius Arminjon	*Elect. Gall. Medit.*
168. P. Antonius Mruk	*Subst. Pol. Min.*
169. P. Felix Litva	*Subst. Viceprov. Slovak.*
170. P. Emmanuel Antunes	*Elect, Lusitan.*
171. P. Ioannes Kerr	*Elect. Hibern.*

172.	P. Vincentius T. O'Keefe	*Elect. Neo-Ebor.*
173.	P. Robertus Tucci	*Elect. Neapol .*
174.	P. Herbertus Dargan	*Elect. Hong-Kong.*
175.	P. Carolus Orie	*Elect. Indones.*
176.	P. Brendanus Barry	*Elect. Hibern.*
177.	P. Salvator Fruscione	*Elect. Siculae*
178.	P. Emericus Coreth	*Elect. Austriae*
179.	P. Franciscus P. Kelly	*Elect. Australiae*
180.	P. Bernwardus Brenninkmeyer	*Elect. Germ. Or.*
181.	P. Franciscus Braganza	*Elect. Gujaraten.*
182.	P. Ioannes P. Leary	*Elect. Oregon.*
183.	P. Aloisius Achaerandio	*Elect. Centro-Am.*
184.	P. Michael A. Fiorito	*Elect. Argentin.*
185.	P. Eusebius García Manrique	*Elect. Arag.*
186.	P. Ferdinandus Larrain	*Elect. Chilen.*
187.	P. Ricardus M. Rosenfelder	*Elect. Patnen.*
188.	P. Mauritius Eminyan	*Elect. Melit.*
189.	P. Andreas Dupont	*Elect. Madecass.*
190.	P. Mauritius Rycx	*Elect. Afric. Centr.*
191.	P. Abdallah Dagher	*Elect. Prox. Or.*
192.	P. Petrus Beltrão	*Elect. Bras. Merid.*
193.	P. Henricus Portilla	*Elect. Maxic. Merid.*
194.	P. Parmananda C. A. Divarkar	*Elect. Bomb.*
195.	P. Lucas Verstraete	*Elect. Ranch.*
196.	P. Iosephus Arroyo	*Elect. Tolet.*
197.	P. Michael Rondet	*Elect. Gall. Medit.*
198.	P. Philippus Gentiloni	*Subst. Elect. Rom.*
199.	P. Lachlan Hughes	*Elect. Salisb.*
200.	P. Iosephus Ćurić	*Elect. Croat.*
201.	P. Antonius P. Roberts	*Elect. Jamshedpur.*
202.	P. Ioannes Calvez	*Elect. Paris.*
203.	P. Marcellus Azevedo	*Elect. Goian Min.*
204.	P. Hervaeus Carrier	*Elect. Quebec.*
205.	P. Iulianus Harvey	*Elect. Quebec.*
206.	P. Marius Schoenenberger	*Elect. Helvet.*
207.	P. Rodulfus de Roux	*Elect. Colomb. Occ.*
208.	P. Ioannes L. Thomas	*Elect. Wiscons.*
209.	P. Ignatius Iglesias	*Elect. Legion.*
210.	P. Geraldus Freitas	*Elect. Bras. Sept.*
211.	P. Paulus C. Reinert	*Elect. Missour.*
212.	P. Emmanuel Segura	*Elect. Paraquar.*
213.	P. Ioannes Ochagavía	*Elect. Chilens.*
214.	P. Paulus Shan	*Elect. Extr. Or.*
215.	P. Albertus Wautier	*Elect. Calcutt.*
216.	P. Fridericus Arvesú	*Elect. Antill.*
217.	P. Carolus Bresciani	*Elect. Bahiens.*
218.	P. Daniel Pasupasu	*Elect. Afr. Centr.*

OFFICIALS OF THE CURIA

219.	P. Iacobus W. Naughton	*Secr. Soc.*
220.	P. Romulus Durocher	*Oecon. Gen.*

PROCURATORS

221.	P. Thomas Byrne	*Subst. Assist. Angl.*
222.	P. Venceslaus F. Feřt	*Proc. Bohem. disp.*
223.	P. Paulus Mailleux	*Deleg. pro rit. Byzant.*
224.	P. Bruno Markaitis	*Proc. Lithuan. disp.*

THE 32nd GENERAL CONGREGATION
OF THE
SOCIETY OF JESUS

December 2, 1974—March 7, 1975

LETTER OF PROMULGATION
FROM FATHER GENERAL

To the Whole Society

Reverend Fathers and dear Brothers in Christ,
Pax Christi

The decrees of the Thirty-second General Congregation which the Supreme Pontiff had asked to be sent to him at the end of the Congregation so that he might consider them before their publication, he has recently returned to me through His Eminence, Jean Cardinal Villot, Secretary of State. Together with the decrees I received from Cardinal Villot on May 2 a letter and some special recommendations with regard to certain of the decrees, which the Holy Father sends to us in order that we might take account of them in putting the decrees into effect.*

Now therefore by this present letter I am sending the decrees of the Thirty-second General Congregation, in the name of the Congregation itself, to all the provinces, vice-provinces and missions, so that they might be published to all the houses of the Society in accord with the norms of the Formula of the General Congregation.¹ The decrees enter into force from the day of their promulgation, that is, from the date of this present letter, which is being sent along with the formal communication of the decrees.

The Supreme Pontiff, who followed the work of the Congregation "with keen, loving and personal concern,"²

---

*See page 545.
1 Form. Congr. Gen., n. 144, §2, 1°.
2 Letter from the Cardinal Secretary of State to Father General, May 2, 1975.

desires that these decrees "be put into effect according to the needs of the Society, with the hope that your worthy Jesuit brothers may draw strength from these decrees as they continue their progress in genuine fidelity to the charisma of St. Ignatius and the Formula of the Institute."[3]

The General Congregation itself was very solicitous about arranging for the implementation of these decrees. It asserted that they could not be put into practice without "the cooperation of all Jesuits under the leadership of their Superiors,"[4] and they thought it necessary for this that the documents be "commended to personal reading and community dialogue in a spirit of prayer and discernment."[5]

Only in this way can the decrees of the Thirty-second General Congregation be a strong instrument for that hoped-for renewal and adaptation of our Society to the contemporary needs of the Church and of the world. I would also ask, as far as I am concerned, that along with the decrees all will wish to consider with the greatest attention the documents of the Holy See which pertain to the Congregation, especially the address given by the Supreme Pontiff on December 3, 1974, and the recommendations which in his name are attached to the letter sent to us by His Eminence, the Cardinal Secretary of State on May 2.

In brief: it is our responsibility to put into practice with the greatest fidelity and with a ready disposition these decrees along with the recommendations of the Holy Father, so that what the General Congregation decided, with the Lord's inspiration and under the fatherly guidance of the Vicar of Christ on earth, may have happy results for our whole Society and for all those for whom the Society desires to work in the vineyard of the Lord.

---

3 Ibid.
4 GC 32, Introductory Decree, no. 10.
5 Ibid., no. 9.

With the intercession of Mary, Mother of the Society, let us try ardently to beg the Lord for a faithful fulfillment of the decrees.

I commend myself to your Sacrifices and prayers.

> *The servant of all of you*
> *in Christ,*
> *Pedro Arrupe*
> *General of the Society of Jesus*

Rome, May 8, 1975
Feast of the Ascension of Our Lord Jesus Christ

A.

HISTORICAL PREFACE

TO THE DECREES

OF THE 32nd GENERAL CONGREGATION

Excerpted from the Official Minutes of the Congregation

A.

HISTORICAL PREFACE
TO THE DECREES
OF THE 32nd GENERAL CONGREGATION

Excerpted from the Official Minutes of the Congregation

1. Steps Taken Prior to the Congregation Itself

The 32nd General Congregation was formally summoned by Very Reverend Father General Pedro Arrupe in his letter of September 8, 1973.[1] However, preparations for the Congregation had been going on long before its convocation, and the first steps in that preparation began already in 1970.

In the 65th Congregation of Procurators, September 17-October 6, 1970, Father General said that although the procurators had decided that a General Congregation was not immediately to be called, that is, within a year and a half, nonetheless he was aware that they had clearly enough indicated that a new General Congregation ought to be held within a few years because of the problems of contemporary change and that for such a Congregation there ought to be a longer preliminary preparation than Society law would allow in the case of a formal convocation of a Congregation by a decision of the procurators.[2] He therefore announced that such preparation was to begin immediately, and, indeed, that this preparation was to arise from an effort in depth and breadth to assimilate the Ig-

---

[1] *ActRSJ*, XVI, 109-115.
[2] " , XV, 613.

natian spirit, to engage in reflection in common and to experience a conversion of the whole Society. The General Congregation itself was to be, as it were, the final step or the juridical expression of such an effort.[3]

A few months later, after consultation with the provincials, Father General set up a preparatory commission of six members: Father Jean Calvez (Atlantic France Province) as chairman, along with Fathers Parmananda Divarkar (Bombay), Walter Farrell (Detroit), Johannes G. Gerhartz (Lower Germany), Luciano Mendes de Almeida (East Central Brazil), and Tomás Zamarriego (Toledo).[4] Over a period of almost three years this commission worked in preparing studies, with the help of almost thirty task forces, on those points which, as a result of consultations in the whole Society, it seemed necessary to treat, as well as in fostering reflection on those matters on the level both of communities and of provinces.

Several times in the course of those years, Father General himself wrote to the Society about the coming Congregation. Especially on December 25, 1971, he sent a letter about spiritual discernment to be used in common preparatory reflection.[5] Then on April 22, 1972, in light of the progress of this preparatory reflection, he announced that he had decided, with the approval of the Supreme Pontiff, that the Congregation of Provincials which would have been held in 1973 was not going to be called.[6]

In addition to this remote preparation the General was also seriously engaged, even after the calling of the Congregation, in its proximate preparation. He ordered that the Provincial Congregations should be completed before the end of April, 1974, in order that there might be for those called to be members of the Congregation a sufficiently

---

3 *ActRSJ*, XV, 616 and 620-621.
4   "   , XV, 631-634, 721, and 755.
5   "   , XV, 767-773.
6   "   , XV, 878.

long period of time available to spend on final preparations. The members were to be in Rome on December 1, 1974. As a result, therefore, the postulata sent by the Provincial Congregations could, toward the end of May, 1974 be arranged by topics and sent to all the members of the Congregation.

In accord with decree 38, n. 7, of the 31st General Congregation,[7] three preliminary committees were called to Rome to finish the preparatory work. Those committees dealt with poverty (toward the end of July), with studies (at the beginning of September), and with the preparation of a list of points which were first to be treated and with other final preparatory matters (from the 18th of November on).

2. The Beginning of the Congregation, the Regulations on Publicity and on Procedural Matters

(From the Minutes, Acta 1, 11, 15)

The General Congregation was convoked in Rome at the General Curia of the Society of Jesus.

Present in Rome on the designated day, December 1, 1974, were all the members of the Congregation except one, the elector of the vice-province of Rumania. In that vice-province, just as in four other provinces or vice-provinces (Hungary, Bohemia, Lithuania, and Slovakia), provincial congregations could not be held. However, there was one member of the General Congregation from each of these four places; he was appointed either by the major superior of the province or vice-province or by Father General according to the norms of the Formula of Provincial Congregations, no. 95, §§2-3.

Three procurators *ad negotia* were appointed by Father General as members of the Congregation from the province

---

7 *ActRSJ,* XIV, 970.

of New York[8] and one from the independent region of Cuba.

The first session was held on the morning of December 2, 1974. Father General began by reading a selection from Sacred Scripture on the action of the Holy Spirit in the Church. All immediately spent some time reflecting on these texts, and then the hymn *Veni Creator* was sung. After Father General had greeted the assembled members, they decided that the Congregation should not be delayed in waiting for the absent elector from the vice-province of Rumania. The Congregation by a unanimous vote then formally declared itself fully and legitimately in session.

After that, the first action taken was to approve of simultaneous translations from the plenary sessions. From this point on, during the whole Congregation there were simultaneous translations from six languages (English, French, German, Spanish, Italian, and Latin) into three languages (English, French, and Spanish). Approximately twenty Fathers and Scholastics worked tirelessly in taking turns as translators under the direction of Father Nicolás Rodríguez Verástegui (Léon).

Father General then spoke at length on the responsibilities of the Congregation, on the great expectations which the members of the Society had, about the attitude of spiritual discernment and prayer to be employed in the Congregation, and on the fundamental motive of our hope, a motive thoroughly theological and in accord with the Spiritual Exercises of St. Ignatius and the Constitutions.

Following this, the Congregation turned to the approval of the regulations for public information proposed by Father General: it set up the Office of Information under the direction of Father Donald Campion (New York). During the whole Congregation this office prepared and published news releases in five languages—English, French, German,

---

8 *ActRSJ*, XV, 103.

Spanish, and Italian. The Congregation also appointed a group of delegates who would exercise supervision over the Office of Information. Provisionally, the group was made up of five Fathers designated by Father General: Fathers Stefan Bamberger (Switzerland), William Daniel (Australia), Julien Harvey (French Canada), Juan Ochagavía (Chile), and Roberto Tucci (Naples). After two weeks they received definitive appointments, and Fathers Tomás Zamarriego (Toledo) and Stefan Moysa-Rosochacki (Lesser Poland) were added as members.

Provisionally and experimentally the "Additions" to the procedural formula (the "rules of order") were approved. They had been worked out before the Congregation and sent to the members before they arrived in Rome. These additions rounded out the Formula of the General Congregation without changing it. If one looks at the norms of procedure which were used in the 31st General Congregation,[9] these present additions introduced certain new practices especially through the use of small groups of members, set up by language (often two languages) or by Assistancy. These groups were used at the beginning of deliberations on matters of greater moment before those matters came to the Aula (where the Congregation held its plenary sessions) for further and final action. The "Additions" also provided that at the beginning of its work the Congregation would decide upon a list of points to be treated first in order of priority in such a way that no other points would be brought up for deliberation by the Congregation as a whole except by a new explicit decision. After some weeks these "Additions" were definitively approved for this present Congregation after they had been slightly modified in accord with suggestions from the procedural commission and from some members of the Congregation.

At the end of the first session the Congregation decided that five Fathers who were not members would be admitted

---

9 See *ActRSJ,* 819-820.

to the meetings of the full Congregation in order to help the secretary of the Congregation in the difficult task of writing the Minutes (the "Acta") of the Congregation.

Later, before noon, meetings of the Assistancy groups were held in order to confer on names for elections to be held by the whole Congregation for Secretary, for his assistants, and for members of the deputations on the state of the Society and on the screening of postulata.

That evening at the Gesù a Mass was concelebrated by all of the members of the Congregation. Hundreds of other Jesuits living in Rome also participated. This was the first of the liturgical celebrations which, along with a variety of groups which gathered for common prayer, became in a way a new characteristic of this Congregation. Every day around noon the Eucharist was celebrated in various languages. In addition there were other special Eucharistic celebrations which took place in the course of the Congregation. Also in the first three days of the Congregation, a fair amount of time was left free especially in order that the delegates might spend time in prayer and spiritual reflection. Material for this prayer and reflection was presented by Father General himself.

3. The Address of the Supreme Pontiff to the Members of the Congregation, and Further Communications from Him to the Congregation

(From the Minutes, Acta 6, 10, 11, 15, 25, 26, 29, 30, 54, 55, 61, 63)

On the following day, December 3, the Feast of St. Francis Xavier, the Supreme Pontiff, Paul VI, graciously received the Fathers of the Congregation in audience and gave a very important address on the affairs of the Society.[10]

It is helpful to recall here that already before the Con-

---

10 See pp. 519-536 below.

gregation he had expressed his mind on its importance and his expectations, desires, even his will. This he did in letters, both at Easter, 1972, when he first received the announcement that a Congregation was to be called, and on September 15, 1973, at the time of its formal convocation.[11] In the same way, the Holy Father wished to follow its work most attentively throughout its whole course.

Before the Congregation, the postulata sent to it were candidly put before him, and he received Father General in audience on November 21, 1974. Throughout the whole time of the Congregation Father General endeavored to inform him regularly of what was taking place in it.

On his part, on the same day, December 3, on which he received the members of the Congregation in audience, the Supreme Pontiff sent through the Secretary of State a letter[12] in which he let Father General know his mind about the innovation by which the fourth vow might be extended to all members of the Society, even those who were not priests (see n. 15 *infra*). In the course of the month of December he again let Father General know his mind.

Toward the end of January, when he had been informed of the actions of the Congregation in treating of this matter with a view to a possible "representation" (see n. 15 *infra*), the Supreme Pontiff asked for an account of the reasons which had thus moved the Congregation. At the same time he ordered the Congregation to forego any deliberations which could be opposed to the norms contained in his letter of September 15, 1973, and in his address of December 3, 1974. In particular they were to do nothing contrary to what he had made clear in the letter of December 3 from the Secretary of State.

---

11 *ActRSJ,* XV, 827-829 (Letter of the Cardinal Secretary of State, April 18, 1972); *ActRSJ,* XVI, 11-15 (Autograph letter of the Supreme Pontiff, September 15, 1973).

12 See pp. 537-538 below.

After he had received that account, the Supreme Pontiff sent an autograph letter to Father General on February 15, 1975, in which he confirmed that no change could be introduced relative to the fourth vow. He asked the members of the Congregation again to give most careful consideration to what decisions were to be made in the light of his previous letters and of his address of December 3, 1974, and he requested that decisions already made by the Congregation or soon to be made should be sent to him before their publication.[13] He further explained himself in an audience with Father General on February 20. He expressed fear lest the Congregation would give less weight to those matters concerned with the renewal of the spiritual life and of religious life, lest it look at the problems of the promotion of justice in a socio-economic aspect, in a way that is less in conformity with the proper nature of the Society which is a sacerdotal order, and lest it give insufficient care to correcting certain lamentable deviations in doctrinal and disciplinary matters which had in recent years often been manifested with respect to the magisterium and the hierarchy.

On each of these points referred to by the Supreme Pontiff the Congregation entered into long reflection and prayerful meditation, and it accepted them in a spirit of deep faith and obedience. One can consider, in several points later to be indicated and in the decrees themselves, how the Congregation attempted to meet the expectations of the Supreme Pontiff.

4. Elections and Appointments to the Principal Offices of the Congregation

(From the Minutes, Acta 2, 3, 4, 5)

For the beginning of the Congregation, the following are still to be mentioned.

---

13 See pp. 539-541 below.

On December 4, Father Johannes G. Gerhartz (Lower Germany) was duly elected Secretary of the Congregation. Fathers Luciano Mendes de Almeida (East Central Brazil) and Simon Decloux (Southern Belgium) were elected Sub-Secretaries.

The following were elected to the deputation on the state of the Society from their respective Assistancies: African, Father Pasupasu (Central Africa); American, Father Michael Buckley (California); Southern Latin American, Father Laercio Dias de Moura (East Central Brazil); Northern Latin American, Father Enrique Gutiérrez (Mexico); English, Father Simon Decloux (Southern Belgium); East Asian, Father Benigno Mayo (Philippines); French, Father Claude Viard (Mediterranean France); German, Father Bernward Brenninkmeyer (East Germany); Spanish, Father Urbano Valero (Castile); Indian, Father Casimir Gnanadickam (Madurai); Italian, Father Paolo Molinari (Turin); Slavic, Father Petar Galauner (Croatia). These twelve members, along with Father General and the four General Assistants, made up the deputation on the state of the Society.

As deputies for the screening of postulata, the following were elected from their respective Assistancies: African, Father Philibert Randriambololona (Madagascar); American, Father Robert Mitchell (New York); Southern Latin American, Father Juan Ochagavía (Chile); Northern Latin American, Father Federico Arvesú (Antilles); English, Father Cecil McGarry (Ireland); East Asian, Father Horacio de la Costa (Philippines); French, Father André Costes (Mediterranean France); German, Father Peter Huizing (Netherlands); Spanish, Father Manuel Segura (Baetica); Indian, Father José Aizpún (Gujarat); Italian, Father Carlo Martini (Turin); Slavic, Father Tadeusz Koczwara (Greater Poland).

Then, in order to set up the President's Council *(Consilium Praesidis),* the deputation on the state of the Society

353

elected from among the members Father Jean Calvez; the deputation for screening postulata likewise elected Father Cecil McGarry. The Secretary of the Congregation was *ex officio* a member of that Council. In accord with the "Additions" to the norms of procedure, to these three were added two other members whom Father General (the presiding officer) with his council named as "Moderators" (to help him by presiding over sessions when he so designated them). They were Fathers Robert Mitchell and Roberto Tucci. Father Jean Calvez, already a member of the council, was also named a "Moderator."

5. Selection of topics "to be treated first"

(*From the Minutes,* Acta 6, 7, 8, 9, 10, 12, 13, 14)

Taking into consideration the suggestions produced by the preliminary preparatory committee near the end of November, the Congregation on December 9 and 10 set to work in small groups made up of members able to deal with a particular language or languages and in Assistancy gatherings to determine which topics were to have priority of treatment. The discussion continued in plenary session on December 11 and 12, and finally the matter came to a vote. Out of the forty-six proposed topics on the list, each of the following six got better than half of the votes (in order of number of votes obtained): the criteria of our apostolic service today; the "mission" of the Society as drawn from its apostolic character and purpose; poverty, in its more institutional or juridical aspects; the promotion of justice as a criterion of our life and apostolate; the fourth vow and its relation to the Church and to the hierarchy; formed members of the Society.

Then, at the proposal of certain members, the Congregation agreed to decide, besides, on a first priority or on a priority of priorities, in the sense that it would from the beginning be treated in a rather special manner. As this type of first priority the Congregation selected two topics together, namely, the criteria of our apostolic service today and the promotion of justice. It was thereupon decided to spend two or three days immediately in considering these topics in language groups, in Assistancy meetings, and in plenary sessions. This was done from December 13 to 20 (cf. n. 11 *infra*).

6. The Commissions of the Congregation

(*From the Minutes,* Acta 2, 8, 10, 17, 18)

Although in its first days the Congregation had decided that Father General should set up the necessary commissions along with the deputation for screening postulata, the greater part of them could not be established until decisions had been made on what topics to treat first. However, two special commissions were organized previous to this. They were the commissions on juridical matters (five members) and on procedural matters (seven members).

The commissions to deal with substantive matters (*"ad paranda negotia"*) were set up after the discussion on priorities. There were ten of them, each with a fairly large membership of from fifteen to thirty as circumstances dictated.

I: The criteria of our apostolate today
II: Mission and apostolic obedience
III: Poverty
IV: The promotion of justice
V: The fourth vow and relationships with the Church and the hierarchy
VI: Formed members
VII: Formation of Jesuits
VIII: Spiritual life, community life, and union
IX: Government and Congregations
X: Final incorporation and tertianship

At the same time a kind of inter-commission on the identity and charism of the Society was established, made up of members of several commissions. As the Congregation went on, certain other groups or commissions or sub-commisions were set up: on the educational apostolate, on the institutions of higher studies in Rome which are the responsibility of the whole Society, on chastity, on inculturation, on the implementation of the Congregation. Near the end of February, a special committee was also established, made up of four members of the Congregation and of the four General Assistants, the task of which was to compare the documents already prepared by the Congregation with the things asked for in the letter and in the address of the Supreme Pontiff. Most of these groups submitted reports to the consideration and approval of the Congregation just as other commissions did. However, the group which dealt with the institutions of higher studies in Rome submitted their conclusions only to Father General and to a special meeting of provincials, without the Congregation being able to deal with the materials because of lack of time. The sub-commission on the educational apostolate produced two reports, but there was no deliberation on them in the meetings of the full Congregation; this group, however, was able to work at preparing a paragraph on education for the decree on our mission today. The group dealing with chastity worked together with the eighth commission, and in addition gave to Father General for his ordinary government some useful observations on the matter. The commission on implementation of the Congregation's decisions prepared material which afterwards was further worked out in Assistancy meetings.

As for the commissions, it should be added that gradually it became clear that those rather large ones which had been set up at the beginning were laboring under some difficulty. Hence, on January 14, 1975, the Congregation decided that a small editorial committee should be elected for each commission by its members, with the provision that when

356

the definitive revised report *(relatio secunda)* which the editorial committee had prepared was to be presented, the whole commission would present its judgment on it at the same time.

Besides these ordinary commissions, the Congregation had recourse to "Definitors of the second type" in order to deal with postulata on the Formula of the Provincial Congregation, except for the question of active and passive voice (the capability of voting or being voted for) in the election of delegates to such a Congregation. That point the Congregation wanted to deal with itself in the usual manner (see n. 20 *infra*).

7. Examination of the State of the Society

(From the Minutes, Acta 2, 3, 8, 11, 15)

Before going on to recount the history of the individual position papers prepared by the commissions, in the order in which the decrees are here published, something should be said about the examination of the state of the Society. The Congregation placed great importance on this examination. It wanted consideration to be given both to the positive elements of recent change which ought to be favored, those elements, that is, which would give promise of great future results, and to the negative elements for which a remedy ought to be supplied.

The discussions began in the small language groups (December 6 and 9). After that, the principal points which were therein proposed were put in order and a preliminary report was distributed (December 16). The Assistancy groups and individual members of the Congregation then had time to hand in their comments. The remarks received were put together and distributed on December 22. At that, the deputation set to work at its own specific task and prepared a report which put together both the negative and the positive elements with which at least the majority of the deputation agreed (December 30).

On January 2 there was an explanatory session in the Aula. On that day Father General presented to the delegates his own opinion on the state of the Society, and at the same time he provided information on relations with the Supreme Pontiff and with the Holy See. Whatever questions the members of the Congregation wished to ask about all these matters Father General freely and fully answered.

As can be seen further on in this history, many of the topics which arose in this examination of the state of the Society were later brought up and treated as the documents of the Congregation were prepared and as several of the documents became decrees, for example in the introductory decree (Decree 1), in the decree on fidelity to the magisterium and the Supreme Pontiff (Decree 3), in the decrees on the formation of Jesuits, on the union of minds and hearts, on poverty . . . (Decrees 6, 11, 12).

8.   The Introductory Decree

(From the Minutes, Acta 61, 64, 70, 71, 72, 79, 81, 82, 83)

The introductory decree (Decree 1) had its origin in the work of the committee (see n. 6 above) set up toward the end of February, 1975, to compare the texts still in process with the letters which had been received from the Supreme Pontiff and with the address he had given on December 3. After careful consideration the committee judged that almost all the points indicated by the Supreme Pontiff were to be found in the documents being prepared by the commissions, even though those documents were still in rather different stages of being worked out. They thought this all the more the case if, as was proper, these decrees in preparation were taken together with the decrees of the 31st General Congregation, to which the present assembly often

358

referred with the intention of explicitly confirming them. The members of this committee also judged that it would be opportune for the documents of the present Congregation to be preceded by a prefatory decree which would contain three points: 1) a confirmation of the 31st General Congregation; 2) a reaffirmation of the principal essential points about the Society which had been emphasized by the Supreme Pontiff; 3) an introduction to the decrees of the present Congregation which looked to implementation. They prepared a text as an example; it was discussed in the Assistancy meetings and in the Aula. Not a few amendments were suggested.

So a second report was prepared, which took into account the previous discussions and which contained in a shorter form the same three points, but especially with an alternative version of the second point. With this in front of them, the members of the Congregation voted on March 5 that there was to be an introductory decree. They decided that the text of the second report was to be used as a basis for that decree, but was to be again revised and put in finished form through amendments. The revised text, along with the amendments, was proposed for a final vote on March 7, and the present decree was definitively passed in the second session on that day.

In its final form the introductory decree confirms the 31st General Congregation, gives thanks to God for the progress which the Society has made, and expresses sorrow at the resistance on the part of some to a desirable renewal and also at the exaggerations on the part of some others. It sincerely recognizes the defects pointed out by the Holy Father and reaffirms in accord with his mind that the Society is a priestly, apostolic, and religious body bound to the Supreme Pontiff by a special vow regarding missions. It seeks a deeper renewal and a closer unity among ourselves and with the Supreme Pontiff. Finally, it introduces the other decrees and stresses the need for their spiritual assimilation and practical implementation.

9. The Declaration "Jesuits Today"

(From the Minutes, Acta 10, 47, 48, 65, 66, 73, 81)

This document (Decree 2) is the fruit of the last phase of the Congregation's work. It was not until the end of December, 1974, that the previously announced inter-commission (see n. 6) on identity and charisma was set up. Its first task was to gather together from the work of the various commissions the principal points which might be especially significant in delineating our charism for today. Then it had to put them together in a single document which might furnish a description of the identity of a Jesuit as it would emerge from the present Congregation.

As the work of many of the commissions went forward, it became possible for the inter-commission to give to the Congregation on February 12 a first report. It provided as examples seven different possible formats for setting forth our identity today (a declaration, confession, profession of faith, offering or oblation, contemporary reading of the Formula of the Institute . . .) After the question was considered in the language groups and in the Aula, the Congregation first decided that some document on identity should be developed. Then it selected from among the various possibilities the format of a declaration which would express in a rather new way "what it meant today to be a Jesuit."

After almost one hundred suggestions had been considered, a definite text was prepared. The editors then accepted informal "friendly amendments" to it. Some formal amendments were also proposed, but the Congregation accepted only a few of these. Finally on March 1 the Declaration passed almost unanimously. However, it had to be modified in one particular. A formal "intercession" took place; the Congregation agreed to it, and so the words "human liberation" were changed in n. 11 to the present text, "the total and integral liberation of man, leading to participation in the life of God himself."

Another "intercession" was approved. Previously, the Congregation had decided that the English text was to be regarded as the official version. Now on March 6 it decided that the Latin text would be the official one, and that the English text would be the original to which reference was to be made in preparing translations.

10. Fidelity to the Magisterium and the Supreme Pontiff

(*From the Minutes,* Acta 42, 43, 44, 76, 79-83)

At the beginning of the Congregation, Commission V received the postulata which dealt both with the meaning and significance of the fourth vow and with the three points of fidelity to the magisterium, the way of acting by Jesuits in doctrinal matters and censures. All of these topics had obvious multiple interconnections. Since the question of the meaning and significance of the fourth vow was among those topics listed as priority items the Commission presented a first report in which as far as possible it dealt separately with the fourth vow, on one hand, and, on the other, with the other questions for which it had responsibility.

When the part of the report which dealt with the significance of the fourth vow was discussed, it became rather evident that the attention of many of the members was on the implications which followed from our relation to the magisterium and to the hierarchy especially in doctrinal matters. This was all the more the case in that the report on the state of the Society had acknowledged many defects in this regard. On the other hand, a great number thought that questions of doctrine and of doctrinal fidelity should not be treated together with the questions of the fourth vow but rather separately and in their own right. After this discussion, the Commission tried to prepare a new report on the fourth vow which would be more satisfactory in the light of the questions raised in the Aula.

Meanwhile, the Supreme Pontiff again in February, 1975,

asked that the Congregation give greater care to this fidelity and to the correcting of errors and defects which had crept into the Society in this matter. He had already earlier, in his letter of September 15, 1973, and in his address of December 3, 1974, publicly treated of doctrinal and disciplinary fidelity toward the magisterium and the hierarchy. On February 21, 1975, under the pressure of time, Father General, as presiding officer of the Congregation and with advice and counsel of the General Assistants and the Council of the President, had to present a new schedule of the more urgent business yet to be dealt with by the Congregation. He did not therefore include in that schedule of business a *separate* document on the fourth vow itself, although its reaffirmation should easily be found in certain of the documents (e.g., the documents on identity and on our mission today). He did, however, take care that an explicit treatment of our fidelity to the magisterium and the Supreme Pontiff would not be neglected.

In order to make progress in treating this matter, Father General asked five of the members of the Congregation each to write a brief document on "thinking with the Church," having before their eyes also the previous work done on this topic by Commission V. From these five texts a single new version was developed and presented to the Congregation. After deliberations in Assistancy meetings and in plenary sessions, the Congregation decided that this question—not yet formally introduced in accord with the Additions to the procedural regulations—should be introduced and dealt with and that it should be done in the form of a brief separate decree. There was an opportunity to offer amendments. Finally voting took place on a revised text and on several formal amendments. The decree thus put together was approved on March 7, 1975. It stressed our obligation of reverence and fidelity and our responsibility toward the Church. It confirms our tradition of service to the Church by explaining, propagating and defending the faith. It deplores shortcomings in recent years in these matters, and it recommends a vigilance at once fatherly and firm in preventing and correcting failings which tarnish our fidelity to the magisterium and service to the faith and the Church (Decree 3).

11. Our Mission Today: The Service of Faith and the Promotion of Justice

(*From the Minutes,* Acta 9, 10, 12-14, 16, 26-28, 33, 46, 63, 74-76)

The document on our mission today (Decree 4) is one of the principal results of this Congregation, and the work on the complex problems involved in it went on all the way through the Congregation.

Many postulata were received on the fundamental criteria of the apostolate of the Society; even more were received on the promotion of justice as an essential dimension of our apostolate as well as of our whole lives. The importance of these problems became evident right in the opening discussions to decide on the topics which were to have priority in treatment. Among the six topics which received a majority of votes were *"The criteria of our apostolic service today"* (first place) and *"The promotion of justice"* (fourth place). When the Congregation came to deciding on a "first priority" some proposed that we should take these two topics together, and that is what the Congregation did (cf. n. 5 *supra*).

If, in addition, one notes that the topic *"Our mission as drawn from the apostolic character and purpose of the Society"* had taken second place in the voting on priorities and was later added by the Congregation to the two topics above, it is easy to understand the general importance which problems of the apostolate held in this Congregation.

However, differing perspectives were at work which only

little by little came together in a single document. The postulata on the criteria of our apostolic service today looked especially to the particular characteristics of our apostolate as a priestly work and to the significance in today's circumstances of the ministries set down in the Formula of the Institute. Those postulata dealt with the place to be given (and under what conditions) to professional work, the response of the Society to the apostolic needs which arise from atheism or religious indifference, the apostolic meaning of our educational endeavors, the ecumenical dimension of our apostolates, etc. The postulata on mission dealt rather with the essential reality of mission (being sent) in the life of each individual Jesuit as something constitutive of our vocation, with all its consequences in the area of apostolic obedience and of the corporate body of the Society. Serious problems, ones also considered in the examination of the state of the Society, for example, apostolic dispersal or even as it were disintegration, individualism, independence in selecting apostolic activities . . . all urged that there be a strengthening of the awareness of an apostolic body, of an apostolic community, of obedience for a mission, and that the function of the superior in individual and community apostolic discernment be reinvigorated. Finally, the postulata on the promotion of justice, although in a different way and with a different insistence, tended to give more importance to this latter aspect of the apostolate today.

In the initial phase (when treating of the first priority), there was an attempt to join the two topics, "the criteria of our apostolic service" and "the promotion of justice." See, for example, the first report, "The mission of the Society and justice in the world," distributed to the Congregation on December 14, 1974. There was no lack of tension between the differing perspectives during the discussions on this report. Commissions I and IV, to whom belonged the responsibility for these two topics, began to work collaboratively. They soon saw the need for unifying

in one document those matters which the Congregation
might decide on with regard to the promotion of justice
and those detailed explanations which it might make about
the fundamental criteria of our apostolate. On the other
hand, it rather quickly became evident that the Congregation ought not descend into a minutely drawn out consideration of particular areas of the apostolate, but rather
that it ought to be concerned with the criteria, the style,
the manner, the form of our apostolic involvement.

In the next phase of the work, in January, at the suggestion of several members, Father General, as presiding
officer of the Congregation, asked not only that Commissions I and IV should try to combine their work, but also
that Commission II should join them, since the topic of
"mission" was itself obviously of great importance for a
correct understanding and decision on our apostolic criteria
today. So the editorial committees of the three commissions,
I, II, and IV, worked at the same time at the preparation
of a second and unified report, "On the mission of the
Society with regard to the service of faith and the promotion of justice." This was approved by the vote of each of
the three commissions (January 24, 1975). The report then
came up for discussion, carried on at length through
several sessions. On February 1 the Congregation decided
by several straw votes or indicative ballots that the text
should be shortened, that the experience of and proclamation of the Faith ought to have greater emphasis, that the
mission of the Society with regard to atheism should be
more prominently put, and finally that a few carefully
worked out criteria on participation in politics should be
proposed.

A new text was prepared in French and presented at the
same time to the Congregation in English and Spanish versions also (third report). There was an opportunity to propose amendments in all three of these languages as well as
in Latin.

365

Once again the text had to be thoroughly revised due to a huge mass of suggestions which came in. So a new version, a fourth report, came before the Congregation on February 21.

This time, too, there was no scarcity of amendments. A vote was taken on them and on the body of the text (in its original French version) on March 1 and 3. Here again amendments were proposed and passed which put the text more in conformity with the wishes of the Congregation. Among those amendments it seems good to point out especially those which again introduced several points which had been left out in the fourth report as originally presented. They came from the early work of Commission II, and they dealt with the community as apostolic, the function of the Superior, obedience in its mission aspect, and the awareness of the Society as a corporate body.

If one compares the earlier versions of *"Our mission today"* with the version of the decree as it was finally passed, one will probably find that the special and most important note of the last version is that it gives pride of place to the notion of the service of the faith as primary to the whole apostolate of the Society, while it presents the promotion of justice as an absolute requirement of such service, especially in today's circumstances. The decree also stressed, but this time in the same manner as in earlier versions, the necessity for a deeper knowledge of men and women, of their aspirations and of their way of thinking and feeling, as well as a real involvement among them, especially among those who lead a modest, indeed a poor, life and who personally suffer injustice. All Jesuits are invited to a serious examination of their relationships, their style of life, their ability to communicate their deepest convictions with those who do not share our faith, and to a thoroughgoing conversion of mind and heart. This examination is to be furthered for the whole Society under the inspiration of Father General by a systematic, well-established program in all the provinces.

12. The Work of Inculturation of the Faith and the Promotion of Christian Life

(From the Minutes, Acta 69, 70, 80)

The question of "inculturation" has relationship to problems of the apostolate, and as a matter of fact it is rather broadly treated in the document "Our mission today." It is a matter especially of inculturation of the faith and of Christian life in those areas of the world where Christianity is now growing among peoples of non-Western culture. The topic, however, and the recommendations reach out more broadly to those regions which were once Christian but which today are distinguished by the rapid process of secularization and by almost new cultures. Nor should we omit the obvious service which the Society can render to the Church for the inculturation of the Gospel in the context of the more universal values which are coming into being all over the world through the multiple relationships among nations (Decree 4, nn. 36 and 53-56). There are similar indications in the decree on the formation of Jesuits (Decree 6, nn. 27, 29, and *passim*).

But the Congregation wanted to pass a particular decree prepared by the commission on this "work of inculturation of the faith and the promotion of Christian life," especially in the cultures of the non-Western world, Africa, Asia, and many of the areas of Latin America. This was something new. Even though the Society in its traditions and its practices had often taken account of a needed inculturation, none at least of the more recent General Congregations had passed a specific decree on this subject.

Given its convocation toward the end of 1974, the General Congregation could hardly fail to follow in the footsteps of the recently held Synod of Bishops *"on evangelization."* But, in addition, it had also received many postulata on inculturation. Besides, the more numerous membership in the Congregation of Jesuits who were born in East Asia, India, and Africa was a new and very important fact.

The commission which was going to deal with this topic was first entitled "on indigenization"; later, and more correctly it seems, it took the name "on inculturation." After the commission presented proposals in two reports, the Congregation by an almost unanimous vote decided on a brief but explicit decree on the participation of the Society in this work, and at the same time it recommended that Father General take further measures in the matter (Decree 5).

13. The Formation of Jesuits, Especially with Regard to the Apostolate and Studies

(From the Minutes, Acta 48, 49, 51, 52, 53, 67, 75, 77, 81)

An international commission on studies functioned as a preparatory committee for this Congregation in accord with decree 38, n. 7, of the 31st General Congregation. Already in September, 1974, it had a rather fully worked-out study of the postulata on the formation of Jesuits. Commission VII started off from this study and took into account the many elements both positive and negative in Jesuit formation as they became clear in the examination of the state of the Society. The commission judged that a very large number of the items asked for had already been satisfactorily taken care of in the eighth and ninth decrees of the 31st General Congregation, as well as in the *General Norms for Studies* which had been promulgated on October 10, 1967, as the outline of a new *Ratio* for studies in the Society[14] and just as well in Father General's Instruction on the spiritual formation of Jesuits, promulgated on December 15, 1967.[15] What was obviously needed was especially a more accurate and more thorough putting into practice of these documents.

---

14 *ActRSJ,* XV, 238-268.
15   "   , XV, 103-133.

However, supported by comments from individual members as well as from Assistancy meetings, the commission judged that some matters ought to be insisted upon. These matters had recently attained new importance and were related to some of the other decrees of the present Congregation (for example, on our mission today). They were: the apostolic integration of Jesuit formation and, in particular, the integration of studies into the apostolic life, the integration of younger members into the body of the Society, personal integration in the formation of each of us, and the continued formation of all Jesuits as necessary for the renewal of the whole apostolic body of the Society. The following recommendations were also made: the commission thought that the responsibility for formation incumbent on the provincial and the responsibility of all those engaged in formation work, including professors of Jesuits, ought to be highlighted. Care should be taken that the younger Jesuits gain familiarity with the sources of the spirituality of the Church and of the Society. So, too, should there be a care for the connection between special studies, undertaken for apostolic purposes, and philosophical and theological studies as well as spiritual formation, both personal and communitarian. The more widespread modern languages are to be learned, since they make it possible to enter into communication with other cultures and with the universal Society. Philosophical and theological studies are to be strengthened, adapted, of course, to the diversity of cultures and regions of the world. In general, the quality of studies in the Society must by every possible exertion be maintained or raised. On all of these matters the Congregation put its stamp of approval by means of the guidelines and regulations of its sixth decree. At the same time the Congregation somewhat changed the examination *ad gradum* for the profession of the four vows. This examination is to be taken by all those who have not acquired in ecclesiastical studies at least the academic degree of the licentiate. The essential prescriptions of the Constitutions which deal with this examination are to be observed, but

369

particular details are now left to regional regulations on studies. The provincials are to take care that in accord with the new decree all should generally acquire the licentiate in philosophy or in theology. Finally, the Congregation definitively abrogated all the decrees of previous General Congregations which are in opposition to the ninth decree of the 31st General Congregation, the sixth decree of this Congregation, and the *General Norms for Studies.*

14. The Time of Last Vows and Tertianship

(From the Minutes, Acta 37, 38, 39, 43)

In recent years it became evident throughout the Society that last vows were being pronounced later than before, partly because of our legislation, whether traditional or more recent (see decree 11 of the 31st General Congregation), and partly because of the abnormal delay, at least in certain provinces, in entering tertianship. Many postulata requested that last vows be able to be taken much more quickly, always supposing the necessary spiritual preparation which takes place through tertianship. Other postulata, though fewer of them, insisted on the rather profound connection which seems to exist between the decision by which the Society presents one of its members for Holy Orders and the final incorporation into the body of the Society by final vows. Mention was made that aptitude for the ministries of the Society can now better than previously be known before the end of studies, since scholastics engage in far more types of apostolic works in the course of their formation.

Commission X, whose responsibility this matter was, sought information from the provincials on the number of those who even several years after completing studies had not begun tertianship and on the reasons for this delay. The commission also heard from the several tertian instructors who were members of the Congregation about the positive results obtained from recent experiments as well as about their shortcomings.

On a great number of points there was large agreement, even if not all of those points were later retained as part of the Congregation's decree:

a) The advantage of not putting off final incorporation into the Society as had been done in these last years. Hence, there was a revision of the eleventh decree of the 31st Congregation; now the requirements consist only of ten years completed in the Society, the tertianship, and, for scholastics, priestly ordination (Decree 10).

b) The importance of tertianship according to the norms set down in the Constitutions and the necessity that those who have not yet begun it after several years since the completion of studies do so soon. As for the Brothers, it was judged good, in accord with the practice of recent years, to reaffirm that they prepare themselves for final vows by a period of more intense spiritual life which in the decree is called "tertianship" and which thus can more easily be made together with the Fathers if the provincial so judges (Decree 7).

c) A strong insistence at the present time on solid spiritual preparation before one receives Holy Orders.

d) The importance of apostolic experiments and of the study of the Institute not only during tertianship but also throughout the whole course of formation.

e) The significance of last vows as an act of definitive incorporation by which the Society sees fully ratified the total consecration which had already been expressed in first vows. This presupposes a long and serious probation throughout the whole period of formation.

f) The usefulness of providing for everyone, even after tertianship, the benefit of some period of time for spiritual renewal (see decree 6, n. 36).

g) The need to prepare tertian instructors who are capable of exercising toward their brethren the Society's care, and the appropriateness of setting up a team of instructors who work together, who mutually complement each other and who give witness to union among themselves as they help those who are making tertianship.

In order to attain the goals of tertianship, it seemed to the Congregation that two different procedures (A and B) could be used, according to provinces or regions, with the approval of Father General. In *Formula A* tertianship is made rather soon after the completion of studies, and ordination to the priesthood takes place during it, keeping of course the condition of full liberty of spirit in taking on Holy Orders. *Formula B* is similar to the experiment of recent years in many provinces, carried out in the ways approved by Father General in 1970.[16]

As for the *days* on which last vows are pronounced, the Congregation wanted to permit greater flexibility, which circumstances of the apostolate or of the community today demand. When it came to changing the rite used at last vows, on the contrary, the Congregation did not wish to act, since according to expert studies there seems to be no obstacle to retaining even today the usage of the Society which goes back in origin to the very rite used for the vows of our founder.

Finally it is to be noted that as far as first incorporation into the Society goes, and specifically with reference to the vows taken after the noviceship, the Congregation made no changes. Neither a consultation made throughout the Society, nor the opinions received from the provincial congregations, nor the mind of by far most of the members of the Congregation favored any change in this matter. There was, however, clearly a desire that the novices know still better the import of the promise contained in the first vows, namely, the promise of entering the Society and of striving with all their strength to become truly apt for this.

---

16 *ActRSJ*, XV, 557.

15. Formed Members, or Grades in the Society of Jesus

(*From the Minutes,* Acta 20, 21, 22, 23, 24, 25, 26, 29, 30, 53, 54, 68)

Very many postulata were sent on the subject of formed members or grades. Fifty-eight of them came from provincial congregations. A special commission had worked through 1967-1969 and in accord with the mandate of the 31st General Congregation had investigated "the whole problem of distinction of grades." The International Congress of Brothers (Villa Cavalletti, 1970) and four task forces which met in 1972 then completed this work.

Thirty-seven provincial congregations, as well as the four task forces and the Congress of Brothers asked that all Jesuits, including those who were not priests, might be admitted to the four solemn vows. On the other hand, through a letter from the Secretary of State on December 3, 1974, the Supreme Pontiff said that the extension to all, even non-priests, of the fourth vow with regard to missions seemed to present serious difficulties which would impede the approval necessary on the part of the Holy See.

In these circumstances, the Congregation by vote (228 positive and 8 negative) decided that the question of grades should be treated, thinking that there was still place for a "representation." It wanted to start a discernment in depth on the whole matter, both in order to determine the mind of the Congregation and in order, if it so turned out, to be able to present its reasons in a spirit of obedience and filial reverence to the Supreme Pontiff for his consideration.

The question was broadly discussed in the language groups and afterwards in many plenary sessions. To one of the sessions ten Brothers came, chosen from among those whose names already before the Congregation had been proposed by the members. Two of these Brothers, designated by the others, presented their opinions to the Congregation. Towards the end of these deliberations, on

January 22, 1975, from an indicative or straw vote of the members it became clear that the Congregation really was tending to "represent" to the Supreme Pontiff, in the Ignatian sense of "representation," the opinion which favored the suppression of grades so that all Jesuits would pronounce the same four vows "in the conviction that thus the priestly character of the Society can and must be preserved."

This result, even though it was still only an indication of opinions, was communicated to the Supreme Pontiff in accord with the procedures of constant information employed all during the Congregation.

The Holy Father informed the Congregation that this had been done contrary to his will; he asked that the Congregation take no further action on this matter, and that it send to him a report of the reasons which had led to the members of the Congregation to choose that line which had found expression in the indicative or straw vote. After he received that report, he confirmed in an autograph letter that as supreme guarantor of the essentials of the Society which were contained in the Formula of the Institute he could in no way grant a change in this matter.

The Congregation soon concluded the whole affair, deciding by vote that in the historical preface to the Acts of the Congregation the following paragraphs should be inserted, by which in the name of the whole Society it would declare its spirit of faithful acceptance:

"The 32nd General Congregation, keeping in mind both Decree 5 of the 31st General Congregation and the discussion that took place in the Congregation of Procurators in 1970, subjected to careful examination those postulates dealing with the question of grades in the Society, which had been submitted by a number of provincial congregations. The Congregation presented the whole question, together with the reasons, to the Holy See.

"Since, however, His Holiness, Pope Paul VI, after care-

*fully considering the matter, expressed his will and con-
firmed that the fourth vow of special obedience to the Holy
Father regarding missions should remain reserved, according to the Institute, to those priests of the Society who successfully complete the required spiritual and doctrinal
preparation, the General Congregation, in the name of the
whole Society, accepted the decision of His Holiness
obediently and faithfully.*

*"The Congregation, however, wanted by means of the
present decree to have us continue to strengthen the unity
of vocation of all of our members of whatever grade and to
encourage the fuller execution both of Decree 7 of the 31st
General Congregation concerning temporal coadjutors
and of the norms given by that same Congregation as regards the promotion of priests to the profession of four
vows."*

16. The Permanent Diaconate

(*From the Minutes,* Acta 40, 42, 68)

Once the Second Vatican Council had restored the
permanent diaconate, the 31st General Congregation removed the obstacles to the possibility of permanent deacons
in the Society (Decree 6). However, "as for the religious
vows to be pronounced by such deacons, whether in the
future they will be the vows of temporal coadjutors or
spiritual coadjutors, the Congregation abstained from
passing a decree, because their functions are not yet clearly
defined in the documents of the Church, and the Holy See
will give further precisions on this for all religious."[17] Since
these determinations have now been given, and since the
Holy See is asking that the general chapters of religious
institutes of men clearly determine the juridical status of
their permanent deacons, the 32nd General Congregation,

---

17 Historical preface to the decrees of GC **XXXI**, *ActRSJ,* XIV, 823.

in order that such deacons can be an ordinary part of our institute, first of all in a more positive manner gave permission that some of the members of the Society become permanent deacons when the good of souls was seen to demand it. Then it decided that these deacons should stay in the religious state which they already had in the Society. This, however, was to be such that if they were approved temporal coadjutors (Brothers without last vows) they could be promoted to the grade of formed temporal coadjutors (Brothers with last vows); and if they were scholastics who for just causes could not be ordained priests (for example because of being completely worn out from studies), they could, in due accord with law and by way of exception, be promoted to the grade of spiritual coadjutor. As for other precisions, such as the necessary time in the Society or proper preparation for diaconate ordination, the Congregation thought they ought to be left to general or particular regulations from Father General in accord with the norms both of the Holy See and of conferences of bishops (Decree 9).

17.   The Union of Minds and Hearts in the Society

(From the Minutes, Acta 40, 41, 59, 63, 75, 77, 78, 82)

The Congregation received a rather large number of postulata on the spiritual life, especially on prayer and on obedience and community life in the Society, as well as on spiritual discernment in common and the proper role of superiors in it. There was also no dearth of postulata on union in the Society; and in the examination of the state of the Society which the Congregation made, it did not fail to take into account the defects in our union which over the last years had shown up among us.

It seemed to the Congregation that both series of problems ought to be approached simultaneously, the personal and communitarian spiritual life and union in the Society.

It also seemed that the problems of such union should not be dealt with separately in a decree which was exhortatory and perhaps abstract, but rather that it ought to make an effort to strengthen the union among ourselves through those means which the eighth part of the Constitutions points out as capable of bringing this about. As a matter of fact, the Congregation thought that the needed orientations ought to be arranged in sections bearing titles which more or less corresponded to the principal means set down in that part of the Constitutions' first chapter ("Aids toward the union of hearts"), namely, "love of God and of our Lord Jesus Christ," relationships among the brethren, and obedience. This, then, is the origin of the decree "On union of minds and hearts," which at one and the same time treats of union with God in Christ, brotherly communion, and obedience as the bond of union (Decree 11).

Under each of these headings the Congregation put together those points which at present seem more needed. For example, with respect to personal prayer, it looked into present day difficulties, recommended mutual help, consultation with one's spiritual director, openness with superiors, shared prayer with one's brethren. To questions on community spiritual discernment it also responded, and it acted similarly in treating of the various types of fraternal communication and relationship which should flourish among us. While the 31st General Congregation pointed out the importance of community life for the Jesuit as such, now its apostolic dimensions were more forcefully recommended. The same was done vigorously with regard to the apostolic dimension of chastity. In general, the mutually necessary relationships between the religious vows and community life were highlighted. Obedience finally was considered in the context of its present circumstances which, perhaps more than those described in the Constitutions, impede union in the Society.

The Congregation then wished to commend the position of the local superior. In that same context, it dealt with the partly new question of the extent of religious authority in at least some of the directors of apostolic works and of the relationships between their positions and the responsibilities of religious superiors.

Some had sought a clarification on how to apply number 10 of the seventeenth decree of the 31st General Congregation, dealing with a possible case of conflict between the order of a superior and a member of the Society who believed in conscience that he could not obey it. The commission and the Congregation, too, at first doubted the usefulness of adding anything to the determinations set down by the 31st General Congregation other than to point out the internal dispositions needed in the persons who were involved. The question was however brought up again by means of a rather long amendment at the time when the decree was being voted on. Discussion took place on March 4; many, though not denying the usefulness of some further explanation, still thought it would be enough to have Father General give such an explanation. But at the wish of Father General himself and of some of the provincials, the discussion started up again on March 6, and the conclusion was that the Congregation itself would produce a brief explanatory statement. This statement was voted on on that same day (to be found at the end of Decree 11).

To the "orientations" on union of minds and hearts the Congregation wished to add certain "guidelines" which flowed from the former and which were to be proposed for all the members of the Society. Once this was done, the Congregation simply abrogated the Common Rules, which the 31st General Congregation had earlier dealt with in recommending to Father General that they be revised, a task which up to the present Congregation could not be done. It also recommended to Father General that, besides the "guidelines" produced by the Congregation, he put together a kind of summary and index of the cardinal points of our religious life, drawn from the decrees of the 31st and 32nd General Congregations and from the letters that he had sent to the whole Society.

18. Poverty

(From the Minutes, Acta 18, 19, 33-36, 38, 57-59, 68, 69)

The new statutes on poverty, prepared by order of the 31st General Congregation, were promulgated by Father General on September 15, 1967.[18] They were, however, only to be use experimentally, until the next General Congregation.[19] Already in 1970 Father General set up a committee of expert consultants who could give their advice for applying the statutes and for revising them in the future. This committee later evolved into the subcommission for revising the statutes on poverty when preparations began for the 32nd General Congregation. In the following years, the subcommission published three reports (July, 1972; December, 1972; July, 1973), taken for this purpose, from the hundreds of letters and comments from major superiors and local superiors and treasurers and expert consultants from all over the Society. In addition, it published two booklets (*CPCG Documenta Complementaria 8A* [116 pages] and *8B* [172 pages]) in order to encourage reflection during the preparatory phase of the Congregation on the problems connected with poverty.

After about 250 postulata on poverty came from the provincial congregations, a preparatory committee was set up to examine them, according to the norms of General Congregation XXXI, decree 38, n. 7. After a meeting at the end of July, 1974, it published *Documentum ad Congregandos n. 12* for the members coming to the Congregation. At one and the same time, the booklet furnished a history of the work done on poverty from the 31st to the

---

18 *ActRSJ,* XV, 60 ff.
19 GC 31, D. 18, n. 20; *ActRSJ,* XIV, 917.

32nd General Congregation, an analytic summary of the postulata, and the main lines of the proposals to be considered by the Congregation.

At the Congregation itself it soon became clear that it would be necessary to prepare a draft document which would have two distinct parts, one more spiritual and ascetic (which would also look to the apostolic characteristics of poverty) and the other more juridical, even though the earlier material had concerned itself almost only with institutional poverty or poverty in its juridical aspects. In this second, or juridical section, rather profound changes were proposed. For example, in place of the distinction between professed houses and colleges, the distinction would be between all the religious communities and any apostolic institute [or institutionalized apostolic work]. Or, to all the communities would be applied the regimen of poverty of the professed houses as that has been adapted by the 31st General Congregation to current economic circumstances; or, again, from the apostolic institutes no goods could be transferred to the religious communities except for a suitable remuneration for the work done by Jesuits in those institutions; or, finally, that every community was to prepare a budget to be approved by the provincial and was to distribute whatever money was left after the expenses of the year so that no surplus would be accumulated.

Because of the importance of the subject, an indicative or straw vote was first taken on these more juridical elements. In that way, the Congregation expressed its mind, for example, on not normally allowing stable revenues for the communities.

A revised draft, together with a draft of the more spiritual-ascetical part, was submitted for a vote. There was still some doubt, before the vote, whether a particularly central part of the decree, by which communities or houses could have the simple ownership of the apostolic institutes (Sec-

380

tion B, v, 1), would contradict the Formula of the Institute and the Constitutions. Although the Congregation was aware that it had the power to resolve such a doubt by an authoritative declaration on its own part, it abstained from doing this and decided rather that a qualified majority (two-thirds) would be required in the voting, according to norm n. 118 of the Formula of a General Congregation, and that if the decree obtained this majority it would be submitted to the Holy See for confirmation.

The proposal in question passed by a vote of 191 for it and 23 against it. The decree as a whole was approved by an almost unanimous vote.[20]

It is useful to add here that it did not seem opportune to the Definitors chosen by the 31st General Congregation to ask the Holy See for the faculty of setting up non-collegial foundations which would enjoy exemption from the local Ordinary as the Congregation had recommended because this kind of privilege seemed little in accord with current tendencies in church law. Hence, other adaptations of our law of poverty had to be found by the Definitors. To this end, after a historical study, and with the deliberative vote of those Fathers of the General's curia who had an *ex officio* right to attend a General Congregation, Father General by his own authority promulgated statutes nn. 52 and 83 (on the capacity of the Society as a whole and of the provinces to possess goods). By this, decree 197, n. 1, of the *Collectio Decretorum* (Epitome 522, §1) was abrogated. Since the incapacity in that earlier decree was proved to take its force neither from the Formula of the Institute nor from the Constitutions, Father General indubitably had such a right, in the light of the Apostolic Letter *Ecclesiae Sanctae* II, nn. 6 and 7, as well as decree 18, n. 20, and decree 56, n. 1, of the 31st General Congre-

20 See the confirmation given by the Holy See for experimental implementation; letter of the Cardinal Secretary of State, May 2, 1975: here, p. 546.

gation.[21] Those statutes, that is, nn. 52 and 83 mentioned above, were submitted to the examination of this present Congregation, which authoritatively confirmed them and made them part of its own decree on poverty (Section C).

The other more particular dispositions of the new decree the reader can easily understand (Sections D, E, F). The general tenor and meaning of the new regulations on material goods in the Society are set forth in the first part of the decree in A, IV, nn. 11-12.

19. The General Congregation and Congregations of Procurators and Provincials

(From the Minutes, Acta 45-46, 56, 69, 79, 83)

Much was done about questions dealing with the General Congregation itself in the preparatory studies (especially *CPCG Documentum 8* and *Documenta Complementaria,* n. 7), and on those same questions there were many postulata.

In the Congregation itself the following topics were the ones which were especially brought up: the periodicity and the length of a General Congregation, reduction in the number of its members, more equitable representation for independent vice-provinces, participation by members of the Society who are not professed of the four vows, the possibility of two types of General Congregations with a corresponding difference in the number of participants (one type, that is, for the election of a General and the other, with fewer participants, for business matters alone), the rights of Procurators *"ad negotia"* in a General Congregation, a more official and complete preparation before the Congregation, and a more expeditious set of procedures in the Congregation itself.

Among all these topics, the one on reducing the number

---

21 *ActRSJ,* XIV, 917; 994.

of participants was discussed at the greatest length. In an indicative or straw vote, there was a majority, even though slender, in favor of a reduction. Afterwards, however, the discussion got down to methods to bring this about, and they were not fully satisfactory. So finally the Congregation decided that it did not itself want to deal further with this matter. It recommended to Father General that he establish a commission which would investigate the situation more deeply with a view to treating it and acting on it in the next Congregation, especially in relation to stabilizing or even reducing the number of members, and in relation to setting not only quantitative but also qualitative criteria in the distribution of members.

As to periodicity and length of General Congregations, this Congregation did not wish to make any changes. On the other hand, by a decree in the final session on March 7 it ordered that in the future the preparation for a General Congregation be more complete and official, that is, that it go up to and include the preparation of the *relationes praeviae* or first official reports (similar to those which are at present provided for in n. 119, §3 of the Formula of a General Congregation). It also decided that Procurators *"ad negotia"* could be elected as Secretary or Vice-Secretary of the Congregation, as members of the deputations on the state of the Society and on the screening of postulates and also as definitors. In addition, it asked that in the light of the experience of this present Congregation, the Formula of the General Congregation be thoroughly revised, both as to the procedural rule and the rules for dealing with substantive matters (cf. Decree 13).

As to congregations of procurators and provincials, the 32nd General Congregation made clear in an indicative vote that it was not of a mind to abolish the congregation of provincials, and so no more was done on that matter. But on the other hand, the Congregation did not act on certain postulata which tended to remove the limitation imposed by the last General Congregation by which a provincial cannot change the decision *de cogenda* taken by the congregation of his own province. It did decide to broaden the power of the congregations, both of procurators and provincials, such that both of them could in case of necessity suspend a decree of a previous general congregation until the next general congregation, and both could publish for the whole Society a report on the state of the Society (Also in Decree 13).

Lastly, the Congregation commissioned Father General to apply these decisions and to insert them in the Formulae of the various congregations. It also commissioned him to revise the Formula of the General Congregation, spoken of earlier, with the help of a commission appointed by him and with the deliberative vote of those members of the General's curia who have an *ex officio* right to be members of a general congregation.

20. Provincial Congregations

(*From the Minutes,* Acta 33, 40, 60, 62-64, 71, 77, 80, 83)

Many postulata were received which dealt with the provincial congregation and its Formula. Fifty-eight such postulata spoke of enlarging participation in the election to its membership. On February 5 the General Congregation decided to reserve to itself the question of active and passive voice (voting and being voted for) in the election to a provincial congregation. The other points to be dealt with it confided to five definitors of the second type who would make decisions on them, keeping intact however the nonlegislative character of a provincial congregation.

The General Congregation asked Father General, after consulting the council of the presidency and the editorial committee of the ninth commission, to propose five names before the Congregation itself elected the definitors. Father General proposed Fathers Bruce Biever (Wisconsin), Tarcisio Botturi (Bahia), Eugeen De Cooman (North Belgium), Casimir Gnanadickam (Madurai), and Mariano Madurga (Aragon). They were all elected by the Congregation on a single ballot despite the provision of n. 126, §2, of the Formula of the General Congregation, after a decision had been made to do it thus following upon a brief discussion.

Meanwhile, with the help of the editorial committee of Commission IX, the Congregation itself took action on the question of active and passive voice in elections to the provincial congregation. The matter, however, could only be decided late in the Congregation because it was dependent on other questions about grades, about final incorporation into the Society, and about the General Congregation. After an indicative vote on February 24 and after a decision not to change the required proportion of professed fathers in the provincial congregation, the commission prepared a greatly shortened text for a definitive vote on February 28. At that vote, the Congregation decided that the not-yet-formed members of the Society would have the same active and passive voice in a single election to a provincial congregation as other members of the Society enjoyed. However it was conditioned as follows: active voice (the right to vote) would be given five years after entrance into the Society; passive voice (the right to be voted for) after eight years; the not-yet-formed members could not be more than five in number in the congregation of a province and not more than three in the congregation of a vice-province. In addition, there would have to be at least one non-formed Jesuit as a member.

The Congregation did not assent to the proposal that in certain provinces the non-formed could make up a voting group distinct from the rest of the province.

As to the other details of the Formula of a Provincial Congregation, not a few changes were introduced by the decisions of the definitors, approved on March 5, 1975, by the Congregation itself. One can easily see them in the text of Decree 14. It is useful in addition to mention some things which the Congregation did not wish to change, despite postulata on these matters. They deal especially with the following: the participation of Jesuits who are bishops, extension of the limits of the powers of a provincial congregation, a variety of proposals offered with respect to the election to a provincial congregation (for example, that the election be by age groups, that one indicate an order of preference among those voted for, that a specified "substantial" number of votes be needed for a person to be elected, that from the list of the eligibles for a provincial congregation be removed those who upon being asked declare that they would be impeded from participating in a provincial congregation, that the numerical results of the election to a provincial congregation be made public). Other items that the Congregation did not wish to act on were: the introduction of multiple preferential voting for the persons to be members of a provincial congregation and the suppression of the double vote which a provincial has.

To Father General was given the commission, with the deliberative vote of the members of the curia who have a right *ex officio* to be present at a general congregation, to revise the Formula of the Provincial Congregation in accord with the decisions taken. To him, also, were left the decisions, with the deliberative vote of the same persons, on other minor points contained in postulatum n. 947.

21. Government, Especially Central Government

(*From the Minutes,* Acta 30-32, 44, 56)

By order of the 31st General Congregation, its forty-fourth decree which dealt with the assistants and counsellors of Father General was to be reviewed by the present Congregation. The question was given careful examination already during the preparatory phase of the Congregation (cf. *CPCG Documentum* 9 and *Documenta Complementaria*, n. 7). The topics most discussed were the following: the appropriateness or inappropriateness of the distinction between the general assistants *ad providentiam* and the general counsellors; the need for the general counsellors to make up a true council for Father General in order to enter into discernment on more difficult and more serious matters; as a consequence, the usefulness of having more general counsellors. It was also suggested that each general counsellor have a special responsibility, either sectional or regional, and that some limit of time be set for the office of counsellor. The request was also made that all the general counsellors, or at least some of them, be elected by the General Congregation.

In the Congregation itself, Commission IX not only examined the earlier studies and the postulata, but also it heard almost all the assistants, counsellors, and major officials of the curia, as well as Father General himself. It soon turned out to be clear that before anything else there was need for a more structured coordination among the various counsellors and officials. It was likewise seen that the general assistants elected *ad providentiam* ought to be *ipso facto* general counsellors. The other main provisions of Decree 44 of the 31st General Congregation could remain in place. The commission also thought that it ought to recommend a very careful inquiry by experts after the Congregation into the whole organization of the curia.

Discussions took place in the Assistancy meetings and on January 31, 1975, in the Aula. Father General himself made known his views and then left the Aula so that matters which dealt with him rather personally might be treated with full freedom. Questions were asked of the assistants and counsellors of various kinds and of the officials, some of whom also gave their own opinions. After an indicative vote, a definitive report was prepared which also served as the document to be voted on. On February 10 a decree was passed which followed the general lines set out above, and it was promulgated on the same day (Decree 15).

Certain other requests came up in some postulata. For example: that at least in some parts of the Society regional superiors should take the place of regional assistants; that a permanent vicar-general should be established to help Father General in day by day business; that the length of office of the General should be limited; that the Secretary of the Society should be one of the general counsellors. On these neither the commission nor the Congregation thought it opportune to take action. However, the Congregation did deal with and voted affirmatively for a postulatum on reorganizing the international secretariats of the Society. It gave Father General the powers necessary to bring this about.

There were also postulata on provincial and local government, and Commission IX acted on them in two reports. The questions dealt mainly with general principles of good government in the Society today (participation, implementation, timely evaluation), with the choice and preparation of superiors, with the distinction and interrelationship between religious government and the government of apostolic works (or between the superior of a community and the director of an apostolate). On all of these the Congregation passed no specific decree, but with at least some of them it dealt either in the decree "On the mission of the Society today" or in "Union of minds and hearts." Others it thought more opportune to leave to the ordinary government of Father General.

22. Election of the General Assistants and Appointment of Some of the New Regional Assistants

(From the Minutes, Acta 50, 51, 52, 83)

Once the revised decree on the general assistants and the general counsellors had been passed and promulgated, the Congregation acceded to the request presented by the four general assistants then in office that during this Congregation a new election for general assistants take place, according to the norms of Decree 44, n. 4, of the 31st General Congregation. After four days of gathering and exchanging information, the Congregation proceeded to the election in three sessions and in separate ballots on January 14 and 15, 1975. The following in alphabetical order were elected: Father Jean Calvez from the Province of Atlantic France, already General Assistant (fourth ballot); Father Parmananda Divarkar from the Province of Bombay (fourth ballot); Father Cecil McGarry from the Province of Ireland (third ballot); Father Vincent O'Keefe from the Province of New York, already General Assistant (second ballot).

After the election, Father General expressed special thanks to Father Paolo Dezza and Father Horacio de la Costa for the extraordinarily helpful collaboration they had given to the whole Society in their capacity of general assistants and to Father General in their capacity as general counsellors.

On the last day of the Congregation, Father General announced that after consulting the provincials and the other members of the Congregation from those respective regions he had appointed three new Regional Assistants: Father Petar Galauner (Croatia) for the Slavic Assistancy, Fr. Casimir Gnanadickam (Madurai) for the Indian Assistancy, and Father Gerald Sheahan (Missouri) for the American Assistancy.

23. Members to Whom Permission was Granted to Leave the Congregation Before its Conclusion

(*From the Minutes,* Acta 27, 32, 33, 49, 64, 73, 82)

Because the work of the Congregation went on beyond the time which many had foreseen, it had, before its termination, to grant permission to thirty-one members to leave on account of urgent business. Thus, five Fathers took final leave in the last days of January: Noël Barré (Atlantic France), Edouard Boné (Southern Belgium), Heinrich Krauss (Upper Germany), Stefan Miecznikowski (Greater Poland), Ladislas Orsy (New York). Then, up to February 13, two others: Josip Ćurić (Croatia) and Peter Huizing (Netherlands). Between February 14 and 24, seven members: Miljenko Belić (Croatia), Guy Bourgeault (French Canada), Joseph Knecht (Patna), Francis Prucha (Wisconsin), Alberto Sily (Argentina), Roger Troisfontaines (Southern Belgium), and Edmond Vandermeersch (Paris). Later, up to March 1, ten members: Thomas Clancy (New Orleans), Thomas Clarke (New York), Roman Darowski (Lesser Poland), Julien Harvey (French Canada), Gediminas Kijauskas (Lithuania), Herbert Roth (East Germany), Antonius Soenarja (Indonesia), Alain de Survilliers (Atlantic France), Louis de Vaucelles (Paris), and Quirino Weber (Southern Brazil). Then, after March 2, another seven: Luk De Hovre (Northern Belgium), Enrique Fabbri (Argentina), Paolo Molinari (Turin), John O'Malley (Detroit), Pasupasu (Central Africa), William Ryan (Upper Canada), and John Sheets (Wisconsin).

At the beginning, the members of the Congregation numbered 236; on February 1, 232; on February 13, 229; on February 24, 222; on March 1, 212; on March 7, the last day, 205.

To some Fathers, the Congregation gave permission to be away for a few days. Permission to be absent insofar as it was necessary from one or another session could be gotten from Father General as presiding officer, without a vote of the Congregation, in accord with the usage already in force in the 31st General Congregation.

24. The End of the Congregation

(*From the Minutes,* Acta 41, 42, 66, 82, 83)

On February 7, at the proposal of the deputation for the screening of postulata, a final date, February 9, was set for the reception of new postulata. Then on February 25 the Congregation set March 8 as the date beyond which it would not continue in session.

On March 6, as the end of the work of the Congregation drew near, all the members took part in a penance service for the Holy Year and in a concelebrated Eucharist at the altar of the Chair of St. Peter in St. Peter's Basilica. At that liturgy, Father General gave a homily in which he summed up the spiritual journey of St. Ignatius from Manresa to Rome.

On the morning of March 7, Father General and the four general assistants left the plenary session to go to an audience with the Supreme Pontiff. At that audience, the Pontiff gave a farewell address which Father General read to the Congregation immediately upon his return to the plenary session.[22]

On this same day, late in the afternoon, once the business at hand was completed, the General Congregation, in almost the same way as the 31st General Congregation (Decree 56), gave to Father General certain special faculties. They included: to finish the legislative work of the Congregation insofar as it was necessary, to dissolve colleges and professed houses until the next General Congregation, to give approval to the minutes of the last sessions, as well as to make whatever corrections might be necessary and to do stylistic emendations in preparing the decrees of the Congregation for publication (Decree 16).

Father General then spoke for the last time to the members assembled, and the 32nd General Congregation ad-

---

22 This address of the Holy Father can be found on pp. 542-544.

journed. The members recited the hymn, *Te Deum*. Before they left the Aula, Father General invited in as many as could be present of those Fathers and Brothers who had helped the Congregation in every way; and in the name of the Congregation, he thanked all for such great assistance. After supper that evening there was an informal recreation period during which many of the members of the Congregation from a variety of cultural backgrounds put on a display of their artistic and humorous talents.

The Congregation lasted 96 days. There were 83 plenary sessions in the Aula (14 in December, 18 in January, 40 in February, 11 in March). In 26 smaller meeting rooms there were many sessions of the council of the presidency, of the deputations on the state of the Society and for screening postulata, of other commissions, of 18 language groups (the membership of which, after an initial grouping, was regrouped once again) and of the 12 Assistancy groups.

B.

DECREES

OF THE

32nd GENERAL CONGREGATION

B.

DECREES
OF THE
32nd GENERAL CONGREGATION

1   INTRODUCTORY DECREE

I.

1. The past decade in the life of the Society has been   1
an effort under the leadership of Father General to implement the decrees of the 31st General Congregation, which
aimed at adapting our life to the directives of the Second
Vatican Council. The success of this effort has been significant in our apostolic work as a community, in our prayer
and our faith. This is clearly a gift of God's generosity,
though not realized without a painful struggle for sincere
renewal.

2. The 32nd General Congregation makes its own and   2
confirms all of the declarations and dispositions of the 31st
General Congregation unless they are explicitly changed in
the present decrees. The documents of the preceding Congregation accurately and faithfully express the genuine
spirit and tradition of the Society. Therefore, the whole
Society is urged to reflect thoughtfully and sincerely upon
those documents once again, and superiors are directed to
see to their ever fuller implementation.

II.

3   3.   One reason for this directive is that the progress mentioned above has not been uniform. Some Jesuits have resisted renewal and have even criticized the 31st General Congregation publicly, as though it were somehow a departure from the genuine Ignatian spirit. Others, at times, have carried new orientations to excess in their impatience to accommodate themselves and their work to the needs of the world. Out of their desire to overcome a distorted emphasis upon the transcendence of the Christian religion—one which would divorce it from experience of the world—they have fallen into a type of "immanentism" which runs counter to the Gospel message.

4   4.   These two exaggerations, each tending in an opposite direction, have threatened unity within the Society and have given non-Jesuits cause for concern and wonder. Some among them fear that the Society may have lost the forcefulness and precision with which it once exercised its priestly and apostolic mission of service to the faith. Others, when they read publications in which Jesuits unsympathetically criticize one another, their own Father General, the magisterium of the Church, and even the Holy Father, ask whether Jesuits have lost their traditional loyalty, obedience, and devotion to the Society and the Church. Sometimes they wonder, too, and not without reason, about the depth and sincerity of faith in those Jesuits who live independent lives, unmarked by poverty, and comfortably accommodated to the world.

5   5.   Out of his deep affection and concern for the Society, the Holy Father brought these points to the attention of the Congregation in his allocution of December 3, 1974.[1] He took that occasion to request that the 32nd General Congregation preserve and reaffirm the Society as a priestly, apostolic, and religious body, bound to the Holy Father by

---

1 See pp. 519-536 below.

a special vow regarding missions. It was to a balanced renewal of religious life and a discerning rededication to apostolic service that the Holy Father clearly wished to call us. In his various letters to the whole Society, Father General has expressed the same desire.

6. The whole Society ought to take the firm and paternal words of the Holy Father gratefully and humbly to heart. We sincerely acknowledge our failings and seek, with God's grace, a more radical renewal and closer unity, both among ourselves and with the Holy Father.

III.

7. Mindful that for the majority of Jesuits the years since the 31st General Congregation have been a time of grace and spiritual and apostolic growth, the 32nd General Congregation has formulated these decrees as an invitation to even greater progress in the way of the Lord. We offer them now to our fellow Jesuits in a spirit of humility and hope—not forgetful of past shortcomings, but, with God's help, looking confidently to the future.

8. The following documents treat of challenges and opportunities arising out of our life and work; of our identity as companions of Jesus in today's world; of the Society's apostolic mission as the service of faith and the promotion of justice; of prayer and obedience, and of discernment of spirits in common, nourished by and further strengthening our union together; of a more authentic poverty and of the formation of young Jesuits.

9. These documents are commended to personal reading and community dialog in a spirit of prayer and discernment. They look far beyond words and verbal analysis. They are offered as a stimulus for conversion of heart and apostolic renewal.

10. These decrees, then, are meant for practical implementation. Only the cooperation of all Jesuits under the leadership of their superiors can achieve this goal.

I

THE SOCIETY'S RESPONSE
TO THE CHALLENGES OF OUR AGE

A response of the 32nd General Congregation to requests for a description of Jesuit identity in our time.

1. What is it to be a Jesuit? It is to know that one is **11** a sinner, yet called to be a companion of Jesus as Ignatius was: Ignatius, who begged the Blessed Virgin to "place him with her Son,"[1] and who then saw the Father himself ask Jesus, carrying his Cross, to take this pilgrim into his company.[2]

2. What is it to be a companion of Jesus today? It is **12** to engage, under the standard of the Cross, in the crucial struggle of our time: the struggle for faith and that struggle for justice which it includes.

3. The Society of Jesus, gathered together in its 32nd **13** General Congregation, considering the end for which it was founded, namely, the greater glory of God and the service of men,[3] acknowledging with repentance its own failures in

---

1 Ignatius Loyola, MI, *Fontes Narrativi* I, "Autobiografia," n. 96.
2 Ibid., II, 133.
3 *FI* [3] (1); *Cons.* 136, 156, 307, 603, 813.
   [Reference numbers to the *Formula of the Institute* present a special problem, since several ways of numbering them have arisen through the centuries. The numbers used here are those employed in *The Constitutions of the Society of Jesus,* Translated, with an Introduction and a Commentary by George E. Ganss, S.J. The Institute of Jesuit Sources: St. Louis, 1970. This is the only practically accessible English translation of the *Formula of the Constitutions* themselves, and so it is the one to which English-language readers will refer in pursuing their further study of the documents of the Congregation. In addition, it makes clear (page 66, fn. 9) the reason for and inter-relation of the two differing sets of reference numbers, either of which might be employed in the Latin or other language versions of these documents.]

keeping faith and upholding justice, and asking itself before Christ crucified what it has done for him, what it is doing for him, and what it is going to do for him,[4] chooses participation in this struggle as the focus that identifies in our time what Jesuits are and do.[5]

A. WHENCE THIS DECISION

14   4. We arrive at this decisive choice from several different points of departure. The postulata received from the provinces, the panorama of the state of the Society presented at the Congregation, and the instructions given us by the Pope, all direct our attention to the vast expanse and circuit of this globe and the great multitude and diversity of peoples therein.[6]

15   5. Two-thirds of mankind have not yet had God's salvation in Jesus Christ proclaimed to them in a manner that wins belief, while in societies anciently Christian a dominant secularism is closing men's minds and hearts to the divine dimensions of all reality, blinding them to the fact that while all things on the face of the earth are, indeed, created for man's sake, it is only that he might attain to the end for which he himself was created: the praise, reverence, and service of God.[7]

16   6. Ignorance of the Gospel on the part of some, and rejection of it by others, are intimately related to the many grave injustices prevalent in the world today. Yet it is in the light of the Gospel that men will most clearly see that injustice springs from sin, personal and collective, and that it is made all the more oppressive by being built into economic, social, political, and cultural institutions of worldwide scope and overwhelming power.[8]

---

4 *SpEx,* 53.
5 GC 32, "Our Mission Today."
6 *SpEx,* 103.
7 *SpEx,* 23.
8 GS, 10, 13, 22, 23, 37; Pope Paul VI, "Populorum progressio," 21, 56 ff.; "Octogesima adveniens," 45.

7.   Conversely, the prevalence of injustice in a world   **17**
where the very survival of the human race depends on men
caring for and sharing with one another is one of the principal obstacles to belief: belief in a God who is justice because he is love.

8.   Thus, the way to faith and the way to justice are   **18**
inseparable ways. It is up this undivided road, this steep
road, that the pilgrim Church must travel and toil. Faith
and justice are undivided in the Gospel which teaches that
"faith makes its power felt through love."[9] They cannot
therefore be divided in our purpose, our action, our life.[10]

9.   Moreover, the service of faith and the promotion of   **19**
justice cannot be for us simply one ministry among others.
It must be the integrating factor of all our ministries; and
not only of our ministries but of our inner life as individuals, as communities, and as a world-wide brotherhood.
This is what our Congregation means by a decisive choice.
It is the choice that underlies and determines all the other
choices embodied in its declarations and directives.

B.   ORIGINAL INSPIRATION OF THE SOCIETY

10.   We are confirmed in this basic choice by being led   **20**
to it from another point of departure, namely, the original
inspiration of the Society as set forth in the Formula of the
Institute and the Constitutions.

11.   Our Society was founded principally for the de-   **21**
fense and propagation of the faith and for the rendering
of any service in the Church that may be for the glory of
God and the common good.[11] In fact, the grace of Christ
that enables and impels us to seek "the salvation and perfection of souls"—or what might be called, in contemporary terms, the total and integral liberation of man, leading
to participation in the life of God himself—is the same

---

9 Gal. 5.6.
10 Synod of Bishops (1971), "Justice in the World," Introduction.
11 *FI,* [3] (1)

grace by which we are enabled and impelled to seek "our own salvation and perfection."[12]

22   12.   Not only does the insight of Ignatius justify our basic choice, it specifies it. It enables us to determine what must be our specifically Jesuit contribution to the defense and propagation of the faith and the promotion of justice in charity.

23   13.   At the very center of that insight is the sense of mission. No sooner was our companionship born than it placed itself at the disposal of "the Roman Pontiff, Christ's Vicar on earth,"[13] to be sent wherever there is hope of God's greater glory and the service of men.

24   14.   A Jesuit, therefore, is essentially a man on a mission: a mission which he receives immediately from the Holy Father and from his own religious superiors, but ultimately from Christ himself, the one sent by the Father.[14] It is by being sent that the Jesuit becomes a companion of Jesus.

25   15.   Moreover, it is in companionship that the Jesuit fulfills his mission. He belongs to a community of friends in the Lord who, like him, have asked to be received under the standard of Christ the King.[15]

C.   FULFILLMENT IN COMPANIONSHIP

26   16.   This community is the entire body of the Society itself, no matter how widely dispersed over the face of the earth. The particular local community to which he may belong at any given moment is, for him, simply a concrete —if, here and now, a privileged—expression of this world-wide brotherhood.

27   17.   The local Jesuit community is thus an apostolic community, not inward but outward looking, the focus of

---

12 *Cons,* General Examen [3] −2.
13 *FI,* [3] (1)
14 John 17.18.
15 *SpEx,* 147.

its concern being the service it is called upon to give men. It is contemplative but not monastic, for it is a *communitas ad dispersionem*. It is a community of men ready to go wherever they are sent.

18.   A *communitas ad dispersionem,* but also a *koi-* **28** *nonia,* a sharing of goods and life, with the Eucharist at its center: the sacrifice and sacrament of the Deed of Jesus, who loved his own to the end.[16] And each member of every Jesuit community is ever mindful of what St. Ignatius says about love, that it consists in sharing what one has, what one is, with those one loves.[17] When we speak of having all things in common, that is what we mean.

19.   The Jesuit community is also a community of dis-   **29** cernment. The missions on which Jesuits are sent, whether corporately or individually, do not exempt us from the need of discerning together in what manner and by what means such missions are to be accomplished. That is why we open our minds and hearts to our superiors and our superiors, in turn, take part in the discernment of our communities, always on the shared understanding that final decisions belong to those who have the burden of authority.

D.   DISTINGUISHING MARK OF THE SOCIETY

20.   Not only our community life, but our religious vows   **30** are apostolic. If we commit ourselves until death to the evangelical counsels of poverty, chastity, and obedience, it is that we may be totally united to Christ and share his own freedom to be at the service of all who need us. In binding us, the vows set us free:

   —free, by our vow of poverty, to share the life of the poor and to use whatever resources we may have not for our own security and comfort, but for service;
   —free, by our vow of chastity, to be men for others, in friendship and communion with all, but especially

---

16 John 13.1.
17 *SpEx,* 231.

with those who share our mission of service;

—free, by our vow of obedience, to respond to the call of Christ as made known to us by him whom the Spirit has placed over the Church, and to follow the lead of our superiors, especially our Father General, who has all authority over us *ad aedificationem.*

31   21.   In our Society, the call to the apostolate is one, though shared in manifold ways. We are many members, but one body, each member contributing what in him lies to the common task of continuing Christ's saving work in the world, which is to reconcile men to God, and men among themselves, so that by the gift of his love and grace they may build a peace based on justice.

32   22.   Because this is its common task, the Society of Jesus is, in its entirety, a sacerdotal society. But it is sacerdotal not merely in the sense of the priesthood of all the faithful. For the Society began as, and continues to be, a band of ordained ministers of the Gospel which comprises in the self-same company both those willing to share the presbyteral function of being coadjutors of the episcopal order and those willing to give themselves to those aspects of our apostolic mission for which priestly orders are not required.

33   23.   Moreover, following Ignatius, we have asked Christ our Lord to let us render this service in a manner that gives us a personality of our own. We have chosen to give it in the form of a consecrated life according to the evangelical counsels, and we have placed ourselves at the service not only of the local churches but of the universal Church, by a special vow of obedience to him who presides over the universal Church, namely, the Successor of Peter.

34   24.   This, then, is the distinguishing mark of our Society: it is a companionship that is, at one and the same time, "religious, apostolic, sacerdotal, and bound to the Roman Pontiff by a special bond of love and service."[18]

---

18 Pope Paul VI, "Address to the Members of the 32nd General Congregation," December 3, 1974, on p. 524 below.

E.   WHAT OUR MISSION DEMANDS OF US

25.   Because the missions on which the Holy Father and   35
our superiors are likely to send us will demand well trained
minds and dedicated spirits, we test the vocation of those
whom we admit to our ranks in various ways over an
extended period of time, and we try to give them, to the
best of our ability, a spiritual and intellectual formation
more than ordinarily exacting. But even during their period
of training these young men are already our companions,
in virtue of the perpetual vows they take after the noviceship.

26.   Coming from many different countries, cultures,   36
and social backgrounds, but banded together in this way,
we try to focus all our efforts on the common task of
radiating faith and witnessing to justice. We are deeply
conscious of how often and how grievously we ourselves
have sinned against the Gospel; yet it remains our ambition
to proclaim it worthily: that is, in love, in poverty, and in
humility.

27.   In *love:* a personal love for the Person of Jesus   37
Christ, for an ever more inward knowledge of whom we
daily ask, that we may the better love him and follow
him[19]; Jesus, whom we seek, as St. Ignatius sought, to
experience; Jesus, Son of God, sent to serve, sent to set free,
put to death, and risen from the dead. This love is the
deepest well-spring of our action and our life. It was this
personal love that engendered in Ignatius that divine dis-
content which kept urging him to the *magis*—the ever more
and more giving—the ever greater glory of God.

28.   *In poverty:* relying more on God's providence than   38
on human resources; safeguarding the freedom of the
apostle by detachment from avarice and the bondage imposed by it; following in the footsteps of Christ, who
preached good news to the poor by being poor himself.

19 *SpEx,* 104.

39   29. *In humility:* realizing that there are many enterprises of great worth and moment in the Church and in the world which we, as priests and religious inspired by one particular charism, are not in a position to undertake. And even in those enterprises which we can and should undertake, we realize that we must be willing to work with others: with Christians, men of other religious faiths, and all men of good will; willing to play a subordinate, supporting, anonymous role; and willing to learn how to serve from those we seek to serve.

40   30. This availability for the meanest tasks, or at least the desire to be thus available, is part of the identity of the Jesuit. When he offers to distinguish himself in the service of the Eternal King,[20] when he asks to be received under his standard,[21] when he glories with Ignatius in being placed by the Father "with the Son,"[22] he does so not in any spirit of prideful privilege, but in the spirit of him who "emptied himself to assume the condition of a slave, even to accepting death, death on a cross."[23]

F.   CONCLUSION: A JESUIT TODAY

41   31. Thus, whether we consider the needs and aspirations of the men of our time, or reflect on the particular charism that founded our Society, or seek to learn what Jesus has in his heart for each and all of us, we are led to the identical conclusion that today the Jesuit is a man whose mission is to dedicate himself entirely to the service of faith and the promotion of justice, in a communion of life and work and sacrifice with the companions who have rallied round the same standard of the Cross and in fidelity to the Vicar of Christ, for the building up of a world at once more human and more divine.

---

20 *SpEx,* 97.
21 *SpEx,* 147.
22 Ignatius Loyola, MI, *Fontes Narrativi* I, "Diario espiritual," n. 67.
23 Phil. 2. 7-8.

32.   Deeply conscious of our utter unworthiness for so **42** great a mission, relying only on God's love and grace, we offer together the prayer of Ignatius[24]:

> Take, O Lord, and receive
> all my liberty,
> my memory, my understanding, and my entire will.
> Whatever I have or hold,
> You have given to me;
> I restore it all to You
> and surrender it wholly
> to be governed by your will.
> Give me only your love and your grace,
> and I am rich enough
> and ask for nothing more.

---

24 *SpEx,* 234.

3   FIDELITY OF THE SOCIETY TO THE MAGISTERIUM AND THE SUPREME PONTIFF

43   1.   In considering the reverence and fidelity which all Jesuits should have toward the magisterium of the Church and in a special way toward the Supreme Pontiff, the 32nd General Congregation makes the following declaration:

44   2.   The Congregation acknowledges the obligation of this reverence and fidelity as well as our proper responsibility to the Church.

45   3.   Mindful of the long and venerable tradition in the Society of serving the Church by explaining, propagating, and defending the Faith, the Congregation supports our Jesuits who are working in scholarly research, in publishing, or in other forms of the apostolate, and urges all of them to continue to remain faithful to this tradition. At the same time, the Congregation regrets particular failings in this matter on the part of some members of the Society in recent years. This behavior can undermine our apostolic effectiveness and firm commitment to serving the Church.

46   4.   The Congregation recommends to all superiors that they apply the norms of the Church and the Society in a firm and fatherly way. Freedom should be intelligently encouraged, but care should be taken to prevent and correct the failings which weaken fidelity to the magisterium and service to the faith and the Church, virtues in which the Society has always striven to be outstanding.

4 OUR MISSION TODAY: THE SERVICE OF FAITH AND THE PROMOTION OF JUSTICE

Introduction and Summary

1. To the many requests received from all parts of the Society for clear decisions and definite guidelines concerning our mission today, the 32nd General Congregation responds as follows.

47

2. The mission of the Society of Jesus today is the service of faith, of which the promotion of justice is an absolute requirement. For reconciliation with God demands the reconciliation of people with one another.

48

3. In one form or another, this has always been the mission of the Society;[1] but it gains new meaning and urgency in the light of the needs and aspirations of the men and women of our time, and it is in that light that we examine it anew. We are confronted today, in fact, by a whole series of new challenges.

49

4. There is a new challenge to our apostolic mission in a fact without precedent in the history of mankind: today, more than two billion human beings have no knowledge of God the Father and His Son, Jesus Christ, whom He has sent,[2] yet feel an increasing hunger for the God they

50

---

1 See *FI,* especially [3] (1). The Formula was approved by Popes Paul III and Julius III.
2 See *SpEx* 102.

already adore in the depths of their hearts without knowing Him explicitly.

51   5.   There is a new challenge to our apostolic mission in that many of our contemporaries, dazzled and even dominated by the achievements of the human mind, forgetting or rejecting the mystery of man's ultimate meaning, have thus lost the sense of God.

52   6.   There is a new challenge to our apostolic mission in a world increasingly interdependent but, for all that, divided by injustice: injustice not only personal but institutionalized: built into economic, social, and political structures that dominate the life of nations and the international community.

53   7.   Our response to these new challenges will be unavailing unless it is total, corporate, rooted in faith and experience, and multiform.

—total: While relying on prayer, and acting on the conviction that God alone can change the human heart, we must throw into this enterprise all that we are and have, our whole persons, our communities, institutions, ministries, resources.

54   *—corporate:* Each one of us must contribute to the total mission according to his talents and functions which, in collaboration with the efforts of others, give life to the whole body. This collaborative mission is exercised under the leadership of Peter's Successor who presides over the universal Church and over all those whom the Spirit of God has appointed Pastors over the churches.[3]

55   *—rooted in faith and experience:* It is from faith and experience combined that we will learn how to respond most appropriately to new needs arising from new situations.

---

3 See LG, 22.

—*multiform:* Since these situations are different in dif- **56**
ferent parts of the world, we must cultivate a great adaptability and flexibility within the single, steady aim of the
service of faith and the promotion of justice.

8.   While offering new challenges to our apostolic mis- **57**
sion, the modern world provides new tools as well: new
and more effective ways of understanding man, nature and
society; of communicating thought, image and feeling; of
organizing action. These we must learn to use in the service
of evangelization and human development.

9.   Consequently we must undertake a thoroughgoing **58**
reassessment of our traditional apostolic methods, attitudes
and institutions with a view to adapting them to the new
needs of the times and to a world in process of rapid
change.

10.   All this demands that we practice discernment, **59**
that spiritual discernment which St. Ignatius teaches us in
the Exercises. Moreover discernment will yield a deeper
grasp of the movements, aspirations and struggles in the
hearts of our contemporaries, as well as those in the heart
of mankind itself.

11.   In short, our mission today is to preach Jesus Christ **60**
and to make Him known in such a way that all men and
women are able to recognize Him whose delight, from the
beginning, has been to be with the sons of men and to take
an active part in their history.[4]

12.   In carrying out this mission, we should be con- **61**
vinced, today more than ever, that "the means which unite
the human instrument with God and so dispose it that it
may be wielded dexterously by His divine hand are more
effective than those which equip it in relation to men."[5]

---

4 See Prov. 8. 22-31; Col. 1. 15-20.
5 *Cons.* [13].

A.

OUR MISSION YESTERDAY AND TODAY

The Charism of the Society

62   13.   The mission we are called to share is the mission of the Church itself, to make known to men and women the love of God our Father, a love whose promise is eternal life. It is from the loving regard of God upon the world that the mission of Jesus takes its rise, Jesus who was sent "not to be served but to serve, and to give His life as a ransom for many."[6] The mission of Christ, in turn, gives rise to the mission shared by all Christians as members of the Church sent to bring all men and women the Good News of their salvation and that "they may have life and have it to the full."[7]

63   14.   St. Ignatius and his first companions, in the spiritual experience of the Exercises, were moved to a searching consideration of the world of their own time in order to discover its needs. They contemplated "how the Three Divine Persons look down upon the whole expanse or circuit of all the earth, filled with human beings" and decide "that the Second Person should become man to save the human race." Then they turned their eyes to where God's gaze was fixed, and saw for themselves the men and women of their time, one after another, "with such great diversity in dress and in manners of acting. Some are white, some black; some at peace, and some at war; some weeping, some laughing; some well, some sick; some coming into the world, some dying, etc."[8] That was how they learned to respond to the call of Christ and to work for the establishment of His Kingdom.[9]

---

6 Matt. 20:28.
7 John 10.10. See Matt. 9.36, 10.1-42; John 6.
8 *SpEx,* 102, 106 (Contemplation on the Incarnation).
9 Ibid., 91-100 (Contemplation of the "Kingdom").

15.   United in a single vision of faith, strong in a com-   **64**
mon hope and rooted in the same love of Christ whose
companions they wished to be, Ignatius and his first band
of apostles believed that the service they could give to the
people of their time would be more effective if they were
more closely bound to one another as members of a single
body, at once religious, apostolic and priestly, and united
to the Successor of Peter by a special bond of love and
service reflecting their total availability for mission in the
universal Church.

16.   It is in this light that we are asked to renew our   **65**
dedication to the properly apostolic dimension of our
religious life. Our consecration to God is really a prophetic
rejection of those idols which the world is always tempted
to adore, wealth, pleasure, prestige, power. Hence our poverty, chastity and obedience ought visibly to bear witness
to this. Despite the inadequacy of any attempt to anticipate the Kingdom which is to come, our vows ought to
show how by God's grace there can be, as the Gospel pro-
claims, a community among human beings which is based
on sharing rather than on greed; on willing openness to all
persons rather than on seeking after the privileges of caste
or class or race; on service rather than on domination and
exploitation. The men and women of our time need a hope
which is eschatological, but they also need to have some
signs that its realization has already begun.

17.   Finally, the Apostolic Letters of Paul III (1540)   **66**
and Julius III (1550) recognize that the Society of Jesus
was found "chiefly for this purpose: to strive especially for
the defense and propagation of the faith, and for the
progress of souls in Christian life and doctrine, by means
of public preaching, lectures, and any other ministrations
whatsoever of the word of God, and further, by means of
the Spiritual Exercises, the education of children and un-
lettered persons in Christianity, and the spiritual consolation
of Christ's faithful through hearing confessions and ad-
ministering the other sacraments," as well as "in reconciling

the estranged, in holily assisting and serving those who are found in prisons and hospitals, and indeed in performing any other works of charity, according to what will seem expedient for the glory of God and the common good."[10] This primordial statement remains for us a normative one.

67   18.   The mission of the Society today is the priestly service of the faith, an apostolate whose aim is to help people become more open toward God and more willing to live according to the demands of the Gospel. The Gospel demands a life freed from egoism and self-seeking, from all attempts to seek one's own advantage and from every form of exploitation of one's neighbor. It demands a life in which the justice of the Gospel shines out in a willingness not only to recognize and respect the rights of all, especially the poor and the powerless, but also to work actively to secure those rights. It demands an openness and generosity to anyone in need, even a stranger or an enemy. It demands towards those who have injured us, pardon; toward those with whom we are at odds, a spirit of reconciliation. We do not acquire this attitude of mind by our own efforts alone. It is the fruit of the Spirit who transforms our hearts and fills them with the power of God's mercy, that mercy whereby he most fully shows forth His justice by drawing us, unjust though we are, to His friendship.[11] It is by this that we know that the promotion of justice is an integral part of the priestly service of the faith.

68   19.   In his address of December 3, 1974,[12] Pope Paul VI confirmed "as a modern expression of your vow of obedience to the Pope" that we offer resistance to the many forms of contemporary atheism. This was the mission he entrusted to us at the time of the 31st General Congregation, and in recalling it he commended the way in which

---

10 *FI,* [3] (1), approved by Julius III.
11 See Rom. 5:89.
12 Pope Paul VI, "Address to the Members of the 32nd General Congregation," December 3, 1974, pp. 519-536.

the Society down the years has been present at the heart of
ideological battles and social conflicts, wherever the crying
needs of mankind encountered the perennial message of the
Gospel. Thus if we wish to continue to be faithful to this
special character of our vocation and to the mission we
have reecived from the Pope, we must "contemplate" our
world as Ignatius did his, that we may hear anew the call
of Christ dying and rising in the anguish and aspirations
of men and women.

20.   There are millions of men and women in our world,   **69**
specific people with names and faces, who are suffering
from poverty and hunger, from the unjust distribution of
wealth and resources and from the consequences of racial,
social, and political discrimination. Not only the quality of
life but human life itself is under constant threat. It is becoming more and more clear that despite the opportunities
offered by an ever more serviceable technology, we are
simply not willing to pay the price of a more just and more
humane society.[13]

21.   At the same time, people today are somehow aware   **70**
that their problems are not just social and technological,
but personal and spiritual. They have a feeling that what
is at stake here is the very meaning of man: his future and
his destiny. People are hungry: hungry not just for bread,
but for the Word of God. (Deut. 8.3; Mt. 4.4). For this
reason the Gospel should be preached with a fresh vigor,
for it is in a position once again to make itself heard. At
first sight God seems to have no place in public life, nor
even in private awareness. Yet everywhere, if we only knew
how to look, we can see that people are groping towards

---

13 We find a Gospel echo, a truly apostolic echo of the anguish and
   questioning of our times, in *Gaudium et Spes, Mater et Magistra,*
   Pacem in Terris, Populorum Progressio, Octogesima Adveniens. In
   these documents of the church's magisterium the needs of our
   world touch us and break in upon us both on the level of our
   personal lives and of our apostolic service.

an experience of Christ and waiting in hope for His Kingdom of love, of justice and of peace.

71   22. Of these expectations and converging desires the last two Synods of Bishops have reminded us in their reflections on *Justice in the World* and *Evangelization in the Modern World*. They point to concrete forms which our witness and our mission must take today.

72   23. The expectations of our contemporaries—and their problems—are ours as well. We ourselves share in the blindness and injustice of our age. We ourselves stand in need of being evangelized. We ourselves need to know how to meet Christ as He works in the world through the power of His Spirit. And it is to this world, our world, that we are sent. Its needs and aspirations are an appeal to the Gospel which it is our mission to proclaim.

B.

THE CHALLENGES WE FACE

New Demands, New Hopes

73   24. The first thing that must be said about the world which it is our mission to evangelize is this: everywhere, but in very different situations, we have to preach Jesus Christ to men and women who have never really heard of Him, or who do not yet know of Him sufficiently.

a) In what were once called "mission lands" our predecessors endeavored by their preaching of the Gospel to set up and foster new Christian communities. This task of direct evangelization by the preaching of Jesus Christ remains essential today, and must be continued, since never before have there been so many people who have never heard the Word of Christ the Savior. At the same time dialog with the believers of other religions is becoming for us an ever more important apostolate.

b) In the traditionally Christian countries, the works we established, the movements we fostered, the institutions —retreat houses, schools, universities—we set up, are still necessary for the service of faith. But there are many in these countries who can no longer be reached by the ministries exercised through these works and instiutions. The so-called "Christian" countries have themselves become "mission lands."

25. The second decisive factor for our preaching of **74** Jesus Christ and his Gospel is this: the new opportunities —and problems—disclosed in our time by the discoveries of technology and the human sciences. They have introduced a relativism, often of a very radical kind, into the picture of man and the world to which we were accustomed, with the result that traditional perspectives have altered almost beyond recognition. Changes of this kind in the mind-sets and structures of society inevitably produce strong repercussions in our lives as individuals and as members of society. As a result, there has been gradual erosion of traditional values, and gradual diminution of reliance on the power of traditional symbols. Simultaneously, new aspirations arise which seek to express themselves in the planning and implementation of practical programs.

26. The secularization of man and the world takes **75** different forms in different groups, classes, ages and parts of the world, and in all its forms offers challenges to the preaching of the Gospel to which there is no ready-made answer.

a) On the one hand, certain false images of God which prop up and give an aura of legitimacy to unjust social structures are no longer acceptable. Neither can we admit those more ambiguous images of God which appear to release man from his inalienable responsibilities. We feel this just as much as our contemporaries do; even more, perhaps, given our commitment to proclaim the God who has revealed himself in Christ. For our own sake, just as much as for the sake of our contemporaries, we must find a new language, a new set of symbols, that will enable us to leave our fallen idols behind us and rediscover the true God: the God who, in Jesus Christ, chose to share our human pilgrimage and make our human destiny irrevocably his own. To live our lives "in memory of Him" requires of us this creative effort of faith.

b) On the other hand, part of the framework within which we have preached the Gospel is now perceived as being inextricably linked to an unacceptable social order, and for that reason is being called into question. Our apostolic institutions, along with many of those of the Church herself, are involved in the same crisis that social institutions in general are presently undergoing. Here again is an experience we share with our contemporaries, and in a particularly painful way. The relevance of our work as religious, priests and apostles is often enough not evident to the men and women around us. Not only that; despite the firmness of our faith and our convictions the relevance of what we do may not be clear, sometimes, even to ourselves. This unsettles us, and in our insecurity we tend to respond to questioning with silence and to shy away from confrontation. Yet there are signs of a contemporary religious revival which should encourage us to reaffirm our commitment with courage, and not only to welcome but to seek new opportunities for evangelization.

76   27.   Finally, a third characteristic of our world particularly significant to our mission of evangelization is this: it is now within human power to make the world more just— but we do not really want to. Our new mastery over nature and man himself is used, often enough, to exploit individuals, groups and peoples rather than to distribute the resources of the planet more equitably. It has led, it is leading, to division rather than union, to alienation rather than communication, to oppression and domination rather than to a greater respect for the rights of individuals or of groups, and a more real brotherhood among men. We can no longer pretend that the inequalities and injustices of our world must be borne as part of the inevitable order of things. It is now quite apparent that they are the result of what man himself, man in his selfishness, has done. Hence there can be no promotion of justice in the full and Christian sense unless we also preach Jesus Christ and the mystery of reconciliation He brings. It is Christ who, in the last analysis, opens the way to the complete and definitive liberation of mankind for which we long from the bottom of our hearts. Conversely, it will not be possible to bring Christ to people or to proclaim His Gospel effectively unless a firm decision is taken to devote ourselves to the promotion of justice.

28.   From all over the world where Jesuits are working, **77** very similar and very insistent requests have been made that, by a clear decision on the part of the General Congregation, the Society should commit itself to work for the promotion of justice. Our apostolate today urgently requires that we take this decision. As apostles we are bearers of the Christian message. And at the heart of the Christian message is God revealing Himself in Christ as the Father of us all whom through the Spirit He calls to conversion. In its integrity, then, conversion means accepting that we are at one and the same time children of the Father and brothers and sisters of each other. There is no genuine conversion to the love of God without conversion to the love of neighbor and, therefore, to the demands of justice. Hence, fidelity to our apostolic mission requires that we propose the whole of Christian salvation and lead others to embrace it. Christian salvation consists in an undivided love of the Father and of the neighbor and of justice. Since evangelization is proclamation of that faith which is made

operative in love of others,[14] the promotion of justice is indispensable to it.

78   29.   What is at stake here is the fruitfulness of all our apostolic endeavors, and notably of any coherent attempt to combat atheism. The injustice that racks our world in so many forms is, in fact, a denial of God in practice, for it denies the dignity of the human person, the image of God, the brother or sister of Christ.[15] The cult of money, progress, prestige and power has as its fruit the sin of institutionalized injustice condemned by the Synod of 1971, and it leads to the enslavement not only of the oppressed, but of the oppressor as well—and to death.

79   30.   At a time when so many people are sparing no effort to put the world to rights without reference to God, our endeavor should be to show as clearly as we can that our Christian hope is not a dull opiate, but a firm and realistic commitment to make our world other than it is, to make it the visible sign of another world, the sign—and pledge—of "a new heaven and a new earth."[16] The last Synod vigorously recalled this for us: "The Gospel entrusted to us is the good news of salvation for man and the whole of society, which must begin here and now to manifest itself on earth even if mankind's liberation in all its fullness will be achieved only beyond the frontiers of this life."[17] The promotion of justice is, therefore, an integral part of evangelization.

80   31.   We are witnesses of a Gospel which links the love of God to the service of man, and that inseparably. In a

---

14 See Gal. 5.6; Eph. 4.15.
15 On the dignity of man, image of God and brother of Christ see: LG, 42; GS, 22, 24, 29, 38, 93; *Nuntium Councilii Vaticani II ad omnes homines,* December 20, 1962; Declarations of the Synods of Bishops of 1971, 1974; Addresses of Pope Paul Vi.
16 Apoc. 21.1.
17 Final Declaration of the Synod of Bishops of 1974, n. 12; see also the address of Pope Paul VI at the closing session of the Synod.

world where the power of economic, social and political structures is now appreciated and the mechanisms and laws governing them are now understood, service according to the Gospel cannot dispense with a carefully planned effort to exert influence on those structures.

32. We must bear in mind, however, that our efforts to **81** promote justice and human freedom on the social and structural level, necessary though they are, are not sufficient of themselves. Injustice must be attacked at its roots which are in the human heart by transforming those attitudes and habits which beget injustice and foster the structures of oppression.

33. Finally, if the promotion of justice is to attain its **82** ultimate end, it should be carried out in such a way as to bring men and women to desire and to welcome the eschatological freedom and salvation offered to us by God in Christ. The methods we employ and the activities we undertake should express the spirit of the Beatitudes and bring people to a real reconciliation. In this way our commitment to justice will simultaneously show forth the spirit and the power of God. It will respond to humanity's deepest yearnings, not just for bread and freedom, but for God and His friendship—a longing to be sons and daughters in His sight.

34. The initiatives required to respond to the challenges **83** of our world thoroughly surpass our capabilities. Nonetheless we must set ourselves to the task with all the resourcefulness we have. By God's grace, a new apostolic awareness does seem to be taking shape gradually in the Society as a whole. There is evidence of a widespread desire, and often of a whole-hearted effort, to renew and adapt our traditional apostolates and to embark on new ones. The guidelines that follow are meant to confirm or focus decisions and to urge us to more definite programs of action.

35. *Our involvement with the world*. Too often we are **84** insulated from any real contact with unbelief and with the

hard, everyday consequences of injustice and oppression. As a result we run the risk of not being able to hear the cry for the Gospel as it is addressed to us by the men and women of our time. A deeper involvement with others in the world will therefore be a decisive test of our faith, of our hope, and of our apostolic charity. Are we ready, with discernment and with reliance on a community which is alive and apostolic, to bear witness to the Gospel in the painful situations where our faith and our hope are tested by unbelief and injustice? Are we ready to give ourselves to the demanding and serious study of theology, philosophy and the human sciences, which are ever more necessary if we are to understand and try to resolve the problems of the world? To be involved in the world in this way is essential if we are to share our faith and our hope, and thus preach a Gospel that will respond to the needs and aspirations of our contemporaries.

85   36.   New forms of apostolic involvement, adapted to different places, have already been developed. The success of these initiatives, whatever form they take, requires of us a solid formation, intense solidarity in community and a vivid awareness of our identity. Wherever we serve we must be attentive to "inculturation"; that is, we must take pains to adapt our preaching of the Gospel to the culture of the place so that men and women may receive Christ according to the distinctive character of each country, class or group and environment.

86   37.   *Our collaboration with others.* The involvement we desire will be apostolic to the extent that it leads us to a closer collaboration with other members of the local church- es, Christians of other denominations, believers of other religions, and all who hunger and thirst after justice; in short, with all who strive to make a world fit for men and women to live in, a world where brotherhood opens the way for the recognition and acceptance of Christ our Brother and God our Father. Ecumenism will then become not just a particular ministry but an attitude of mind and a way of life. Today it is essential for the preaching and acceptance of the Gospel that this spirit of ecumenism embrace the whole of mankind, taking into account the cultural differences and the traditional spiritual values and hopes of all groups and peoples.

38.   *The wellspring of our apostolate.* We are also led   **87** back again to our experience of the Spiritual Exercises. In them we are able continually to renew our faith and apostolic hope by experiencing again the love of God in Christ Jesus. We strengthen our commitment to be companions of Jesus in His mision, to labor like Him in solidarity with the poor and with Him for the establishment of the Kingdom. This same spiritual experience will teach us how to maintain the objectivity needed for a continuing review of our commitments. Thereby we gradually make our own that apostolic pedagogy of St. Ignatius which should characterize our every action.

C.

APOSTOLIC DECISIONS FOR TODAY

People and Structures

39.   For the greater glory of God and salvation of men,   **88** Ignatius desired that his companions go wherever there was hope of the more universal good; go to those who have been abandoned; go to those who are in greatest need. But where is the greatest need today? Where are we to locate this hope for the more universal good?

40.   It is becoming more and more evident that the   **89** structures of society are among the principal formative influences in our world, shaping people's ideas and feelings, shaping their most intimate desires and aspirations; in a

word, shaping mankind itself. The struggle to transform these structures in the interest of the spiritual and material liberation of fellow human beings is intimately connected to the work of evangelization. This is not to say, of course, that we can ever afford to neglect the direct apostolate to individuals, to those who are the victims of the injustice of social structures as well as to those who bear some responsibility or influence over them.

90   41.   From this point of view of desire for the more universal good is perfectly compatible with the determination to serve the most afflicted for the sake of the Gospel. Our preaching will be heard to the extent that witness accompanies it, the witness of commitment to the promotion of justice as an anticipation of the Kingdom which is to come.

Social Involvement

91   42.   Our faith in Christ Jesus and our mission to proclaim the Gospel demand of us a commitment to promote justice and to enter into solidarity with the voiceless and the powerless. This commitment will move us seriously to verse ourselves in the complex problems which they face in their lives, then to identify and assume our own responsibilities to society.

92   43.   Our Jesuit communities have to help each of us overcome the reluctance, fear and apathy which block us from truly comprehending the social, economic, and political problems which exist in our city or region or country, as well as on the international scene. Becoming really aware of and understanding these problems will help us see how to preach the Gospel better and how to work better with others in our own particular way without seeking to duplicate or compete with their strengths in the struggle to promote justice.

93   44.   We cannot be excused from making the most rigorous possible political and social analysis of our situation.

This will require the utilization of the various sciences, sacred and profane, and of the various disciplines, speculative and practical, and all of this demands intense and specialized studies. Nothing should excuse us, either, from undertaking a searching discernment into our situation from the pastoral and apostolic point of view. From analysis and discernment will come committed action; from the experience of action will come insight into how to proceed further.

45.   In the discernment mentioned above, the local superior, and at times the provincial as well, will take part. This will help to overcome the tensions that arise and to maintain union of minds and hearts. The superior will enable the members of the community not only to understand and appreciate the particular—and possibly unusual —apostolates undertaken by their companions under obedience, but also to take joint responsibility for them. And if contradictions arise as a result of a particular course of action, the community will be better prepared to "suffer persecution for justice's sake" if the decision to take that course has been prepared for by a discernment in which it had taken part or was at least represented by its superior.[18]   **94**

46.   Any effort to promote justice will cost us something. Our cheerful readiness to pay the price will make our preaching of the Gospel more meaningful and its acceptance easier.   **95**

Solidarity with the Poor

47.   A decision in this direction will inevitably bring us to ask ourselves with whom we are identified and what our apostolic preferences are. For us, the promotion of justice is not one apostolic area among others, the "social apostolate"; rather, it should be the concern of our whole life and a dimension of all our apostolic endeavors.   **96**

18 See Matt. 5.10.

97   48.   Similarly, solidarity with men and women who live a life of hardship and who are victims of oppression cannot be the choice of a few Jesuits only. It should be a characteristic of the life of all of us as individuals and a characteristic of our communities and institutions as well. Alterations are called for in our manner and style of living so that the poverty to which we are vowed may identify us with the poor Christ, who identified Himself with the deprived.[19] The same questions need to be asked in a review of our institutions and apostolic works, and for the same reasons.

98   49.   The personal backgrounds of most of us, the studies we make, and the circles in which we move often insulate us from poverty, and even from the simple life and its day-to-day concerns. We have access to skills and power which most people do not have. It will therefore be necessary for a larger number of us to share more closely the lot of families who are of modest means, who make up the majority of every country, and who are often poor and oppressed. Relying on the unity we enjoy with one another in the Society and our opportunity to share in one another's experience, we must all acquire deeper sensitivity from those Jesuits who have chosen lives of closer approximation to the problems and aspirations of the deprived. Then we will learn to make our own their concerns as well as their preoccupations and their hopes. Only in this way will our solidarity with the poor gradually become a reality.

99   50.   If we have the patience and the humility and the courage to walk with the poor, we will learn from what they have to teach us what we can do to help them. Without this arduous journey, our efforts for the poor will have an effect just the opposite from what we intend, we will only hinder them from getting a hearing for their real wants and from acquiring the means of taking charge of their own destiny, personal and collective. Through such humble

---

19 See *SpEx*, 90, 147, 167; Matt. 25.35-45; also the decisions of the present General Congregation on poverty.

service, we will have the opportunity to help them find, at the heart of their problems and their struggles, Jesus Christ living and acting through the power of the Spirit. Thus can we speak to them of God our Father who brings to Himself the human race in a communion of true brotherhood.

The Service of Faith

51. The life we lead, the faith-understanding we have **100** of it and the personal relationship to Christ which should be at the heart of all we do are not three separate realities to which correspond three separate apostolates. To promote justice, to proclaim the faith and to lead others to a personal encounter with Christ are the three inseparable elements that make up the whole of our apostolate.

52. We must therefore review not only our commitment **101** to justice but our effectiveness in communicating the truths which give it meaning and in bringing men to find Christ in their daily lives. We must attentively examine our efforts to strengthen the faith of those who already believe in Christ, taking into account the formidable forces that in our time tend to undermine that faith. We must subject to a similarly searching examination our efforts to bring the Gospel to unbelievers (according to Decree 3 of the 31st General Congregation, especially n. 11).

53. In recent years the Church has been anxious to give **102** fuller expression to her catholicity by paying more attention to the differences among her various members. More, perhaps, than in the past, she tries to take on the identity of nations and peoples, to align herself with their aspirations, both toward a socio-economic development and an understanding of the Christian mystery, in accord with their own history and traditions.

54. The incarnation of the Gospel in the life of the **103** Church implies that the way in which Christ is preached and encountered will be different in different countries,

different for people with different backgrounds. For some Christian communities, especially those in Asia and Africa, this "economy of the Incarnation" calls for a more intensive dialog with the heirs of the great non-Christian traditions. Jesuits working in these countries will have to take account of this. In some Western countries which can hardly be called Christian any longer, the language of theology and of prayer will also have to be suitably adapted. In those countries dominated by explicity atheist ideologies, a renewed preaching of the Gospel demands not merely that our lives be, and be seen to be, in conformity with the commitment to justice Christ demands of us, but also that the structures of theological reflection, catechesis, liturgy and pastoral ministry be adapted to needs perceived through a real experience of the situation.

104   55.   We are members of a Society with a universal vocation and a missionary tradition. We therefore have a special responsibility in this regard. We have a duty to ensure that our ministry is directed toward incarnating the faith and life of the Church in the culture and traditions of the people among whom and with whom we work and, at the same time, toward communion with all who share the same Christian faith.

105   56.   Moreover, the Church is aware that today the problematic of inculturation must take into account not only the cultural values proper to each nation but also the new, more universal values emerging from the closer and more continuous interchange among nations in our time. Here, too, our Society is called upon to serve the Church; take part in her task of *aggiornamento,* of "bringing-up-to-date"; that is, of incarnating the Gospel in these values as well, these new values that are becoming increasingly planetary in scope.

The Spiritual Exercises

106   57.   The ministry of the Spiritual Exercises is of particular importance in this regard. A key element in the pedagogy of the Exercises is that its aim is to remove the barriers between God and man so that the Spirit speaks directly with man. Inherent in this Ignatian practice of spiritual direction is a deep respect for the exercitant as he is and for the culture, background and tradition that have gone into making him what he is. Moreover, the pedagogy of the Exercises is a pedagogy of discernment. It teaches a man to discover for himself where God is calling him, what God wants him to do, as he is, where he is, among his own people.

58.   The Exercises also help to form Christians who, **107** having personally experienced God as Savior, are able to stand back from the spurious absolutes of competing ideologies, and because of this detachment can play a constructive part in the reform of social and cultural structures. Thus, the ministry of the Spiritual Exercises is one of the most important we can undertake today. We should by all means encourage studies, research and experiment directed toward helping our contemporaries experience the vitality of the Exercises as adapted to the new needs which are theirs. Moreover the spirit of the Exercises should pervade every other ministry of the Word that we undertake.

Guidelines for Concerted Action

59.   In presenting this review of our apostolate in its **108** various dimensions, the General Congregation wishes to continue along the lines given by Father General to the Congregation of Procurators of 1970* and to emphasize once more the importance of theological reflection, social action, education and the mass media as means of making our preaching of the Gospel more effective. The importance of these means rests in the fact that, in touching its most profound needs, they permit a more universal service to humankind.

---

*See the Yearbook of the Society of Jesus, 1971-1972.

109   60.   In the concrete:

—We must be more aware of the need for research and for theological reflection, carried on in a context which is both interdisciplinary and genuinely integrated with the culture in which it is done and with its traditions. Only thus can it throw light on the main problems which the Church and humanity ought to be coming to grips with today.

—Greater emphasis should be placed on the conscientization according to the Gospel of those who have the power to bring about social change, and a special place given to service of the poor and oppressed.

—We should pursue and intensify the work of formation in every sphere of education, while subjecting it at the same time to continual scrutiny. We must help prepare both young people and adults to live and labor for others and with others to build a more just world. Especially we should help form our Christian students in such a way that animated by a mature faith and personally devoted to Jesus Christ, they can find Him in others and having recognized Him there, they will serve Him in their neighbor. In this way we shall contribute to the formation of those who by a kind of multiplier-effect will share in the process of educating the world itself.

—We have to take a critical look at our ability to communicate our heart-felt convictions not only to persons we deal with directly, but also with those we cannot meet individually, and whom we can only help to the extent that we succeed in humanizing the social climate—attitudes and behavior—where we are engaged. In this regard the communications media would seem to play a role of great importance.

110   61.   We should pursue these objectives not separately, in isolation, but as complementary factors of a single apostolic thrust toward the development of the whole person and of every person.

D.

A MISSIONARY BODY

62.   The dispersal imposed on us today by our vocation **111**
as Jesuits makes it imperative that we strengthen and renew
the ties that bind us together as members of the same
Society.

63.   That is why it is so important that our communities **112**
be apostolic communities, and it is the primary responsibility of the local superior to see to it that his community
approach this ideal as closely as possible. Each one of us
should be able to find in his community—in shared prayer,
in converse with his brethren, in the celebration of the
Eucharist—the spiritual resources he needs for the apostolate. The community should also be able to provide him
with a context favorable to apostolic discernment.

64.   It is this stress on the apostolic dimension of our **113**
communities that this 32nd General Congregation wishes
to add to what the 31st General Congregation has already
set forth in detail regarding the requirements of community
life in the Society.[20] Our communities, even those whose
members are engaged in different ministries, must have for
their principle of unity the apostolic spirit.[21]

65.   It is important that whether a Jesuit works in a **114**
team or whether he works alone, he must be, and must
feel himself to be, sent. It is the responsibility of the superior, after he has shared with the individual Jesuit in
his discernment, to see to it that the apostolic work of each
is properly integrated into the global mission of the Society.

---

20 GC 31, D. 19.
21 See the directives of the present General Congregation in the
document "The Union of Minds and Hearts," especially those
regarding spiritual and community life.

The individual Jesuit normally receives his mission from his provincial superior; but it belongs to the local superior to adapt that mission to local circumstances and to promote the sense of solidarity of the members of the community with each other and with the whole body of the Society to which they belong.

115   66.   This solidarity with the Society is primary. It ought to take precedence over loyalties to any other sort of institution, Jesuit or non-Jesuit. It ought to stamp any other commitment which is thereby transformed into "mission." The "mission" as such is bestowed by the Society and is subject to her review. She can confirm or modify it as the greater service of God may require.

116   67.   This kind of responsibility on the part of the superior cannot be exercised without the living practice of the account of conscience, by which the superior is made capable of taking part in the discernment done by each of the members and can help him therein.[22] It presupposes that, with the help of his companions, he engage in a continual, communitarian reflection upon fresh needs of the apostolate and upon the ways and means by which they can best be met. And it asks the superior to encourage the shy and the hesitant and to see to it that each individual finds a place in the community and a place in the apostolate which will bring out the best in him and enable him to cope with the hardships and risks he may encounter in God's service.

117   68.   The apostolic body of the Society to which we belong should not be thought of just in terms of the local community. We belong to a province, which should itself constitute an apostolic community in which discernment and coordination of the apostolate on a larger scale than at the local level can and should take place. Moreover, the

22 Ibid.

province is part of the whole Society, which also forms one single apostolic body and community. It is at this level that the over-all apostolic decisions and guidelines must be made and worked out, decisions and guidelines for which we should all feel jointly responsible.

69. This demands of all of us a high degree of avail- **118**
ability and a real apostolic mobility in the service of the universal Church. Father General, with the help of his advisers, has the task of inspiring the Society as a whole to serve the cause of the Gospel and its justice. But we ask all our brothers, especially the provincials, to give Father General all the support, all the ideas and assistance which they can, as he tries to carry out this task of inspiring and coordinating, even if this should shake up our settled habits or stretch horizons sometimes all too limited. The extent to which our contemporaries depend on one another in their outlook, aspirations and religious concepts, to say nothing of structural connections that span our planet, makes this over-all coordination of our efforts indispensable if we are to remain faithful to our mission of evangelization.

E.

PRACTICAL DISPOSITIONS

70. The decisions and guidelines about our apostolic **119**
mission set forth above have certain practical consequences which we now propose to detail in some points.

A Program for Deepening Awareness and for Apostolic Discernment

71. Considering the variety of situations in which Je- **120**
suits are working, the General Congregation cannot provide

the programs each region will need to reflect upon and implement the decisions and guidelines presented here. Each province or group of provinces must undertake a program of reflection and a review of our apostolates to discover what action is appropriate in each particular context.

121   72.   What is required is not so much a research program as a process of reflection and evaluation inspired by the Ignatian tradition of spiritual discernment, in which the primary stress is on prayer and the effort to attain "indifference," that is, an apostolic readiness for anything.

122   73.   The general method to be followed to produce this awareness and to engage in this discernment may be described (see *Octogesima Adveniens,* n. 4) as a constant interplay between experience, reflection, decision and action, in line with the Jesuit ideal of being "contemplative in action." The aim is to insure a change in our habitual patterns of thought, a conversion of heart as well as of spirit. The result will be effective apostolic decisions.

123   74.   The process of evaluation and discernment must be brought to bear principally on the following: the identification and analysis of the problems involved in the service of faith and the promotion of justice and the review and renewal of our apostolic commitments. Where do we live? Where do we work? How? With whom? What really is our involvement with, dependence on, or commitment to ideologies and power centers? Is it only to the converted that we know how to preach Jesus Christ? These are some of the questions we should raise with reference to our membership individually, as well as to our communities and institutions.

Continuing Evaluation of Our Apostolic Work

124   75.   With regard to the choice of ministries and the setting up of priorities and programs, the General Congregation asks that the following guidelines be taken into account.

76.   The review of our ministries and the deployment of **125** our available manpower and resources must pay great attention to the role in the service of faith and the promotion of justice which can be played by our educational institutions, periodicals, parishes, retreat houses, and the other apostolic works for which we are responsible. Not only should our structured activities undergo this review, so should our individual apostolates.

77.   In each province or region, or at least at the Assist- **126** ancy level, there should be a definite mechanism for the review of our ministries.[23] Now is a good time to examine critically how these arrangements are working and, if need be, to replace them by others which are more effective and allow for a wider participation in the process of communal discernment. The appropriate major superior should make an annual report to Father General on what has been accomplished here.

Some Special Cases

78.   The General Congregation recognizes how impor- **127** tant it is that we should be present and work with others in different areas of human activity, especially in those parts of the world which are most secularized. It also recognizes the real opportunities for apostolic work afforded, in some cases, by the practice of a profession or by taking a job not directly related to the strictly presbyteral function.[24]

79.   The General Congregation considers that such com- **128** mitments can be a part of the Society's mission, provided they meet the following conditions: They must be undertaken as a mission from our superiors. Their aim must be

23 See GC 31, D. 22.
24 See GC 31, D. 23, n. 12.

clearly apostolic. Preference should be given to work in an area which is de-Christianized or underprivileged. The activity must be in harmony with the priestly character of the Society as a whole. It must be compatible with the essential demands of the religious life—an interior life of prayer, a relationship with a Jesuit superior and a Jesuit community, poverty, apostolic availability.

129   80.   Any realistic plan to engage in the promotion of justice will mean some kind of involvement in civic activity. Exceptional forms of involvement must conform to the general practice of the Church[25] and the norms laid down by Father General.[26] If, in certain countries, it seems necessary to adopt more detailed norms and directives, this must be seen to by provincials—as far as possible in regional conferences. These norms and directives should be submitted to Father General for approval. It will then be for the provincial—with the agreement, where the case demands it, of the local bishop or the bishops' conference—to give or refuse the permission that may be required.

International Cooperation

130   81.   All the major problems of our time have an international dimension. A real availability and openness to change will thus be necessary to foster the growth of co-operation and coordination throughout the whole Society. All Jesuits, but especially those who belong to the affluent world, should endeavor to work with those who form public opinion, as well as with international organizations, to promote justice among all peoples. To this end, the General Congregation asks Father General to make one or other of his advisers specifically responsible for the necessary organization of international cooperation within the Society, as required by our service of faith and promotion of justice.

---

25 See Synod of Bishops, 1971.
26 *ActRSJ*, XV, 942.

5 THE WORK OF INCULTURATION OF THE FAITH AND PROMOTION OF CHRISTIAN LIFE

1.   In furthering the mission of evangelization and the **131** building up of Christ's Church, the 32nd General Congregation is aware of the great importance that must be given today to the work involving inculturation of both faith and Christian life in all the continents of the world, but especially in the regions of Asia and Africa[1] and in some countries of Latin America. Mindful that from its very beginning the Society has had a long and venerable missionary tradition of promoting inculturation, the Congregation judges that this work must be pursued with even greater determination in our own day and that it deserves the progressively greater concern and attention of the whole Society. Therefore, the Congregation urgently requests all Jesuits to promote this effort according to the mind and authentic teaching of the Church[2] in order to provide greater help and service not only to the local Churches but especially to the universal Church under the Vicar of Christ on earth, to the end that all peoples and nations may be restored to unity in Christ Jesus, Our Lord.

2.   The Congregation entrusts to Father General the **132** further development and promotion of this work through-

---

1 See GC 32, "Our Mission Today: The Service of Faith and the Promotion of Justice," nn. 53-56, and "The Formation of Jesuits," nn. 27-29 and passim.

2 E.g., LG, 13, 17; AG, 16-18, 22, 26; GS, 53-58.
 Pope Paul VI, *Populorum Progressio,* n. 65; *Insegnamenti di Paolo VI,* V/1967, 576-600, 635; VII/1969, 528-31, 542, 548-49, 609-13; VIII/1970, 1215-16, 1249; *AAS,* LXVI (1974), 625-29, 631-39.
 Statement of the First Plenary Assembly of the Federation of Asian Bishops' Conferences (FABC, April 27, 1974; Statement of African Bishops (AMECEA/SECAM) present at the 4th Synod of Bishops, Rome, October 20, 1974.

out the Society. In the first place, it recommends that, after he has considered the whole question with the help of expert assistance, Father General write a letter or instruction to the entire Society, in order to further this work in and by the Society. His purpose in writing will be to clarify for all of Ours the true meaning and theological understanding of the task and process of inculturation as well as its importance for the apostolic mission of the Society today. The Congregation also recommends to Father General that he further this effort in any other ways which seem to him more conducive to God's greater glory.[3]

---

3 For example, by establishing a commission to promote the work of inculturation in the Society. The members of this commission could be chosen principally from the three Assistancies of Africa, East Asia, and India, as seems best to Father General. In addition, by recommending strongly to other institutions and centers of the Society, e.g., those engaged in theological studies, the renewal of pastoral works, the publication of magazines and periodicals, the preparation of audio-visual materials, etc., studies and projects which would promote inculturation.

II

DEVELOPING THE
APOSTOLIC BODY OF THE SOCIETY

6   THE FORMATION OF JESUITS

Especially with Regard to the Apostolate and Studies

1. Since the 31st General Congregation the many **133** changes in the world at large have brought influences to bear on the training of our scholastics and brothers. Among these changes we might mention: the development of new structures, institutions, and mentalities in many nations; a deeper appreciation of the identity and autonomy of different cultures; the profound renewal of the Church in recent years; new arrangements in many provinces for the education of our men, which is often pursued in institutions not belonging to the Society or in circumstances where the academic program is distinct from religious formation; a restructuring of community life located now in urban centers; new cultural values which often have an influence on our young men; new aspirations of young Jesuits: their sensitivity to the world of today and the problems of society, their desire to be more closely associated with their peers; the difficulty—affecting most young people today—of remaining for a long time in the status of students while desirous of taking a genuine role in the active life of the Society; their regret oftentimes at what appears an isolated existence; their desire, finally, that the Society embrace an apostolic perspective more suited to the growth of their own vocations.

2. In this context, an adequate evaluation of the pres- **134** ent formation of Jesuits—which has not yet been done sufficiently—seems all the more necessary because, in continually changing times, constant adaptation is required in order to be sure of achieving the essential purpose of our formation. Moreover, certain defects which are apparent

both in formation generally and in the organization of studies sometimes stem from a failure to fulfill the prescribed norms, as found in the following documents: Decrees 8 and 9 of the 31st General Congregation, *An Instruction of Father General on the Spiritual Training of Jesuits,* and the *General Norms for Studies* (1968).[1]

135 3. Therefore, the 32nd General Congregation proposes some practical norms for the evaluation of various features of formation and their execution. At the same time, it provides, in declarative form, some preliminary reflections which may help to give both young Jesuits and those who in various ways help to educate them, and indeed all of our men, a perspective on formation adapted to our times. Within this perspective the above-mentioned documents can be re-read and explained. Little is said, however, about spiritual formation, because in this area the General Congregation confirms and stresses what has been prescribed in the eighth decree of the 31st General Congregation.

136 4. The present document, then, although dealing principally with the formation of young Jesuits, looks, in a certain sense, to all our members since all are involved in formation as that task is presented here. All of us, after all, constitute an apostolic body into which the younger members are gradually integrated. Moreover, older Jesuits themselves need a permanent and continuing formation, which our formal training must have in view from the start. Our apostolic calling requires personal and ever-deepening study not only on the part of the young but on the part of all Jesuits.

A. THE INTEGRATED CHARACTER OF APOSTOLIC FORMATION

137 5. The decision made by the 32nd General Congregation concerning the mission of the Society in today's world[2] calls us to give renewed emphasis to the apostolic charac-

---

1 *ActRSJ,* XV, 105-33.
2 See above, pp. 97-124.

ter of our formation process. This was already clearly affirmed by the 31st General Congregation.[3] Moreover, the total formation of Jesuits, both scholastics and brothers, must be equal to the demands of evangelization in a world deeply troubled by atheism and social injustice.

6. It is with this world in view that our formation must **138** prepare witnesses and ministers of the faith who, as members of the Society, are ready to be sent for the greater service of the Church into situations which are characterized by uncertainty. Their formation must make our men capable of dialogue with others, capable of confronting the cultural problems of our day. For these are the circumstances under which they must labor to promote the spiritual growth of mankind according to the tradition of the Society.

7. To respond to this apostolic vision, the whole forma- **139** tion of our members must be understood and promoted as a process of integration into the apostolic body of the Society.

8. This notion of integration expresses, in a synthetic **140** way, a most important aspect of contemporary Jesuit formation which is used in this document in two different senses: as meaning both personal integration and integration into the apostolic body of the Society. These aspects should not be separated. Integration among disciplines and structures of the formation process will be treated later.

a) Personal Integration

9. First of all, it might be good to recall some of the **141** elements by which an apostolic personality is formed:

a) The process of apostolic formation must favor the personal assimilation of Christian experience. This demands a deep knowledge of revelation based on Sacred Scripture and on the living tradition of the Church and the ability, in the light of this knowledge, to reflect in a

---

3 GC 31, D. 8, n. 4 and D. 9, n. 1; *ActRSJ,* XIV, 872, 877.

discerning way on the apostolate as it is concretely experienced.

b) In an apostolic formation an important place must be given to spiritual experience which is personal, vital, rooted in faith, nourished by daily prayer and the Eucharist: an experience that makes us capable of witnessing to the gift of faith before nonbelievers and of cooperating with God for the spiritual growth of those who do believe.

c) Our style of life and its attendant circumstances, both personal and communitarian, ought to favor apostolic formation. It should have the young Jesuits live in real conditions and come to know themselves, where responsibilities prevent a lapse into carelessness and individualism. This should mean that young Jesuits should not, during their time of formation, be oblivious of the actual living conditions of the people of the regions in which they live. Their style of life therefore must help them to know and understand what the people around them seek, what they suffer, what they lack.

142   10. Accordingly, an experience of living with the poor for at least a certain period of time will be necessary for all, so that they may be helped to overcome the limitations of their own social background. For this reason, the conditions of such an experience must be thought out carefully, so that it will be genuine, free of illusions, and productive of an inner conversion. And it must be added that our whole personal and community life ought to be characterized by the radical standard of the Gospel, in the sense that our fidelity to the evangelical choice we have made by our vows must lead us to a critical vision of ourselves, of the world, and of society. This radical standard must be appropriate to a personal insertion into the human culture of the region where the apostolate is carried out, so that one's own faith may be intelligible to other people and influence their life and culture.

143   11. In the whole course of formation, these diverse elements, necessary for an apostolic and priestly mission in today's world, must be harmoniously united. We should conceive and plan for the total formation of our men as a process of progressive integration of the spiritual life, of the apostolate, and of studies in such a way that the richness of the spiritual life should be the source of the apostolate, and the apostolate, in turn, the motive for study and for a more profound spiritual life.

12.   This process of integration begins in the novitiate, **144** which may be common for both scholastics and brothers, and whose purposes are formation and probation. Right from the novitiate members of the Society are to be carefully instructed in spiritual discernment. This Ignatian discernment is an essential ingredient of our apostolic formation. Indeed, today's conditions demand that a member of the Society during the whole course of formation should practice spiritual discernment about the concrete choices which, stage by stage, the service of Christ and the Church require of him. It is through this discernment that a sense of personal responsibility and true freedom will be achieved.

b) *Integration into the Apostolic Body of the Society*

13.   The whole process of formation, through its various **145** stages from novitiate to tertianship, should favor this integration. It should prepare our young men to be eager to fulfill the missions and perform the ministries which the Society may wish to assign to them.

14.   To achieve this, the provincial must follow the en- **146** tire course of development of each individual; he must take care that each understand the purpose of the stage of formation in which he is involved and profit from it according to the measure of grace granted to him. Moreover, through the whole course of this development, each young man should also be assisted by his local superior, the spiritual father, the director or prefect of studies, and his teachers to integrate intellectual reflection with apostolic experience—both personal and communitarian—in order to prepare his own apostolic orientation. Those who direct the

young must therefore challenge them to develop a sense of responsibility. Ultimately, all who work in formation must try to become so filled with God's own wisdom that they teach and form our young as much by the lively sharing of their personal knowledge of God and man as by the communication of academic learning.

147   15.   This integration, moreover, is to be aided by the continual experience of participating in the life of the Society as an apostolic body. On the one hand, such experience is fostered in houses of formation by a community, which the young constitute among themselves and with other Jesuits, in which there is real communication and a sharing of life, even on the spiritual level, as well as cooperation and mutual responsibility in studies and in apostolic works. If, indeed, young Jesuits live at times in apostolic communities, care must be taken that: (a) the communities are such as can willingly assume the responsibility of formation, along with those who have special charge of formation in the province; and (b) a priest, designated by the provincial, be responsible for helping them to pursue serious studies and carry on their apostolic work while still maintaining close ties with their companions.

148   16.   On the other hand, this experience supposes a formation that is closely bound up with the activities of the province or region; those in charge of formation therefore must be men who are capable both of assisting other Jesuits and of receiving help from others. Contact, information and cooperation with other communities and works, especially with those in the same province, should help young Jesuits to experience the whole province, indeed the whole Society, as an apostolic body united in one spirit. To achieve this, the provincial, or someone designated by him, should see that the young are given this apostolic orientation in progressive stages and by a variety of experiences, according to the talents of each and with a view to the apostolic works of the province and the Society.

17.   The goal of the whole process of integration should **149** be to assist each one, with the help of spiritual discernment, to learn not to indulge his own aspirations in an individualistic way, but to come to understand that he is a member of the body of the whole Society and shares its apostolic mission.

c)   Continued Formation as the Renewal of the Whole Apostolic Body of the Society

18.   Especially in our times, when everything is subject **150** to such rapid change and evolution, and when new questions and new knowledge, both in theology and in other branches of learning, are constantly developing, a truly contemporary apostolate demands of us a process of permanent and continuing formation. Thus formation is never ended, and our "first" formation must be seen as the beginning of this continuing process.

19.   Continuing   formation   is   achieved   especially **151** through a constant evaluation of and reflection on one's apostolate, in the light of faith and with the help of one's apostolic community. It also needs the cooperation of our professors and experts, whose theory can shed light on our praxis, even while they themselves are led to more profound reflection by the apostolic experience of their fellow Jesuits. This kind of communication will also assist the integration of the young into the apostolic life of the province, and the contact between formation and the apostolate will profit the whole Society.

20.   This continuing formation demands that definite **152** periods of time be given to formal courses or simply to private study, whether in theology or other disciplines, as required for one's apostolate.

B.   INTEGRATION OF STUDIES INTO THE APOSTOLIC LIFE

21.   Since our mission today is the proclamation of our **153** faith in Jesus Christ, which itself involves the promotion of justice, our studies must be directed toward this mission and

derive their motivation from it. In a world where faith is fostered only with great difficulty and in which justice is so broadly violated, our wish is to help others arrive at a knowledge and love of God and a truly fraternal love of men, to help them lead lives according to the Good News of Christ and to renew the structures of human society in justice. Ministers of the Word of God can bring such help to others only if they have themselves acquired a profound vision of reality, from personal reflection on the experience of man in the world and on his transcendent finality in God. They must make their own God's revelation of Himself in Jesus Christ, as it is contained in Sacred Scripture and expressed in the life of the Church and in the teaching of the Magisterium. Such personal and accurate assimilation cannot be obtained without continued discipline and the labor of tireless and patient study.

154   22.   Thus the Society has opted anew for a profound academic formation of its future priests—theological as well as philosophical, humane and scientific—in the persuasion that, presupposing the testimony of one's own life, there is no more apt way to exercise our mission. Such study is itself an apostolic work which makes us present to men to the degree that we come to know all the more profoundly their possibilities, their needs, their cultural milieu. Our studies should foster and stimulate those very qualities which today are often suffocated by our contemporary style of living and thinking: a spirit of reflection and an awareness of the deeper, transcendent values. For this reason, our young men should be reminded that their special mission and apostolate during the time of study is to study. Thus, the desire for a more active service, which the young feel so deeply, ought to be itself the animating force which penetrates all their studies.

155   23.   The brothers also who participate in the apostolic activity of the Society according to Decrees 7 and 8 of the 31st General Congregation,[4] should receive appropriate

---

4 *ActRSJ*, XIV, 861, 871; see also *ActRSJ*, XV, 567-570.

theological instruction and a better formation in what concerns their work, according to the measure of the gifts they have received from God.

24.   From different parts of the Society it has been reported that our philosophical studies in recent years have, for various reasons, suffered deterioration. The General Congregation urges both superiors and professors to take the necessary means to strengthen the philosophical training of our men. Sufficient time must be given to it, and it must be done in a mature, unified and coherent fashion, reaching a serious level of academic quality. The Society expects from its scholastics the kind of long-term philosophical training which is in touch with the radical problems of human existence and which is a mature reflection on the different intellectual traditions of mankind, in such a way that it can be integrated with subsequent or concomitant theological reflection. **156**

25.   The numerous points of contact between philosophy and other fields of learning, contact with contemporary problems and with the present and future lives of students, ought to be pointed out. Because of today's diversity of cultures, sciences, ideologies and social movements, priests in the Society ought to be men who possess balance and depth in their thinking and who can communicate to others with credibility their own convictions regarding meaning and values. **157**

26.   Theological training should be well integrated, sufficiently systematic, adapted to the exigencies of our mission and conducted according to the norms of the Church. The whole of this training supposes above all a personal experience of the faith which must be developed and explained by a knowledge of Sacred Scripture, Christian doctrine, and moral theology. Students should be encouraged to establish a critical dialogue between theology and human culture, between faith and the real questions and problems which occupy the minds of the people among whom we exercise our apostolate. This reflection cannot be effective **158**

today except through an integration of the human sciences with philosophy and theology, both in teaching and in learning. Cooperation and communication among professors can be a great help towards this.

159   27.   In accord with the norm of Decree 9, n. 18, of the 31st General Congregation,[5] those studies should be fostered that readily help our young men attain a harmonious, balanced human and religious maturity; studies leading not only to a living knowledge of man and his modern world, but also suited to expressing ourselves to the people of our times. Also, our formation must be such that the Jesuit can be one with the people to whom he is sent, capable of communicating with them. He must be able to share their convictions and values, their history, their experience and aspirations; at the same time, he must be open to the convictions and values of other peoples, traditions, and cultures. Hence training in the sciences, in languages, in literature, in the classic "liberal arts," in modern media of communication, and in the cultural traditions of the nation, must be undertaken with much greater care.[6]

160   28.   Moreover, the apostolic activities of the scholastics and brothers, accepted as a genuine mission from superiors, must be so directed and so subjected to evaluation that a real connection will be possible between apostolic activities and studies. Such activities are a part of apostolic formation for everyone, and part of the strictly priestly formation for those who are called to the ministerial priesthood: they ought to be integrated into the curriculum of studies as a basis for further reflection. For studies can be so tied in with these different experiences that by the experiences, the studies themselves can be appreciated in a new light.[7]

161   29.   In the whole course of formation, especially during philosophical and theological studies, a deep and authentic

---

5 *ActRSJ,* XIV, 880.

6 See NG 85-95; *ActRSJ,* XV, 258-260.

7 See Ibid., 116-117; *ActRSJ,* XV, 263-264.

involvement with the local culture should be fostered, according to regional differences; yet care should also be taken to promote unity of minds and hearts in the Society. To foster this union, all the young members of the Society must cultivate Ignatian spirituality and be taught a theology which is grounded in the tradition and official teaching of the Church, though adapted to the needs of the times and of local cultures. For this purpose, meetings of those responsible for formation and professors of Ours in the various regions and in the whole Society can be very helpful. The young men themselves, by communication among the various provinces and regions, should acquire better knowledge of the unity and diversity of the Society, which will lead them to a true sense of its universality.

30. Those who teach our men ought to manifest by **162** their labor and living example this integration of the intellectual, spiritual and apostolic life. To them is committed a prime role in the intellectual apostolate of the Society. They teach in the name and by the mandate of the Church.[8] By their scholarship and with openness of mind, they seek out ways to develop a more profound understanding of the faith and to make it known to men, taking into account the questions and the needs of our times and of their own nations. They are called by the Society not only to teach their disciplines and to carry on scholarly research, but are also responsible for fostering each in his own way, the integral formation of our men—intellectual and spiritual, priestly and apostolic—in the spirit of the Society.

C. NORMS

31. The provincial is responsible for all aspects of the **163** formation of those who belong to his province. He is responsible for both the persons and the institutions of the Society charged with formation. However, it is appropriate

---

8 GC 31, D. 9, n. 43.

that there be a delegate who should have the immediate care for the various aspects of formation of each young Jesuit in the province (or in the region, where circumstances so dictate).

a) There should be regional or provincial commissions to advise superiors in the direction of formation in accord with local conditions.[9]

b) These commissions should be made up both of those who are in charge of formation and also of some who are working in various apostolic ministries. They should evaluate the status of formation in the province or region on a regular basis.

164   32.   The General Congregation suggests to Father General that one of the general counsellors should have special concern for the integral formation of Jesuits throughout the Society. He ought also to help Father General in insisting on the execution of the decrees of this Congregation on formation, in adapting the *General Norms for Studies* and in evaluating experiments relative to formation.

165   33.   Those who are in charge of formation should take care that our scholastics and brothers, especially in the period immediately after the novitiate, become familiar with the sources of the spirituality of the Church and the Society and with its history and traditions and that they study them with a view toward their own progress and the progress of others.

166   34.   Provincials should be mindful of poverty in the matter of expenses for new arrangements of formation communities and institutions and in the pursuit of special studies.

167   35.   In accord with the resources and the apostolic needs of the different regions or provinces, provincials should provide for the spiritual, intellectual, and apostolic

---

9 See GC 31, D. 9, n. 16; *ActRSJ*, XIV, 819 and NG 10; *ActRSJ*, XV, 241.

renewal of all our men. At determined times, all should be given sufficient opportunity for study and for reflection about their apostolic life. This program should be carried out with serious application according to a plan approved by the provincial.

36.   It is suggested that, more or less ten years after **168** completing tertianship, Jesuits who have had experience in apostolic ministries and offices be given the opportunity for intensive spiritual renewal during two or three months.

37.   Studies in the Society are governed by the common **169** law of the Church and by Decree 9 of the 31st General Congregation unless this present decree in a particular case provides otherwise. All the decrees of previous General Congregations which are contrary either to this decree or to Decree 9 of the 31st General Congregation or to the *General Norms for Studies* are definitively abrogated. These *General Norms* which Father General promulgated in place of the previous *Ratio Studiorum* are to be continually revised and adapted to new needs.[10]

38.   Because of the importance of philosophical and **170** theological studies in the tradition and apostolic life of the Society, provincials should see to it that in general all acquire the licentiate in either theology or philosophy and that those who manifest greater interest and talent should continue further studies in order to acquire higher degrees. What is said in Decree 9, nn. 33-40, of the 31st General Congregation concerning special studies should also be implemented.

39.   In faculties or institutions where the curriculum **171** in philosophy and theology is flexible, the superior of the scholastics or the prefect of studies, according to the determination of the provincial, is responsible for arranging the curriculum of each scholastic according to his ability and his future apostolic work.

---

10 See GC 31, D. 9, n. 15; *ActRSJ*, XIV, 879.

172   40.   The studies of brothers should be in accord with the needs of the province as well as their ability, interest, and future apostolic work. Their education in religious studies should be commensurate with their ability and adapted to their other studies.

173   41.   Scholastics are to devote at least two years to the study of philosophy.[11] But when these studies are combined with other subjects or with the study of theology, they must be pursued in such a way that the equivalent of two years is devoted to them.

174   42.   a)   The four year study of theology, prescribed by the Church for all who are preparing for the priesthood, is to be observed. But when the regular curriculum of theology is completed in three years, a fourth year is to be added which should be dedicated either to preparation for a degree in theology or, in an approved program, to the integration of theological studies into one's formation, especially one's pastoral formation.

175   b)   If, however, there is an introductory course in theology, under the direction of a faculty of theology, beginning in the novitiate and continued through the period of philosophical studies, a careful evaluation should be made to determine whether the quality of this program is such that it might be equivalent to the first year of the theological curriculum.

176   43.   Special studies, understood according to their apostolic character, should be earnestly fostered by superiors. Those who undertake such studies, especially in secular universities, should be assisted to understand and personally to assimilate the interrelationship between these studies and their philosophy and theology. They should have special spiritual assistance and should be integrated into the life of a community of the Society.

177   44.   A solid education should also be fostered in litera-

---

11 GC 31, D. 9, n. 22.

ture, the arts, sciences, history, and the various aspects of the culture of the region where the apostolate will be carried on. The study of modern means of social communication should also be encouraged. An academic degree should be required as the usual means to evaluate our education in these fields in order to make our apostolic service more effective.

45. Besides their own language, our young men should **178** learn one or other of the more common modern languages which would facilitate communication with other cultures and with the universal Society.

46. Although the curriculum of studies for the scholas- **179** tics may be arranged in a number of ways, such unity ought to be observed in the regional programs as to make it possible for the scholastics, without extreme difficulty, to take part of their training in another province or region.

47. Formation in apostolic activities ought to be car- **180** ried on in a progressive fashion under the direction of a competent coordinator who should direct the young Jesuits in their activities, bring them to examine the activities critically, and help them to carry them out. Such activities, which are to be undertaken as a mission from superiors, should be so arranged that they lead to a deeper level of spiritual and intellectual reflection. For this purpose, it will be especially helpful, according to the mind of the Constitutions, for the scholastics to become accustomed to directing others in the Spiritual Exercises under the supervision of an experienced director.[12] Moreover, these apostolic experiences should be an integral part of the curriculum of studies.

48. In institutions where scholastics are taught by Jesu- **181** its, these Jesuit professors should remember that the mission which they have received from the provincial extends also to the formation of scholastics. Therefore, a team of professors should be chosen which has the aptitude for

---

12 *Cons.* [408-09].

carrying on scholarly work, for teaching, and for cooperating in the integral formation of the scholastics. With regard to this point, professors should be conscious of their responsibility toward the Society.

182   49.   a)   In provinces where scholastics study in faculties or institutions which do not belong to the Society, superiors should see to it that the formation proper to the Society is provided with all the necessary means, for example: by complementing the curriculum with special courses.

183   b)   Where, however, the faculty or institution is directed by the Society but the academic direction is separate from the religious direction (of the community), superiors are responsible for promoting mutual cooperation in order to achieve the integral formation of our men.

184   50.   The *Regional Orders of Studies* are to be sufficiently revised so that they will truly correspond to the requirements of this decree. Such revisions are, in good time, to be submitted to Father General for approval.

185   51.   To establish the level of learning required of those who may be admitted to the profession of four vows, of all those who have not acquired a higher degree, at least a licentiate, in sacred studies[13] an *examen ad gradum* is required according to the Constitutions.[14] It must be an oral examination in philosophy and theology, before four examiners. Decree 9, n. 29, of the 31st General Congregation is abrogated. Everything else dealing with the length of the examination, its program, and the way of giving the grades for the examination is to be determined in the Regional Orders of Studies approved by Father General.

186   52.   In each province there should be a serious consideration of how this decree is to be implemented. A report on this matter is to be sent to Father General.

---

13 See GC 31, D. 11, n. 3 (1 and 2); *ActRSJ,* XIV, 887.
14 *Cons.* [518].

1.   Just as the 31st General Congregation, so also the   **187**
32nd General Congregation holds the institution of tertianship in high regard.[1] Therefore, provincials should urge
priests and coadjutor brothers who have not yet made
their tertianship to do so as soon as possible.

2.   The tertianship of the coadjutor brothers enjoined   **188**
by the 30th General Congregation[2] is to be observed faithfully, for it has contributed much to the spiritual advancement of the brothers. When it is judged opportune, and
the provincial permits, this period of formation may be
made together with our priests or candidates for the priesthood.

3.   The 32nd General Congregation approves two ter-   **189**
tianship plans, A and B, understanding that, with Father
General's approval, they may be adopted in different provinces and regions:

Plan A: After completing the Society's required studies of theology, the candidate will enter his third probation.
The experiment of the month-long Spiritual Exercises is to
be made within the first months of the tertianship. Then,
allowing for a suitable interval after the retreat, ordinations to the diaconate and priesthood will take place. During the course of the tertianship, a solid knowledge of the
Institute and a deeper understanding of the spirit of the
Society are to be fostered; but a notable part of the time
after priestly ordination is to be devoted to ministries, primarily pastoral, under competent supervision. At the end
of this tertianship year, the priests can be promoted to final

---

1 GC 31, D. 10, n. 1; *ActRSJ,* XIV, 885.
2 GC 30, D. 42; *ActRSJ,* XIII, 333; (CD, 387).

vows. In individual cases, and for a just cause, the provincial is authorized to postpone a scholastic's entry into tertianship; but if this is done, priestly ordination and final vows will likewise be postponed.

190   *Plan B:*   When the third year of theology is completed and an appropriate spiritual preparation has been made, the scholastic can receive ordination to the priesthood. After ordination, and some time after the course of studies is finished, tertianship is to be made; this should be done not later than three years after priestly ordination, except for a just cause, with the provincial's approval.

It is better that the tertian have an assignment and work in an apostolic community, provided that, in the judgment of the Instructor, this assignment and work are compatible with the experiments and duration of residence required in the forms of tertianship approved by Father General,[3] so that while in an active life, the tertian may be formed to be a Jesuit contemplative in action.

---

3   *ActRSJ,* XV, 557, letter of April 15, 1970.

8   GRADES IN THE SOCIETY OF JESUS

1.   The 32nd General Congregation again lays very **191**
great stress on promoting the unity of vocation of the entire
body of the Society, as enshrined in our Constitutions. It
asks each and every member to make this unity shine forth
in the life, work, and apostolate of all communities; to ensure that grades be not a source of division, let there rather
be, by means of the day-to-day efforts of everyone, a complete union of the one religious, priestly, and apostolic body
in the love of Christ the Lord and the service of the
Church.

2.   Furthermore, the Congregation commends and **192**
urges:

a)   that the participation of the temporal coadjutors
in the life and apostolic activity of the Society be further
promoted, fulfilling the recommendations of the 31st General Congregation completely;[1]

b)   that the norms for the promotion of priests to the
profession of four vows, better adapted by the 31st General
Congregation to today's circumstances, be put into practice
both for those who are at present spiritual coadjutors and
for approved scholastics. Candidates, however, are to be
selected in such a way as in fact to meet the demands of
those criteria of selection.

---

1 GC 31, D. 7, nn. 2, 3, 4; *ActRSJ*, XIV, 862.

9   THE PERMANENT DIACONATE

The 32nd General Congregation amends Decree 6 of the 31st General Congregation[1] as follows: •

193   1.   In willing compliance with the desire of the Church, which commends the restoration of the permanent diaconate in the Eastern Churches, where the custom was discontinued,[2] and also in the Western Church, where in the judgment of the bishops and with the approval of the Holy See such renewal may lead to the spiritual progress of the faithful,[3] the General Congregation declares that our Society can be helped by having some members who are permanently engaged in the service of the Church by means of the holy order of the diaconate.

194   2.   Those members who for good reasons approved by Father General are ordained permanent deacons will retain the grade that they already have in the Society; if they are approved coadjutors, they are to be advanced to the grade of formed temporal coadjutors, all requisites having been observed; if they are scholastics, they can be admitted by Father General to the grade of spiritual coadjutors, by way of exception, once all requisites have been observed, but they cannot be made superiors in the strict sense.

195   3.   It is entrusted to Father General to obtain the necessary faculties from the Holy See so that there can be permanent deacons in the Society; and also to establish, whenever he judges it opportune, general or particular norms concerning the permanent diaconate in the Society.

---

1 *ActRSJ*, XIV, 861.
2 See OE, 17.
3 See LG, 29; AG, 16.

1.   As to decree 11, of the 31st General Congregation:[1]   **196**

a)   n. 2, 6°, is abrogated.

b)   n. 2, 7°, shall be revised to read: *"At least ten full years in the Society, including the years spent in initial studies of philosophy and theology in the Society."*

c)   n. 2, 8°, is abrogated.

d)   n. 6, 3°, shall be revised to read: *"If they are temporal coadjutors, they have completed ten years of religious life and have made the tertianship required by Decree 42 of the 30th General Congregation*[2]*; if they are approved scholastics, they have completed the length of time in the Society prescribed in n. 1.b above."*

2.   In the case of scholastics, ordination to the priesthood (which, generally, is not to be deferred more than three years after studies of theology are completed) and the tertianship prescribed in the Constitutions must precede final vows.   **197**

3.   The 9th Decree of the 12th General Congregation[3] is abrogated; but the days on which final vows have traditionally been pronounced in the Society are commended anew.   **198**

---

1 *ActRSJ,* XIV, 887, 888.
2 CollDecr 387.
3 CollDecr 167.

III

WITNESS TO THE GOSPEL
IN TODAY'S CIRCUMSTANCES

11 THE UNION OF MINDS AND HEARTS

Orientations and Guidelines for our Spiritual Life and our Life in Community

199

1.   The 32nd General Congregation confirms and commends the declarations and directives of the 31st General Congregation on the religious life contained in its Decrees 13-17 and 19.[1] We believe them to be as helpful today in promoting our continual progress in spirit as when they were formulated, and hence they are implicitly assumed throughout the following statement.

2.   It must, however, be added that our experience during the last ten years of trying to live up to those declarations and directives, and the choices we have now made regarding our mission today, seem to call upon us, as well as to enable us, to give a sharper focus to our religious life as Jesuits. We believe that focus is *the union of minds and hearts [unio animorum] in the Society*. It is toward preserving and strengthening that union of minds and hearts under present-day conditions that the following orientations and practical norms are directed.

201

3.   We see our mission today as this: with renewed vigor to bear witness to the Gospel and, by the ministry of the Word, made operative in Christian charity, to help bring about in our world the reign of Christ in justice, love, and peace.[2] For just as Christ by his words and deeds, by his death and resurrection, made God's justice the world's salvation, and by so doing gave all men hope of becoming

---

1   *ActRSJ*, XIV, 889-926. D. 18, on Poverty, of the 31st GC, has been revised by the present GC.
2   See GC 32, D. 4. "Our Mission Today: The Service of Faith and the Promotion of Justice."

truly and wholly free, so we, his followers, are called upon to bear the witness of word and life to God's salvific love of the world in which we live.[3]

202 4. The carrying out of this mission demands a very wide dispersion both of men and of ministries, given the great social and cultural diversity of our world. Hence, what St. Ignatius says about the need for union of minds and hearts among us was never more true than now: "The more difficult it is for members of this congregation to be united with their head and among themselves, since they are so scattered among the faithful and among unbelievers in diverse regions of the world, the more ought means to be sought for that union. For the Society cannot be preserved, or governed, or, consequently, attain the end it seeks for the greater glory of God, unless its members are united among themselves and with their head."[4]

203 5. Moreover, that very union of minds and hearts which participation in Christ's mission requires will at the same time be a powerful aid to that mission, since it will be a visible sign of the love of the Father for all men. In the following orientations, therefore, we treat of our *union with God in Christ,* from which flows our *brotherly communion* with one another, a communion strengthened and made apostolically efficacious by the *bond of obedience.*

A. UNION WITH GOD IN CHRIST

204 6. Where, then, do we begin? We begin with the Ignatian insight that the unity of an apostolic body such as ours must be based on the union of each and all with God in Christ.[5] For if we have come together as a companionship, it is because we have, each of us, responded to the call of the Eternal King.[6]

---

3 See Luke 4. 18-19, 6. 20-21; Matt. 11. 5, 12. 18-21; Gal. 2. 10; James 2. 1-18

4 *Cons* [655].

5 *Cons* [671].

6 *SpEx* 98.

7.   In seeking this union with God in Christ, we experi-   **205**
ence a *difficulty peculiar to our times,* and we must be prepared to meet it. The material conditions of our world—a
world of sharply contrasted affluence and misery—and the
spiritual climate engendered by them, tend to produce in
our contemporaries an inner emptiness, a sense of the absence of God. The expressions, signs, and symbols of God's
presence which reassured men in the past do not seem to
be able to fill the present emptiness. We are still groping
for the new expressions, signs, and symbols that can do so.
In the meantime, we ourselves are sometimes plunged in
this climate of emptiness; and so it is crucial for us somehow to regain that continual *familiarity* with God in both
prayer and action which St. Ignatius considered absolutely
essential to the very existence of our companionship.

8.   We are thus led, inevitably, to the absolute necessity   **206**
of *personal prayer,* both as a value in itself and as a source
of energy for apostolic action. "The charity of Christ urges
us to personal prayer and no human person can dispense
us from that urgency."[7] We need it for the familiarity with
God which consists in finding him in all things, and all
things in him. Christ himself gave us an example of this.
St. Ignatius urges it in both the Exercises and the Constitutions. Our own personal experience confirms it. For while
it is "in action" that we are called to be contemplative,
this cannot obscure the fact that we *are* called to be "contemplative."

9.   And yet, many of us are troubled because, although   **207**
we want to pray, we cannot pray as we would like and as
our apostolic commitments demand we should. In the midst
of our individual, isolated efforts to pray as we should, perhaps we should listen to Christ's reminder that "where two
or three are gathered in my name, there am I in their
midst."[8] Does this not suggest that if we need assistance it

---

7 GC 31, D. 14, n. 7; *ActRSJ,* XIV, 893.
8 Matt. 18. 20.

is in our companionship that we must seek it: in dialogue with the spiritual counsellor, in openness to the superior, in shared prayer with our brothers?

208   10.   Moreover, let us not forget that while our world poses obstacles in the way of our search for union with God in Christ, it also offers suggestions for surmounting those obstacles, which we should submit to an Ignatian discernment of spirits in order to determine where in them the Spirit of God is moving us. There is, for instance, the contemporary stress on spontaneous prayer, with a minimum of formalism. There is the interest in, and understanding of, the different approaches to union with God developed by the non-Christian religions. There are the various forms of prayer in community which lead to a mutually enriching exchange of faith experiences. There is, finally, the remarkable renewal taking place today in the giving and the making of the Spiritual Exercises, whose vivifying influence extends beyond the limits of the formal retreat into the daily life of prayer.[9]

209   11.   Not only that; fidelity to the Exercises energizes our apostolic action. It enlarges our inner freedom to respond readily to the demands which the service of faith may make of us. It deepens in us the self-abnegation that unites us to Christ crucified,[10] and thus to the poverty, humiliations, and sufferings by which he saved the world.[11] And, not least, it fills us with joy: the joy of service which, more than anything else, will attract others to join our companionship;

---

9 There is steady growth in the practice of shared prayer which can greatly help our awareness of both God and our fellow men. Schools of prayer and houses of prayer have also developed. Different kinds of community prayer are facilitating the sharing of faith and spiritual experiences with others in the community. Eucharistic concelebrations, meetings on spiritual topics, spiritual conversations, reading of Sacred Scripture or part of the liturgical hours in common, the review of life in community: all these practices can strengthen our fraternal union as members of an apostolic community as well as our personal relationship with Christ.

10 Phil. 2. 5-8.

11 *SpEx* 167.

the abiding joy of men whom nothing can separate from the love of God which is in Christ Jesus our Lord.[12] Thus, the Spiritual Exercises, in which as Jesuits we especially experience Christ and respond to his call, lie at the heart of our Jesuit vocation. Returning every year to the Exercises, each Jesuit renews in them his dedication to Christ.

12.   Our union with God in Christ is furthered not only **210** by formal prayer, personal and communitarian, but also by the offering of Christ's sacrifice and the reception of his sacraments. Every Jesuit community is a faith community, and it is in the Eucharist that those who believe in Christ come together to celebrate their common faith. Our participation at the same table in the Body and Blood of Christ, more than anything else, makes us one companionship totally dedicated to Christ's mission in the world.

13.   Inwardly strengthened and renewed by prayer and **211** the sacraments, we are able to make apostolic action itself a form of union with God. Our service of the faith [*diakonia fidei*] and our service of men then become, not an interruption of that union but a continuation of it, a joining of our action with Christ's salvific action in history. Thus contemplation flows into action regularly, and we realize to some extent our ideal of being contemplatives "in action."

B.   BROTHERLY COMMUNION

14.   From union with God in Christ flows, of necessity, **212** brotherly love. Love of the neighbor, which union with Christ and with God in Christ implies and includes,[13] has for its privileged object in our case, the companions of Jesus who compose our Society.[14] They are our companions; and it is our community ideal that we should be companions not only in the sense of fellow workers in the apostolate, but truly brothers and friends in the Lord.

---

12 Rom. 8. 39.
13 1 John 3. 14-15; 4. 7-8, 16; 5. 1.
14 *Cons* [671].

213   15. a)   By forming in this way a community of brothers, we bear witness to the presence of God among men:
God who, as Trinity, is, beyond all imagining, a community
of Love; God who, made Man, established with men an
everlasting covenant.[15] Even our interpersonal relationship
within the community, then, has an apostolic dimension,
in that it must set the tone of our relationship with those
outside the community who serve in the apostolate with
us, and, indeed, with all men of good will who work for
justice or sincerely seek the real meaning of human life.
Not only that; it must set the tone of our relationship with
those we seek to serve: with those who are our neighbors
not simply by local propinquity, but by a sharing of concerns and aspirations.

214   16.   But let us realistically face the facts that make community building difficult today. More so today than in the
past, our membership is drawn from very different social
and cultural backgrounds. Moreover, the modern world
places a much heavier stress on individual freedom than on
the subordination of the individual to the group. Our response to these realities will be to transform them from obstacles to aids in community building. Our basic attitude
toward cultural differences will be that they can enrich
our union rather than threaten it. Our basic attitude
toward personal freedom will be that freedom is fulfilled
in the active service of love.

215   17.   Not that we should adopt an attitude of indiscrimi-
nate tolerance, a weary attitude of "peace at any price."
Our attitude should be, rather, that of the Contemplation
for Obtaining Love: "to consider how all blessings and
gifts descend from above, such as my limited power from
the supreme and limitless power on high, and so with justice, goodness, piety, mercy; as rays from the sun, as water
from the spring."[16] We come to the Society from many

---

15 John 13. 34 sq.
16 *SpEx* 237.

lands, many ways of thought and life, each one of which has received a particular grace from God's infinite bounty. As companions of Jesus and each other, we wish to share with one another what we have and are, for the building up of communities dedicated to the apostolate of reconciliation.

18. b) Hence the need of opening up and maintain- **216** ing clear channels of communication within our communities and among them, a need which St. Ignatius foresaw when, in terms of the communication facilities of his time, he called for regular and frequent letter writing back and forth between communities and individuals, and between head and members.[17] In any case, it is clear that our communities should not be self-enclosed but most open; they are *communities for mission.* They receive their mission from authority; but authority itself expects the community to discern, in union with its superior and in conformity with his final decision, the concrete ways whereby that mission is to be accomplished and the procedure by which it is to be evaluated and revised in the light of actual performance. In other words, it is with the community as with the individual: it is from the inner life of grace and virtue that force flows outward to the works proposed to us.[18] Hence the need to structure in our communities, flexibly, to be sure, but firmly, a way of life that favors personal and community prayer, provides for the relaxation of tensions and the celebration of life, and establishes a climate in which men dedicated to apostolic service can—as the apostles of Jesus did—gradually grow to the height of their vocation.[19]

19. Fraternal communication within the community **217** can take many forms according to different needs and circumstances. But its basic presupposition is, at the human

---

17 *Cons* [673, 821].
18 *Cons* [813].
19 Mark 6. 30-31.

level, sincerity and mutual trust[20] and, at the level of grace, those gifts of God with which our companionship began and by which it is maintained.[21]

218 20. Certain features of our Ignatian heritage can be given a communitarian dimension; provided, of course, the personal practice for which they were originally intended is not abandoned. For instance, the examination of conscience could, at times, be made a shared reflection on the community's fidelity to its apostolic mission. Similarly, fraternal correction and personal dialogue with the superior can usefully become a community review of community life style.

219 21. c) We can go further and say that community spiritual interchange can, under certain conditions, become *communitarian discernment*. This is something quite distinct from the usual community dialogue. It is "a corporate search for the will of God by means of a shared reflection on the signs which point where the Spirit of Christ is leading,"[22] and the method to follow in such communitarian discernment is analogous to that which St. Ignatius teaches for the making of a personal decision on a matter of importance.[23]

220 22. There are prerequisites for a valid communitarian discernment. On the part of the individual member of the community, a certain familiarity with the Ignatian rules for the discernment of spirits, derived from actual use[24]; a determined resolution to find the will of God for the community whatever it may cost; and, in general, the dispositions of mind and heart called for and cultivated in the First and Second Weeks of the Exercises. On the part of the community as such, a clear definition of the matter to be discerned, sufficient information regarding it, and "a

---

20 *SpEx* 22.
21 *Cons* [134, 812].
22 R.P. Arrupe, "De Nostrorum in spiritu institutione," *ActRSJ*, XV (1967), 123-4.
23 *SpEx* 169-89.
24 *SpEx* 313-36.

capacity to convey to one another what each one really thinks and feels."[25]

23. Clearly, the requisite dispositions for true com- **221** munitarian discernment are such that they will not be verified as often as those for ordinary community dialogue. Nevertheless, every community should seek to acquire them, so that when need arises it can enter into this special way of seeking the will of God. Indeed, inasmuch as it should be characteristic of a Jesuit to be in familiar contact with God and to seek his will constantly in a spirit of true Ignatian indifference, even ordinary community meetings and house consultations can incorporate elements of true communitarian discernment, provided we seriously seek God's will concerning the life and work of the community.

24. What is the role of the superior in communitarian **222** discernment? It is, first, to develop, as far as he can, the requisite disposition for it; second, to decide when to convoke the community for it, and clearly to define its object; third, to take active part in it as the bond of union within the community and as the link between the community and the Society as a whole; and, finally, to make the final decision in the light of the discernment, but freely, as the one to whom both the grace and the burden of authority are given. For in our Society the discerning community is not a deliberative or capitular body but a consultative one, whose object, clearly understood and fully accepted, is to assist the superior to determine what course of action is for God's greater glory and the service of men.

25. d) Times of stress and trial that might threaten **223** our fraternal communion from time to time can become moments of grace, which confirm our dedication to Christ and make that dedication credible. For, obviously, there is a reciprocal relationship between the religious vows and

---

25 R.P. Arrupe, "De spirituali discretione," *ActRSJ,* XV (1971), 767-73.

community life.[26] The living of the vows promotes and
strengthens community life; community life, in turn, if truly
fraternal, helps us to be faithful to our vows.

224   26.   The orientations of this 32nd General Congregation regarding the *vow of poverty* are to be found in a
separate declaration.

225   Our *vow* of *chastity* consecrates a celibacy freely chosen
for the sake of the Kingdom of God. By it, we offer an undivided heart to God, a heart capable of a self-giving in service approaching the freedom from self-interest with which
God himself loves all his creatures. This is the witness we
are called upon to give to a world which calls the value of
celibacy into question; and the 32nd General Congregation
simply and wholly confirms what the 31st General Congregation declared regarding the apostolic value of the vow of
chastity.[27] We might simply add that celibacy for the sake
of the Kingdom has a special apostolic value in our time,
when men tend to put whole classes of their fellow human
beings beyond the margins of their concern, while at the
same time identifying love with eroticism. In such a time,
the self-denying love which is warmly human, yet freely
given in service to all, can be a powerful sign leading men
to Christ who came to show us what love really is: that
God is love.

C.   obedience: the bond of union

226   27.   "This union is produced, in great part, by the bond
of obedience."[28] And precisely because it is our bond of
union, it is the guarantee of our apostolic efficacy. Today,
especially, given the wide dispersion of our apostolic enterprises, the need for us to acquire highly specialized skills in
highly specialized works, and the consequent need, in many
places, to make a distinction between our apostolic institutes

---

26 See GC 31, D. 19, n. 4; *ActRSJ*, XIV, 919.

27 GC 31, D. 16; *ActRSJ*, XIV, 898 sq.

28 *Cons* [659; see 662, 664, 666].

and our religious communities, the preservation of unity of purpose and direction becomes a prime necessity.

28. In this task of unification the role of the major **227** superior has been well defined by the 31st General Congregation.[29] What this 32nd General Congregation would like to stress is the equally important *role of the local or community superior*. Given the conditions alluded to above, even if the local superior does not have the direction of the apostolic work owing to the appointment of a director of the apostolate, he nevertheless retains the responsibility to confirm his brethren in their apostolic mission and to see to it that their religious and community life is such as to enable them to fulfill that mission with God's grace. Moreover, the task of the superior is not only to support the mission of the members of his community, but at times to determine it more precisely, "in such wise that the individuals dwelling in some house or college have recourse to their local superior or rector and are governed by him in every respect."[30]

29. His part is to stimulate as well as to moderate the **228** apostolic initiatives of the members of his community. But, above all, the preservation of the community as a fraternal union depends on him. Whatever the kind of community over which he presides—and our mission today demands an astonishing variety of them—his task is to keep it together in love and obedience by that spiritual mode of governance "in all modesty and charity in the Lord" recommended and exemplified by St. Ignatius.[31]

In addition to superiors, there are also *directors of works*. **229** Where fitting, and in accord with norms that must be approved by Father General, the director of a work can have true religious authority in directing the efforts of those who have been assigned to work in that apostolate so that

---

29 GC 31, D. 46; *ActRSJ,* XIV, 978 sq., cf. D. 22; ibid. XIV, 931.
30 *Cons* [662].
31 *Cons* [667].

everything may be directed to the greater glory of God and the progress of others in Christian life and teaching. In carrying out his office, the director of the work should be alert to the advice and suggestions of his brother Jesuits and ready to receive their help. If any difficulties arise in reconciling the duties of the superior or superiors of communities and the director of the work, they should be resolved in statutes drawn up for this purpose.

230   30.   Today, more than ever before, that spiritual mode of governance is needed. The contemporary stress on individual initiative mentioned earlier, combined with the wide range of opportunities open to that initiative, tends to obscure the sense of mission essential to Ignatian obedience and may dislodge it altogether, unless we make fuller use of the special instrument for spiritual governance bequeathed to us by St. Ignatius: the *account of conscience*.

231   31.   Vowed obedience, whether in humdrum or in heroic matters, is always an act of faith and freedom whereby the religious recognizes and embraces the will of God manifested to him by one who has authority to send him in the name of Christ. He does not necessarily have to understand why he is being sent. But both the superior who sends and the companion who is sent gain assurance that the mission is really God's will if it is preceded by the dialogue that is the account of conscience. For by it the superior acquires an inner knowledge of those subject to his authority: what they can and what they cannot do, and what help they need by way of counsel or resource to do what they can. The companion, in turn, learns what the mission on which he is being sent involves and what, concretely, he must do to discharge his responsibility.

232   32.   The more the account of conscience is genuinely practiced, the more authentic will our discernment be of God's purpose in our regard and the more perfect that union of minds and hearts from which our apostolate derives its dynamism. A community from which sincerity and

openness in mutual relationships are absent soon becomes immobilized in purely formal structures which no longer respond to the needs and aspirations of the men of our time, or else it disintegrates altogether.

33.   Beyond the limits of the strict matter of our vow of   **233**
obedience extends our duty of *thinking with the Church*. Our being united among ourselves depends, in the last analysis, on our being united in both mind and heart to the Church that Christ founded. The historical context in which St. Ignatius wrote his Rules for Thinking with the Church is, of course, different from ours. But there remains for us the one pillar and ground of truth, the Church of the living God,[32] in which we are united by one faith and one baptism to the one Lord and to the Father.[33] It behooves us, then, to keep undimmed the spirit of the Ignatian rules and apply them with vigor to the changed conditions of our times.

34.   Clearly, the union of minds and hearts of which we   **234**
speak is difficult of achievement. Equally clearly, it is demanded by our apostolic mission. Our witness to the Gospel would not be credible without it. The sincere acceptance and willing execution of these orientations and norms set forth by this present Congregation will help toward that union. But human means fall short. It is the Spirit of God, the Spirit of love, that must fill the Society. For this we humbly pray.

D.   GUIDELINES

35.   Because "the work of our redemption is constantly   **235**
carried on in the mystery of the Eucharistic Sacrifice,"[1] all of our members should consider daily celebration of the

---

32 1 Tim. 3. 15.
33 Eph. 4. 5.

The official Latin text begins here a newly numbered set of reference notes for the "Guidelines" in this decree.

1 GC 31, D. 14, n. 10; *ActRSJ,* XIV, 894.

Eucharist as the center of their religious and apostolic life.[2] Concelebrations are encouraged, especially on days when the community can more easily gather together.

236   36.   In order to respond to the interior need for familiarity with God, we should all spend some time each day in personal prayer. Therefore, for those still in formation, "the Society retains the practice of an hour and a half as the time for prayer, Mass, and thanksgiving. Each man should be guided by his spiritual father as he seeks that form of prayer in which he can best advance in the Lord. The judgment of superiors is normative for each."[3]

For others, "our rule of an hour's prayer is to be adapted so that each Jesuit, guided by his superiors, takes into account his particular circumstances and needs, in the light of a discerning love."[4]

237   37.   The time order of the community should include some brief daily common prayer and at times, in a way that is appropriate for each apostolic community, a longer period for prayer and prayerful discussion. Shared prayer, days of recollection, and the Spiritual Exercises in common are recognized as fruitful means for increasing union, since they provide the opportunity for reflecting before God on the mission of the community and, at the same time, express the apostolic character of our prayer.

238   38.   Our entire apostolic life should be examined with the spiritual discernment proper to the Exercises, so that we might increasingly put into practice what God expects of us and purify the motivation of our lives. One means available to us is the daily examination of conscience, which was recommended by St. Ignatius so that we might be continually guided by the practice of spiritual discernment.

---

2 R.P. Arrupe, "De Nostrorum in spiritu institutione," *ActRSJ,* XV, 121 sq.

3 GC 31, D. 14, n. 12, 2°; *ActRSJ,* XIV, 895.

4 GC 31, D. 14, n. 11; *ActRSJ,* XIV, 895.

39.   Since we need the grace of continual conversion of   **239**
heart "to the love of the Father of mercies"[5] that the purity
and freedom of our lives in God's service might increase,
all should frequent the Sacrament of Reconciliation.[6] We
should also willingly participate in communal penitential
services and strive to promote the spirit of reconciliation in
our communities.

40.   Dialogue with a spiritual director on a regular basis   **240**
is a great help for growing in spiritual insight and learning
discernment. Every Jesuit, especially during formation but
also when he is engaged in an active apostolate, should
make every effort to have a spiritual director with whom
he can speak frequently and openly. The provincials should
endeavor to identify and prepare spiritual fathers who are
experienced in personal prayer and who have good judgment. This is especially true for the formation communities.

41.   The local superior is also responsible for the spiritual   **241**
vitality of the community. He should take care that the
community is a true faith community precisely because he
is concerned with its apostolic mission. For this reason, he
should consider it part of his job to provide the conditions
that foster personal and community prayer, the sacramental
life, and communication on a spiritual level. He should also
take care that every Jesuit be able to find in the organization of community life whatever is necessary for recollection
and for a suitable balance between work and rest.

42.   The Spiritual Exercises are a privileged means for   **242**
achieving renovation and union in the Society and for re-
vitalizing our apostolic mission. They are a school of prayer
and a time when a man has the spiritual experience of
personally encountering Christ.

---

5 PO, 186.
6 Sacred Congregation for Religious: "Circa usum et Administra-
   tionem Sacramenti Paenitentiae et circa idoneitatem ad Profes-
   sionem Religiosam," n. 3; Dec. 8, 1970.

243   For this reason, the 32nd General Congregation confirms n. 16 of Decree 14 of the 31st General Congregation.[7] In addition, it recommends:

a)   That, especially at the time of the annual visitation, the provincials inquire about the way our members are making the Spiritual Exercises;

b)   That, especially during this period of renovation in the Society, those who are already formed be encouraged to make the full Exercises extended over a month. This can be an effective means of implementing the conclusions of the 32nd General Congregation;

c)   That, in the provinces, the greatest care be given to the formation of those who have the talent to direct the Exercises;

d)   That those already formed should at times make the annual retreat under the personal direction of a skilled director.

244   43.   The 32nd General Congregation confirms and recommends all that is contained in the decrees of the 31st General Congregation concerning devotion to the Sacred Heart and Our Lady, as they pertain to both the spiritual life of Ours and the apostolate. In the promotion of these devotions, account should be taken of the differences which exist in various parts of the world.[8]

245   44.   All Jesuits, even those who must live apart because of the demands of their apostolate or for other justifiable reasons, should take an active part in the life of some community. To the extent that the bond with a community and its superior is more than merely juridical, that union of minds and hearts which is so desirable will be kept intact.

246   45.   Every community of the Society should have its own superior.

---

7 GC 31, D. 14, n. 16; *ActRSJ,* XIV, 896.
8 GC 31, D. 15; *ActRSJ,* XIV, 897; and D. 16, n. 7e; *ActRSJ,* XIV, 901.

46.   The account of conscience is of great importance for the spiritual governance of the Society, and its practice is to be esteemed and cultivated. Therefore, all should give an account of conscience to their superiors, according to the norms and spirit of the Society.[9] In addition, the relationships between superiors and their brethren in the Society should be such as to encourage the account of conscience and conversation about spiritual matters.

47.   Taking into account the mission it has been given, every community should after mature deliberation establish a time order for community life. This time order should be approved by the major superior and periodically revised.

48.   Since our communities are apostolic, they should be oriented toward the service of others, particularly the poor, and to cooperation with those who are seeking God or working for greater justice in the world. For this reason, under the leadership of superiors, communities should periodically examine whether their way of living sufficiently supports their apostolic mission and encourages hospitality. They should also consider whether their style of life testifies to simplicity, justice, and poverty.

250

49.   Communities will not be able to witness to Christian love unless each member contributes to community life and gives sufficient time and effort to the task. Only in this way can an atmosphere be created which makes communication possible and in which no one goes unnoticed or is neglected.[10]

50.   To the extent possible, superiors should strive to build an Ignatian apostolic community in which many forms of open and friendly communication on a spiritual level are possible. Since it is a privileged way to find God's will, the use of communal spiritual discernment is en-

---

9   GC 31, D. 17, n. 8; *ActRSJ,* XIV, 908.
10   *SpEx* 22, "It is necessary to suppose that every good Christian is more ready to put a good interpretation on another's statement than to condemn it as false."

couraged if the question at issue is of some importance and the necessary preconditions have been verified.

252   51.   Solidarity among communities in a province as well as fraternal charity require that communities be open to men of different ages, talent, and work.

253   52.   The dwelling and arrangement of the community should be such that it allows for needed privacy and encourages the spiritual, intellectual, and cultural development of community members. These are necesary conditions for the fulfillment of our apostolic mission.

254   53.   Within limits imposed by our profession of poverty, communication and union among members of the Society should be strengthened in the following ways:

a)   gatherings of communities in the same city or region should be encouraged;

b)   workshops and task forces should be established for each area of the apostolate;

c)   regular meetings should be held of the superiors of each province and the provincials of each assistancy or major region.

E.   THE COMMON RULES

255   54.   The Common Rules approved by the 4th General Congregation and revised by the 27th General Congregation are abrogated. Number 14 of Decree 19 of the 31st General Congregation is also abrogated.[11]

a)   This Congregation recommends to Father General that at his discretion he publish a *summary* of the decrees of the 31st and 32nd General Congregations, together with a summary of the letters he has written to the Society since the 31st General Congregation. This summary can serve as an index of principal features of our religious life.

b)   It is left to provincials, with the approval of Father General, to determine for each province or group of

---

11 See *ActRSJ*, XIV, 925.

provinces more particular norms which shall be adapted to local circumstances.

F. DECLARATION CONCERNING DECREE 17, NUMBER 10 OF
THE 31ST GENERAL CONGREGATION[12]

55. What is contained in Decree 17, n. 10, should be **256** understood in the following way:

a) The ordinary means of dealing with a conflict of this type is through sincere dialogue, according to the Ignatian principle of representation and following upon prayer and appropriate consultation.

b) A Jesuit is always free to approach a higher superior.

c) If the conflict cannot be resolved either through dialogue or recourse to a higher superior, other persons— some of whom may be from outside the Society—may be called by mutual consent to assist in forming one's conscience more clearly. This should be done privately and without publicity.

d) The procedure cannot be imposed on either the superior or the Jesuit involved. It is entirely voluntary and unofficial. It is nothing more than a new effort to find the divine will.

e) The opinion of those consulted has no juridical effect on the authority of the superior. It is merely advisory.

f) If, after this procedure, a Jesuit still feels he cannot obey in good conscience, the superior should determine what should be done. "But a man who, time after time, is unable to obey with a good conscience, should take thought regarding some other path of life in which he can serve God with greater tranquility."[13]

---

12 See *ActRSJ*, XIV, 909. [See p. 163-164 in this translation.]
13 GC 31, D. 17, n. 10; *ActRSJ*, XIV, 910.

For a More Authentic Poverty

257   1.   In recent times and especially since the Second Vatican Council, the Church, her families of religious, indeed the whole Christian world have been striving for a deeper understanding and new experiential knowledge of evangelical poverty. This Congregation, like its predecessor, has tried earnestly to enter into this movement and to discern its implications for our Society.

258   2.   Voluntary poverty in imitation of Christ is a sharing in that mystery revealed in the self-emptying of the very Son of God in the Incarnation. The Jesuit vocation to poverty draws its inspiration from the experience of St. Ignatius and the Spiritual Exercises and is specified by the Formula of the Institute and by the Constitutions.[1] It is the charism of the Society to serve Christ poor and humble. The principle and foundation of our poverty, therefore, is found in a love of the Word made Flesh and crucified.

A.   SIGNS OF THE TIMES

259   3.   Reflection on the Gospel in the light of the signs of our times has illumined new aspects of this religious poverty. Contemporary man has become very aware of massive, dehumanizing poverty, not only material but spiritual as well. Everywhere there are to be found men of good will working for a social order of greater justice and the abolition of oppressive structures. At the same time, the appetite for

---

1 *SpEx* 98, 147, 167; *ConsMHSJ* I, "Deliberatio de Paupertate," pp. 78 sq.; Ibid., "Ephemeris S. P.N. Ignatii," p. 86 sq.; *Cons.* [553 sq.].

enjoyment and consumption of material goods spreads everywhere and verges on a practical atheism. The rich, individuals and nations, are thereby hardened in their readiness to oppress others, and all, rich and poor, are duped into placing man's whole happiness in such consumption. Still, there are those who react against this materialism and seek a new liberty and another happiness in a simpler way of life and in the pursuit of higher values. On all sides there is felt a desire to discover new communities which favor a more intimate interpersonal communication, communities of true sharing and communion, concerned for the integral human development of their members. Our lives, our communities, our very poverty can and should have a meaning and a message for such a world.

4. These common experiences of contemporary man are **260** signs of the times which prompt us to seek a deeper insight into the mystery of Christ. Religious poverty still calls to the following of Christ poor, but also to a following of Christ at work in Nazareth, identifying with the needy in his public life, the Christ of heartfelt compassion, responding to their needs, eager to serve them.[2] For centuries, the perfection of religious poverty was found in mendicancy. He was counted poor who lived on alms, placing all his hopes in the providence of God operative through benefactors. With growing clarity the Church invites religious to submit to the common law of labor.[3] "Earning your own living and that of your brothers or sisters, helping the poor by your work—these are duties incumbent upon you."[4] Indeed the Church encourages religious "to join the poor in their situation and to share their bitter cares."[5] Response to such invitations is presented as an expression of vowed poverty suited to our times. Calling all the faithful more

---

2 Pope Paul VI, Adhortatio Apostolica, "Evangelica Testificatio," June 29, 1971; AAS (1971), p. 497 sq., 17.
3 PC, 13; see ET, 20.
4 ET, 20.
5 Ibid., 18.

urgently than ever to spend themselves in the promotion of social justice, the Church shows that she places high hopes in the efforts of those who have consecrated themselves and all they have to Christ by the vow of poverty.[6] Something of an evolution seems to have taken place: today the primary import of religious poverty is found not only in an ascetic-moral perfection through the imitation of Christ poor, but also, and more in the apostolic value of imitating Christ, forgetful of self in his generous and ready service of all the abandoned.

261   5.   The Society cannot meet the demands of today's apostolate without reform of its practice of poverty. Jesuits will be unable to hear the "cry of the poor"[7] unless they have greater personal experience of the miseries and distress of the poor. It will be difficult for the Society everywhere to forward effectively the cause of justice and human dignity if the greater part of her ministry identifies her with the rich and powerful, or is based on the "security of possession, knowledge, and power."[8] Our life will be no "witness to a new and eternal life won by Christ's redemption or to a resurrected state and the glory of the heavenly kindgom,"[9] if individually or corporately, Jesuits are seen to be attached to earthly things, even apostolic institutions, and to be dependent on them. Our communities will have no meaning or sign value for our times, unless by their sharing of themselves and all they possess, they are clearly seen to be communities of charity and of concern for each other and all others.

B.   OUR RESPONSE

262   6.   That the Society has long been uneasy about the practice of poverty by individuals, communities, and apostolic institutes is evidenced by hundreds of postulates from

---

6 Ibid., 17.
7 Ps. 9.13; Job 34.28; Prov. 21.13; ET, 17.
8 ET, 19.
9 LG, 44.

all parts of the world. The Congregation, mindful of its duty, has tried to answer this call of the Society, not so much by words and exhortation as by new structures of temporal administration. The single intent is to strengthen and confirm the practice of poverty.

7.   The first aim of the reform to be outlined below is **263** finally to "answer the demands of this real and not pretended poverty."[10] In a world of mass starvation, no one can lightly call himself poor. It is perhaps regrettable that we have no other word to designate this note of religious life, since poverty means very different things to different people. At the very least, religious poverty should try hard to limit rather than to expand consumption. It is not possible to love poverty or experience its mysterious consolations, without some knowledge of its actuality. The standard of living of our houses should not be higher than that of a family of slender means whose providers must work hard for its support. The concrete exigencies of such a standard are to be discerned by individuals and communities in sincere deliberation with their superiors. It should look to food and drink, lodging and clothing, but also and perhaps especially to travel, recreation, use of automobiles, and of villas, vacations, etc. Some should scrutinize their leisure, sometimes such as hardly the rich enjoy. The need for reform is so frequently evident and demanded by so many Provincial Congregations that no person or community may decline this examination.

8.   The grace of our vocation demands loyal and gener- **264** ous effort to live that poverty required by the Society's spirit and law. The frequent engagement of Ours in professions and salaried offices is not without dangers, not only for the spirit of gratuity, but even for the observance of common life itself. Such work is to be chosen only as a more effective means to the communication of the faith or to spiritual advancement, without thought of remuneration

---

10 GC 31, D. 18, n. 7; *ActRSJ,* XIV, 913.

or of the privileges attached to an office. Independence from the community in acquisition or expenditure, a vice with manifold disguises, cannot be tolerated. Every Jesuit must contribute to the community everything he receives by way of remuneration, stipend, alms, gift or in any other way. He receives from the community alone everything he needs. In the same way, by cheerfully and gratefully accepting the community's standard of living, each undertakes to support his brothers in their efforts to live and to love poverty. Those who are unwilling to observe this double law of common life, separate themselves from the fraternity of the Society in spirit if not in law.

265   9.   The voluntary poverty of religious is the attempt of fallen men to achieve that liberty from inordinate attachment, which is the condition of any great and ready love of God and man. In the Society this very liberty to love is in the service of the apostolate. Every Jesuit, no matter what his ministry, is called "to preach in poverty,"[11] according to the *sacra doctrina* of the Two Standards,[12] and this poverty has a spiritual power not to be measured in human terms. Apostolic efficiency and apostolic poverty are two values to be held in an on-going tension, and this is a rule for apostolic institutes as well as for individuals. The expedience of retaining rich and powerful institutions, requiring great capital outlay, is to be weighed prudently and spiritually. Since these institutions are but means, the attitude of the Society should be that of the Third Class of Men, and according to the rule of *tantum-quantum,* fully as ready to abandon as to retain, to the greater service of God. The faithful practice of religious poverty is apostolic, too, in its contempt of personal gain, which commends the Gospel and frees the apostle to preach it in all its integrity. It is apostolic, finally, in that communities which are really poor, by their simplicity and fraternal union, proclaim the

---

11 *MHSJ,* MI "S. Ignatii . . . Epistolae et Instructiones," I, 96.
12 *SpEx,* 147.

beatitudes, "manifesting to all believers the presence of heavenly goods already possessed here below."[13]

10. This Congregation has spoken elsewhere of the **266** necessity of commitment to the cause of justice and to the service of the poor. The Church regards such ministry as integral to the contemporary practice of poverty.[14] Such commitment is everywhere needed, but in many places it is a very condition of credibility for the Society and for the Church. The insertion of communities among the poor so that Jesuits may work for them and with them, or at least may acquire some experience of their condition, is a testimony of love of the poor and of poverty to which the Church encourages religious.[15] Implementation of this proposal will have to be different in our widely differing circumstances. Unless there be evident reason to the contrary, however, provincials should encourage those communities which, in union and charity with the rest of the province, choose to practice a stricter poverty, or to live among the poor, serving them and sharing something of their experience.[16]

C. NEW STRUCTURES

11. The better to meet the new demands of our poverty, **267** the Congregation has undertaken a reform of the structures of temporal administration. The keystone of this reform is the distinction between apostolic institutes and the communities which serve them. The former are governed by the present law of the "colleges," [technically so called in the law of the Society] and so may possess endowments and needful revenue. Communities, however, are assimilated to "professed houses," [also technically so called] and may have no stable revenues from capital.

12. With the recognition of remuneration for work as a **268**

---

13 LG, 44; GS, 72; GC 31, D. 18, nn. 4, 7, 16a; D. 19, 7 sq.; AA, 4.
14 ET, 18, 20.
15 Ibid.
16 *Cons* [580] ; *Examen Generale* 81.

legitimate source of support, there is less emphasis on alms as the only legitimate source of income for a community.[17] On the other hand, there is greater stress on the apostolic use of all revenues. Communities must live a simple and frugal life within an approved budget. They may not accumulate capital but must dispose of any annual surplus, according to a provincial plan which will look to the needs of communities, of apostolates, and of the poor. As far as possible, apostolic institutes, too, are bound by this law of fraternity and solidarity towards other ministries. Neither the capital nor the revenues of our institutes may profit our communities, except for approved remuneration for services rendered. If an institute is suppressed, its assets are reserved for use in other apostolic enterprises.

D. CONCLUSION

269   13.   It is clear that admission of sin and true conversion of heart will help more toward a lived poverty than any revision of law. For that favor we must pray God earnestly as part of the grace of our vocation, to which we must remain open. While law can support spirit, no legal reform will profit anything unless all our members elect evangelical poverty with courage at the invitation of the Eternal King, Christ Our Lord. Let all superiors in meditation and prayer become deeply conscious of their responsibility to forward this renovation of poverty. Each member should recall that this reformed poverty will never be realized unless all unitedly and generously support superiors in this task.

270   14.   This is the desire of the Congregation, this its prayer to God for the Society, a poverty profoundly renewed,

> —simple in community expression and joyous in the following of Christ;
> —happy to share with each other and with all;

---

17 GC 31, D. 18, n. 15; *ActRSJ*, XIV, 915.

—apostolic in its active indifference and readiness for any service;

—inspiring our selection of ministries and turning us to those most in need;

—spiritually effective, proclaiming Jesus Christ in our way of life and in all we do.

The authenticity of our poverty after all does not consist **271** so much in the lack of temporal goods, as in the fact that we live, and are seen to live, from God and for God, sincerely striving for the perfection of that ideal which is the goal of the spiritual journey of the Exercises: "Give me only your love and your grace, and I am rich enough, and ask for nothing more."[18]

15.   The following norms are the principles for the re- **272** vision of the statutes on poverty. It will take time to reduce them to familiar practice. It is the internal law of charity and love which will be their best interpreter, that law which leads all of us to "love poverty as a mother, and . . . when occasions arise, feel some effects of it."[19] The Congregation earnestly commends this decree to the faithful observance of all.

E.   NORMS

Terminology

16.   In this decree by *community* is understood any **273** group of Jesuits legitimately constituted under the authority of a local superior.

17.   *Apostolic institutes* are those institutions or works **274** belonging to the Society which have a certain permanent unity and organization for apostolic purposes, such as universities, colleges, retreat houses, reviews, and other such in which our members carry on their apostolic work.

---

18 *SpEx,* 234.
19 *Cons* [287].

All communities can have apostolic institutes

275   18.   All communities can have attached to them one or more apostolic institutes in which the whole community or some of its members exercise their apostolate.

The separation to be put into effect

276   19.   By the law of the Society, there is to be established a distinction between communities and apostolic institutes, at least with regard to the destination and usufruct of their goods and between the financial accounts of each.

277   20.   A distinction of moral persons, canonical or civil, is also recommended, where this can be effected without great inconvenience, preserving always the apostolic finality of the institutes and the authority of the Society to direct them to such ends.

The resources of institutes may not be diverted to the use of the communities

278   21.   The goods of apostolic institutes of the Society may not be diverted to the use or profit of our members, except for a suitable remuneration, to be approved by the provincial, for work in such institutes or for services rendered to the same.

Poverty of communities

279   22.   All communities dedicated to pastoral work or to any other apostolic functions are equated to professed houses in what pertains to poverty.[20] However, all may be the juridical subject of all rights, including ownership, pertaining to the apostolic institutes attached to such communities.

280   23.   Seminaries for our members[21] retain their own

---

20 See GC 31, D. 27, n. 7; *ActRSJ,* XIV, 948.
21 See *Epitome Instituti Societatis Jesu,* n. 29.

regime of poverty. Houses or infirmaries for our aged or sick are equated to the former.

Annual community budgets

24. In each community the responsible administrators will draft each year at the appointed times and according to the norms established by the provincial, a projected budget as well as a statement of revenues and expenses. These will be communicated to the community as soon as convenient and are to be approved by the provincial. **281**

Disposition of surplus

25. That the life of our communities may be "removed as far as possible from all infection of avarice and as like as possible to evangelical poverty,"[22] the surplus of each community will be distributed yearly according to the provision of nn. 27-31 except for a moderate sum to be approved by the provincial for unforeseen expenses. This sum is never to exceed the ordinary expenses of one year. **282**

26. The first beneficiary of such surplus in each community will be the apostolic institute or institutes attached to the same if these stand in need, unless the provincial with his consultors should decide otherwise. **283**

Sharing resources

27. According to the norms to be established by the provincial and approved by Father General, there is to be provision for the distribution of the communities' surplus mentioned in n. 25, for the benefit of those communities or works of the province which are in greater need. **284**

28. In this sharing of resources, the needs of other provinces, of the whole Society, and of non-Jesuits will be considered.[23] **285**

---

22 *FI*, n. 7.
23 See GC 31, D. 48, n. 4; *ActRSJ,* XIV, 981.

286   29.   Major superiors can require that individual communities, according to their capacities, contribute a certain sum of money to the relief of the needs of other communities or apostolic institutes of the province or of other provinces, even if this should require some reduction in their standard of living, which in any case must always be frugal.[24]

287   30.   Provinces are permitted to provide insurance for old age and for sickness, either through their own "Arca," or with other provinces, or by participation in governmental or in private plans.

288   31.   A Charitable and Apostolic Fund of the Society is to be established for the benefit of communities and works of the Society, and, should need arise, for externs as well. It is not to be permanently invested but what it receives is to be distributed.

Father General is to determine the sources of this fund, its administration and manner of distributing benefits, with the assistance of advisers from different parts of the Society.

Poverty of apostolic institutes

289   32.   Apostolic institutes, churches excepted, can have revenue-bearing capital and stable revenues, adequate to their purposes, if such seem necessary to the provincial.

290   33.   Superiors and directors, mindful that we are sent to preach in poverty, will take great care that our apostolic institutes avoid every manner of extravagance and limit themselves strictly to the functional, attentive to the standards of similar institutes or works of their region and to the apostolic finality of our institutes. It is the responsibility of the provincial to determine what is required so that the apostolic institutes belonging to the Society manifest this character and mark of apostolic evangelical poverty.

291   34.   With due respect for the needs of apostolic institutes

---

24 See GC 31, D. 18, n. 9; *ActRSJ*, XIV, 914.

and, if this applies, for the statutes of the institute and the will of benefactors, provincials, with the approval of the General, will provide for a more equitable and apostolically effective sharing of resources among the apostolic institutes of the province, looking always to God's greater service.

35.   Those responsible for the administration of apostolic   **292**
institutes will present to the provincial at the appointed times, the annual budget of the institute, a statement of the year's revenues and expenses, and, if required, a balance sheet.

36.   If an apostolic institute be suppressed, the superiors,   **293**
according to their respective competence, will take care that its assets be devoted to another apostolic work or placed in the fund for apostolic works of the province or of the Society, respecting always, if this applies, the statutes of the institute and the will of benefactors. Such assets may never be destined to the use or benefit of a community, of a province, or of the Society.

Norms of transition

37.   The Statutes on Poverty, promulgated by Father   **294**
General on September 15, 1967, continue in force with the same authority as at promulgation, except for those norms which are contrary to the provisions of this decree.

38.   The General Congregation charges Father General,   **295**
with the help of a commission to be constituted by himself, to have the Statutes revised according to the principles, prescriptions, and recommendations of this decree and to promulgate them as soon as possible on his own authority.

Recommendations to the commission for the revision of the statutes on poverty

39.   The General Congregation recommends the follow-   **296**
ing to the commission for the revision of the statutes on poverty:

a)   The statutes should prescribe that in temporal administration and especially in investments of the Society, of provinces, or communities and apostolic institutes, care be had for the observance and due promotion of social justice.

b) In editing the revised statutes, the provisions which look to the personal and community practice of poverty should be so published in a compendium as to serve in the best manner possible for reflection and spiritual discernment, while those matters which have little to do with the daily practice of poverty of our members should be relegated to an appendix or to an Instruction on Temporal Administration.

c) The commission should give serious study to many well considered postulates, either of provincial congregations or of individuals, to the end that according to the diligent prudence of the commission,

—provision may be made in the Statutes for those matters which do not exceed the competence of Father General;

—those which exceed his authority may be thoroughly investigated so that clear proposals in their regard can be made to the 33rd General Congregation.

F. CAPACITY OF THE SOCIETY AND OF PROVINCES TO POSSESS TEMPORAL GOODS

297   40. The General Congregation, confirming the provisions of the statutes on poverty promulgated September 15, 1967, concerning the capacity of the Society and of provinces to possess temporal goods,[25] decrees the following:

1) The Society, provinces, vice-provinces, and missions dependent and independent, as distinguished from communities and apostolic institutes, are capable of possessing even revenue-bearing capital and of enjoying fixed and stable revenues, within the limits here defined, provided

---

25 See Statutes on Poverty, nn. 52, 83; *ActRSJ*, XV, 81, 88.

always that such goods and revenues are not applied to the support of the professed or formed coadjutors, except as permitted below, 3), a) and b).

2) The Society may possess such revenue-bearing capi- **298** tal and fixed and stable revenues only to promote certain apostolic works of a more universal kind or to relieve the needs of missions and provinces.

The Society is owner of the Charitable and Apostolic Fund mentioned above in n. 31.

3) Provinces, vice-provinces, and missions dependent **299** and independent, can possess revenue-bearing capital and can enjoy fixed and stable revenues, only for the following purposes:

a) For the support and education of those in probation or engaged in studies *(Arca Seminarii)*;

b) For the support of the aged and the sick;

c) To set up or develop houses or foundations, whether these have already been established or are yet to be established, according as necessity or opportunity may indicate *(Arca Fundationum)*;

d) To promote certain works, such as retreat houses, especially for non-Jesuits, centers for the social apostolate or for the diffusion of Catholic teaching by means of the media of social communication, for charitable enterprises both in and outside the Society, and for other apostolates which otherwise would lack sufficient resources *(Arca Operum Apostolicorum)*.

G. DEFINITION OF REVENUES PROHIBITED TO COMMUNITIES

41. The 32nd General Congregation authentically de- **300** clares that the fixed and stable revenues prohibited to our communities are completely defined to be those revenues from property, moveable or immoveable, either belonging to the Society or so invested in foundations, which the Society can claim in law.

H. AMENDMENT OF DECREE 18 OF GENERAL CONGREGATION XXXI

301   42. In Decree 18, n. 16, d, of the 31st General Congregation[26] after the words "may be accepted;" the following is to be added: "so also the remuneration attached to certain stable ministries, such as those of hospital chaplains, catechists, and the like."

I. A FACULTY OF DISPENSATION TO BE ASKED OF THE HOLY SEE

302   43. The General Congregation charges Father General to request of the Holy See, at least as a precaution, the faculty to dispense in individual cases, both communities and churches of Jesuits from the prohibition of having stable revenues, in the case of revenues not deriving from investment with the intention of gain, and which are judged necessary or very useful.[27]

---

26 See *ActRSJ*, XIV, 916.

27 See the letter from Jean Cardinal Villot, Secretary of State, May 2, 1975, p. 546, by which this faculty has been granted under certain conditions, and also by which the Holy See has confirmed as experimental the Norms under E, as well as the declaration under H.

IV

CONGREGATIONS AND GOVERNMENT

13 THE GENERAL CONGREGATION AND CONGREGATIONS OF PROCURATORS AND PROVINCIALS

1. The 32nd General Congregation confirms Decree 38   **303**
of the 31st General Congregation on the preparation for a
general congregation.[1] It further defines this decree in the
following ways:

a) The preparation for a general congregation should
be complete, in the sense that it should include the drafting
of the preliminary reports which are now described in the
first sentence of n. 119, No. 3, of the Formula of the General Congregation. In as far as possible, these reports should
be prepared for all the topics which the coming general
congregation will be likely to treat.

b) The preparation for a general congregation should   **304**
also be authoritative, in the sense that the preliminary reports and studies described in a) above, to the extent that
they are produced or approved by the official preparatory
committee described in c) below, should be recognized by
the general congregation as part of its official work, although the congregation retains the power to complete
this preparatory work itself.

c) If it seems useful, the preliminary committees fore-   **305**
seen in n. 7 of Decree 38 of the 31st General Congregation
may be set up, but, in any case, an official preparatory committee should be established in due time. Its members are
to be chosen by the General or the Vicar General, acting
with his council, from among those who will attend the
coming congregation. This committee should meet early
enough to complete the preparations described in a) and b)
above.

---

1 GC 31, D. 38; *ActRSJ,* XIV, 970.

306   2.   The Formula of the General Congregation should be revised with regard to both its procedure and its method of handling business from the calling of the congregation until its closing.

307   3.   The additional procedural norms adopted by the 32nd General Congregation for its own use should also be reviewed.

308   4.   In the future, those who attend the congregation only *"ad negotia"* (according to the norm contained in n. 7, of the Formula of the General Congregation) may be elected secretary or assistant secretary of the congregation and members of the committee on the state of the Society and the committee for screening postulates. They may also be elected *"Definitores."*

309   5.   In addition to what is contained in n. 3 of Decree 39 of the 31st General Congregation,[2] the power of both the congregation of procurators and the congregation of provincials is augmented so that they may:
   1° prepare and present to the Society a report on the state of the Society;
   2° suspend decrees of previous general congregations until the next general congregation, if this seems necessary.

310   6.   The 32nd General Congregation gives the following commission and authority to Father General: That, with the help of a commission and with the deliberative vote of those fathers of the General Curia who have a right by reason of their office to attend a general congregation, he should:
   a)   revise the Formula of the General Congregation as well as the additional procedural norms, as described in nn. 2 and 3 above, in light of the experience of this general congregation;
   b)   introduce into the Formula of the General Congregation the changes mentioned in nn. 1 and 4 above and

---

2 Ibid., 971.

determine the particulars which may be required to carry out the decisions of this General Congregation regarding these changes.

c) as far as necessary, adapt and change the Formula of the General Congregation to accomplish the above;

d) make any decisions, of a more particular nature, which may be required to implement n. 5 above. As far as necessary, he may also change the Formulas of both the congregation of procurators and the congregation of provincials to include the new decisions which pertain to those congregations.

7. The 32nd General Congregation recommends to   **311**
Father General that he establish a commission to examine the following questions in more detail in preparation for their consideration and decision by the next general congregation:

> —stabilizing the number of those who attend a general congregation;
> —apportioning the members of the general congregation according to criteria which are not only quantitative but also qualitative;
> —reducing the numbers of those who attend a general congregation.

14   THE PROVINCIAL CONGREGATION

The 32nd General Congregation has decided the following about the provincial congregation.

A.   THE CONGREGATION IN GENERAL

312   1.   The power of the provincial congregation is not to be increased. However, before the provincial congregations meet, Father General may send to the delegates questions about the state of the province so that on these questions action might be taken in the provincial congregation.

313   2.   In the Formula of the Provincial Congregation:
—n. 6; the clause is omitted: *"The day of arrival of the delegates be so set that the next day is the first day of the congregation."*
—n. 32, §1, is to begin: *"The members legitimately begin the congregation immediately, and at the appointed time . . ."*
—n. 49 is thus corrected: *"From the beginning of the congregation there be posted . . ."*
—n. 50 is thus corrected: *"At the time established by the provincial for the first session, whoever are present . . ."*
—n. 58 is thus corrected: *"Ninth, unless the congregation should prefer to make the choice in the following session, it should determine the day after which it will not be allowed to present any other postulatum, which should be the second day or at most the fourth day after the day on which the first session was held."*

314   3.   In the Formula, n. 95, the following fourth paragraph is to be added: *"In cases of provinces which have*

506

been dispersed both within and outside their native country because of religious persecution or other adverse conditions and in which the group existing outside the province constitutes a quasi-province, even if the provincial himself or a delegate elected according to the norm of n. 10 can come from the province to the general congregation, the General or Vicar-General, having consulted and received the approval of the general assistants, can name as a full delegate one of the professed of four vows from among those working outside the territory of their native country."

4. The minor questions treated in Postulatum 947[1] are to be left to the decision of Father General with a deliberative vote of those fathers of the General's Curia who have a right *ex officio* to attend a general congregation.   **315**

5. With reference to the Formula of the Provincial Congregation, the General Congregation directs and empowers Father General, with a deliberative vote of those fathers of the General's Curia who have a right, *ex officio,* to attend a general congregation, to bring that Formula up to date and, where necessary, change it and introduce those points on which the General Congregation gave an affirmative vote.   **316**

B. PARTICIPATION IN THE CONGREGATION

6. As to the number of delegates to be elected to a provincial congregation, Father General has the power to allow vice-provinces which have a large number of members to use the norms of provinces for that number, without increasing the number of delegates whom they may send to the general congregation.   **317**

7. The number of those who attend the provincial congregation *ex officio* should be in some way decreased.   **318**
a) To be retained *ex officio* are those superiors ordinarily named by Father General. But at this time it is rec-

---

1 See the postulata sent to the 31st General Congregation.

ommended that Father General review the list of superiors whom he names in each province and use criteria based on the importance of different offices and even the separation of office of superior from that of director of the apostolic work so that he move toward reducing the number of superiors named by himself.

b) The consultors of the province do not attend the provincial congregation *ex officio;* the treasurer of the province, however, does.

319   8. In the Formula of the Provincial Congregation: —n. 19, §1, 2° is changed to read as follows: *"That there be included in the congregation and computed within the forty members of the congregation (twenty in a vice-province) two or more persons from this territory to be determined by the General or Vicar-General according to the number of Jesuits within the territory and its distance from the province. The General or Vicar-General will designate one of these because of the office he holds. The others will be elected from the list of those who have passive voice by those who have active voice in the territory. The election will be conducted by the superior of the territory. This election process will take place and the results will be reviewed by the superior with his consultors before the rest of the province proceeds to vote on naming the other delegates to the congregation. In the case of such a special election, the members of that territory lose active and passive voice in the election of delegates from the rest of the province."*

320   9. To n. 21, §1, 1°, the following is to be added: *"It is recommended, however, that as far as possible, they choose delegates from different apostolic works and houses."* In his letter convoking the congregation, the provincial should make the same recommendation.

321   10. To n. 21, §1, 4°, in place of *"It is permitted to seek in confidence information from one or another prudent man,"* the following is to be substituted: *"It is permitted,*

with discretion and charity, to seek information from other persons."

11. To Jesuits without final vows, participation in the provincial congregation is granted under the following conditions: 322

a) All scholastics and brothers without final vows have active voice five years after their entrance into the Society; they have passive voice eight years after their entrance into the Society. With regard to the number of those without final vows in the provincial congregation: there should be at least one; there may not be more than five in the provinces, nor more than three in the vice-provinces.

b) More specific norms concerning this participation should be determined by Father General with the deliberative vote of those fathers of the General Curia who have the right, *ex officio,* to attend a general congregation. This should be done in a flexible way but within the norms given above.

c) These norms and determinations should be reviewed by the next general congregation.

12. In the Formula of the Provincial Congregation, n. 29, §3, the first words are to be changed to read as follows: *"Those who according to the judgment of the committee of assessors mentioned in paragraph 2 or the preparatory committee . . . etc."* In n. 13 the following words are to be added: *"5th—Those exclaustrated according to the Code of Canon Law, n. 639; 6th—Those who have sought a change to the lay state or to be dismissed from the Society. If the petition is still secret and the person seeking a change to the lay state or dismissal wishes his name to remain on the list of those having passive voice so that his petition remain secret, his name can be kept on the list. But if it happens that he is elected, he must, ipso facto, be considered ineligible by the committee of assessors."* 323

C. ACTIONS WITHIN THE CONGREGATION

13. In the Formula of the Provincial Congregation n. 324

26 is to be changed to read as follows: *"Before the beginning of the congregation, let two lists be prepared and sent in due time to the delegates to the provincial congregation . . . etc."*

325 14. The Formula of the Provincial Congregation is so to be changed as to meet the concerns expressed below without imposing on all provinces the obligation of following this method of procedure:

a) Setting a deadline beyond which postulata may not be sent for consideration by the congregation, without however limiting the right of delegates to submit postulata during the course of the congregation;

b) Sending the postulata to the delegates to the provincial congregation early enough to permit them to study them and to propose amendments before the congregation;

c) Establishing small committees to arrange the postulata in order, and to develop further the topics proposed;

d) All the above should be done in such a way that the anonymity of the authors of the postulata is preserved. It should also be done in a way that preserves the obligation of secrecy and without prejudice to any decision which the committee for screening postulata may wish to make.

326 15. The Formula of the Provincial Congregation is to be changed to meet the concerns expressed below without however ordering that this method be followed. In this revision, provision should be made for harmonizing these changes with the power of the committee for screening postulata.

a) That there be committees to study the postulata;

b) That the conclusions of these committees be explained to the congregation by a reporter;

c) That after receiving suggestions, the committee can again study or reshape the postulata;

d) That all the above be carried out according to the regulations of the Formula of the Provincial Congregation concerning the method of voting.

16.   The Formula, n. 44, §2, is to read as follows: *"In public votes different methods can be used at the discretion of the provincial according to the importance of the different subjects involved, but the directive in n. 83, §1, must be maintained."*   **327**

17.   In the election of the committee for screening postulata, if it seems fitting to the provincial congregation, a prior indicative vote can be taken.   **328**

18.   In the Formula, n. 73, §2, is to be changed so that the phrase *"immediately before the election of all substitutes"* replaces the phrase *"immediately after the election of all substitutes."*   **329**

15   CENTRAL GOVERNMENT
OF THE SOCIETY

330   1.   Decree 44 of the 31st General Congregation, in force experimentally until now,[1] is definitively confirmed by the 32nd General Congregation, with however the following modifications:

a)   At the end of I, 1, should be added: *"who will also be general counsellors."*

b)   I, 4, now reads as follows: *"Even a general congregation called for business should proceed to a new election of general assistants. Former assistants may be re-elected to the same office."*

c)   At the end of II, 7, should be added: *"At least the general counsellors will normally give their advice gathered together in council."*

d)   At the end of II, 8, is added: *"In addition to the four general counsellors elected by the general congregation as general assistants, Father General should name at least two more general counsellors, having first consulted the regional assistants and obtained the deliberative vote of the general assistants."*

331   2.   All the contrary dispositions of previous general congregations, which were suspended by the 31st General Congregation[2] (cf. I, 6; II, 9), are now definitively abrogated.

B.   RECOMMENDATIONS MADE TO FATHER GENERAL

332   3.   The General Congregation recommends to Father General the following:

---

1 *ActRSJ*, XIV, 976-978.
2 GC 31, D. 44, I-6 and II-9; *ActRSJ*, XIV, 977.

a) The general counsellors should form a council which in its manner of working goes beyond the consultation of the individual counsellors. It will be a regular and stable working group to collaborate organically with Father General in the formation of policy, in decision-making and in planning execution. It will not only take up problems proposed to it but also propose matters to be considered. Its members should examine together what matters ought to be treated, especially in the light of the varied perspectives of the different members. Finally, it will promote discernment regarding serious and universal matters.

b) Father General should give the care of some sector of the life of the Society or of some geographical region, or even of both, to each of the general counsellors.

c) A general assistant or general counsellor should not ordinarily remain in office for more than about eight years, nor should all of them be changed at the same time.

d) The regional assistants should be brought together as a group once a month for discussion of business.

e) A review should be undertaken of the organization and coordination of the administration of the General Curia by people expert in this matter.

In this review, the possibility of lessening the number of Jesuits engaged in the central administration should be considered.

Meanwhile, every effort should be made to coordinate as much as possible the work of the different counsellors and officials of the Curia; some form of structural intercommunication and collaboration should be encouraged. Father General should commit the special care of this matter to the Secretary of the Society.

C. REVIEWING THE SYSTEM OF WORLD SECRETARIATS

4. The 32nd General Congregation gives the General   333
the mandate and the authority to review the system of world secretariats of the Society, suspending contrary de-

crees of previous general congregations until the next general congregation. In this review of the secretariats, however, the purposes intended by the previous general congregations should be kept in mind.

1.   For the proper completion of the legislative work of **334** the 32nd General Congregation, Father General is empowered, after obtaining the deliberative vote of those fathers of the General Curia who have a right *ex officio* to attend a general congregation, and without prejudice to the powers given him in other decrees, to abrogate or modify decrees of past general congregations that seem not to be in accord with the decrees of this 32nd General Congregation.

2.   Moreover, the 32nd General Congregation grants to **335** Father General the following:

1° That he himself, if it should be a matter of necessity, can suppress colleges and professed houses, with the deliberative votes, however, of the general counsellors and of the provincial of the province in whose territory the house to be suppressed is located and after consulting the regional assistant.

2° That the minutes of some sessions that could not be **336** distributed to the fathers of the Congregation should be approved by Father General and the general assistants.

3° That with respect to decrees that must be promul- **337** gated after the close of the Congregation, it should be permitted to Father General:

a) to make whatever corrections seem obviously needed;

b) to reconcile contradictions, if any are detected, according to the mind of the Congregation, but after having ascertained the deliberative vote of those fathers of the General Curia who have a right *ex officio* to attend a general congregation;

c) to edit the decrees with regard to style;

d) where necessary, to combine different decrees into one, while preserving the meaning and intent of each;

e) to fix a *vacatio legis* or delay with respect to enforcement, in the light of circumstances, when promulgating the decrees.

C.

DOCUMENTS

OF THE HOLY SEE

WHICH PERTAIN TO THE CONGREGATION

DOCUMENTS

OF THE HOLY SEE

WHICH PERTAIN TO THE CONSECRATION

I. Address of Pope Paul VI to the members of the Extraordinary General Congregation, December 4, 1974.

II. Letter of the Cardinal Secretary of State to Father Arrupe, December 3, 1974.

III. Autograph Letter of Pope Paul VI to Father Arrupe, February 15, 1975.

IV. Address of Pope Paul VI in the presence of Father General and the General Assistants, March 7, 1975.

V. Letter of the Cardinal Secretary of State to Father Arrupe, May 2, 1975.

Appendix: Particular Observations about Certain Decrees

I. ADDRESS OF POPE PAUL VI
TO THE MEMBERS OF THE 32nd
GENERAL CONGREGATION

December 3, 1974

Esteemed and beloved Fathers of the Society of Jesus,

As we receive you today, there is renewed for us the joy and trepidation of May 7, 1965, when the Thirty-first General Congregation of your Society began, and that of November 15 of the following year, at its conclusion. We have great joy because of the outpouring of sincere paternal love which every meeting between the Pope and the sons of St. Ignatius cannot but stir up. This is especially true because we see the witness of Christian apostolate and of fidelity which you give us and in which we rejoice. But there is also trepidation for the reasons of which we shall presently speak to you. The inauguration of the 32nd General Congregation is a special event, and it is usual for us to have such a meeting on an occasion like this; but this meeting has a far wider and more historic significance. It is the whole Ignatian Society that has gathered at Rome before the Pope after a journey of more than four hundred years, and is reflecting, perhaps, on the prophetic words that were heard in the vision of La Storta: "I will be favorable to you in Rome." (P. Tacchi-Venturi, SI, *Storia della Compagnia di Gesu in Italia narrata col sussidio di fonti inedite,* Vol. II, part 1, Rome, 1950, 2nd ed., p. 4, n. 2; P. Ribadeneira, *Vita Ignatii,* Chapter IX: *Acta Sanctorum Julii,* t. VII, Antwerp, 1731, p. 683).

There is in you and there is in us the sense of a moment

of destiny for your Society, which in our hearts concentrates memories, sentiments and the presages of your role in the life of the Church. Seeing you here as representatives of all your provinces throughout the world, our glance embraces the whole Ignatian family, some thirty thousand men, working on behalf of the Kingdom of God and making a contribution of great value to the apostolic and missionary works of the Church—religious men who are dedicated to the care of souls, often passing their whole lives in hiddenness and obscurity. Certainly each one of your confreres sends forth from his heart towards this Congregation profound desires, many of which are expressed in the postulata, and which therefore require from you, the delegates, a careful understanding and a great respect. But more than the number, it seems to us that there must be taken into account the quality of such wishes, whether they be expressed or silent, which certainly embrace conformity to the vocation and charism proper to Jesuits—transmitted by an uninterrupted tradition—conformity to the will of God, humbly sought in prayer, and conformity to the will of the Church in the tradition of the great spiritual impulse that has sustained the Society in the past, sustains it now, and will always sustain it in the future.

We realize the special seriousness of the present moment. It demands of you more than a routine performance of your function: it demands an examination of the present state of your Society, one that will be a careful synthesis, free and complete, to see how it stands with regard to the difficulties and problems that beset it today. It is an act that must be accomplished with extreme lucidity and with a supernatural spirit—to compare your identity with what is happening in the world and in the Society itself—listening exclusively, under the guidance and illumination of the magisterium, to the voice of the Holy Spirit, and consequently with a disposition of humility, of courage, and of resoluteness to decide on the course of action to be adopted, lest there be prolonged a state of uncertainty that would become dangerous. All this with great confidence.

And we give you the confirmation of our confidence: we love you sincerely, and we judge that you are able to effect that renewal and new balance which we all desire.

This is the meaning of today's meeting, and we want you to reflect on it. We already made known our thought in this regard through the letters that the Cardinal Secretary of State sent in our name on March 26, 1970, and on February 15, 1973, and with that letter of September 13, 1973, *In Paschae Sollemnitate,* which we sent to the General and through him to all the members of the Society.

Continuing along the line of thought of the last-mentioned document, which we hope has been meditated and reflected upon by you, as was our wish, we speak to you today with special affection and a particular urgency. We speak to you in the name of Christ and—as you like to consider us—as the highest Superior of the Society, by reason of the special bond which from the time of its foundation links the Society itself to the Roman Pontiff. The Popes have always placed special hope in the Society of Jesus.

On the occasion of the previous Congregation, we entrusted to you, as a modern expression of your vow of obedience to the Pope (*AAS* 57 (1965), p. 514; 58 (1966), p. 1177), the task of confronting atheism. And today we are turning to you, at the beginning of your work to which the entire Church is looking, to strengthen and stimulate your reflections. We observe you in your totality as a great religious family, which has paused for an instant and is deliberating about the road to be followed.

And it seems to us, as we listen in this hour of anxious expectation and of intense attention "to what the Spirit is saying" to you and to us (see Rev. 2:7 ff.), that there arise in our heart three questions which we feel bound to answer: "Where do you come from?", "Who are you?", "Where are you going?"

So we stand here before you, like a milestone, to measure in one sweeping glance, the journey you have already made.

I. Hence, *where do you come from?* Our thought goes back to that complex sixteenth century, when the foundations of modern civilization and culture were being laid, and the Church, threatened by schism, began a new era of religious and social renewal founded on prayer and on the love of God and the brethren, that is, on the search for genuine holiness. It was a moment bound up with a new concept of man of the world, which often—although this was not the most genuine humanism—attempted to relegate God to a place outside the course of life and history. It was a world which took on new dimensions from recent geographical discoveries, and hence in very many of its aspects—upheavals, rethinking, analyses, reconstructions, impulses, aspirations, etc.—was not unlike our own.

Placed against this stormy and splendid background is the figure of St. Ignatius. Yes, where do you come from? And we seem to hear a united cry—a "voice like the sound of the ocean" (Rev 1:15)—resounding from the depths of the centuries from all your confreres: We come from Ignatius Loyola, our Founder—we come from him who has made an indelible imprint not only on the Order but also on the spirituality and the apostolate of the Church.

With him, we come from Manresa, from the mystical cave which witnessed the successive ascents of his great spirit: from the serene peace of the beginner to the purifications of the dark night of the soul, and finally to the great mystical graces of the visions of the Trinity (cf. Hugo Rahner, *Ignatius von Loyola u. das geschichtliche Werden seiner Frömmigkeit*, Graz, 1947, Chapter III).

There began at that time the first outlines of the Spiritual Exercises, that work which over the centuries has formed souls, orienting them to God, and which, among other things, teaches the lesson of treating "the Creator and Lord with great openheartedness and generosity, offering him all one's will and liberty, so that his divine Majesty may avail himself, in accordance with his most holy will, of the person and of all that he has" (*Annotaciones,* 5: *Monumenta Ignatiana,* second series, *Exercitia Spiritualia S. Ignatii de Loyola et eorum Directoria,* new edition, t. I, *Exerc.Spir.:* MHSI, Vol. 100, Rome, 1969, p. 146).

With St. Ignatius—you answer us again—we come from Montmartre, where our Founder on August 15, 1534, after the Mass celebrated by Peter Faber, pronounced with him, with Francis Xavier, whose feast we celebrate today, with Salmeron and Lainez and Rodrigues and Bobadilla, the vows which were to mark as it were the springtime bud from which in Rome the Society would flower (See P. Tacchi-Venturi, *op. cit.,* Vol. II, part I, p. 63 ff.).

And with St. Ignatius—you continue—we are in Rome, whence we departed fortified by the blessing of the Successor of Peter, from the time when Paul III, responding to the ardent appeal of Cardinal Gaspare Contarini in September, 1539, gave the first verbal approval—the prelude to that Bull *Regimini Ecclesiae Militantis* of September 27, 1540, which sanctioned with the supreme authority of the Church the existence of the new Society of Priests. It seems to us that its originality consisted in having grasped that the times required people who were completely available, capable of detaching themselves from everything and of following any mission that might be indicated by the Pope and called for, in his judgment by the good of the Church, putting always in first place the glory of God: *ad maiorem Dei gloriam.* But St. Ignatius also looked beyond those times, as he wrote at the end of the *Quinque Capitula* or *First Sketch of the Institute of the Society of Jesus:* "These are the matters which we were able to explain about our profession in a kind of sketch. We now complete this explanation in order to give brief information both to those who ask us about our plan of life and also to those who will later follow us if, God willing, we shall ever have imitators along this path." (P. Tacchi-Venturi, *op. cit.,* Vol. I, part II, Rome, 2nd ed., 1931, p. 189)

This is what your predecessors wanted of you, this is how you came to be: it can be said that these facts give the definition of the Society. This definition is extracted from the origins of the Society; it indicates the Society's constitutional lines and imprints upon it the dynamism which has supported it throughout the centuries.

II. We know then *who you are.* As we summarized in our Letter, *In Paschae Sollemnitate,* you are members of an Order that is religious, apostolic, priestly, and united with the Roman Pontiff by a special bond of love and service, in the manner described in the *Formula Instituti.*

You are religious, and therefore men of prayer, of the evangelical imitation of Christ, and endowed with a supernatural spirit, guaranteed and protected by the religious vows of poverty, chastity and obedience. These vows are not an obstacle to the freedom of the person, as though they were a relic of periods that have sociologically been superseded, but rather a witness to the clear desire for freedom in the spirit of the Sermon on the Mount. By means of these commitments, the one who is called as Vatican II has emphasized—"in order to derive more abundant fruit from the grace of Baptism . . . intends to be freed from the obstacles which might draw him away from the fervor of charity and the perfection of divine worship and consecrates himself to the service of God" (*Lumen Gentium,* 44; See *Perfectae Caritatis,* 12-14). As religious you are men given to austerity of life in order to imitate the Son of God, who "emptied himself to assume the condition of a slave" (Phil 2:7) and who "was rich but became poor for your sake, to make you rich out of his poverty" (2 Cor 8:9). As religious you must flee—as we wrote in the above-mentioned Letter—"from those facile compromises with a desacralized mentality, which is evidenced in so many aspects of modern behavior," and you must likewise recognize and live—courageously and in an exemplary way—"the ascetical and formative value of the common life," guarding it intact against the tendencies of individualism and singularity.

You are, moreover, *apostles,* that is, preachers of the Gospel, sent in every direction in accordance with the most authentic and genuine character of the Society. You are men whom Christ himself sends into the whole world to spread his holy doctrine among the people of every state and condition (See Spiritual Exercises, n. 145: See MHSI, Vol. 100, Rome, 1969, p. 246). This is a fundamental and irreplaceable characteristic of the true Jesuit, who indeed finds in the Exercises, as in the Constitutions, continuous inducements to practice the virtues proper to him, those virtues indicated by St. Ignatius, and this practice even more strongly, with greater striving, in a continual search for the better, for the *"magis,"* for the greater (See the *criteria* of the Constitutions). The very diversity of ministries to which the Society dedicates itself takes from these sources its most profound motive of that apostolic life which must be lived *pleno sensu.*

You are likewise *priests*: this, too, is an essential character of the Society, without forgetting the ancient and established tradition of enlisting the help of Brothers who are not in Sacred Orders and who have always had an honored and effective role in the Society. Priesthood was formally required by the Founder for all professed religious, and this with good reason, because the priesthood is necessary for the Order he instituted with the special purpose of the sanctification of men through the Word and the sacraments. Effectively, the sacerdotal character is required by your dedication to the active life—we repeat—*pleno sensu.* It is from the charism of the Order of priesthood, which conforms a man to Christ sent by the Father, that there principally springs the apostolic character of the mission to which, as Jesuits, you are deputed. You are therefore priests, trained for that *familiaritas cum Deo* on which St. Ignatius wished to base the Society; priests who teach, endowed with the *sermonis gratia* (*See Monumenta Ignatiana, Sancti Ignatii de Loyola Constitutiones Societatis Iesu,* t. III, textus latinus, p. 1, c. 2, 9 (59-60); MHSI, Vol. 65, Rome, 1938, p. 49); oriented to see "that the Lord's message may spread quickly and be received with honor" (2 Thess 3:1). You are priests who serve or minister the grace of God through the sacraments; priests who receive the power and have the duty to share organically in the apostolic work of sustaining and uniting the Christian community, especially with the celebration of the Eucharist; priests who are therefore aware, as we mentioned in one of our talks in 1963, of "the antecedent and consequent relationship (of the priesthood) with the Eucharist, through which the priest is the minister of so great a sacrament and then its first adorer, wise teacher, and tireless distributor" (Address to the Italian clergy at the Thirteenth National Week of Pastoral Renewal, September 6, 1963: *AAS* 55 (1963), p. 754).

And finally you are *united with the Pope* by a special vow: since this union with the Successor of Peter, which is the principal bond of the members of the Society, has always given the assurance—indeed it is the visible sign—of your communion with Christ, the first and supreme head of the Society which by its very name is his—the Society of Jesus. And it is union with the Pope that has always rendered the members of the Society truly free, that is, placed under the direction of the Spirit, fit for all missions —even the most arduous and most distant ones—not hemmed in by the narrow conditions of time and place, and endowed with truly Catholic and universal energy.

In the combination of this fourfold note we see displayed all the wonderful richness and adaptability which has characterized the Society during the centuries as the Society of those "sent" by the Church. Hence there have come theological research and teaching, hence the apostolate of preaching, of spiritual assistance, of publications and writings, of the direction of groups, and of formation by means of the Word of God and the Sacrament of Reconciliation in accordance with the special and characteristic duty committed to you by your holy Founder. Hence there have come the social apostolate and intellectual and cultural activity which extends from schools for the solid and complete education of youth all the way to all the levels of advanced university studies and scholarly research. Hence the *puerorum ac rudium in christianismo institutio,* which St. Ignatius gives to his sons, from the very first moment of his *Quinque Capitula,* or *First Sketch,* as one of their specific aims (See P. Tacchi-Venturi, *op. cit.,* Vol. I, part II, p. 183). Hence the missions, a concrete and moving testimony of the "mission" of the Society. Hence the solicitude for the poor, for the sick, for those on the margins of society. Wherever in the Church, even in the most difficult and extreme fields, in the crossroads of ideologies, in the front line of social conflict, there has been and there is confrontation between the deepest desires of man and the perennial message of the Gospel, there also there have been, and there are, Jesuits. Your Society is in accord with and blends with the society of the Church in the multiple works which you direct, also taking account of the necessity that all should be unified by a single aim, that of God's glory and the sanctification of men, without dissipating its energies in the pursuit of lesser goals.

And why then do you doubt? You have a spirituality strongly traced out, an unequivocal identity and a centuries-old confirmation which was based on the validity of methods, which, having passed through the crucible of history, still bear the imprint of the strong spirit of St. Ignatius. Hence there is absolutely no need to place in doubt the fact that a more profound commitment to the way up till now followed—to the special charism—will be the source of spiritual and apostolic fruitfulness. It is true that there is today widespread in the Church the temptation characteristic of our time: systematic doubt, uncertainty about one's identity, desire for change, independence, and individualism. The difficulties that you have noticed are those that today seize Christians in general in the face of the profound cultural change which strikes at one's very sense of God. Yours are the difficulties of all today's apostles, those who experience the longing to proclaim the Gospel and the difficulty of translating it into a language accessible to modern man; they are the difficulties of other religious orders. We understand the doubts and the true and serious difficulties that some of you are undergoing. You are at the head of that interior renewal which the Church is facing in this secularized world, especially after the Second Vatican Council. Your Society is, we say, the test of the vitality of the Church throughout the centuries; it is perhaps one of the most meaningful crucibles in which are encountered the difficulties, the temptations, the efforts, the perpetuity and the successes of the whole Church.

Certainly it is a crisis of suffering, and perhaps of growth, as has been said many times. But we, in our capacity as Vicar of Christ, who must confirm the brethren in faith (See Lk 22:32), and likewise you, who have the heavy responsibility of consciously representing the aspirations of your confreres—all of us must be vigilant so that the necessary adaptation will not be accomplished to the detriment of the fundamental identity or essential character of the role of the Jesuit as is described in the *Formula Instituti,* as the history and particular spirituality of the Order propose it, and as the authentic interpretation of the very needs of the times seem still today to require it. This image must not be altered; it must not be distorted.

One must not call apostolic necessity what would not be other than spiritual decadence. Just as St. Ignatius is said to have clearly advised, any confrere sent on mission must by all means take care not to forget his own salvation in order to attend to that of others. Not only was it wrong to commit even the slightest sin for the greatest possible spiritual gain; it was not even right to put himself in danger of sinning. (See *Monumenta Ignatiana,* first series, *Sancti Ig-*

natii de Loyola Epistolae et Instructiones, t. XII, fasc. II:
MHSI, Annus 19, fasc. 217, January, 1912, Madrid, pp.
251-52). If your Society puts itself at risk, if it enters onto
paths full of danger which are not its own, there suffer also
thereby all those who, in one way or another, owe to the
Jesuits so very much of their Christian formation.

You are as well aware as we are that today there appears
within certain sectors of your ranks a strong state of uncertainty, indeed a certain fundamental questioning of your
very identity. The figure of the Jesuit, as we have traced
it out in its principal aspects, is essentially that of a spiritual
leader, an educator of his contemporaries in Catholic life,
within, as we have said, his proper role, as a priest and as
an apostle. But we are asking, and you are asking yourselves, as a conscientious verification and as a reassuring
confirmation, what is the present state of the life of prayer,
of contemplation, of simplicity of life, of poverty, of the use
of supernatural means? What is the state of acceptance
and loyal witness in regard to the fundamental points of
Catholic faith and moral teaching as set forth by the ecclesiastical magisterium? The will to collaborate with full
trust in the work of the Pope? Have not the "clouds on the
horizon" which we saw in 1966, although "in a great measure dispersed" by the Thirty-first General Congregation
(*AAS* 58 (1966), p. 1174), unfortunately continued to
cast a certain shadow on the Society? Certain regrettable
actions, which would make one doubt whether the man
were still a member of the Society, have happened much
too frequently and are pointed out to us from many sides,
especially from bishops of dioceses; and they exercise a sad
influence on the clergy, on other religious, and on the
Catholic laity. These facts require from us and from you
an expression of sorrow, certainly not for the sake of dwelling on them, but for seeking together the remedies, so that
the Society will remain, or return to being, what is needed,
what it must be in order to respond to the intention of the
Founder and to the expectations of the Church today.

There is needed an intelligent study of what the Society is, an experience of situations and of people. But there is also needed—and it is as well to insist on this—a spiritual sense, a judgment of faith on the things we must do and on the way that lies ahead of us, taking into account God's will, which demands an unconditioned availability.

III. Therefore, *where are you going?* The question cannot remain unanswered. You have in fact been asking it for some time, asking it with lucidity, perhaps with risk.

The goal to which you are tending, and of which this General Congregation is the opportune sign of the times, is and must be without doubt the pursuit of a healthy, balanced, and suitable *aggiornamento* to the right desires of our day in essential fidelity to the specific character of the Society and in respect for the charism of your Founder. This was the desire of the Second Vatican Council, with the Decree *Perfectae Caritatis* which hoped for "the continued return to the sources of every Christian life and to the original spirit of institutes, and the adaptation of the institutes themselves to the changed conditions of the times" (*op. cit.*, 2). We would like to inspire you with full confidence and encourage you to keep pace with the attitudes of the world of today, recalling to you, nevertheless, as we did in a general way in the Apostolic Exhortation *Evangelica Testificatio*, that such necessary renewal would not be effective if it departed from the particular identity of your religious family which is so clearly described in your fundamental rule or *Formula Instituti*. As we said: "For a living being, adaptation to its surroundings does not consist in abandoning its true identity, but rather in asserting itself in the vitality that is its own. Deep understanding of present tendencies and of the needs of the modern world should cause your own sources of energy to spring up with renewed vigor and freshness. It is a sublime task in the measure that it is a difficult one" (*op. cit.*, 5: *AAS* 63 (1971), p. 523).

Hence we encourage you with all our heart to pursue the

aggiornamento willed so clearly and authoritatively by the Church. But at the same time, we are all aware of both its importance and its innate risk. The world in which we live places in crisis our religious outlook and sometimes even our option of faith: we live in a dazzling perspective of worldly humanism, bound up with a rationalistic and irreligious attitude with which man wants to complete his personal and social perfection exclusively by his own efforts. On the other hand for us, who are men of God, it is a question of the divinization of man in Christ, through the choice of the Cross and of the struggle against evil and sin. Do you remember the *"sub crucis vexillo Deo militare et soli Domino atque Romano Pontifici . . . servire?"* (Bull *Regimini Militantis Ecclesiae,* in P. Tacchi-Venturi, *op. cit.,* Vol. I, part II, *Documenti,* Rome, 1931, pp. 182-83).

The century of Ignatius underwent a humanistic transformation equally powerful even though not as turbulent as that of the succeeding centuries which have seen in action the teachers of systematic doubt, of radical negation, of the idealistic utopia of an exclusively temporal kingdom on earth, closed to every possibility of true transcendence. But "where is the master of worldly argument? Has not God turned the wisdom of this world into folly? Since in God's wisdom the world did not come to know him through 'wisdom,' it pleased God to save those who believe through the absurdity of the preaching of the Gospel" (1 Cor 1:20-21). We are the heralds of this paradoxical wisdom, this proclamation. But as we recalled to our brethren in the Episcopate at the end of the Synod, so we also repeat to you, that, notwithstanding the difficulties: "Christ is with us, he is in us, he speaks in us and by means of us and will not let us lack the necessary help" (*L'Osservatore Romano,* October 27, 1974, p. 2) in order that we may pass on the Christian message and wisdom to our contemporaries.

A realistic glance at this world makes us alert to another danger: the phenomenon of novelty for its own sake— novelty which questions everything. Novelty is the stimulus for human and spiritual progress. This is true only when it is willing to be anchored to fidelity to him who makes all things new (Rev. 21:5), in the ever self-renewing mystery of his death and resurrection, to which he assimilates us in the sacraments of his Church. This is not true when novelty becomes a relativism that destroys today what it built up yesterday. It is not difficult to see what you should use to combat these temptations, and these same means will keep you moving forward yourselves—they are faith and love.

Hence, in the road that opens before you in this remaining part of the century, marked by the Holy Year as a hopeful presage for a radical conversion to God, we propose to you the double charism of the apostle—the charism which must guarantee your identity and constantly illumine your teaching, your centers of study, your periodical publications. On the one hand, *fidelity*—not sterile and static, but living and fruitful—to the faith and to the institution of your Founder, in order that you may remain the salt of the earth and the light of the world (see Mt 5:13, 14). Guard what has been entrusted to you (see 1 Tim 6:20; 2 Tim 1:14). "Put on the armor of God so that you may be able to stand firm against the tactics of the devil. Our battle is not against human forces but against the principalities and powers, the rulers of this world of darkness . . . You must put on the armor of God if you are to resist on the evil day; do all that your duty requires, and hold your ground" (Eph 6:11-13).

On the other hand, there is the charism of love, that is of generous *service* to all men, our brethren traveling with us towards the future. It is that anxiety of Paul which every true apostle feels burning within him: "I made myself all things to all men in order to save some at any cost . . . I try to be helpful to everyone at all times, not anxious for my own advantage but for the advantage of everybody else, so that they may be saved" (1 Cor 9:22; 10:33).

Perfection lies in the simultaneous presence of two charisms—fidelity and service—without letting one have the advantage over the other. This is something that is certainly difficult, but it is possible. Today the attraction of the second charism is very strong: the precedence of action over being, of activity over contemplation, of concrete existence over theoretical speculation, which has led from a deductive theology to an inductive one; and all this could cause one to think that the two aspects of fidelity and love are mutually opposed. But such is not the case, as you know. Both proceed from the Holy Spirit, who is love. People are never loved too much, provided they are loved only in the love and with the love of Christ. "The Church endeavors to show in every argument that revealed doctrine, to the extent that it is Catholic—embraces and completes all the right thoughts of men, which in themselves always have something of the fragmentary and paltry" (H. de Lubac, *Catholicisme*, Paris, 1952, Chapter 9, p. 248). But if this is not the case, readiness to serve can degenerate into relativism, into conversion to the world and its immanentist mentality, into assimilation with the world that one wanted to save, into secularism and into fusion with the profane. We exhort you not to be seized by the *spiritus vertiginis* (Is 19:14).

For this purpose, we wish to indicate to you some further orientations which you can develop in your reflections:

A) *Discernment,* for which Ignatian spirituality especially trains you, must always sustain you in the difficult quest for the synthesis of the two charisms, the two poles of your life. You will have to be able always to distinguish with absolutely lucid clarity between the demands of the world and those of the Gospel, of its paradox of death and life, of Cross and Resurrection, of folly and wisdom. Take your direction from the judgment of St. Paul: "But because of Christ, I have come to consider all these advantages that I had as disadvantages. Not only that, but I believe nothing can happen that will outweigh the supreme advantage of knowing Christ and the power of his resurrection and to share his sufferings by reproducing the pattern of his death. That is the way I can hope to take my place in the resurrection of the dead" (Phil. 3:7-8, 10-11). We recall always that a supreme criterion is the one given by Our Lord: "You will be able to tell them by their fruits" (Mt. 7:16); and the effort which must guide your discernment will be that of being docile to the voice of the Spirit in order to produce the fruit of the Spirit, which is "love, joy, peace, patience, kindness, goodness, trustfulness, gentleness and self-control" (Gal 5:22).

B) It will also be opportune to remember the need to make a proper *basic choice* among the many appeals that come to you from the apostolate in the modern world. Today—it is a fact—one notes the difficulty of making properly thought-out and decisive choices; perhaps there is a fear that full self-realization will not be achieved. Hence there is the desire to be everything, the desire to do everything and to follow indiscriminately all the human and Christian vocations—those of the priest and the lay person, those of the Religious Institutes and of the Secular Institutes—applying oneself to spheres that are not one's own. Hence then arise lack of satisfaction, improvisation and discouragement. But you have a precise vocation, that which we have just recalled, and an unmistakably specific character in your spirituality and in your apostolic vocation. And this is what you must profoundly study in its main guidelines.

C) Finally, we once more remind you of *availability of obedience*. This, we would say, is the characteristic feature of the Society: "In other Orders," St. Ignatius wrote in his famous letter of March 26, 1553, "one can find advantages in fastings, vigils, and other austerities . . .; but I greatly desire, beloved brothers, that those who serve our Lord God in this Society may be marked by the purity and perfection of obedience, with true renunciation of our wills and the abnegation of our judgments" (*Monumenta Ignatiana,* first series, *Sancti Ignatii de Loyola Societatis Iesu Fundatoris Epistolae et Instructiones,* t. IV, fasc. V: MHSI, Annus 13, fasc. 153, September, 1906, Madrid, p. 671).

In obedience there is the very essence of the imitation of Christ, "who redeemed by obedience the world lost by its lack, *factus obediens usque ad mortem, mortem autem crucis*" (ibid.). In obedience lies the secret of apostolic fruitfulness. The more you do the works of pioneers, the more you need to be closely united with him who sends you: "All apostolic boldness is possible, when the apostles' obedience is certain" (Loew, *Journal d'une mission ouvrière,* p. 452). We are certainly aware that if obedience demands much from those who obey, it demands even more of those who exercise authority. The latter are required to listen without partiality to the voices of all of their sons, to surround themselves with prudent counsellors in order to evaluate situations sincerely, to choose before God what best corresponds to his will and to intervene with firmness whenever there is departure from that will. In fact, every son of the Church is well aware that obedience is the proof and foundation of his fidelity: "the Catholic knows that the Church only commands because of the fact that she first obeys God. He wants to be a 'free man,' but recoils from being among those 'who make use of freedom as a pretext for evil' (1 Peter 2:16). Obedience is for him the price of freedom, just as it is the condition for unity" (H. de Lubac, *Meditation sur l'Eglise,* p. 224, cf. pp. 222-30).

Beloved sons!

At the end of this encounter we believe that we have given you some indications concerning the path which you must take in today's world; and we have also wanted to indicate to you the path which you must take in the world of the future. Know it, approach it, serve it, love it—this world; and in Christ it will be yours. Look at it with the same eyes as St. Ignatius did; note the same spiritual requirements; use the same weapons: prayer, a choice for the side of God, of his glory, the practice of asceticism, absolute availability. We think that we are not asking you too much when we express the desire that the Congregation should profoundly study and restate the essential elements (*essentialia*) of the Jesuit vocation in such a way that all your confreres will be able to recognize themselves, to strengthen their commitment, to rediscover their identity, to experience again their particular vocation, and to recast their proper community union. The moment requires it, the Society expects a decisive voice. Do not let that voice be lacking!

We are following with the most lively interest this work of yours, work which ought to have a great influence upon your holiness, your apostolate, and your fidelity to your charism and to the Church. We accompany your work especially with our prayer that the light of the Holy Spirit, the Spirit of the Father and of the Son, may illumine you, strengthen you, guide you, rouse you, and give you the incentive to follow ever more closely Christ crucified. So let us now together turn to Jesus in prayer, in the very words of St. Ignatius:

"Receive, Lord, my entire liberty. Take my memory, my intellect, and my whole will. Whatever I have or possess you gave to me. I give it all back to you, Lord. Dispose of it according to your will. All that I ask and desire is your holy will; give me your love and your grace. That is enough for me, and I ask for nothing more." (*Spiritual Exercises,* n. 234, *op. cit.,* MHSI, Vol. 100, Rome, 1969, pp. 308-09).

This is the way, this is the way, brothers and sons. Forward, *in Nomine Domini.* Let us walk together, free, obedient, united to each other in the love of Christ, for the greater glory of God. Amen.

II. LETTER OF THE CARDINAL SECRETARY OF STATE TO FATHER GENERAL

December 3, 1974

Secretariat of State

The Vatican, December 3, 1974

Most Reverend Father:

His Holiness has given me the responsibility to convey to you and to the members of the Society his sincere satisfaction with the meeting held this morning, the feast of St. Francis Xavier, with those that are to take part in the 32nd General Congregation.

In the address which the Holy Father gave to those present, he certainly indicated his lively concern—expressed also in the letter which he sent to you on September 15, 1973—that the Society itself, in its praiseworthy and responsible attempt at *"aggiornamento"* in accord with the needs of the times, would remain faithful in its essential characteristics set down in the fundamental rule of the Order, that is, in the Formula of the Institute.

To this end the Supreme Pontiff did not fail to consider the possibility which might be proposed and which you yourself brought up in the recent audience with him on November 21st; that is, the proposal to extend to all the religious of the Society of Jesus, even those who were not priests, the fourth vow of special obedience to the Supreme Pontiff "with regard to missions"—reserved according to the Institute to those religious who are priests and who have satisfactorily completed the required spiritual and doctrinal preparation. He desires to let you know that such

537

a change in the light of more careful examination seems to present grave difficulties which would impede the approval necessary on the part of the Holy See.

I am sending this communication to you so that you may have it before you as the work of the General Congregation develops.

I am happy to take the occasion of professing myself with religious respect,

> Most devotedly yours,
> Jean Cardinal Villot

III. AUTOGRAPH LETTER OF HIS HOLINESS
PAUL VI TO FATHER GENERAL

February 15, 1975

To his beloved son, Pedro Arrupe, S.J.,
General of the Society of Jesus

We have received the letter which you sent to us and the account which we requested of the reasons which moved the General Congregation in its voting on the problem of grades and the fourth vow. We have not failed duly to consider it.

As regards more recent events, we confirm what our Cardinal Secretary of State wrote to you at our request on December 3 last. Again we repeat with all regard for you and for the Fathers of the Congregation: no change can be introduced related to the fourth vow.

As the supreme guarantor of the "Formula of the Institute," and as universal pastor of the Church, we cannot allow this point in any way to be infringed upon, since it constitutes one of the pivotal points of the Society of Jesus. In excluding the extension of the fourth vow what moves us is not some less important feeling or an anguish-free knowledge of the problems. Rather it is that profound respect and deep love which we have for the Society as well as the persuasion of the great good which the Society in the future is called upon to provide for the ever more difficult work of the Church, if it is kept what its founder wished it to be—obviously with opportune adaptations which do not go beyond the limits of its basic identity.

Precisely in this view of things we want to express to you a doubt which arises in us from certain orientations and dispositions which are emerging from the work of the General Congregation: Is the Church able to have faith in you here and now, the kind of faith it has always had? What will the relationship of the ecclesiastical hierarchy toward the Society be? How will the hierarchy itself in a spirit free from fear be able to trust the Society to carry on works of such moment and of such a nature? The Society now enjoys a prosperity and an almost universal extension which as it were set it apart and which are in proportion to the trust which was always placed in it. It has a spirituality and doctrine and discipline and obedience and service and an example which it is bound to maintain and to witness to. Therefore we repeat confidently the question which we asked in our address on the 3rd of December at the beginning of the Congregation "Where are you going?"

In the days which you still have left to you for your common work, we ardently exhort you, my dear son, you and your brethren, to a yet deeper reflection on your responsibilities, and on your great potentialities as well as on the dangers which threaten the future of that farsighted and deserving "Society of Priests" founded by St. Ignatius.

As we wrote to you on September 15, 1973, this is a decisive hour "for the Society of Jesus, for its future and also for all religious congregations." Let us think of the innumerable repercussions that a line of action which—God forbid—was contrary to what we set out above could have on the Society and even on the Church. For this reason we "most insistently" ask you to consider seriously before the Lord the decisions to be made. It is the Pope who humbly but with an intense and sincere affection for you repeats with fatherly alarm and utter seriousness: Think well, my dear sons, on what you are doing.

For this reason we request that you send to us before their publication the decisions already made or soon to be made by the General Congregation.

In this serious hour we pray intensely for our beloved

Society of Jesus while with a full heart we impart to you and to all its members all over the world, in the name of the Lord our apostolic benediction.

From the Vatican, February 15, 1975, the twelfth year of our Pontificate.

Paul VI

IV. ADDRESS OF POPE PAUL VI
IN THE PRESENCE OF FATHER GENERAL
AND THE GENERAL ASSISTANTS

March 7, 1975

Beloved Members of the Society of Jesus:

Almost three months ago, on the third of last December, it was a consolation for Us to receive in audience all the Fathers of the Society of Jesus who are members of the 32nd General Congregation just when they were undertaking their work. We were happy to indicate to them, the representatives before our eyes of the entire Ignatian family, our esteem for all the members "who labor for the Kingdom of God and carry on very valuable work for the apostolic and missionary endeavors of the Church" (*AAS* 66; 1974; p. 712). We now have, therefore, a great occasion for rejoicing since we have yet another opportunity of once again giving evidence of our great, paternal and sincere good will for this religious order that is so clearly joined with Us and is certainly very dear to Us.

For our part, We admit that We were impelled by the very spirit of love, by which We embrace all of you, to interpose our authority with the superiors of your Society—as you well know—in rather recent circumstances. We thought that this action had to be taken because of our consciousness that We are the supreme protector and guardian of the Formula of the Institute, as well as the Shepherd of the Universal Church. Actually, at that time We were not a little pleased by the fact that the members of the General Congregation favorably understood the force and meaning of our recommendations and showed that they received them with a willingness to carry them out. Now We wish once again to cite the words of the Apostle Paul: "I wrote (what) I did . . . (confident that) you all know that I could never be happy, unless you were. When I wrote to you, in deep distress and anguish of mind, and in tears, it was not to make you feel hurt but to let you know how much love I have for you" (2 Cor. 2:3-4).

Some of you, perhaps in order to inject new vigor into the life of your Society, thought that it would be necessary to introduce substantially new elements into the Formula of the Institute, that is, into its primary norms or into its adaptation to the present social milieu. For our part, We cannot allow changes based on such reasoning to enter into your religious institute, which is of its very nature so special and so fully approved, not only by historical experience but also by hardly doubtful indications of divine protection. We feel that the Society must indeed be adapted and adjusted to this age of ours and must be enriched with new vitality, but always in accord with the principles of the Gospel and the Institute. It must not be transformed or deformed.

In view of this persuasion and our abundant love, We shall continue to take a solicitous part in all your affairs as often as the good of the Society or the Church seems to demand such involvement.

At the close of this Congregation, We gladly take advantage of the occasion to give this reminder to each and every son of St. Ignatius, scattered as they are throughout the world: Be loyal! This loyalty, which is freely and effectively shown to the Formula of the Institute, will safeguard the original and true form of the companions of Ignatius and strengthen the fruitfulness of their apostolate. This same loyalty must be considered a condition that is absolutely necessary to every type of ministry to which you are called, so that the name of Jesus may be spread and glorified throughout the world in the many and diverse areas of endeavor where you labor as members of a priestly and apostolic religious order that is united to the Supreme Pontiff by a special vow.

When We consider the great quantity of works which have been entrusted to you and which demand minds of proven maturity of judgment and firm wills outstanding in humility and generosity, it is our wish that all the members of the Society of Jesus be supported by supernatural helps and that they always rely on them! For no salvation can be brought to the world except through the selfless outpouring of the cross of Jesus Christ (see Phil. 2:7-8) and "the foolishness of the message that we preach" (1 Cor. 1:21).

Therefore We exhort all the companions of Ignatius to continue with renewed zeal to carry out all the works and endeavors upon which they have so eagerly embarked in the service of the Church and that they be aware of the importance of their tasks while at the same time they rely on the help and assistance of God who alone suffices just as he alone was always sufficient for Ignatius and Francis Xavier in the midst of the great needs which they experienced. You should be aware of the fact that not only the eyes of contemporary men in general but also and especially those of so many members of other religious orders and congregations and even those of the universal Church are turned toward you. May such grandly conceived hopes, then, not be frustrated! Go, therefore, and proceed in the name of the Lord. As sons and brethren, go forth always and only in the name of the Lord.

With our Apostolic Blessing, We wish to confirm this desire of our heart.

V. LETTER OF THE CARDINAL SECRETARY OF STATE TO FATHER GENERAL

May 2, 1975

The Secretary of State
N. 281428
Vatican City, May 2, 1975

Very Reverend Father,

In fulfillment of my office, I submitted to the Holy Father for his consideration the decrees of the 32nd General Congregation of the Society of Jesus which the Congregation presented to him in accord with the desire he expressed to you in a letter dated the 15th of last February.

The Holy Father carefully examined these texts which represent the culmination of the work of the General Congregation, whose progress he followed with keen, loving, and personal concern. He has commissioned me to return these decrees to you, together with the following observations.

From an examination of the decrees, it appears that well-known circumstances prevented the General Congregation from achieving all that His Holiness had expected from this important event, and for which, at different times and in various ways, he gave some paternal suggestions, especially in his allocution of the 3rd of December, 1974, when he indicated his hopes for the Congregation. In any case, he has directed that the decrees be returned to you so that they can be put into effect according to the needs of the Society, with the hope that your worthy Jesuit brothers may draw strength from these decrees as they continue their progress in genuine fidelity to the charism of St. Ignatius and the Formula of the Institute.

However, while some statements in the decrees merit total acceptance, others are somewhat confusing and could, because of the way they are expressed, give grounds for mis-interpretation. Therefore, the Holy Father desires that some particular recommendations pertaining to certain decrees be sent to you and to your companions. You will find them appended to this letter, and I would ask that you regard them in that spirit of obedience which has always character-ized the Society.

Finally, with reference to the decree, "On Poverty," which you presented to him in your filial letter of the 14th of last March, His Holiness could not help but notice how thoroughly you undertook the complicated task of adapting the Society's legislation in this area to contemporary needs in accord with the norms I conveyed in my letter of Febru-ary 26, 1973. Because of the sensitive nature of this subject, however, and because of the character of the innovations introduced, it would be well if this decree were implemented "experimentally," in such a way that the next general congregation can reexamine the whole question in depth against the background of experience gained in the years ahead. As to the faculty for dispensing from the vow of poverty which you requested in your letter, I am to inform you that the Vicar of Christ grants you this in the individual cases where, with the deliberative vote of your council, it seems necessary.

Questions may arise about the interpretation of the decrees as a whole. In this event, the Holy Father sincerely desires that reference always be made to the norms and directives contained either in his address to you on the 3rd of December or in other documents of the Holy See per-taining to the Congregation.

The Holy Father hopes that these remarks will be taken as the context within which the decrees of the 32nd General Congregation are accurately understood and correctly implemented. For this reason, it seems most appropriate that this letter and the added reflections be published along with the decrees and thus be available to those responsible for reading and applying these decrees.

The Holy Father follows the work of the Society with special and fervent prayer to the Lord that it always remain true—as he said in his final talk of March 7th last—to itself and to its mission in the bosom of the Church. It is also his prayer that the Society continue to perform those ministries of apostolic service and evangelical witness, in the name of Jesus, which are expected of it today. These desires the Holy Father confirms with his special blessing.

Devotedly yours,

J. Cardinal Villot

APPENDIX

Particular Observations about Certain Decrees

The decree, *"Our Mission Today: Diakonia Fidei and the Promotion of Justice,"* and the declaration, *"Jesuits Today"*

The promotion of justice is unquestionably connected with evangelization, but—as the Holy Father said in his closing remarks to the last Synod of Bishops in October of 1974—"Human development and social progress in the temporal order should not be extolled in such exaggerated terms as to obscure the essential significance which the Church attributes to evangelization and the proclamation of the full Gospel." (*AAS* 66, 1974, 637)

This applies to the Society of Jesus in a special way, founded as it was for a particularly spiritual and supernatural end. Every other undertaking should be subordinated to this end and carried out in a way appropriate for an Institute which is religious, not secular, and priestly. Moreover, we must not forget that the priest should inspire lay Catholics, since in the promotion of justice theirs is the more demanding role. The tasks proper to each should not be confused.

It is also helpful to recall that work for the promotion of justice should be undertaken in accord with directives drawn up by the local hierarchy and in consideration of the conditions peculiar to each region.

The decree, *"On Fidelity to the Magisterium and the Roman Pontiff"*

It is most opportune that the General Congregation has confirmed the traditional fidelity of the Society to the magisterium and the Holy Father. However, the expression, "Freedom should be intelligently encouraged," should not be allowed to provide grounds for disregarding the rules for "Thinking with the Church," which are proper to the Society.

The decree, *"Concerning the Formation of Jesuits"*

There is laudable insistence upon solid philosophical and theological education. However, in keeping with the Conciliar Decree, *Optatam Totius,* those engaged in philosophical instruction should bear in mind that organized body of solid doctrine gathered—as a patrimony—by the Church.

Moreover, in theological studies, after a careful investigation of the sources, "by way of making the mysteries of salvation known as thoroughly as they can be, students should learn to penetrate them more deeply with the help of speculative reason exercised under the tutelage of St. Thomas, and they should learn, too, how these mysteries are interconnected." (#16)

The decree, *"On Poverty"*

Superiors should take very seriously their responsibility to see that the distinction between the apostolic institute and·the religious community is properly observed so that ways of acting which are contrary to the genuine Ignatian poverty may be avoided. Furthermore, the performance of ministries which, by tradition, are undertaken gratuitously should not be lightly abandoned.

The decree, *"Concerning the Province Congregation"*

The extension of active and passive voice to nonformed members significantly expands the process of election to a provincial congregation. However, since the decree itself stipulates that the norms therein contained should be reviewed by the next general congregation, timely and serious study should be given to this whole question, so that it can be resolved in a way which is both more equitable and more in keeping with the spirit of the Society.

D.

MEMBERS OF THE

32nd GENERAL CONGREGATION

(In Alphabetical Order)

President: VERY REV. FR. PEDRO ARRUPE

Elected General on May 22, 1965

SURNAME AND NAME	TITLE TO MEMBERSHIP
1. Abellán Pedro	*Proc. Gen. (Tolet.)*
2. Acévez Manuel	*Ass. Reg. (Mex.)*
3. Achaerandio Luis	*Elect. Centr. Am.*
4. Adám John	*Elect. Hung.*
5. Adami Leopoldo	*Prov. Bras. Mer.*
6. Agúndez Melecio	*Elect. Cast.*
7. Aizpún José	*Elect. Guj.*
8. Aldecoa José Antonio	*Elect. Loy.*
9. Alfaro Juan	*Elect. Loy.*
10. Alvarez-Bolado Alfonso	*Elect. Cast.*
11. Amet Henri	*Prov. Gall. Atl.*
12. Antunes Manuel	*Elect. Lusit.*
13. Arango Gerardo	*Prov. Colomb.*
14. Arevalo Catalino	*Elect. Philipp.*
15. Arroyo José	*Elect. Tolet.*
16. Arrupe Pedro	*Praepos. Gen. (Japon.)*
17. Arvesú Federico	*Elect. Antill.*
18. Athazhapadam Thomas	*Elect. Patn.*
19. Bamberger Stefan	*Elect. Helvet.*
20. Baragli Enrico	*Elect. Rom.*
21. Barré Noël	*Elect. Gall. Atl.*
22. Begley John	*Elect. Austral.*
23. Belic Miljenko	*Elect. Croat.*
24. Berden Pavel	*Elect. Sloven.*
25. Bergoglio Jorge	*Prov. Argent.*
26. Besanceney Paul	*Prov. Detroit.*

27.	Biever Bruce	*Prov. Wiscons.*
28.	Blanco Benito	*Elect. Antill.*
29.	Boné Edouard	*Elect. Belg. Mer.*
30.	Bortolotti Roberto	*Prov. Rom.*
31.	Botturi Tarcisio	*Elect. Bah.*
32.	Bourgeault Guy	*Elect. Gallo-Can.*
33.	Brenninkmeyer Bernward	*Prov. Germ. Or.*
34.	Browne Joseph	*Proc. Neo Ebor.*
35.	Buckley Michael	*Elect Calif.*
36.	Cachat Leo	*Elect. Patn.*
37.	Calvez Jean-Yves	*Ass. Gen. (Gall. Atl.)*
38.	Casassa Charles	*Elect. Calif.*
39.	Chabert Henri	*Prov. Gall. Med.*
40.	Chu Bernard	*Prov. Sin.*
41.	Clancy Thomas	*Prov. Neo Aur.*
42.	Clarke Thomas	*Proc. Neo Ebor.*
43.	Cleary Richard	*Prov. Nov. Angl.*
44.	de Colnet Yves	*Elect. Gall Sept.*
45.	Connery John	*Elect. Chicag.*
46.	Connor James	*Elect. Maryl.*
47.	Coreth Emerich	*Prov. Austr.*
48.	Correia-Afonso John	*Ass. Reg. (Bomb.)*
49.	de la Costa Horacio	*Ass. Gen. (Philipp.)*
50.	Costes André	*Prov. tot. Gall. (Gall. Med.)*
51.	Counihan John	*Elect. Zamb.*
52.	Cruz Luis A.	*Elect. Aequat.*
53.	Curic Josip	*Elect. Croat.*
54.	Cuyás Manuel	*Elect. Tarrac.*
55.	Daniel William	*Elect. Austral.*
56.	Dargan Herbert	*Ass. Reg. (HongK.)*
57.	Dargan Joseph	*Elect. Hibern.*
58.	Darowski Roman	*Elect. Pol. Min.*
59.	Decloux Simon	*Prov. Belg. Mer.*
60.	De Cooman Eugeen	*Prov. Belg. Sept.*
61.	van Deenen Jan	*Prov. Neerl.*
62.	De Hovre Luk	*Elect. Belg. Sept.*
63.	De Mello Anthony	*Elect. Bomb.*
64.	Dezza Paolo	*Ass. Gen. (Ven. Med.)*
65.	Díaz Bertrana Marcos	*Prov. Baet.*
66.	Divarkar Parmananda	*Elect. Bomb.*
67.	D'Mello Ambrose	*Elect. Kanar.*
68.	Domínguez Héctor	*Elect. Baet.*
69.	Dortel-Claudot Michel	*Elect. Gall. Sept.*
70.	D'Souza Noel	*Elect. Calcutt.*
71.	D'Souza Romuald	*Elect. Goa-Poo.*
72.	Dullard Maurice	*Elect. Ranch.*
73.	Echeverría José Luis	*Prov. Venezol.*
74.	Egaña Francisco	*Prov. Loy.*

75.	Ekka Philip	*Prov. Ranch.*
76.	Ekwa bis Isal	*Elect. Afr. Centr.*
77.	Fabbri Enrique	*Elect. Argent.*
78.	Fang Chih-Jung Marc	*Elect. Sin.*
79.	Farrell Walter	*Elect. Detroit.*
80.	Fernández Avelino	*Elect. Legion.*
81.	Fernández-Castañeda José Luis	*Prov. Peruv.*
82.	Flaherty Daniel	*Prov. Chicag.*
83.	Fragata Julio	*Prov. Lusit.*
84.	Galauner Petar	*Prov. Croat.*
85.	Galbraith Kenneth	*Prov. Oreg.*
86.	Ganzi Igino	*Ass. Reg. (Taurin.)*
87.	Gerhartz Johannes Günter	*Prov. Germ. Inf.*
88.	Giorgianni Giovanni	*Prov. Sic.*
89.	Gnanadickam Casimir	*Prov. Madur.*
90.	Gordon Douglas	*Elect. Madur.*
91.	Grez Ignacio	*Elect. Chil.*
92.	Guidera John	*Elect. Jamshed.*
93.	Guindon William	*Elect. Nov. Angl*
94.	Gutiérrez Enrique	*Elect. Mex.*
95.	Gutiérrez Semprún Manuel	*Prov. Cast.*
96.	Hall Bernard	*Prov. Angl.*
97.	Hannan Michael	*Elect. Salisb.*
98.	Hardawirjana Robert	*Elect. Indon.*
99.	Harvanek Robert	*Elect. Chicag.*
100.	Harvey Julien	*Prov. Gallo-Can.*
101.	Hayashi Shogo	*Prov. Japon.*
102.	Hebga Meinrod	*Elect. Afr. Occ.*
103.	Hillengass Eugen	*Oec. Gen. (Germ. Sup.)*
104.	Hoël Marc	*Prov. Gall. Sept.*
105.	Hoffmann Georg	*Elect. Germ. Or.*
106.	Hortal Jesús	*Elect. Bras. Mer.*
107.	Huarte Ignacio	*Elect. Venezol.*
108.	Huber Eduard	*Elect. Germ. Sup.*
109.	Hughes Gerard J.	*Elect. Angl.*
110.	Huizing Peter	*Elect. Neerl.*
111.	Iglesias Ignacio	*Ass. Reg. (Legion.)*
112.	Jiménez Gustavo	*Elect. Colomb.*
113.	Kaufmann Leo	*Elect. Oreg.*
114.	Kern Walter	*Elect. Austr.*
115.	Kijauskas Gediminas	*Elect. Lit.*
116.	Knecht Joseph	*Prov. Patn.*
117.	Koczwara Tadeusz	*Prov. Pol. Mai.*
118.	Kolacek Josef	*Elect. Boh.*
119.	Kolvenbach Peter Hans	*Elect. Prox. Or.*
120.	Krauss Heinrich	*Elect. Germ. Sup.*
121.	Kullu Patrick	*Elect. Ranch.*
122.	Kunz Erhard	*Elect. Germ. Inf.*

123.	Kyne Michael	*Elect. Angl.*
124.	Lambert Louis	*Elect. Neo Aur.*
125.	Lapize de Salée Bernard	*Elect. Gall. Med.*
126.	Lariviere Florian	*Elect. Gallo-Can.*
127.	Laurendeau Louis	*Secr. Soc. (Gallo-Can.)*
128.	Leäo Joaquim	*Elect. Mozamb.*
129.	van Leeuwen Hans	*Elect. Neerl.*
130.	Leite Antonio	*Elect. Lusit.*
131.	Lesage Jacques	*Ass. Reg. (Gall. Par.)*
132.	Londoño Fernando	*Elect. Colomb.*
133.	Lucey Paul	*Elect. Nov. Angl.*
134.	Macchi Angelo	*Elect. Ven. Med.*
135.	Mac Gregor Felipe	*Elect. Peruv.*
136.	Madurga Mariano	*Elect. Arag.*
137.	Mahoney Martin	*Elect. Neo Ebor.*
138.	Malone Patrick	*Elect. Can. Sup.*
139.	Marranzini Alfredo	*Elect. Neap.*
140.	Martini Carlo	*Elect. Taurin.*
141.	Mayo Benigno	*Prov. Philipp.*
142.	McCarthy Charles	*Elect. Sin.*
143.	McGarry Cecil	*Prov. Hibern.*
144.	McPolin James	*Elect. Hibern.*
145.	Meharu Carlos	*Elect. Urug.*
146.	Menacho Antonio	*Elect. Bol.*
147.	Mendes de Almeida Luciano	*Elect. Bras. Centr. Or.*
148.	Mendizábal Miguel	*Elect. Japon.*
149.	Mertens Victor	*Ass. Reg. (Afr. Centr.)*
150.	Miecznikowski Stefan	*Elect. Pol. Mai.*
151.	Mitchell Robert	*Elect. Neo Ebor.*
152.	Molinari Paolo	*Elect. Taurin.*
153.	Montes Fernando	*Elect. Chil.*
154.	Moragues Ignacio	*Prov. Arag.*
155.	Moreland Gordon	*Elect. Oreg.*
156.	Dias de Moura Laercio	*Ass. Reg., Elect. Bras. C. Or.*
157.	Moysa-Rosochacki Stefan	*Elect. Pol. Min.*
158.	Mruk Anton	*Ass. Reg. (Pol. Min.)*
159.	Muguiro Ignacio	*Elect. Peruv.*
160.	Navarrete Urbano	*Elect. Arag.*
161.	Ochagavía Juan	*Prov. Chil.*
162.	O'Keefe Vincent	*Ass. Gen. (Neo Ebor.)*
163.	O'Malley John	*Elect. Detroit.*
164.	Orsy Ladislas	*Proc. Neo Ebor.*
165.	O'Sullivan Patrick	*Prov. Austral.*
166.	Padberg John	*Elect. Missour.*
167.	Panuska Joseph	*Prov. Maryl.*
168.	Pasupasu	*Prov. Afr. Centr.*
169.	Pelenda Bikakala	*Elect. Afr. Centr.*
170.	Pereira Joaquim	*Prov. Bras. Centr. Or.*

171.	Pérez-Lerena Francisco	*Prov. Antill.*
172.	Perniola Vito	*Elect. Ceyl.*
173.	Perz Zygmunt	*Elect. Pol. Mai.*
174.	Petrucelli Donato	*Prov. Neap.*
175.	Philipps Bertram	*Prov. Bomb.*
176.	Pilz Johann Chr.	*Elect. Austr.*
177.	Piña Joaquín	*Elect. Paraq.*
178.	Popiel Jan	*Prov. Pol. Min.*
179.	Prucha Paul	*Elect. Wiscons.*
180.	Rakotonirina Charles-Remy	*Elect. Madec.*
181.	Randriambololona Philibert	*Prov. Madec.*
182.	Rendina Sergio	*Prov. Ven. Med.*
183.	Roth Herbert	*Elect. Germ. Or.*
184.	Russell John	*Elect. HongK.*
185.	Russo Biagio	*Elect. Sic.*
186.	Ryan William	*Elect. Can. Sup.*
187.	San Juan Vicente	*Elect. Philipp.*
188.	Santana Hindenburg	*Elect. Bras. Sept.*
189.	Sanz Criado Luis M.	*Prov. Tolet.*
190.	Scaduto Mario	*Elect. Sic.*
191.	Schasching Johann	*Ass. Reg. (Austr.)*
192.	Scheifler Xavier	*Elect. Mex.*
193.	Segura Manuel	*Elect. Baet.*
194.	Seibel Vitus	*Prov. Germ. Sup.*
195.	Sencik Stefan	*Elect. Slovak.*
196.	Sheahan Gerald	*Elect. Missour.*
197.	Sheets John	*Elect. Wiscons.*
198.	Sheridan Edward	*Ass. Reg. (Can. Sup.)*
199.	Sily Alberto	*Elect. Argent.*
200.	Small Harold	*Ass. Reg. (Oreg.)*
201.	Soenarja Antonius	*Prov. Indon.*
202.	Soltero Carlos	*Prov. Mex.*
203.	Sorge Bartolomeo	*Elect. Ven.-Med.*
204.	Sucre Gustavo	*Elect. Venezol.*
205.	Suradibrata Paul	*Elect. Indon.*
206.	de Survilliers Alain	*Elect. Gall. Atl.*
207.	ʲTabao Francois-Xavier	*Elect. Madec.*
208.	Taylor Eamon	*Prov. Neo Ebor.*
209.	Tejerina Angel	*Prov. Legion.*
210.	Tomé Mariano	*Proc. Cuban.*
211.	Torres Gasset Juan	*Prov. Tarrac.*
212.	Troisfontaines Roger	*Elect. Belg. Mer.*
213.	Tucci Roberto	*Elect. Neap.*
214.	Vadakel Paul	*Elect. Ker.*
215.	Valero Urbano	*Prov. tot. Hisp. (Cast.)*
216.	Van Bladel Louis	*Elect. Belg. Sept.*
217.	Vandermeersch Edmond	*Elect. Gall. Par.*
218.	Vanni Ugo	*Elect. Rom.*

219.	Varaprasadam Arul Maria	*Elect. Madur.*
220.	de Varine-Bohan Jean	*Prov. Gall. Par.*
221.	de Vaucelles Louis	*Elect. Gall. Par.*
222.	Vaughan Richard	*Prov. Calif.*
223.	Vela Luis	*Elect. Legion.*
224.	Vella Arthur	*Elect. Melit.*
225.	Vergnano Carlo	*Prov. Taur.*
226.	Viard Claude	*Elect. Gall. Med.*
227.	Vives José	*Elect. Tarrac.*
228.	Walsh Maurice	*Elect. Jamaic.*
229.	Walsh Terence	*Prov. Can. Sup.*
230.	Weber Leo	*Prov. Missour.*
231.	Weber Quirino	*Elect. Bras. Mer.*
232.	Whelan Joseph	*Elect. Maryl.*
233.	Wulf Friedrich	*Elect. Germ. Inf.*
234.	Yamauchi James	*Elect. Neo Aur.*
235.	Yanase Mutsuo	*Elect. Japon.*
236.	Zamarriego Tomás	*Elect. Tolet.*

THE GENERAL CONGREGATIONS

G.C.	Year	No. of Jesuits	Members in GC	% in GC	Father General	Days
I	1558	1,000	20	2	Laynez	92
II	1565	3,500	31	0.88	Borgia	75
III	1573	3,905	40	1.11	Mercurian	65
IV	1581	5,165	57	1.10	Acquaviva	74
V	1593	8,519	63	0.73	Acquaviva	76
VI	1608	10,640	65	0.61	Acquaviva	36
VII	1615	13,112	75	0.57	Vitelleschi	144
VIII	1645	—	92	—	Carafa	145
IX	1649	—	80	—	Piccolomini	73
X	1652	—	77	—	Gottifredi & Nickel	73
XI	1661	—	78	—	Nickel & Oliva	79
XII	1682	17,655	85	0.48	de Noyelle	76
XIII	1687	—	86	—	González	77
XIV	1696	—	86	—	González	60
XV	1706	19,998	92	0.46	Tamburini	74
XVI	1730	—	80	—	Retz	91
XVII	1751	22,589	91	0.40	Visconti	76
XVIII	1755	—	87	—	Centurione	73
XIX	1758	—	89	—	Ricci	44
XX	1820	1,307	24	1.83	Brzozowski Fortis	66
XXI	1829	2,137	28	1.31	Roothaan	49
XXII	1853	5,209	55	1.05	Beckx	71
XXIII	1883	11,221	72	0.64	Beckx & Anderledy	39
XXIV	1892	13,275	73	0.54	Martin	74
XXV	1906	15,661	72	0.45	Wernz	48
XXVI	1915	16,946	87	0.51	Ledóchowski	
XXVII	1923	18,304	102	0.45	Ledóchowski	104
XXVIII	1938	25,683	161	0.61	Ledóchowski	58
XXIX	1946	28,191	168	0.59	Janssens	49
XXX	1957	33,732	185	0.54	Janssens	68
XXXI	1965–66	36,000	226	0.62	Arrupe	140
XXXII	1974–75	28,500	236	0.83	Arrupe	96

INDEX TO THE DECREES
OF THE 31st AND 32nd
GENERAL CONGREGATIONS

The numerical references are to the consecutive marginal numbers in the texts.

[The numbers for the 31st General Congregation were earlier used in several translations of the decrees; the numbers for the 32nd General Congregation are those of the official Latin text of the decrees].

[References to identical terms in the two congregations are given first for the 31st General Congregation. These references are followed by the sign // and then references are given for the 32nd General Congregation].

[The present index is meant to indicate the principal subject headings and to facilitate the beginning of further research in the decrees themselves. An exhaustive index would obviously have to be far lengthier].

of formation, 80, 141;—explains our vows, chastity, 248; obedience, 269; poverty, 288. **// 32:**—character S.J. recalled by Paul VI, 5;—vocation in S.J. one but manifold, 31;—shared by Brothers, 155; —formation process, 137;—community, 26-29, 111-118; young Jesuits in ap. comm. 147-148;—dimension of our religious life and vows, 30, 65, 111, 113;—institutes: defined, 274; some questioned, 75; their witness to poverty reviewed, 97; attachment to them, 97; their poverty, 274-293; their suppression, 293;—message, 77;—options for today, 88-110;—poverty and efficiency, 265;—aim of non-priestly work, 128;—principle of unity of our communities, 113;—value of celibacy, 225.

Apostolic organizations: 31:—362.

Apostolic schools: 31:—533.

Apostolic spirit: 31:—of the first Companions, 4;—of the Society today, 15, 16, 24;—interreactions, 144;—of Brothers, 66- 67;—to be instilled in the young religious, 79, 80;—in the novices, 105;—in the Scholastics, 122, 127;—to be put into practice, 131, 139, 144, 344;—supposes the spirit of prayer, 212, 213, 219;—necessity of permeating every aspect of religious life, 204;—and chastity, 247, 248, 259;—and obedience, 269;—and poverty, 288, 291, 299;—and community life, 313, 315, 327, 339, 340.

Approved Coadjutors: 32:—formation, 155, 160;—tertianship, 188;—final vows time requirements, 196;—and diaconate,

194;—in Prov. Congr. 322. See: BROTHERS.

Approved Scholastics: 32:—promotion to profession, 192;—and diaconate, 194;—final vows requirements, 196, 197; —in Prov. Congr. 322. See: SCHOLASTICS.

Arca: 32:—Seminarii, 299;—for Aged and Sick, 287, 299;—for Foundations, 299;—for Apostolic Works, 293, 299;—Charitable and Apostolic Fund of the Society, 288, 298.

Arts, importance of: 31:—533; —cultivation in the Society, 158, 555;—means of apostolate, 553, 554, 556;—formation of those who are involved, 558;—necessity of fine arts in formation of Jesuits, 557.

Assessment:—See: EVALUATION.

Assistancy: 32:—mechanism for review of ministries, 126;—Regional Conference, 129;—meetings of formation personnel, 161;—of Africa, East Asia and India, 132 note.

Assistants of Father General: 31: —general, 310, 357, 633-635, 639-640, 644-647, 649-656, 664, 669, 766, 773;—regional, 657 2°, 685. **// 32:**—General A, 330-331, 336;—General Counsellors, 330-331, 335;—Regional A, 330, 332, 335.

Atheism: 31:—mission entrusted to Society by Paul VI, 376;—state of the world threatened by, 12, 13;—diffusion, danger of, urgency of the task, 12, 24, 370;—influence on young people, 497;—the fight against atheism by prayer and action, 24, 212;—the understanding of atheism, 25;—its history, 38;—explained in religious instructions, 38;—how to deal with, 27-30;—adaptation of our ministries, 36, 37. **// 32:**

Society's mission today, 67;—today's apostolic task, 108-109; renewed poverty today, 270.

Charism S. J.: 32:—humble service, 39;—foundation, 41;—in our mission today, 62-72;—the same as the Church's, 62;—of apostolic team, priestly and religious, 64;—specially united to the Pope, 64;—vowed repudiation of world's idols, 65; in Formulas of Paul III and Julius III, 66;—in search of greatest need and more universal good, 88;—in social involvement, 92;—serve Christ poor, 258. See: IGNATIUS, JESUITS, SOCIETY.

Charity: 31:—love of God and of neighbor, 29, 77, 86, 126, 148, 216, 223, 245, 257, 267, 275, 290, 295, 317, 343, 345, 366;—fraternal, 81, 100, 131, 251b, 282, 314, 675. // **32:**—internal law of Ch, 272;—works of Ch in the Formula of the Institute, 66;—Charitable and Apostolic Fund, 288, 298. See: DISCRETA CARITAS.

Chastity: 31:—100, 315;—particular nature and importance, 245, 247, 264;—sign of the world to come, 247;—new problems, 243;—necessary requirements, 250;—associating us with the mystery of Christ, 249;—source of spiritual fruitfulness, 248;—friendship with Christ, 252;—supported by true brotherly love, 315; supposes mastery of the affections, 248, 249, 250, 255;—itself a source of apostolic force, 248;—means of preserving, 251, 315. // **32:**—frees us to be men for others, 30;—eschatological dimension, 65;—apostolic value of love and service

to all, 225;—32nd GC confirms decree of 31st, 225.

Choice: 32:—Basic Ch of 32nd GC, 13, 19, 20, 22, 96;—principle for Ch of ministries, 88, 117, 124.

Christ: 32:—sent by the Father, 50, 62;—God's revelation through the Spirit, 30, 75, 99;—His example of prayer, 206;—what the Society does for Ch, 13;—following Christ poor at work, 38, 97, 260;—Crucified, 40, 258;—Savior and Liberator, 15, 201;—personal Christian experience, 141 a, b;—in personal prayer, 206;—encounter with Ch in Spir. Exerc., 107, 242;—our personal relationship with Ch, 100, 109;—union with others in Ch, 191, 203-211;—proclaiming Ch, 270;—Christian mystery and inculturation, 102, 131;—His call in men's anguish, 63, 68;—present in human history, 60. See: JESUS.

Christians and non-Christians: 32:—15, 39, 73, 101, 103, 208;—in Form. Inst., 66;—mission of all Ch, 62;—collaboration with all, 86;—transcendence of Ch religion, 3.

Church: 31:—knowledge of, 86;—sense of, 79;—service of, 270, 277, 374, 473;—Christ present in the Church, 78. // **32:**—our service in the Ch, 4, 21, 45, 118, 191;—hierarchy, 30;—pilgrim Ch, 18;—her mission, 62;—universal, 33, 54, 131;—local, 33, 54, 131;—collaboration with local Ch for involvement, 86;—thinking with the Ch, 233;—profound renewal, 133;—deeper understanding of evangelical poverty, 257;—and inculturation, 102, 105, 131;—and permanent diaconate, 193;

—our churches and poverty, 289. See: BISHOPS, MAGISTERIUM, HOLY FATHER.

Civic activities: 32:—involvement, conditions, directives, 129. See: POLITICAL PROBLEMS.

Coadjutors: 32:—of the episcopal order, 32. See: BROTHERS, SPIRITUAL COADJUTORS, GRADES.

Coeducation: 31:—in our schools, 534.

Collaboration: 31:—among Jesuits, 37, 71, 89, 101, 312-314, 319, 321, 327, 481;—with the Provincial, 379;—between Provincial and General, 670-671; —for the spiritual progress of others, 81;—in the apostolate, 369, 371-374, 408, 409, 473, 501, 676;—with neighboring Provinces, 325, 344, 680;— missionary, 430-431, 441;— ecumenism, 456-462;—with the hierarchy, 371, 401, 407, 431, 446, 468, 473, 521, 573; —with religious, 332, 372, 431, 508;—with the laity, 373, 410, 440, 500, 526, 540, 541, 551, 578, 588;—with the parents of new students, 526;— with our separated brethren, 459-462;—with non-Christian, nonbelievers, 430, 506, 547, 583;—international, in the apostolate of education, 508, 542;—for the social apostolate, 460, 578, 579;—economical, 679. // **32:**—in execution of decrees, 10;—with Church universal and local, 54;—with Christians and non-Christians, 39;—with others in involvement, 86;—to avoid competition and duplication, 92; among professors for integration and reflection, 158;—for mobility in interdependence, 118. See: ALUMNI, BISHOPS, LAITY, INTERNATIONAL.

Colleges and Houses: 32:—poverty, 267, 274;—suppression, 335. See: EDUCATION.

Comfort: 32:—love of, 4;—poverty, 30;—appetite for enjoyment and consumption, 259.

Commission for the ministries: 31:—379, 380-385, 507. See: MINISTRIES.

Commissions: 32:—Regional or Provincial for Formation, 163; —for Statutes of Poverty, 295-296;—for Inculturation, 132 note;—Prov. Cong.: for screening Postulata, 325, 326, 328; for study of Postulata, 326;—Gen. Congr.: 305, 310, 311; for screening Postulata, 308, 325, 326;—State of Society, 308, 309;—for revision of Formula of GC, 310;—on number of members in GC, 311.

Commitment: 32:—to serving the Church, 45;—to work for justice, 77, 90, 91, 96, 101, 266; —will lead to involvement and responsibility, 91;—of individuals and institutions, 97;— work not directly priestly, 127-128;—other contracts must yield to mission, 115;—other commitments to be reviewed, 96;—to social involvement: conscientization, 92; analysis of situation, 93; and discernment, 94; review, 101; solidarity and C, 123; in civic matters, 129; exceptional cases, 129.

Committee: 31:—permanent, on education, 544;—Administrative Council, for works placed under the Society's care by the Holy See, 564;—for Academic planning, 565.

Common Rules: 32:—decree of 27th GC and 31st GC abrogated, 255;—Summary of decrees of 31st GC and 32nd GC

us Companion, 23, 24, 25, 87, 204;—four distinguishing marks, 34;—in the Eucharist, 210;—help to prayer and counsel, 207;—sharing, 215.

Concelebration: 31:—201, 224.

Concerted action: 32:—Guidelines for our Mission today, 108-110.

Confession: 32:—See: CONVERSION OF HEART, PENANCE, RECONCILIATION.

Confidence: 31:—towards superiors, 262;—mutual, 317, 318.

Conflict of conscience and obedience: 32:—256.

Congregation, General 31st: 32: —implementation and Vatican II, 1;—its execution urged, 2; —expresses Ignatian spirit, 2, 3; criticized, 3;—mandate on atheism, 68;—on Gospel to unbelievers, 101;—apostolic dimension of community, 113;— on apostolic character of our formation, 137; norms on spiritual formation, 135;—norms on studies, 134, 169;—directives on religious life, 199;— on Brothers, 192;—apostolic value of chastity, 225;—defined role of Provincial, 227.

Congregation, General 32nd: 32: —(i) Confirms points of 31st—on atheism, 68;—on evangelization, 101;—community life, 113;—spiritual formation, 135;—chastity, 225; —apostolic character of our formation, 137;—religious life, 199; Brothers' formation, 192; —esteem of Tertianship, 187; —Spiritual Exercises, 243;— devotion to Sacred Heart and Our Lady 244;—understanding of poverty, 257; preparation of a GC, 303. (ii) Other points: its decrees an invitation to progress, 7;—main topics, 19;—recommended for

reading and dialogue, 9;— meant for practical implementation, 10, 272;—humility and hope, 7;—fidelity to Magisterium and Pope, 43-46;—its basic choice, 19;—confirms Fr. General's apostolic priorities, 108;—defines role of local superior, 227; and director of work, 229;—answer to postulata on poverty, 262;—modifies decree on General Assistants, 330-331.

Congregation, General 33rd: 32: —proposal to it by the Poverty Commission, 296 c;—revision of norms for participation in Prov. Congr., 322 c; —to review system of Central Secretariates, 333;—on number of participants in a GC, 311.

Congregations, General: 31:— preparation, 22, 23, 605-615; —ability to interpret and modify the Constitutions, 48-59. // **32:**—preparation, 303; —complete and authoritative, 303, 304;—preparatory committee, 305;—revision of its Formula, 306-308.

Congregations, Procurator and Provincial: 31:—formed fathers and brothers summoned by the Provincial, 625;— elected members, 615-627;— "supra numerum," 732, 760-762. // **32:**—C of Procurators: of 1970, 108; its power augmented, 309; change in Formula, 310 d.—C of Provincials: its power augmented, 309; change in Formula, 310 d. 14th Decree, 312-329.— powers not enlarged, 312;— various changes and adaptations in the Formula, 313-329; participation of non-formed, 322;—many Prov. Congr. demanded a reform of poverty,

adapted to individual, 171;—and apostolic activities, 160, 181;—2 years Philosophy, 173; —4 years Theology, 174, 175.

Creatures for man: 32:—15.

Crisis: 32:—of apostolic institutions, 75 b.

Criterion for choice of ministries: 32:—90.

Criticism: 32:—of 31st GC, 3;—of one another, Fr. General, Magisterium, Pope, 4;—of traditional values, 75.

Cross of Christ: 31:—249, 258. // **32:**—Jesus carrying C, 3, 11;—Jesus crucified, 13, 209, 258;—death on the C, 40;—rallied under C for common life and work, 41.

Culture: 31:—universality of mind and openness needed in the Apostolate, 151, 375, 433, 503, 505-507, 526, 528;—and faith, 503, 525;—esteem of all cultures, 426. // **32:**—variety, 36, 63, 86, 214;—identity and autonomy of C influence our formation, 133;—formation to confront C of today, 138;—inculturation, 85, 104, 109, 131, 132;—regional information, 161;—personal insertion into C or region, 142, 177;—languages for cultural communication, 178.

Curia of the General: 32:—central government, 330-333;—reorganization, 332 e;—vote of exofficio members of GC, 310, 315, 316, 322, 334, 337.

Customs: 31:—contrary to our law are not permitted, 59;—those of monastic life, secular priests, or of a worldly spirit are not to be introduced, 330.

Daily order: 31:—222, 322, 335, 443. // **32:**—237, 248.

Decision: 32:—rests with superior, 29, 222;—community takes joint responsibility, 94, 95;—of committing Society to work for justice, 77, 137;—consequences of our decision, 119, 120;—in General Council, 332 a.

Decrees: 31:—abrogation and modification of certain ones, 718-762. // **32:**—of 31st GC, 1, 2, 3;—of 32nd GC, 2, 7-10; —reading of, 9;—promulgation of 32nd GC, 337.

Dedication, total: 32:—35, 41, 42, 53, 65;—in the Exercises, 209;—through Eucharist, 210.

Definitors: 31:—on adaptation, renewal, and revision of our law concerning poverty, 310. // **32:**—in General Congregation, 308.

Degrees, academic: 32:—Licentiate in Ph or Th by all, 170;—in Theology, 174;—a means to evaluate education, 177.

Delegate for Formation: 32:—in Province, 163;—in Society, 164.

Delegation of authority: 31:—given by the General, 689-692;—of the local superior, 320.

Detachment: 32:—from avarice, 38, 265, 282;—for discernment, 220-221;—for reform of structures, 107;—even from apostolic institutes, 261. See: ABNEGATION.

Devotion: 32:—to Sacred Heart and Our Lady, 244.

Diaconate, permanent: 31:—63-64. // **32:**—possible help to Church and Society, 193;—they retain their grade, 194;—approved Coadjutors may be advanced to Formed CC, 194; —Scholastics may be made Spiritual CC. 194;—Fr General will obtain faculties from Holy See and may give norms, 195.

Diakonia Fidei: 32:—continua-

102, 105;—applicable to many countries differently, 103, 131; —our responsibility, 104, 105; —Ignatian method respects personal values and cultures, 106;—integration of cultures, 109 a;—Jesuit tradition of service to Church, 131;—further development and instruction by Fr. General, 131;—in the course of formation, 161.

Independence: 32:—in living, 4; —in acquiring and spending, abuses condemned, 264.

Indifference, Ignatian: 31:—73, 365. // **32:**—and the 'magis', 37;—apostolic readiness for anything, 121;—required for community discernment, 221; —active I in poverty, 270.

Individual: 32:—attention to I, besides transforming structures, 89;—initiative stressed more in diversity of ministries, 114, 230;—sense of mission and integration even if alone, 114; —I freedom stressed 214;— each one's contribution to community life, 250.

Individualism: 31:—how to fight it, 321. // **32:**—an obstacle in formation and life, 141c, 149.

Infirmaries and their poverty: 32:—280, 287, 299 b.

Information in Prov. Congr.: 32: —321.

Informationes: 31:—before admission to theology, orders, last vows, and government, 200.

Initiative: 31:—and obedience, 83, 102, 126, 280. // **32:**— and sense of mission, 114, 228, 230.

Injustice: 32:—prevalent today springs from sin, 16, 17;—institutionalized, 52;—its victims, 69, 76, 89, 98;—to be attacked at the heart of man,

81;—endangers man's sense of destiny, 70;—and false idols, 75 a;—and atheism, 77;—liberation and evangelization, 89; —affects our formation process, 137.

Insertion: 32:—among poor, 66; —into the region, 142.

Institute SJ: 32:—study in Tertianship, 289. See: FORMULA OF THE INSTITUTE.

Institutions: 32:—apostolic I and communities, 267;—described in the Decree, 274;—no financial benefit to community, 278; —ruling for their poverty, 289;—functional character, 290;—in case of suppression, 268, 293;—their promotion, 298.

Instructors of tertianship: 31:— 133-136;—preparation of, 176; —adaptation of tertianship, 190-191;—revision of rules of, 192.

Instrument united with God: 31: —205, 269, 366.

Insurance: 32:—for old age and sickness, 287.

Integration: 32:—individual mission integrated with community, 114;—gradual I of younger Jesuits, 136; I of apostolic formation, 137-152;—formation a process of I, 139;—personal I and I into the Body of the Society, 140;—I of studies into apostolic life, 153-162;—elements of apostolic personality harmoniously united, 141-143; —progressive I of spiritual life, apostolate and studies, 143;— from Novitiate to Tertianship, 144-145;—experimental participation in life and apostolate, 147;—studies with a mission, 153;—human sciences with philosophy and theology, 158.

Intention, right: 31:—85.

Mobility: 32:—117, 118, 138.
See: AVAILABILITY.

Moral theology: 32:—158; ascetico-moral perfection, 260.

Mortification: 31:—251, 259.

Multiform: 32:—response to challenge of Mission, 56;—proclamation of Gospel, 85.

Mystery: 31:—of Christ, 86, 104, 127, 160, 249, 370, 470;—paschal mystery, 249. // **32:** —of Christ poor, 258, 260;—of poverty, 258, 260;—Christian M, 102;—Eucharistic Sacrifice, 235.

Nationalism: 31:—151.

Needs of the world: 32:—of bread, freedom, God, 82;—our answer is involvement, 84;—accommodation to, 13;—greater awareness and concern 98, 141c;—criterion of greatest need, 88, 90, 284-286. See: MANKIND, WORLD.

New: 32:—challenges, 50-57;—instruments, 57;—opportunities, 74;—signs and symbols, 205;—international values, 105;—questions and knowledge, 150;—N heaven and N earth, 79, 261.

Non-Christian religions: 32:—methods of prayer, 208.

Non-formed Jesuits: 32:—participation in Prov. Congr. 322. See: FORMATION.

Norms: 32:—General N of Studies, 134, 138, 164, 169;—on Formation, 163-186;—on union of hearts, 235-255;—on Poverty, 272-293.

Novices: 31:—knowledge of them, 111;—confidence in the master of novices, 102;—formed in self-denial, 103; awakened to their responsibiities, 104-108; —formed in knowledge of the Society, 105.

Novitiate: 31:—91-111;—twofold purpose, 92;—conditions for admission and remaining, 93-95, 109;—site, 107;—to test the vocation of the novices, 96-97;—to form them in the spiritual life, 98;—in community life, 100;—in charity, 102;—equality among scholastics, brothers, 101;—doctrinal and scriptural formation, 104; —relations with the world, 106-108. // **32:**—perpetual vows, 35;—ongoing formation begins in N, 138;—purpose: formation and probation, 144; progress of integration from N, 144-145;—instructed in discernment, 144;—may be common for Scholastics and Brothers, 144;—introductory course of Theology, 175. See: FORMATION.

Numbers: 32:—of members in GC, 311, 317, 318;—of General Assistants and Counsellors, 330 d;—in General Curia, 332 e.

Obedience: 31:—76, 126, 150, 346;—to the Pope, superior of the Society, 5-6, 270;—sign and principle of life in the Society, 268;—favored by a flourishing community life, 315;—condition of renewal, 269;—of faith, 208, 281;—personal, responsible, universal, 102, 276, 279;—absolute availability, 276-277;—apostolic sense, 6;—Ignatian charism, 269;—development, 79;—to the superior, representative of Christ, 270;—bond of unity, 269, 282, 315;—of the novices, 102-103;—and initiative, 125-126;—and objection of conscience, 279;—to bishops, 282, 315, 473, 492, 508, 521, 538. // **32:**—frees us to respond to Christ's call, 30;—implies account of conscience, 230;—an act of faith and freedom

—231;—the bond of union, 226-233;—guarantee of apostolic efficacy, 226;—objection or conflict of conscience, 256. See: AUTHORITY, SUPERIORS.

Offering: 31:—of selves to God, 208, 281; to others, 317. **//** **32:**—"Suscipe" 40, 42;—by chastity, 225.

Office, Divine: 31:—224. **//** **32:** —Hours in common, 208 note.

Older Jesuits: 32:—all involved in formation of Ours, 136;— permanent and continued formation, 136, 150-152;—old age and sick houses, 280; old age and sickness insurance, 287;—infirmaries and poverty, 280.

Openness: 32:—to God and Gospel, 67;—to Superiors, 29, 207, 218, 230, 231, 232;—to Spiritual Father, 240;—sincerity with companions, 217, 232, 251, 252;—within and among communities, 216;—to change, 130;—of service to all men, 65, 67, 73 a.

Opinion, public, to be formed: **32:**—130.

Oppression: 32:—victims of, 76, 78, 97, 109, 259;—structures of, 16, 80, 81, 84, 89.

Options: 32:—for faith and justice, 19, 20;—apostolic for today, 88-110;—preference for more universal good, greatest need, F & J, 90;—profound academic formation needed, 154.

Ordination, Priestly: 31:—171, 200. **//** **32:**—band of ordained ministers of the Gospel, 32;— of deacons and priests, 189, 190, 197;—spiritual preparation, 190;—postponed if Tertianship delayed, 189 a;— permanent diaconate, 193-195;

—required before last vows of Scholastics, 197.

Ordo studiorum: 31:—156.

Orientations: 32:—for spiritual life in community, 199-234;— 0 of 31st GC exaggerated, 3.

Our Lady: See: MARY.

Outsiders: See: EXTERNS.

Pagans: 31:—neo-pagans, 375.

Parishes: 31:—488-490;—wishes of the Church in this regard, 489;—Society able to take on as apostolate, 490;—the approbation of the General, 490. **//** **32:**—role in service of Faith and Justice, 125.

Participation: 32:—in God's life, 21;—in Christ's mission, 203; —in Eucharistic table, 210;— in Prov. Congr. 317-323;—in GC, 308, 311. See: SHARING.

Particularism and egoism: 31:— to be rejected, 675.

Pastoral characteristic of theological studies: 31:—163, 447.

Pastoral ministry: 31:—407, 468, 473-474, 508, 677, 687. **//** **32:** —communities, poverty regime, 279; ministry and local needs, 103;—ministry in Tertianship, 189;—theology course, 174.

Pastoral spirit of the Council: 31: —21.

Patrology: 31:—163, 234.

Paul III: 32:—66.

Paul VI: 32:—Recommendation to SJ, 5; his mandate on atheism, 68;—allocution to GC (3 Dec. 74), Section C;—autograph letter to Fr. General (15 Feb. 75), Section C; alloc. before General and Assistants 7 Mar. 75), Section C;— Octog. Adv. 122 note).

Peace: 31:—in the world, 678. **//** **32:**—in justice, 31, 70;— not at any price, 215.

Peace of soul: 31:—99, 220.

Penance, Sacrament of: 31:—98,

Sciences: 31:—30, 37, 158, 177-178, 375, 528;—of man, 37, 409, 548;—sacred, 177, 409, 548. // 32:—new technological discoveries, 74;—labor of research, 84;—for study of socio-political problems, 93;—solid academic formation, 154, 177.

Scripture: 31: 78, 116, 123, 127, 138, 163, 184, 215, 234;—and the mystery of Christ, 86, 98; —daily reading, 127;—methodical reading with gradual initiation, 160;—and ecumenism, 455. // 32:—reading, 280 note;—deep knowledge of, 141, 158;—to assimilate revelation, 153.

Secret: 32:—in information, 321; —in Formula of Prov. Congr. 323;—in postulata, 325 d; in conflict of conscience, 255.

Secretariats, central: 32:—organization, 333.

Secretary: 32:—of the Society, 322 e;—of the GC, 308, 309.

Secularization: 32:—present threat, 15;—false images of God, 75 a;—evangelization forms linked with rejected order, 75 b;—world has no use for God, 79;—Christian hope no opium, 79;—today's unbelief, 84;—our presence in secularized societies, 127, 128.

Security: 32:—and poverty, 30.

Selection for promotion to four vows: 32:—192 b.

Seminaries: 31: 177, 538.

Seminaries for Ours: 32:—poverty, 280;—arca S, 299 a.

Sense of God: 32:—51, 70, 205; sense of mission, 23.

Senses: 31:—maintaining custody of, 251e.

Separation from Society: 32:—by breach of poverty, 264;—conscientious objector, 256;

exclaustration, laicization, dismissal, 323.

Service: 32:—of the Faith, main topic of this GC, 8;—foundational aim, 21; Jesuit specific contribution, 22;—diminished in the Society, 4; S of Faith and promotion of Justice, 15-19; 47-130;—to men, 23, 27, 30, 39, 65;—to the poor, 30; —of the Eternal King, 40; —Christ serves, 62;—of the Church, 45, 138, 191; S-oriented communities, 249.

Service of God: 31:—goal of every adaptation of the Institute, 21, 56;—goal of the Society, 203; goal of the Church, 374, 668, 675.

Sexual education: 31: 261.

Sexuality: 31: 246, 250.

Sharing: 32:—of goods and life, 28 259, 261, 270;—of life and experience in scholasticates, 147;—basis of community, 65; —help of shared prayer, 112, 207;—the experience of the poor, 266;—wisdom with students, 146;—in Contemplation for Love, 28, 215;—sharing resources, 284-288. See: PARTICIPATION.

Sick: 31:—visiting, 493. // 32: —poverty of infirmaries, 280, 287, 299 b;—Arca, 287.

Signs of the times: 31:—how to observe them, 268, 353, 556. // 32:—religious revival, 75 b;—of God's presence, 205;—reform of poverty, 259-261.

Silence: 31:—favorable to a life of prayer, fraternal charity, the apostolate, 220, 322, 343; —during the annual Spiritual Exercises, 236.

Simplicity: 31: 328, 334. // 32: —of life, 249, 259, 265, 268, 270, 286.

Sincerity: 31: 32. 85, 88, 290-291, 328, 462.

sent to this, secularized, god-
less, 72, 76, 78;—our insertion
into it, 84, 85;—shaped by
structures, 89, 107;—universal
interdependence, 118;—worldly spirit and our Faith, 4. See:
CONTEMPORARIES, NEEDS OF
THE WORLD, MANKIND,
PLANET.

Writers: 31:—186, 766.
Writing, Art of: 31:—158.
Youth: 31:—375, 409, 429, 495,
497. // **32:**—and social order,
109 c;—new cultural values,
133; young Jesuits, 133-136,
145-149, 161. See: EDUCA-
TION, FORMATION, INTEGRA-
TION, SCHOOLS.